Aesthetical and Philosophical Essays

By

Friedrich Schiller

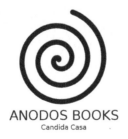

ANODOS BOOKS
Candida Casa

Friedrich Schiller (1775-1805)
Originally published in 1902, translated by Nathan Haskell Dole
Editing, cover, and internal design by Alisdair MacNoravaich for Anodos Books.
Copyright © 2017 Anodos Books. All rights reserved.

Anodos Books
1c Kings Road
Whithorn
Newton Stewart
Dumfries & Galloway
DG8 8PP

Contents

INTRODUCTION.

The special subject of the greater part of the letters and essays of Schiller contained in this volume is Aesthetics; and before passing to any remarks on his treatment of the subject it will be useful to offer a few observations on the nature of this topic, and on its treatment by the philosophical spirit of different ages.

First, then, aesthetics has for its object the vast realm of the beautiful, and it may be most adequately defined as the philosophy of art or of the fine arts. To some the definition may seem arbitrary, as excluding the beautiful in nature; but it will cease to appear so if it is remarked that the beauty which is the work of art is higher than natural beauty, because it is the offspring of the mind. Moreover, if, in conformity with a certain school of modern philosophy, the mind be viewed as the true being, including all in itself, it must be admitted that beauty is only truly beautiful when it shares in the nature of mind, and is mind's offspring.

Viewed in this light, the beauty of nature is only a reflection of the beauty of the mind, only an imperfect beauty, which as to its essence is included in that of the mind. Nor has it ever entered into the mind of any thinker to develop the beautiful in natural objects, so as to convert it into a science and a system. The field of natural beauty is too uncertain and too fluctuating for this purpose. Moreover, the relation of beauty in nature and beauty in art forms a part of the science of aesthetics, and finds again its proper place.

But it may be urged that art is not worthy of a scientific treatment. Art is no doubt an ornament of our life and a charm to the fancy; but has it a more serious side? When compared with the absorbing necessities of human existence, it might seem a luxury, a superfluity, calculated to enfeeble the heart by the assiduous worship of beauty, and thus to be actually prejudicial to the true interest of practical life. This view seems to be largely countenanced by a dominant party in modern times, and practical men, as they are styled, are only too ready to take this superficial view of the office of art.

Many have indeed undertaken to defend art on this score, and to show that, far from being a mere luxury, it has serious and solid advantages. It has been even apparently exaggerated in this respect, and represented as a kind of mediator between reason and sense, between inclination and duty, having as its mission the work of reconciling the conflicting elements in the human heart. A strong trace of this view will be found in Schiller, especially in all that he says about the play-instinct in his "Aesthetical Letters."

Nevertheless, art is worthy of science; aesthetics is a true science, and the office of art is as high as that assigned to it in the pages of Schiller. We admit that art viewed only as an ornament and a charm is no longer free, but a slave. But this is a perversion of its proper end. Science has to be considered as free in its aim and in its means, and it is only free when liberated from all other considerations; it rises up to truth, which is its only real object, and can alone fully satisfy it. Art in like manner is alone truly art when it is free and independent, when it solves the problem of its high destination—that problem whether it has to be placed beside religion and philosophy as being nothing else than a particular mode or a special form of revealing God to consciousness, and of expressing the deepest interests of human nature and the widest truths of the human mind.

For it is in their works of art that the nations have imprinted their favorite thoughts and their richest intuitions, and not unfrequently the fine arts are the only means by which we can penetrate into the secrets of their wisdom and the mysteries of their religion.

It is made a reproach to art that it produces its effects by appearance and illusion; but can it be established that appearance is objectionable? The phenomena of nature and the acts of human life are nothing more than appearances, and are yet looked upon as constituting a true reality; for this reality must be sought for beyond the objects perceived immediately by the sense, the substance and speech and principle underlying all things manifesting itself in time and space through these real existences, but preserving its absolute existence in itself. Now, the very special object and aim of art is to represent the action and development of this universal force. In nature this force or principle appears confounded with particular interests and transitory circumstances, mixed up with what is arbitrary in the passions and in individual wills. Art sets the truth free from the illusory and mendacious forms of this coarse, imperfect world, and clothes it in a nobler, purer form created by the mind itself. Thus the forms of art, far from being mere appearances, perfectly illusory, contain more reality and truth than the phenomenal existences of the real world. The world of art is truer than that of history or nature.

Nor is this all: the representations of art are more expressive and transparent than the phenomena of the real world or the events of history. The mind finds it harder to pierce through the hard envelop of nature and common life than to penetrate into works of art.

Two more reflections appear completely to meet the objection that art or aesthetics is not entitled to the name of science.

It will be generally admitted that the mind of man has the power of considering itself, of making itself its own object and all that issues from its activity; for thought constitutes the essence of the mind. Now art and its work, as creations of the mind, are themselves of a spiritual nature. In this respect art is much nearer to the mind than nature. In studying the works of art the mind has to do with itself, with what proceeds from itself, and is itself.

Thus art finds its highest confirmation in science.

Nor does art refuse a philosophical treatment because it is dependent on caprice, and subject to no law. If its highest aim be to reveal to the human consciousness the highest interest of the mind, it is evident that the substance or contents of the representations are not given up to the control of a wild and irregular imagination. It is strictly determined by the ideas that concern our intelligence and by the laws of their development, whatever may be the inexhaustible variety of forms in which they are produced. Nor are these forms arbitrary, for every form is not fitted to express every idea. The form is determined by the substance which it has to suit.

A further consideration of the true nature of beauty, and therefore of the vocation of the artist, will aid us still more in our endeavor to show the high dignity of art and of aesthetics. The history of philosophy presents us with many theories on the nature of the beautiful; but as it would lead us too far to examine them all, we shall only consider the most important among them. The coarsest of these theories defines the beautiful as that which pleases the senses. This theory, issuing from the philosophy of sensation of the school of Locke and Condillac, only explains the idea and the feeling of the beautiful by disfiguring it. It is entirely contradicted by facts. For it converts it into desire, but desire is egotistical and insatiable, while admiration is respectful, and is its own satisfaction without seeking possession.

Others have thought the beautiful consists in proportion, and no doubt this is one of the conditions of beauty, but only one. An ill-proportioned object cannot be beautiful, but the exact correspondence of parts, as in geometrical figures, does not constitute beauty.

A noted ancient theory makes beauty consist in the perfect suitableness of means to their end. In this case the beautiful is not the useful, it is the suitable; and the latter idea is more akin to that of beauty. But it has not the true character of the beautiful. Again, order is a less mathematical idea than proportion, but it does not explain what is free and flowing in certain beauties.

The most plausible theory of beauty is that which makes it consist in two contrary and equally necessary elements—unity and variety. A beautiful flower has all the elements we have named; it has unity, symmetry, and variety of shades of color. There is no beauty without life, and life is movement, diversity. These elements are found in beautiful and also in sublime objects. A beautiful object is complete, finished, limited with symmetrical parts. A sublime object whose forms, though not out of proportion, are less determined, ever awakens in us the feeling of the infinite. In objects of sense all qualities that can produce the feeling of the beautiful come under one class called physical beauty. But above and beyond this in the region of mind we have first intellectual beauty, including the laws that govern intelligence and the creative genius of the artist, the poet, and the philosopher. Again, the moral world has beauty in its ideas of liberty, of virtue, of devotion, the justice of Aristides, the heroism of Leonidas.

We have now ascertained that there is beauty and sublimity in nature, in ideas, in feelings, and in actions. After all this it might be supposed that a unity could be found amidst these different kinds of beauty. The sight of a statue, as the Apollo of Belvedere, of a man, of Socrates expiring, are adduced as producing impressions of the beautiful; but the form cannot be a form by itself, it must be the form of something. Physical beauty is the sign of an interior beauty, a spiritual and moral beauty which is the basis, the principle, and the unity of the beautiful.

Physical beauty is an envelop to intellectual and to moral beauty.

Intellectual beauty, the splendor of the true, can only have for principle that of all truth.

Moral beauty comprehends two distinct elements, equally beautiful, justice and charity. Thus God is the principle of the three orders of beauty, physical, intellectual, and moral. He also construes the two great powers distributed over the three orders, the beautiful and the sublime. God is beauty par excellence; He is therefore perfectly beautiful; He is equally sublime. He is to us the type and sense of the two great forms of beauty. In short, the Absolute Being as absolute unity and absolute variety is necessarily the ultimate principle, the extreme basis, the finished ideal of all beauty. This was the marvellous beauty which Diotimus had seen, and which is described in the Banquet of Socrates.

It is our purpose after the previous discussion to attempt to elucidate still further the idea of art by following its historic development.

Many questions bearing on art and relating to the beautiful had been propounded before, even as far back as Plotinus, Plato, and Socrates, but recent times have been the real cradle of aesthetics as a science. Modern philosophy was the first to recognize that beauty in art is one of the means by which the contradictions can be removed between mind considered in its abstract and absolute existence and nature constituting the world of sense, bringing back these two factors to unity.

Kant was the first who felt the want of this union and expressed it, but without determining its conditions or expressing it scientifically. He was impeded in his efforts to effect this union by the opposition between the subjective and the objective, by his placing practical reason above theoretical reason, and he set up the opposition found in the moral sphere as the highest principle of morality. Reduced to this difficulty, all that Kant could do was to express the union under the form of the subjective ideas of reason, or as postulates to be deduced from the practical reason, without their essential character being known, and representing their realization as nothing more than a simple you ought, or imperative "Du sollst."

In his teleological judgment applied to living beings, Kant comes, on the contrary, to consider the living organism in such wise that, the general including the particular, and determining it as an end, consequently the idea also determines the external, the compound of the organs, not by an act springing from without but issuing from within. In this way the end and the means, the interior and exterior, the general and particular, are confounded in unity. But this judgment only expresses a subjective act of reflection, and does not throw any light on the object in itself. Kant has the same view of the aesthetic judgment. According to him the judgment does not proceed either from reason, as the faculty of general ideas, or from sensuous perception, but from the free play of the reason and of the imagination. In this analysis of the cognitive faculty, the object only exists relatively to the subject and to the feeling of pleasure or the enjoyment that it experiences.

The characteristics of the beautiful are, according to Kant:—

1. The pleasure it procures is free from interest.

2. Beauty appears to us as an object of general enjoyment, without awakening in us the consciousness of an abstract idea and of a category of reason to which we might refer our judgment.

3. Beauty ought to embrace in itself the relation of conformity to its end, but in such a way that this conformity may be grasped without the idea of the end being offered to our mind.

4. Though it be not accompanied by an abstract idea, beauty ought to be acknowledged as the

object of a necessary enjoyment.

A special feature of all this system is the indissoluble unity of what is supposed to be separated in consciousness. This distinction disappears in the beautiful, because in it the general and the particular, the end and the means, the idea and the object, mentally penetrate each other completely. The particular in itself, whether it be opposed to itself or to what is general, is something accidental. But here what may be considered as an accidental form is so intimately connected with the general that it is confounded and identified with it. By this means the beautiful in art presents thought to us as incarnate. On the other hand, matter, nature, the sensuous as themselves possessing measure, end, and harmony, are raised to the dignity of spirit and share in its general character. Thought not only abandons its hostility against nature, but smiles in her. Sensation and enjoyment are justified and sanctified, so that nature and liberty, sense and ideas, find their justification and their sanctification in this union. Nevertheless this reconciliation, though seemingly perfect, is stricken with the character of subjectiveness. It cannot constitute the absolutely true and real.

Such is an outline of the principal results of Kant's criticism, and Hegel passes high praise on the profoundly philosophic mind of Schiller, who demanded the union and reconciliation of the two principles, and who tried to give a scientific explanation of it before the problem had been solved by philosophy. In his "Letters on Aesthetic Education," Schiller admits that man carries in himself the germ of the ideal man which is realized and represented by the state. There are two ways for the individual man to approach the ideal man; first, when the state, considered as morality, justice, and general reason, absorbs the individualities in its unity; secondly, when the individual rises to the ideal of his species by the perfecting of himself. Reason demands unity, conformity to the species; nature, on the other hand, demands plurality and individuality; and man is at once solicited by two contrary laws. In this conflict, aesthetic education must come in to effect the reconciliation of the two principles; for, according to Schiller, it has as its end to fashion and polish the inclinations and passions so that they may become reasonable, and that, on the other hand, reason and freedom may issue from their abstract character, may unite with nature, may spiritualize it, become incarnate, and take a body in it. Beauty is thus given as the simultaneous development of the rational and of the sensuous, fused together, and interpenetrated one by the other, an union that constitutes in fact true reality.

This unity of the general and of the particular, of liberty and necessity of the spiritual and material, which Schiller understood scientifically as the spirit of art, and which he tried to make appear in real life by aesthetic art and education, was afterwards put forward under the name of idea as the principle of all knowledge and existence. In this way, through the agency of Schelling, science raised itself to an absolute point of view. It was thus that art began to claim its proper nature and dignity. From that time its proper place was finally marked out for it in science, though the mode of viewing it still labored under certain defects. Its high and true distinction were at length understood.

In viewing the higher position to which recent philosophical systems have raised the theory of art in Germany, we must not overlook the advantages contributed by the study of the ideal of the ancients by such men as Winckelmann, who, by a kind of inspiration, raised art criticism from a carping about petty details to seek the true spirit of great works of art, and their true ideas, by a study of the spirit of the originals.

It has appeared expedient to conclude this introduction with a summary of the latest and highest theory of art and aesthetics issuing from Kant and Schiller, and developed in the later philosophy of Hegel.

Our space only allows us to give a glance, first, at the metaphysics of the beautiful as developed by Hegel in the first part of his 'Aesthetik,' and then at the later development of the same system in recent writers issuing from his school.

Hegel considers, first, the abstract idea of the beautiful; secondly, beauty in nature; thirdly, beauty in art or the ideal; and he winds up with an examination of the qualities of the artist.

His preliminary remarks are directed to show the relations of art to religion and philosophy, and he shows that man's destination is an infinite development. In real life he only satisfies his longing partially and imperfectly by limited enjoyments. In science he finds a nobler pleasure, and civil life opens a career for his activity; but he only finds an imperfect pleasure in these pursuits. He cannot then find the ideal after which he sighs. Then he rises to a higher sphere, where all contradictions are effaced and the ideas of good and happiness are realized in perfect accord and in constant harmony. This deep want of the soul is satisfied in three ways: in art, in religion, and in philosophy.

Art is intended to make us contemplate the true and the infinite in forms of sense. Yet even art does not fully satisfy the deepest need of the soul. The soul wants to contemplate truth in its inmost consciousness. Religion is placed above the dominion of art.

First, as to idea of the beautiful, Hegel begins by giving its characteristics. It is infinite, and it is free; the contemplation of the beautiful suffices to itself, it awakens no desire. The soul experiences something like a godlike felicity and is transported into a sphere remote from the miseries of life. This theory of the beautiful comes very near that of Plato.

Secondly, as to beauty in nature. Physical beauty, considered externally, presents itself successively under the aspects of regularity and of symmetry, of conformity with a law, and of harmony, also of purity and simplicity of matter.

Thirdly, beauty in art or the ideal is beauty in a higher degree of perfection than real beauty. The ideal in art is not contrary to the real, but the real idealized, purified, and perfectly expressed. The ideal is also the soul arrived at the consciousness of itself, free and fully enjoying its faculties; it is life, but spiritual life and spirit. Nor is the ideal a cold abstraction, it is the spiritual principle under the form of a living individuality freed from the laws of the finite. The ideal in its highest form is the divine, as expressed in the Greek divinities; the Christian ideal, as expressed in all its highest purity in God the Father, the Christ, the Virgin. Its essential features are calm, majesty, serenity.

At a lower degree the ideal is in man the victory of the eternal principles that fill the human heart, the triumph of the nobler part of the soul, the moral and divine principle.

But the ideal manifested in the world becomes action, and action implies a form of society, a determinate situation with collision, and an action properly so called. The heroic age is the best society for the ideal in action; in its determinate situation the ideal in action must appear as the manifestation of moral power, and in action, properly so called, it must contain three points in the ideal: first, general principles; secondly, personages; thirdly, their character and their passions. Hegel winds up by considering the qualities necessary in an artist: imagination, genius, inspiration, originality, etc.

A recent exponent of Hegel's aesthetical ideas further developed expresses himself thus on the nature of beauty:—

"After the bitterness of the world, the sweetness of art soothes and refreshes us. This is the high value of the beautiful—that it solves the contradiction of mind and matter, of the moral and sensuous world, in harmony. Thus the beautiful and its representation in art procures for intuition what philosophy gives to the cognitive insight and religion to the believing frame of mind. Hence the delight with which Schiller's wonderful poem on the Bell celebrates the accord of the inner and outer life, the fulfilment of the longing and demands of the soul by the events in nature. The externality of phenomena is removed in the beautiful; it is raised into the circle of ideal existence; for it is recognized as the revelation of the ideal, and thus transfigured it gives to the latter additional splendor."

"Thus the beautiful is active, living unity, full existence without defect, as Plato and Schelling have said, or as recent writers describe it; the idea that is quite present in the appearance, the appearance which is quite formed and penetrated by the idea."

"Beauty is the world secret that invites us in image and word," is the poetical expression of Plato; and we may add, because it is revealed in both. We feel in it the harmony of the world; it breaks forth in a beauty, in a lovely accord, in a radiant point, and starting thence we penetrate further and yet further, and find as the ground of all existence the same charm which had refreshed us in individual forms. Thus Christ pointed to the lilies of the field to knit His followers' reliance on Providence with the phenomena of nature: and could they jet forth in royal beauty, exceeding that of Solomon, if the inner ground of nature were not beauty?

We may also name beauty in a certain sense a mystery, as it mediates to us in a sensuous sign a heavenly gift of grace, that it opens to us a view into the eternal Being, teaching us to know nature in God and God in nature, that it brings the divine even to the perception of sense, and establishes the energy of love and freedom as the ground, the bond, and the end of the world.

In the midst of the temporal the eternal is made palpable and present to us in the beautiful, and offers itself to our enjoyment. The separation is suppressed, and the original unity, as it is in God, appears as the first, as what holds together even the past in the universe, and what constitutes the aim of the development in a finite accord.

The beautiful not only presents itself to us as mediator of a foreign excellence or of a remote divinity, but the ideal and the godlike are present in it. Hence aesthetics requires as its basis the system in which God is known as indwelling in the world, that He is not far distant from any one of us, but that He animates us, and that we live in Him. Aesthetics requires the knowledge that mind is the creative force and unity of all that is extended and developed in time and space.

The beautiful is thus, according to these later thinkers, the revelation of God to the mind through the senses; it is the appearance of the idea. In the beautiful spirit reveals itself to spirit through matter and the senses; thus the entire man feels himself raised and satisfied by it. By the unity of the beautiful with us we experience with delight that thought and the material world are present for our individuality, that they utter tones and shine forth in it, that both penetrate each other and blend in it and thus become one with it. We feel one with them and one in them.

This later view was to a great extent expressed by Schiller in his "Aesthetical Letters."

But art and aesthetics, in the sense in which these terms are used and understood by German philosophical writers, such as Schiller, embrace a wider field than the fine arts. Lessing, in his "Laocoon," had already shown the point of contrast between painting and poetry; and aesthetics, being defined as the science of the beautiful, must of necessity embrace poetry. Accordingly Schiller's essays on tragic art, pathos, and sentimental poetry, contained in this volume, are justly classed under his aesthetical writings.

This being so, it is important to estimate briefly the transitions of German poetry before Schiller, and the position that he occupied in its historic development.

The first classical period of German poetry and literature was contained between A. D. 1190 and 1300. It exhibits the intimate blending of the German and Christian elements, and their full development in splendid productions, for this was the period of the German national epos, the "Nibelungenlied," and of the "Minnegesang."

This was a period which has nothing to compare with it in point of art and poetry, save perhaps, and that imperfectly, the heroic and post-Homeric age of early Greece.

The poetical efforts of that early age may be grouped under—(1) national epos: the "Nibelungenlied;" (2) art epos: the "Rolandslied," "Percival," etc.; (3) the introduction of antique legends: Veldeck's "Aeneide," and Konrad's "War of Troy;" (4) Christian legends "Barlaam," "Sylvester," "Pilatus," etc.; (5) poetical narratives: "Crescentia," "Graf Rudolf," etc.; (6) animal legends; "Reinecke Vos;" (7) didactic poems: "Der Renner;" (8) the Minne-poetry, and prose.

The fourth group, though introduced from a foreign source, gives the special character and much of the charm of the period we consider. This is the sphere of legends derived from ecclesiastical ground. One of the best German writers on the history of German literature remarks: "If the aim and nature of all poetry is to let yourself be filled by a subject and to become penetrated with it; if the simple representation of unartificial, true, and glowing feelings belongs to its most beautiful adornments; if the faithful direction of the heart to the invisible and eternal is the ground on which at all times the most lovely flowers of poetry have sprouted forth, these legendary poems of early Germany, in their lovely heartiness, in their unambitious limitation, and their pious sense, deserve a friendly acknowledgment. What man has considered the pious images in the prayer-books of the Middle Ages, the unadorned innocence, the piety and purity, the patience of the martyrs, the calm, heavenly transparency of the figures of the holy angels, without being attracted by the simple innocence and humility of these forms, the creation of pious artists' hands? Who has beheld them without tranquil joy at the soft splendor poured, over them, without deep sympathy, nay, without a certain emotion and tenderness? And the same spirit that created these images also produced those poetical effusions, the same spirit of pious belief, of deep devotion, of heavenly longing. If we make a present reality of the heroic songs of the early German popular poetry, and the chivalrous epics of the art poetry, the military expeditions and dress of the Crusades, this legendary poetry appears as the invention of humble pilgrims, who wander slowly on the weary way to Jerusalem, with scollop and pilgrim's staff, engaged in quiet prayer, till they are all to kneel at the Saviour's sepulchre; and thus contented, after touching the holy earth with their lips, they return, poor as they were, but full of holy comfort, to their distant home.

"While the knightly poetry is the poetry of the splendid secular life, full of cheerful joy, full of harp-tones and song, full of tournaments and joyous festivals, the poetry of the earthly love for the earthly bride, the poetry of the legends is that of the spontaneous life of poverty, the poetry of the solitary cloister cell, of the quiet, well-walled convent garden, the poetry of heavenly brides, who without lamenting the joys of the world, which they need not, have their joy in their Saviour in tranquil piety and devout resignation—who attend at the espousals of Anna and Joachim, sing the Magnificat with the Holy Mother of God, stand weeping beneath the cross, to be pierced also by the sword, who hear the angel harp with St. Cecilia, and walk with St. Theresa in the glades of Paradise. While the Minne-poetry was the tender homage offered to the beauty, the gentleness, the grace, and charm of noble women of this world, legendary poetry was the homage given to the Virgin Mother, the Queen of Heaven, transfiguring earthly love into a heavenly and eternal love."

"For the twelfth and thirteenth centuries were the time of woman cultus, such as has never been before or since seen; it is also the time of the deepest and simplest and truest, most enthusiastic and faithful veneration of the Virgin Mary. If we, by a certain effort, manage to place ourselves back on the standpoint of childlike poetic faith of that time, and set aside in thought the materializing and exaggeration of the hagiology and Mariolatry produced by later centuries, rendering the reaction of the Reformation unavoidable—if now in our age, turned exclusively to logical ideas and a negative dialectic, we live again by thought in those ages of feeling and poetry—if we acknowledge all these things to be something more than harmless play of words and fancy, and as the true lifelike contents of the period, then we can properly appreciate this legendary poetry as a necessary link in the crown of pearls of our ancient poetry."

In short, the first classical period of German literature was a time of youthful freshness, of pure harmony, plunged in verse and song, full of the richest tones and the noblest rhythm, so that rhyme and song alone must be looked for as the form of poetic creations. Accordingly it had no proper prose. Like our own youth, it was a happy, free, and true youth, it knew no prose; like us it dreamed to speechless songs; and as we expressed our youthful language and hopes, woes and joys, in rhyme and song, thus a whole people and age had its beautiful youth full of song and verse tones. The life was poetry and poetry was the life.

Then came degeneracy and artifice; after that the great shock of the Reformation; subsequently a servile and pedantic study of classical forms without imbibing their spirit, but preparing the way for a truer art spirit, extracted from their study by the masterly criticism of Winckelmann and Lessing, till the second classical period of German literature and poetry bloomed forth in full beauty, blending the national and legendary elements so well expressed by Herder with the highest effusions of dramatic poetry, partly creative and partly imitative of the Greek models, in Schiller and Goethe.

Modern German literature presents a very remarkable spectacle, though far from unique in history, for there we see criticism begetting genius.

Lessing, the founder of the modern German drama, sought to banish all pomp from the theatre, and in doing so some critics have thought that he banished the ideal and fell into affectation. At any rate, his "Dramaturgy" is full of original ideas, and when he drew out the sphere of poetry contrasted with that of painting in his "Laocoon," all Germany resounded with his praise. "With that delight," says Goethe, "we saluted this luminous ray which a thinker of the first order caused to break forth from its clouds. It is necessary to have all the fire of youth to conceive the effect produced on us by the 'Laocoon' of Lessing." Another great contemporary, whose name is imperishable as that of art, struck a mortal blow at a false taste in the study of the antique. Winckelmann questioned the works of the Greek chisel with an intelligence full of love, and initiated his countrymen into poetry by a feeling for sculpture! What an enthusiasm he displayed for classical beauty! what a worship of the form! what a fervor of paganism is found in its eloquent pages when he also comments on the admirable group of the Laocoon, or the still purer masterpiece of the Apollo of Belvedere.

These men were the vanguard of the great Germanic army; Schiller and Goethe alone formed its main column. In them German poetry shows itself in its perfection, and completely realizes the ideal designed for it by the critic. Every factitious precept and conventional law was now overthrown; these poetical Protestants broke away entirely from the yoke of tradition. Yet their genius was not without a rule. Every work bears in itself the organic laws of its development. Thus, although they laugh at the famous precept of the three unities, it is because they dig still deeper down to the root of things, to grasp the true principle from which the precept issued. "Men have not understood," said Goethe, "the basis of this law. The law of the comprehensive —'das Fassliche'—is the principle; and the three unities have only value as far as they attain it. When they become an obstacle to the comprehension it is madness to wish to observe them. The Greeks themselves, from whom the rule is derived, did not always follow it. In the 'Phaeton' of Euripides, and in other pieces, there was change, place; accordingly they prefer to give a perfect exposition of their subject, rather than blindly respect a law never very essential in itself. The pieces of Shakspeare violate in the highest degree the unity of time and of place; but they are full of comprehensiveness; nothing is easier to grasp, and for that reason they would have found favor with the Greeks. The French poets tried to obey exactly the law of the three unities; but they violate the law of comprehensiveness, as they do not expound dramatic subjects by dramas but by recitals."

Poetical creation was therefore viewed as free, but at the same time responsible. Immediately, as if fecundity were the reward of correctness, the German theatre became filled with true and living characters. The stage widens under their steps that they may have room to move. History with its great proportions and its terrible lessons, is now able to take place on the stage. The whole Thirty Years' War passes before us in "Wallenstein." We hear the tumult of camps, the disorder of a fanatical and undisciplined army, peasants, recruits, sutlers, soldiers. The illusion is complete, and enthusiasm breaks out among the spectators. Similar merits attach to many other of Schiller's plays.

This new drama, which seemed to give all to the natural sphere, concedes still more to the ideal. An able critic has said the details which are the truth of history are also its poetry. Here the German school professes a principle of the highest learning, and one that seems to be borrowed from its profoundest philosophers; it is that of the universal beauty of life, of the identity of beauty and existence. "Our aesthetics," says Goethe, "speak a great deal of poetical or antipoetical subjects; fundamentally there is no subject that has not its poetry; it is for the poet to find it there."

Schiller and Goethe divide the empire over modern German poetry, and represent its two principal powers; the one, Schiller, impassioned and lyrical, pours his soul over all the subjects he touches; in him every composition, ode, or drama is always one of his noble ideas, borrowing its dress and ornament from the external world. He is a poet especially through the heart, by the force with which he rushes in and carries you with him. Goethe is especially an epic; no doubt he paints the passions with admirable truth, but he commands them; like the god of the seas in Virgil, he raises above the angry waves his calm and sublime forehead.

After this glance at the position and chief characteristics of Schiller, it may be useful to offer a few remarks on those of the principal works in this volume, his Aesthetical Letters and Essays. Schiller, in his Aesthetical Essays, did not choose the pure abstract method of deduction and conception like Kant, nor the historical like Herder, who strove thus to account for the genesis of our ideas of beauty and art. He struck out a middle path, which presents certain deficiencies to the advocates of either of these two systems. He leans upon Kantian ideas, but without scholastic constraint. Pure speculation, which seeks to set free the form from all contents and matter, was remote from his creative genius, to which the world of matter and sense was no hinderance, but a necessary envelop for his forms.

His removal to Jena in 1791, and acquaintance with Reinhold, familiarized him with the Kantian philosophy, but he only appreciated it by halves. The bare and bald dealing with fundamental principles was at this time equally repulsive to Goethe and Schiller, the man of the world and the man of life. But Schiller did not find anywhere at that time justice done to the dignity of art, or honor to the substantial value of beauty.

The Aesthetical Essays in this volume appeared for the most part since 1792, in the "Thalia" and the "Hours" periodicals. The first "On the Ground of our Pleasure in Tragic Subjects" (1792), applies Kantian principles of the sublime to tragedy, and shows Schiller's lofty estimate of this class of poetry. With Kant he shows that the source of all pleasure is suitableness; the touching and sublime elicit this feeling, implying the existence of unsuitableness. In this article he makes the aim and source of art to consist in giving enjoyment, in pleasing. To nature pleasure is a mediate object, to art its main object. The same proposition appears in Schiller's paper on Tragic Art (1792), closely connected with the former. This article contains views of the affection of pity that seem to approximate the Aristotelian propositions about tragedy.

His views on the sublime are expressed in two papers, "The Sublime" and "The Pathetic," in which we trace considerable influence of Lessing and Winckelmann. He is led especially to strong antagonism against the French tragedy, and he indulges in a lengthy consideration of the passage of Virgil on Laocoon, showing the necessity of suffering and the pathetic in connection with moral adaptations to interest us deeply.

All these essays bespeak the poet who has tried his hand at tragedy, but in his next paper, "On Grace and Dignity," we trace more of the moralist. Those passages where he takes up a medium position between sense and reason, between Goethe and Kant, are specially attractive. The theme of this paper is the conception of grace, or the expression of a beautiful soul and dignity, or that of a lofty mind. The idea of grace has been developed more deeply and truly by Schiller than by Wieland or Winckelmann, but the special value of the paper is its constantly pointing to the ideal of a higher humanity. In it he does full justice to the sensuous and to the moral, and commencing with the beautiful nature of the Greeks, to whom sense was never mere sense, nor reason mere reason, he concludes with an image of perfected humanity in which grace and dignity are united, the former by architectonic beauty (structure), the last supported by power.

The following year, 1795, appeared his most important contribution to aesthetics, in his Aesthetical Letters.

In these letters he remarks that beauty is the work of free contemplation, and we enter with it into the world of ideas, but without leaving the world of sense. Beauty is to us an object, and yet at the same time a state of our subjectivity, because the feeling of the conditional is under that which we have of it. Beauty is a form because we consider it, and life because we feel it; in a word, it is at once our state and our art. And exactly because it is both it serves us as a triumphant proof that suffering does not exclude activity, nor matter form, nor limitation the infinite, for in the enjoyment of beauty both natures are united, and by this is proved the capacity of the infinite to be developed in the finite, and accordingly the possibility of the sublimest humanity.

The free play of the faculty of cognition which had been determined by Kant is also developed by Schiller. His representation of this matter is this: Man, as a spirit, is reason and will, self-active, determining, form-giving; this is described by Schiller as the form-instinct; man, as a sensuous being, is determinable, receptive, termed to matter; Schiller describes this as the material instinct, "Stofftrieb." In the midst between these two is situated the beautiful, in which reason and the sensuous penetrate each other, and their enjoyable product is designated by Schiller the play instinct. This expression is not happily chosen. Schiller means to describe by it the free play of the forces, activity according to nature, which is at once a joy and a happiness; he reminds us of the life of Olympus, and adds: "Man is only quite a man when he plays." Personality is that which lasts, the state of feeling is the changeable in man; he is the fixed unity remaining eternally himself in the floods of change. Man in contact with the world is to take it up in himself, but to unite with it the highest freedom and independence, and, instead of being lost in the world, to subject it to his reason. It is only by his being independent that there is reality out of him; only by being susceptible of feeling that there is reality in him. The object of sensuous instinct is life; that of the purer instinct figure; living figure or beauty is the object of the play instinct.

Only inasmuch as life is formed in the understanding and form in feeling does life win a form and form win life, and only thus does beauty arise. By beauty the sensuous man is led up to reason, the one-sided tension of special force is strung to harmony, and man made a complete whole.

Schiller adds that beauty knits together thought and feeling; the fullest unity of spirit and matter. Its freedom is not lack, but harmony, of laws; its conditions are not exclusions, inclusion of all infinity determined in itself. A true work of art generates lofty serenity and freedom of mind. Thus the aesthetic disposition bestows on us the highest of all gifts, that of a disposition to humanity, and we may call beauty our second creator.

In these letters Schiller spoke out the mildest and highest sentiments on art, and in his paper on Simple and Sentimental Poetry (1795) he constructs the ideal of the perfect poet. This is by far the most fruitful of Schiller's essays in its results. It has much that is practically applicable, and contains a very able estimate of German poetry. The writing is also very pointed and telling, because it is based upon actual perceptions, and it is interesting because the contrast drawn out throughout it between the simple and the sentimental has been referred to his own contrast with Goethe. He also wished to vindicate modern poetry, which Goethe seemed to wish to sacrifice to the antique.

The sentimental poetry is the fruit of quiet and retirement; simple poetry the child of life. One is a favor of nature; the sentimental depends on itself, the simple on the world of experience. The sentimental is in danger of extending the limits of human nature too far, of being too ideal, too mystical. Neither character exhausts the ideal of humanity, but the intimate union of both. Both are founded in human nature; the contradictions lying at their basis, when cleared in thought from the poetical faculty, are realism and idealism. These also are sides of human nature, which, when unconnected, bring forth disastrous results. Their opposition is as old as the beginning of culture, and till its end can hardly be set aside, save in the individual. The idealist is a nobler but a far less perfect being; the realist appears far less noble, but is more perfect, for the noble lies in the proof of a great capacity, but the perfect in the general attitude of the whole and in the real facts.

On the whole it may be said, taking a survey of these labors, that if Schiller had developed his ideas systematically and the unity of his intuition of the world, which were present in his feelings, and if he had based them scientifically, a new epoch in philosophy might have been anticipated. For he had obtained a view of such a future field of thought with the deep clairvoyance of his genius.

A few words may be desirable on Schiller's religious standpoint, especially in connection with his philosophical letters.

Schiller came up ten years later than Goethe, and concluded the cyclus of genius that Goethe had inaugurated. But as he was the last arrival of that productive period of tempestuous agitation, he retained more of its elements in his later life and poetry than any others who had passed through earlier agitations, such as Goethe. For Goethe cast himself free in a great measure from the early intoxication of his youthful imagination, devoting himself partly to nobler matter and partly to purer forms.

Schiller derived from the stormy times of his youth his direction to the ideal, to the hostility against the narrow spirit of civil relations, and to all given conditions of society in general. He derived from it his disposition, not to let himself be moulded by matter, but to place his own creative and determining impress on matter, not so much to grasp reality poetically and represent it poetically as to cast ideas into reality, a disposition for lively representation and strong oratorical coloring. All this he derived from the genial period, though later on somewhat modified, and carried it over into his whole life and poetry; and for this very reason he is not only together with Goethe, but before Goethe, the favorite poet of the nation, and especially with that part of the nation which sympathizes with him in the choice of poetic material and in his mode of feeling.

Gervinus remarks that Schiller had at Weimar long fallen off from Christianity, and occupied his mind tranquilly for a time with the views of Spinoza (realistic pantheism). Like Herder and Goethe, he viewed life in its great entirety and sacrificed the individual to the species. Accordingly, through the gods of Greece, he fell out with strict, orthodox Christians.

But Schiller had deeply religious and even Christian elements, as became a German and a Kantian. He receives the Godhead in His will, and He descends from His throne, He dwells in his soul; the poet sees divine revelations, and as a seer announces them to man. He is a moral educator of his people, who utters the tones of life in his poetry from youth upwards. Philosophy was not disclosed to Plato in the highest and purest thought, nor is poetry to Schiller merely an artificial edifice in the harmony of speech; philosophy and poetry are to both a vibration of love in the soul upwards to God, a liberation from the bonds of sense, a purification of man, a moral art. On this reposes the religious consecration of the Platonic spirit and of that of Schiller.

Issuing from the philosophical school of Kant, and imbued with the antagonism of the age against constituted authorities, it is natural that Schiller should be a rationalist in his religious views. It has been justly said of him that while Goethe's system was an apotheosis of nature Schiller's was an apotheosis of man.

Historically he was not prepared enough to test and search the question of evidence as applied to divine things handed down by testimony, and his Kantian coloring naturally disposed him to include all religions within the limits of pure reason, and to seek it rather in the subject than in anything objective.

In conclusion, we may attempt to classify and give Schiller his place in the progress of the world's literary history. Progress is no doubt a law of the individual, of nations, and of the whole race. To grow in perfection, to exist in some sort at a higher degree, is the task imposed by God on man, the continuation of the very work of God, the complement of creation. But this moral growth, this need of increase, may, like all the forces of nature, yield to a greater force; it is an impulsion rather than a necessity; it solicits and does not constrain. A thousand obstacles stay its development in individuals and in societies; moral liberty may retard or accelerate its effects. Progress is therefore a law which cannot be abrogated, but which is not invariably obeyed.

Nevertheless, in proportion to the increase of the mass of individuals, the caprices of chance and of liberty neutralize each other to allow the providential action that presides over our destinies to prevail. Looking at the same total of the life of the world, humanity undoubtedly advances: there are in our time fewer moral miseries, fewer physical miseries, than were known in the past.

Consequently art and literature, which express the different states of society, must share in some degree in this progressive march. But there are two things in literary work: on the one hand the ideas and social manners which it expresses, on the other the intelligence, the feeling, the imagination of the writer who becomes its interpreter. While the former of these elements tends incessantly to a greater perfection, the latter is subject to all the hazards of individual genius. Accordingly the progressive literature is only in the inspiration, and so to speak in the matter; it may and must therefore not be continuous in form.

But more than this: in very advanced societies the very grandeur of ideas, the abundance of models, the satiety of the public render the task of the artist more and more difficult. The artist himself has no longer the enthusiasm of the first ages, the youth of imagination and of the heart; he is an old man whose riches have increased, but who enjoys his wealth less.

If all the epochs of literature are considered as a whole it will be seen that they succeed each other in a constant order. After the period when the idea and the form combined in a harmonious manner comes another where the social idea is superabundant, and destroys the literary form of the preceding epoch.

The middle ages introduced spiritualism in art; before this new idea the smiling untruths of Greek poetry fled away frightened. The classical form so beautiful, so pure, cannot contain high Catholic thought. A new art is formed; on this side the Alps it does not reach the maturity that produces masterpieces. But at that time all Europe was one fatherland; Italy completes what is lacking in France and elsewhere.

The renaissance introduces new ideas into civilization; it resuscitates the traditions of antique science and seeks to unite them to the truths of Christianity. The art of the middle ages, as a vessel of too limited capacity, is broken by the new flood poured into it. These different ideas are stirred up and in conflict in the sixteenth century; they became co-ordinate and attain to an admirable expression in the following age.

In the eighteenth century there is a new invasion of ideas; all is examined and questioned; religion, government, society, all becomes a matter of discussion for the school called philosophical. Poetry appeared dying out, history drying up, till a truer spirit was breathed into the literary atmosphere by the criticism of Lessing, the philosophy of Kant, and the poetry of Klopstock. It was at this transition period that Schiller appeared, retaining throughout his literary career much of the revolutionary and convulsive spirit of his early days, and faithfully reflecting much of the dominant German philosophy of his time.

Part of the nineteenth century seems to take in hand the task of

reconstructing the moral edifice and of giving back to thought a larger form. The literary result of its effects is the renaissance of lyrical poetry with an admirable development in history.

Schiller's most brilliant works were in the former walk, his histories have inferior merit, and his philosophical writings bespeak a deep thinking nature with great originality of conception, such as naturally results from a combination of high poetic inspiration with much intellectual power.

Schiller, like all great men of genius, was a representative man of his country and of his age. A German, a Protestant free-thinker, a worshipper of the classical, he was the expression of these aspects of national and general thought.

The religious reformation was the work of the North. The instinct of races came in it to complicate the questions of dogmas. The awakening of individual nationalities was one of the characters of the epoch.

The nations compressed in the severe unity of the Middle Ages escaped in the Reformation from the uniform mould that had long enveloped them, and tended to that other unity, still very distant, which must spring from the spontaneous view of the same truth by all men, result from the free and original development of each nation, and, as in a vast concert, unite harmonious dissonances. Europe, without being conscious of its aim, seized greedily at the means—insurrection; the only thought was to overthrow, without yet thinking of a reconstruction. The sixteenth century was the vanguard of the eighteenth. At all times the North had fretted under the antipathetic yoke of the South. Under the Romans, Germany, though frequently conquered, had never been subdued. She had invaded the Empire and determined its fall. In the Middle Ages the struggle had continued; not only instincts, but ideas, were in conflict; force and spirit, violence and polity, feudalism and the Catholic hierarchy, hereditary and elective forms, represented the opposition of two races. In the sixteenth century the schism long anticipated took place. The Catholic dogma had hitherto triumphed over all outbreaks— over Arnaldo of Brescia, the Waldenses, and Wickliffe. But Luther appeared, and the work was accomplished: Catholic unity was broken.

And this breaking with authority went on fermenting in the nations till its last great outburst at the French Revolution; and Schiller was born at this convulsive period, and bears strong traces of his parentage in his anti-dogmatic spirit.

Yet there is another side to Germanism which is prone to the ideal and the mystical, and bears still the trace of those lovely legends of mediaeval growth to which we have adverted. For Christianity was not a foreign and antagonistic importation in Germany; rather, the German character obtained its completeness through Christianity. The German found himself again in the Church of Christ, only raised, transfigured, and sanctified. The apostolic representation of the Church as the bride of Christ has found its fullest and truest correspondence in that of Germany. Hence when the German spirit was thoroughly espoused to the Christian spirit, we find that character of love, tenderness, and depth so characteristic of the early classics of German poetry, and reappearing in glorious afterglow in the second classics, in Klopstock, Herder, and, above all, Schiller.

It is this special instinct for the ideal and mystical in German nature that has enabled spirits born of negation and revolution, like Schiller, to unite with those elements the most genial and creative inspirations of poetry.

VOCABULARY OF TERMINOLOGY.

Absolute, The. A conception, or, more strictly, in Kantian language, an idea of the pure reason, embracing the fundamental and necessary yet free ground of all things.

Antinomy. The conflict of the laws of pure reason; as in the question of free will and necessity.

Autonomy (autonomous). Governing itself by the spontaneous action of free will.

Aesthetics. The science of beauty; as ethics of duty.

Cognition (knowledge; Germanice, "Erkenntniss") is either an intuition or a conception. The former has an immediate relation to the object, and is singular and individual; the latter has but a mediate relation, by means of a characteristic mark, which may be common to several things.

Cognition is an objective perception.

Conception. A conception is either empirical or pure. A pure conception, in so far as it has its origin in the understanding alone, and is not the conception of a pure sensuous image, is called notio.

Conceptions are distinguished on the one hand from sensation and perception, and on the other hand from the intuitions of pure reason or ideas. They are distinctly the product of thought and of the understanding, except when quite free from empirical elements.

Feeling (Gefuehl). That part of our nature which relates to passion and instinct. Feelings are connected both with our sensuous nature, our imagination, and the pure reason.

Form. See Matter.

Ideas. The product of the pure reason (Vernunft) or intuitive faculty. Wherever the absolute is introduced in thought we have ideas. Perfection in all its aspects is an idea, virtue and wisdom in their perfect purity and ideas. Kant remarks ("Critique of Pure Reason," Meiklejohn's translation, p. 256): "It is from the understanding alone that pure and transcendental conceptions take their origin; the reason does not properly give birth to any conception, but only frees the conception of the understanding from the unavoidable limitation of possible experience. A conception formed from notions which transcend the possibility of experience is an idea or a conception of reason."

Intuition (Anschauung) as used by Kant, is external or internal. External, sensuous intuition is identical with perception; internal intuition gives birth to ideas.

Matter and Form. "These two conceptions are at the foundation of all other reflection, being inseparably connected with every mode of exercising the understanding. By the former is implied that which can be determined in general; the second implies its determination, both in a transcendental sense, abstraction being made of any difference in that which is given, and of the mode in which it is determined. That which in the phenomenon corresponds to the sensation, I term its matter; but that which effects that the content of the phenomenon can be arranged under certain relations, I call its form."—Kant, "Critique," op. cit.

Objective. What is inherent or relative to an object, or not Myself, except in the case when I reflect on myself, in which case my states of mind are objective to my thoughts. In a popular sense objective means external, as contrasted with the subjective or internal.

Perception, if it relates only to the subject as a modification of its state, is a sensation. An objective perception is a cognition (Erkenntniss).

Phenomena (Erscheinnngen). The undetermined object of an empirical intuition is called phenomenon.

Reason (pure; Germanice, "Vernunft"). The source of ideas of moral feelings and of conceptions free from all elements taken up from experience.

Representation (Vorstellung). All the products of the mind are styled representations (except emotions and mere sensations) and the term is applied to the whole genus.

Representation with consciousness is perceptio.

Sensation. The capacity of receiving representations through the mode in which we are affected by objects is called sensibility. By means of sensibility objects are given to us, and it alone furnishes with intentions meaning sensuous intuitions. By the understanding they are thought, and from it arise conceptions.

Subjective. What has its source in and relation to the personality, to Myself, I, or the Ego; opposed to the objective, or what is inherent in and relative to the object. Not myself, except in the case when my states of mind are the object of my own reflection.

Supersensuous. Contrasted with and opposed to the sensuous. What is exclusively related to sense or imparted through the sensuous ideas is supersensuous. See Transcendental.

Transcendental. What exceeds the limits of sense and empirical observation. "I apply the term transcendental to all knowledge which is not so much occupied with objects as with the mode of our cognition of these objects, so far as this mode of cognition is possible a priori." Kant's "Critique," op. cit. p. 16.

Understanding (Verstand). The thought of faculty, the source of conceptions and notions (Begriffe) of the laws of logic, the categories, and judgment.

LETTERS ON THE AESTHETICAL EDUCATION OF MAN.

LETTER I.

By your permission I lay before you, in a series of letters, the results of my researches upon beauty and art. I am keenly sensible of the importance as well as of the charm and dignity of this undertaking. I shall treat a subject which is closely connected with the better portion of our happiness and not far removed from the moral nobility of human nature. I shall plead this cause of the beautiful before a heart by which her whole power is felt and exercised, and which will take upon itself the most difficult part of my task in an investigation where one is compelled to appeal as frequently to feelings as to principles.

That which I would beg of you as a favor, you generously impose upon me as a duty; and, when I solely consult my inclination, you impute to me a service. The liberty of action you prescribe is rather a necessity for me than a constraint. Little exercised in formal rules, I shall scarcely incur the risk of sinning against good taste by any undue use of them; my ideas, drawn rather from within than from reading or from an intimate experience with the world, will not disown their origin; they would rather incur any reproach than that of a sectarian bias, and would prefer to succumb by their innate feebleness than sustain themselves by borrowed authority and foreign support.

In truth, I will not keep back from you that the assertions which follow rest chiefly upon Kantian principles; but if in the course of these researches you should be reminded of any special school of philosophy, ascribe it to my incapacity, not to those principles. No; your liberty of mind shall be sacred to me; and the facts upon which I build will be furnished by your own sentiments; your own unfettered thought will dictate the laws according to which we have to proceed.

With regard to the ideas which predominate in the practical part of Kant's system, philosophers only disagree, whilst mankind, I am confident of proving, have never done so. If stripped of their technical shape, they will appear as the verdict of reason pronounced from time immemorial by common consent, and as facts of the moral instinct which nature, in her wisdom, has given to man in order to serve as guide and teacher until his enlightened intelligence gives him maturity. But this very technical shape which renders truth visible to the understanding conceals it from the feelings; for, unhappily, understanding begins by destroying the object of the inner sense before it can appropriate the object. Like the chemist, the philosopher finds synthesis only by analysis, or the spontaneous work of nature only through the torture of art. Thus, in order to detain the fleeting apparition, he must enchain it in the fetters of rule, dissect its fair proportions into abstract notions, and preserve its living spirit in a fleshless skeleton of words. Is it surprising that natural feeling should not recognize itself in such a copy, and if in the report of the analyst the truth appears as paradox?

Permit me therefore to crave your indulgence if the following researches should remove their object from the sphere of sense while endeavoring to draw it towards the understanding. That which I before said of moral experience can be applied with greater truth to the manifestation of "the beautiful." It is the mystery which enchants, and its being is extinguished with the extinction of the necessary combination of its elements.

LETTER II.

But I might perhaps make a better use of the opening you afford me if I were to direct your mind to a loftier theme than that of art. It would appear to be unseasonable to go in search of a code for the aesthetic world, when the moral world offers matter of so much higher interest, and when the spirit of philosophical inquiry is so stringently challenged by the circumstances of our times to occupy itself with the most perfect of all works of art—the establishment and structure of a true political freedom.

It is unsatisfactory to live out of your own age and to work for other times. It is equally incumbent on us to be good members of our own age as of our own state or country. If it is conceived to be unseemly and even unlawful for a man to segregate himself from the customs and manners of the circle in which he lives, it would be inconsistent not to see that it is equally his duty to grant a proper share of influence to the voice of his own epoch, to its taste and its requirements, in the operations in which he engages.

But the voice of our age seems by no means favorable to art, at all events to that kind of art to which my inquiry is directed. The course of events has given a direction to the genius of the time that threatens to remove it continually further from the ideal of art. For art has to leave reality, it has to raise itself boldly above necessity and neediness; for art is the daughter of freedom, and it requires its prescriptions and rules to be furnished by the necessity of spirits and not by that of matter. But in our day it is necessity, neediness, that prevails, and lends a degraded humanity under its iron yoke. Utility is the great idol of the time, to which all powers do homage and all subjects are subservient. In this great balance on utility, the spiritual service of art has no weight, and, deprived of all encouragement, it vanishes from the noisy Vanity Fair of our time. The very spirit of philosophical inquiry itself robs the imagination of one promise after another, and the frontiers of art are narrowed in proportion as the limits of science are enlarged.

The eyes of the philosopher as well as of the man of the world are anxiously turned to the theatre of political events, where it is presumed the great destiny of man is to be played out. It would almost seem to betray a culpable indifference to the welfare of society if we did not share this general interest. For this great commerce in social and moral principles is of necessity a matter of the greatest concern to every human being, on the ground both of its subject and of its results. It must accordingly be of deepest moment to every man to think for himself. It would seem that now at length a question that formerly was only settled by the law of the stronger is to be determined by the calm judgment of the reason, and every man who is capable of placing himself in a central position, and raising his individuality into that of his species, can look upon himself as in possession of this judicial faculty of reason; being moreover, as man and member of the human family, a party in the case under trial and involved more or less in its decisions. It would thus appear that this great political process is not only engaged with his individual case, it has also to pronounce enactments, which he as a rational spirit is capable of enunciating and entitled to pronounce.

It is evident that it would have been most attractive to me to inquire into an object such as this, to decide such a question in conjunction with a thinker of powerful mind, a man of liberal sympathies, and a heart imbued with a noble enthusiasm for the weal of humanity. Though so widely separated by worldly position, it would have been a delightful surprise to have found your unprejudiced mind arriving at the same result as my own in the field of ideas. Nevertheless, I think I can not only excuse, but even justify by solid grounds, my step in resisting this attractive purpose and in preferring beauty to freedom. I hope that I shall succeed in convincing you that this matter of art is less foreign to the needs than to the tastes of our age; nay, that, to arrive at a solution even in the political problem, the road of aesthetics must be pursued, because it is through beauty that we arrive at freedom. But I cannot carry out this proof without my bringing to your remembrance the principles by which the reason is guided in political legislation.

LETTER III.

Man is not better treated by nature in his first start than her other works are; so long as he is unable to act for himself as an independent intelligence she acts for him. But the very fact that constitutes him a man is that he does not remain stationary, where nature has placed him, that he can pass with his reason, retracing the steps nature had made him anticipate, that he can convert the work of necessity into one of free solution, and elevate physical necessity into a moral law.

When man is raised from his slumber in the senses he feels that he is a man; he surveys his surroundings and finds that he is in a state. He was introduced into this state by the power of circumstances, before he could freely select his own position. But as a moral being he cannot possibly rest satisfied with a political condition forced upon him by necessity, and only calculated for that condition; and it would be unfortunate if this did satisfy him. In many cases man shakes off this blind law of necessity, by his free spontaneous action, of which among many others we have an instance, in his ennobling by beauty and suppressing by moral influence the powerful impulse implanted in him by nature in the passion of love. Thus, when arrived at maturity, he recovers his childhood by an artificial process, he founds a state of nature in his ideas, not given him by any experience, but established by the necessary laws and conditions of his reason, and he attributes to this ideal condition an object, an aim, of which he was not cognizant in the actual reality of nature. He gives himself a choice of which he was not capable before, and sets to work just as if he were beginning anew, and were exchanging his original state of bondage for one of complete independence, doing this with complete insight and of his free decision. He is justified in regarding this work of political thraldom as non-existing, though a wild and arbitrary caprice may have founded its work very artfully; though it may strive to maintain it with great arrogance and encompass it with a halo of veneration. For the work of blind powers possesses no authority before which freedom need bow, and all must be made to adapt itself to the highest end which reason has set up in his personality. It is in this wise that a people in a state of manhood is justified in exchanging a condition of thraldom for one of moral freedom.

Now the term natural condition can be applied to every political body which owes its establishment originally to forces and not to laws, and such a state contradicts the moral nature of man, because lawfulness can alone have authority over this. At the same time this natural condition is quite sufficient for the physical man, who only gives himself laws in order to get rid of brute force. Moreover, the physical man is a reality, and the moral man problematical. Therefore when the reason suppresses the natural condition, as she must if she wishes to substitute her own, she weighs the real physical man against the problematical moral man, she weighs the existence of society against a possible, though morally necessary, ideal of society. She takes from man something which he really possesses, and without which he possesses nothing, and refers him as a substitute to something that he ought to possess and might possess; and if reason had relied too exclusively on him she might, in order to secure him a state of humanity in which he is wanting and can want without injury to his life, have robbed him even of the means of animal existence, which is the first necessary condition of his being a man. Before he had opportunity to hold firm to the law with his will, reason would have withdrawn from his feet the ladder of nature.

The great point is, therefore, to reconcile these two considerations, to prevent physical society from ceasing for a moment in time, while the moral society is being formed in the idea; in other words, to prevent its existence from being placed in jeopardy for the sake of the moral dignity of man. When the mechanic has to mend a watch he lets the wheels run out; but the living watchworks of the state have to be repaired while they act, and a wheel has to be exchanged for another during its revolutions. Accordingly props must be sought for to support society and keep it going while it is made independent of the natural condition from which it is sought to emancipate it.

This prop is not found in the natural character of man, who, being selfish and violent, directs his energies rather to the destruction than to the preservation of society. Nor is it found in his moral character, which has to be formed, which can never be worked upon or calculated on by the lawgiver, because it is free and never appears. It would seem, therefore, that another measure must be adopted. It would seem that the physical character of the arbitrary must be separated from moral freedom; that it is incumbent to make the former harmonize with the laws and the latter dependent on impressions; it would be expedient to remove the former still farther from matter and to bring the latter somewhat more near to it; in short, to produce a third character related to both the others—the physical and the moral—paving the way to a transition from the sway of mere force to that of law, without preventing the proper development of the moral character, but serving rather as a pledge in the sensuous sphere of a morality in the unseen.

LETTER IV.

Thus much is certain. It is only when a third character, as previously suggested, has preponderance that a revolution in a state according to moral principles can be free from injurious consequences; nor can anything else secure its endurance. In proposing or setting up a moral state, the moral law is relied upon as a real power, and free-will is drawn into the realm of causes, where all hangs together mutually with stringent necessity and rigidity. But we know that the condition of the human will always remains contingent, and that only in the Absolute Being physical coexists with moral necessity. Accordingly, if it is wished to depend on the moral conduct of man as on natural results, this conduct must become nature, and he must be led by natural impulse to such a course of action as can only and invariably have moral results. But the will of man is perfectly free between inclination and duty, and no physical necessity ought to enter as a sharer in this magisterial personality. If, therefore, he is to retain this power of solution, and yet become a reliable link in the causal concatenation of forces, this can only be effected when the operations of both these impulses are presented quite equally in the world of appearances. It is only possible when, with every difference of form, the matter of man's volition remains the same, when all his impulses agreeing with his reason are sufficient to have the value of a universal legislation.

It may be urged that every individual man carries within himself, at least in his adaptation and destination, a purely ideal man. The great problem of his existence is to bring all the incessant changes of his outer life into conformity with the unchanging unity of this ideal. This pure ideal man, which makes itself known more or less clearly in every subject, is represented by the state, which is the objective, and, so to speak, canonical form in which the manifold differences of the subjects strive to unite. Now two ways present themselves to the thought in which the man of time can agree with the man of idea, and there are also two ways in which the state can maintain itself in individuals. One of these ways is when the pure ideal man subdues the empirical man, and the state suppresses the individual, or again when the individual becomes the state, and the man of time is ennobled to the man of idea.

I admit that in a one-sided estimate from the point of view of morality this difference vanishes, for the reason is satisfied if her law prevails unconditionally. But when the survey taken is complete and embraces the whole man (anthropology), where the form is considered together with the substance, and a living feeling has a voice, the difference will become far more evident. No doubt the reason demands unity, and nature variety, and both legislations take man in hand. The law of the former is stamped upon him by an incorruptible consciousness, that of the latter by an ineradicable feeling. Consequently education will always appear deficient when the moral feeling can only be maintained with the sacrifice of what is natural; and a political administration will always be very imperfect when it is only able to bring about unity by suppressing variety. The state ought not only to respect the objective and generic, but also the subjective and specific in individuals; and while diffusing the unseen world of morals, it must not depopulate the kingdom of appearance, the external world of matter.

When the mechanical artist places his hand on the formless block, to give it a form according to his intention, he has not any scruples in doing violence to it. For the nature on which he works does not deserve any respect in itself, and he does not value the whole for its parts, but the parts on account of the whole. When the child of the fine arts sets his hand to the same block, he has no scruples either in doing violence to it, he only avoids showing this violence. He does not respect the matter in which he works any more than the mechanical artist; but he seeks by an apparent consideration for it to deceive the eye which takes this matter under its protection. The political and educating artist follows a very different course, while making man at once his material and his end. In this case the aim or end meets in the material, and it is only because the whole serves the parts that the parts adapt themselves to the end. The political artist has to treat his material—man—with a very different kind of respect than that shown by the artist of fine art to his work. He must spare man's peculiarity and personality, not to produce a defective effect on the senses, but objectively and out of consideration for his inner being.

But the state is an organization which fashions itself through itself and for itself, and for this reason it can only be realized when the parts have been accorded to the idea of the whole. The state serves the purpose of a representative, both to pure ideal and to objective humanity, in the breast of its citizens, accordingly it will have to observe the same relation to its citizens in which they are placed to it; and it will only respect their subjective humanity in the same degree that it is ennobled to an objective existence. If the internal man is one with himself he will be able to rescue his peculiarity, even in the greatest generalization of his conduct, and the state will only become the exponent of his fine instinct, the clearer formula of his internal legislation. But if the subjective man is in conflict with the objective, and contradicts him in the character of a people, so that only the oppression of the former can give victory to the latter, then the state will take up the severe aspect of the law against the citizen, and in order not to fall a sacrifice, it will have to crush under foot such a hostile individuality without any compromise.

Now man can be opposed to himself in a twofold manner; either as a savage, when his feelings rule over his principles; or as a barbarian, when his principles destroy his feelings. The savage despises art, and acknowledges nature as his despotic ruler; the barbarian laughs at nature, and dishonors it, but he often proceeds in a more contemptible way than the savage to be the slave of his senses. The cultivated man makes of nature his friend, and honors its friendship, while only bridling its caprice.

Consequently, when reason brings her moral unity into physical society, she must not injure the manifold in nature. When nature strives to maintain her manifold character in the moral structure of society, this must not create any breach in moral unity; the victorious form is equally remote from uniformity and confusion. Therefore, totality of character must be found in the people which is capable and worthy to exchange the state of necessity for that of freedom.

LETTER V.

Does the present age, do passing events, present this character? I direct my attention at once to the most prominent object in this vast structure.

It is true that the consideration of opinion is fallen; caprice is unnerved, and, although still armed with power, receives no longer any respect. Man has awakened from his long lethargy and self-deception, and he demands with impressive unanimity to be restored to his imperishable rights. But he does not only demand them; he rises on all sides to seize by force what, in his opinion, has been unjustly wrested from him. The edifice of the natural state is tottering, its foundations shake, and a physical possibility seems at length granted to place law on the throne, to honor man at length as an end, and to make true freedom the basis of political union. Vain hope! The moral possibility is wanting, and the generous occasion finds an unsusceptible rule.

Man paints himself in his actions, and what is the form depicted in the drama of the present time? On the one hand, he is seen running wild, on the other, in a state of lethargy; the two extremest stages of human degeneracy, and both seen in one and the same period.

In the lower larger masses, coarse, lawless impulses come to view, breaking loose when the bonds of civil order are burst asunder, and hastening with unbridled fury to satisfy their savage instinct. Objective humanity may have had cause to complain of the state; yet subjective man must honor its institutions. Ought he to be blamed because he lost sight of the dignity of human nature, so long as he was concerned in preserving his existence? Can we blame him that he proceeded to separate by the force of gravity, to fasten by the force of cohesion, at a time when there could be no thought of building or raising up? The extinction of the state contains its justification. Society set free, instead of hastening upward into organic life, collapses into its elements.

On the other hand, the civilized classes give us the still more repulsive sight of lethargy, and of a depravity of character which is the more revolting because it roots in culture. I forget who of the older or more recent philosophers makes the remark, that what is more noble is the more revolting in its destruction. The remark applies with truth to the world of morals. The child of nature, when he breaks loose, becomes a madman; but the art scholar, when he breaks loose, becomes a debased character. The enlightenment of the understanding, on which the more refined classes pride themselves with some ground, shows on the whole so little of an ennobling influence on the mind that it seems rather to confirm corruption by its maxims. We deny nature on her legitimate field and feel her tyranny in the moral sphere, and while resisting her impressions, we receive our principles from her. While the affected decency of our manners does not even grant to nature a pardonable influence in the initial stage, our materialistic system of morals allows her the casting vote in the last and essential stage. Egotism has founded its system in the very bosom of a refined society, and without developing even a sociable character, we feel all the contagions and miseries of society. We subject our free judgment to its despotic opinions, our feelings to its bizarre customs, and our will to its seductions. We only maintain our caprice against her holy rights. The man of the world has his heart contracted by a proud self-complacency, while that of the man of nature often beats in sympathy; and every man seeks for nothing more than to save his wretched property from the general destruction, as it were from some great conflagration. It is conceived that the only way to find a shelter against the aberrations of sentiment is by completely foregoing its indulgence, and mockery, which is often a useful chastener of mysticism, slanders in the same breath the noblest aspirations. Culture, far from giving us freedom, only develops, as it advances, new necessities; the fetters of the physical close more tightly around us, so that the fear of loss quenches even the ardent impulse toward improvement, and the maxims of passive obedience are held to be the highest wisdom of life. Thus the spirit of the time is seen to waver between perversion and savagism, between what is unnatural and mere nature, between superstition and moral unbelief, and it is often nothing but the equilibrium of evils that sets bounds to it.

LETTER VI.

Have I gone too far in this portraiture of our times? I do not anticipate this stricture, but rather another—that I have proved too much by it. You will tell me that the picture I have presented resembles the humanity of our day, but it also bodies forth all nations engaged in the same degree of culture, because all, without exception, have fallen off from nature by the abuse of reason, before they can return to it through reason.

But if we bestow some serious attention to the character of our times, we shall be astonished at the contrast between the present and the previous form of humanity, especially that of Greece. We are justified in claiming the reputation of culture and refinement, when contrasted with a purely natural state of society, but not so comparing ourselves with the Grecian nature. For the latter was combined with all the charms of art and with all the dignity of wisdom, without, however, as with us, becoming a victim to these influences. The Greeks have put us to shame not only by their simplicity, which is foreign to our age; they are at the same time our rivals, nay, frequently our models, in those very points of superiority from which we seek comfort when regretting the unnatural character of our manners. We see that remarkable people uniting at once fulness of form and fulness of substance, both philosophizing and creating, both tender and energetic, uniting a youthful fancy to the virility of reason in a glorious humanity.

At the period of Greek culture, which was an awakening of the powers of the mind, the senses and the spirit had no distinctly separated property; no division had yet torn them asunder, leading them to partition in a hostile attitude, and to mark off their limits with precision. Poetry had not as yet become the adversary of wit, nor had speculation abused itself by passing into quibbling. In cases of necessity both poetry and wit could exchange parts, because they both honored truth only in their special way. However high might be the flight of reason, it drew matter in a loving spirit after it, and while sharply and stiffly defining it, never mutilated what it touched. It is true the Greek mind displaced humanity, and recast it on a magnified scale in the glorious circle of its gods; but it did this not by dissecting human nature, but by giving it fresh combinations, for the whole of human nature was represented in each of the gods. How different is the course followed by us moderns! We also displace and magnify individuals to form the image of the species, but we do this in a fragmentary way, not by altered combinations, so that it is necessary to gather up from different individuals the elements that form the species in its totality. It would almost appear as if the powers of mind express themselves with us in real life or empirically as separately as the psychologist distinguishes them in the representation. For we see not only individual subjects, but whole classes of men, uphold their capacities only in part, while the rest of their faculties scarcely show a germ of activity, as in the case of the stunted growth of plants.

I do not overlook the advantages to which the present race, regarded as a unity and in the balance of the understanding, may lay claim over what is best in the ancient world; but it is obliged to engage in the contest as a compact mass, and measure itself as a whole against a whole. Who among the moderns could step forth, man against man, and strive with an Athenian for the prize of higher humanity.

Whence comes this disadvantageous relation of individuals coupled with great advantages of the race? Why could the individual Greek be qualified as the type of his time; and why can no modern dare to offer himself as such? Because all-uniting nature imparted its forms to the Greek, and an all-dividing understanding gives our forms to us.

It was culture itself that gave these wounds to modern humanity. The inner union of human nature was broken, and a destructive contest divided its harmonious forces directly; on the one hand, an enlarged experience and a more distinct thinking necessitated a sharper separation of the sciences, while, on the other hand, the more complicated machinery of states necessitated a stricter sundering of ranks and occupations. Intuitive and speculative understanding took up a hostile attitude in opposite fields, whose borders were guarded with jealousy and distrust; and by limiting its operation to a narrow sphere, men have made unto themselves a master who is wont not unfrequently to end by subduing and oppressing all the other faculties. Whilst on the one hand a luxuriant imagination creates ravages in the plantations that have cost the intelligence so much labor; on the other hand, a spirit of abstraction suffocates the fire that might have warmed the heart and inflamed the imagination.

This subversion, commenced by art and learning in the inner man, was carried out to fulness and finished by the spirit of innovation in government. It was, no doubt, reasonable to expect that the simple organization of the primitive republics should survive the quaintness of primitive manners and of the relations of antiquity. But, instead of rising to a higher and nobler degree of animal life, this organization degenerated into a common and coarse mechanism. The zoophyte condition of the Grecian states, where each individual enjoyed an independent life, and could, in cases of necessity, become a separate whole and unit in himself, gave way to an ingenious mechanism, when, from the splitting up into numberless parts, there results a mechanical life in the combination. Then there was a rupture between the state and the church, between laws and customs; enjoyment was separated from labor, the means from the end, the effort from the reward. Man himself, eternally chained down to a little fragment of the whole, only forms a kind of fragment; having nothing in his ears but the monotonous sound of the perpetually revolving wheel, he never develops the harmony of his being, and instead of imprinting the seal of humanity on his being, he ends by being nothing more than the living impress of the craft to which he devotes himself, of the science that he cultivates. This very partial and paltry relation, linking the isolated members to the whole, does not depend on forms that are given spontaneously; for how could a complicated machine, which shuns the light, confide itself to the free will of man? This relation is rather dictated, with a rigorous strictness, by a formulary in which the free intelligence of man is chained down. The dead letter takes the place of a living meaning, and a practised memory becomes a safer guide than genius and feeling.

If the community or state measures man by his function, only asking of its citizens memory, or the intelligence of a craftsman, or mechanical skill, we cannot be surprised that the other faculties of the mind are neglected for the exclusive culture of the one that brings in honor and profit. Such is the necessary result of an organization that is indifferent about character, only looking to acquirements, whilst in other cases it tolerates the thickest darkness, to favor a spirit of law and order; it must result if it wishes that individuals in the exercise of special aptitudes should gain in depth what they are permitted to lose in extension. We are aware, no doubt, that a powerful genius does not shut up its activity within the limits of its functions; but mediocre talents consume in the craft fallen to their lot the whole of their feeble energy; and if some of their energy is reserved for matters of preference, without prejudice to its functions, such a state of things at once bespeaks a spirit soaring above the vulgar. Moreover, it is rarely a recommendation in the eye of a state to have a capacity superior to your employment, or one of those noble intellectual cravings of a man of talent which contend in rivalry with the duties of office. The state is so jealous of the exclusive possession of its servants that it would prefer— nor can it be blamed in this—for functionaries to show their powers with the Venus of Cytherea rather than the Uranian Venus.

It is thus that concrete individual life is extinguished, in order that the abstract whole may continue its miserable life, and the state remains forever a stranger to its citizens, because feeling does not discover it anywhere. The governing authorities find themselves compelled to classify, and thereby simplify the multiplicity of citizens, and only to know humanity in a representative form and at second-hand. Accordingly they end by entirely losing sight of humanity, and by confounding it with a simple artificial creation of the understanding, whilst on their part the subject-classes cannot help receiving coldly laws that address themselves so little to their personality. At length, society, weary of having a burden that the state takes so little trouble to lighten, falls to pieces and is broken up—a destiny that has long since attended most European states. They are dissolved in what may be called a state of moral nature, in which public authority is only one function more, hated and deceived by those who think it necessary, respected only by those who can do without it.

Thus compressed between two forces, within and without, could humanity follow any other course than that which it has taken? The speculative mind, pursuing imprescriptible goods and rights in the sphere of ideas, must needs have become a stranger to the world of sense, and lose sight of matter for the sake of form. On its part, the world of public affairs, shut up in a monotonous circle of objects, and even there restricted by formulas, was led to lose sight of the life and liberty of the whole, while becoming impoverished at the same time in its own sphere. Just as the speculative mind was tempted to model the real after the intelligible, and to raise the subjective laws of its imagination into laws constituting the existence of things, so the state spirit rushed into the opposite extreme, wished to make a particular and fragmentary experience the measure of all observation, and to apply without exception to all affairs the rules of its own particular craft. The speculative mind had necessarily to become the prey of a vain subtlety, the state spirit of a narrow pedantry; for the former was placed too high to see the individual, and the latter too low to survey the whole. But the disadvantage of this direction of mind was not confined to knowledge and mental production; it extended to action and feeling. We know that the sensibility of the mind depends, as to degree, on the liveliness, and for extent on the richness of the imagination. Now the predominance of the faculty of analysis must necessarily deprive the imagination of its warmth and energy, and a restricted sphere of objects must diminish its wealth. It is for this reason that the abstract thinker has very often a cold heart, because he analyzes impressions, which only move the mind by their combination or totality; on the other hand, the man of business, the statesman, has very often a narrow heart, because, shut up in the narrow circle of his employment, his imagination can neither expand nor adapt itself to another manner of viewing things.

My subject has led me naturally to place in relief the distressing tendency of the character of our own times and to show the sources of the evil, without its being my province to point out the compensations offered by nature. I will readily admit to you that, although this splitting up of their being was unfavorable for individuals, it was the only open road for the progress of the race. The point at which we see humanity arrived among the Greeks was undoubtedly a maximum; it could neither stop there nor rise higher. It could not stop there, for the sum of notions acquired forced infallibly the intelligence to break with feeling and intuition, and to lead to clearness of knowledge. Nor could it rise any higher; for it is only in a determinate measure that clearness can be reconciled with a certain degree of abundance and of warmth. The Greeks had attained this measure, and to continue their progress in culture, they, as we, were obliged to renounce the totality of their being, and to follow different and separate roads in order to seek after truth.

There was no other way to develop the manifold aptitudes of man than to bring them in opposition with one another. This antagonism of forces is the great instrument of culture, but it is only an instrument: for as long as this antagonism lasts man is only on the road to culture. It is only because these special forces are isolated in man, and because they take on themselves to impose all exclusive legislation, that they enter into strife with the truth of things, and oblige common sense, which generally adheres imperturbably to external phenomena, to dive into the essence of things. While pure understanding usurps authority in the world of sense, and empiricism attempts to subject this intellect to the conditions of experience, these two rival directions arrive at the highest possible development, and exhaust the whole extent of their sphere. While, on the one hand, imagination, by its tyranny, ventures to destroy the order of the world, it forces reason, on the other side, to rise up to the supreme sources of knowledge, and to invoke against this predominance of fancy the help of the law of necessity.

By an exclusive spirit in the case of his faculties, the individual is fatally led to error; but the species is led to truth. It is only by gathering up all the energy of our mind in a single focus, and concentrating a single force in our being, that we give in some sort wings to this isolated force, and that we draw it on artificially far beyond the limits that nature seems to have imposed upon it. If it be certain that all human individuals taken together would never have arrived, with the visual power given them by nature, to see a satellite of Jupiter, discovered by the telescope of the astronomer, it is just as well established that never would the human understanding have produced the analysis of the infinite, or the critique of pure reason, if in particular branches, destined for this mission, reason had not applied itself to special researches, and it, after having, as it were, freed itself from all matter, it had not, by the most powerful abstraction given to the spiritual eye of man the force necessary, in order to look into the absolute. But the question is, if a spirit thus absorbed in pure reason and intuition will be able to emancipate itself from the rigorous fetters of logic, to take the free action of poetry, and seize the individuality of things with a faithful and chaste sense? Here nature imposes even on the most universal genius a limit it cannot pass, and truth will make martyrs as long as philosophy will be reduced to make its principal occupation the search for arms against errors.

But whatever may be the final profit for the totality of the world, of this distinct and special perfecting of the human faculties, it cannot be denied that this final aim of the universe, which devotes them to this kind of culture, is a cause of suffering, and a kind of malediction for individuals. I admit that the exercises of the gymnasium form athletic bodies; but beauty is only developed by the free and equal play of the limbs. In the same way the tension of the isolated spiritual forces may make extraordinary men; but it is only the well-tempered equilibrium of these forces that can produce happy and accomplished men. And in what relation should we be placed with past and future ages if the perfecting of human nature made such a sacrifice indispensable? In that case we should have been the slaves of humanity, we should have consumed our forces in servile work for it during some thousands of years, and we should have stamped on our humiliated, mutilated nature the shameful brand of this slavery— all this in order that future generations, in a happy leisure, might consecrate themselves to the cure of their moral health, and develop the whole of human nature by their free culture.

But can it be true that man has to neglect himself for any end whatever? Can nature snatch from us, for any end whatever, the perfection which is prescribed to us by the aim of reason? It must be false that the perfecting of particular faculties renders the sacrifice of their totality necessary; and even if the law of nature had imperiously this tendency, we must have the power to reform by a superior art this totality of our being, which art has destroyed.

LETTER VII.

Can this effect of harmony be attained by the state? That is not possible, for the state, as at present constituted, has given occasion to evil, and the state as conceived in the idea, instead of being able to establish this more perfect humanity, ought to be based upon it. Thus the researches in which I have indulged would have brought me back to the same point from which they had called me off for a time. The present age, far from offering us this form of humanity, which we have acknowledged as a necessary condition of an improvement of the state, shows us rather the diametrically opposite form. If, therefore, the principles I have laid down are correct, and if experience confirms the picture I have traced of the present time, it would be necessary to qualify as unseasonable every attempt to effect a similar change in the state, and all hope as chimerical that would be based on such an attempt, until the division of the inner man ceases, and nature has been sufficiently developed to become herself the instrument of this great change and secure the reality of the political creation of reason.

In the physical creation, nature shows us the road that we have to follow in the moral creation. Only when the struggle of elementary forces has ceased in inferior organizations, nature rises to the noble form of the physical man. In like manner, the conflict of the elements of the moral man and that of blind instincts must have ceased, and a coarse antagonism in himself, before the attempt can be hazarded. On the other hand, the independence of man's character must be secured, and his submission to despotic forms must have given place to a suitable liberty, before the variety in his constitution can be made subordinate to the unity of the ideal. When the man of nature still makes such an anarchial abuse of his will, his liberty ought hardly to be disclosed to him. And when the man fashioned by culture makes so little use of his freedom, his free will ought not to be taken from him. The concession of liberal principles becomes a treason to social order when it is associated with a force still in fermentation, and increases the already exuberant energy of its nature. Again, the law of conformity under one level becomes tyranny to the individual when it is allied to a weakness already holding sway and to natural obstacles, and when it comes to extinguish the last spark of spontaneity and of originality.

The tone of the age must therefore rise from its profound moral degradation; on the one hand it must emancipate itself from the blind service of nature, and on the other it must revert to its simplicity, its truth, and its fruitful sap; a sufficient task for more than a century. However, I admit readily, more than one special effort may meet with success, but no improvement of the whole will result from it, and contradictions in action will be a continual protest against the unity of maxims. It will be quite possible, then, that in remote corners of the world humanity may be honored in the person of the negro, while in Europe it may be degraded in the person of the thinker. The old principles will remain, but they will adopt the dress of the age, and philosophy will lend its name to an oppression that was formerly authorized by the church. In one place, alarmed at the liberty which in its opening efforts always shows itself an enemy, it will cast itself into the arms of a convenient servitude. In another place, reduced to despair by a pedantic tutelage, it will be driven into the savage license of the state of nature. Usurpation will invoke the weakness of human nature, and insurrection will invoke its dignity, till at length the great sovereign of all human things, blind force, shall come in and decide, like a vulgar pugilist, this pretended contest of principles.

LETTER VIII.

Must philosophy therefore retire from this field, disappointed in its hopes? Whilst in all other directions the dominion of forms is extended, must this the most precious of all gifts be abandoned to a formless chance? Must the contest of blind forces last eternally in the political world, and is social law never to triumph over a hating egotism?

Not in the least. It is true that reason herself will never attempt directly a struggle with this brutal force which resists her arms, and she will be as far as the son of Saturn in the "Iliad" from descending into the dismal field of battle, to fight them in person. But she chooses the most deserving among the combatants, clothes him with divine arms as Jupiter gave them to his son-in-law, and by her triumphing force she finally decides the victory.

Reason has done all that she could in finding the law and promulgating it; it is for the energy of the will and the ardor of feeling to carry it out. To issue victoriously from her contest with force, truth herself must first become a force, and turn one of the instincts of man into her champion in the empire of phenomena. For instincts are the only motive forces in the material world. If hitherto truth has so little manifested her victorious power, this has not depended on the understanding, which could not have unveiled it, but on the heart which remained closed to it and on instinct which did not act with it.

Whence, in fact, proceeds this general sway of prejudices, this might of the understanding in the midst of the light disseminated by philosophy and experience? The age is enlightened, that is to say, that knowledge, obtained and vulgarized, suffices to set right at least on practical principles. The spirit of free inquiry has dissipated the erroneous opinions which long barred the access to truth, and has undermined the ground on which fanaticism and deception had erected their throne. Reason has purified itself from the illusions of the senses and from a mendacious sophistry, and philosophy herself raises her voice and exhorts us to return to the bosom of nature, to which she had first made us unfaithful. Whence then is it that we remain still barbarians?

There must be something in the spirit of man—as it is not in the objects themselves—which prevents us from receiving the truth, notwithstanding the brilliant light she diffuses, and from accepting her, whatever may be her strength for producing conviction. This something was perceived and expressed by an ancient sage in this very significant maxim: sapere aude [dare to be wise.]

Dare to be wise! A spirited courage is required to triumph over the impediments that the indolence of nature as well as the cowardice of the heart oppose to our instruction. It was not without reason that the ancient Mythos made Minerva issue fully armed from the head of Jupiter, for it is with warfare that this instruction commences. From its very outset it has to sustain a hard fight against the senses, which do not like to be roused from their easy slumber.

The greater part of men are much too exhausted and enervated by their struggle with want to be able to engage in a new and severe contest with error. Satisfied if they themselves can escape from the hard labor of thought, they willingly abandon to others the guardianship of their thoughts. And if it happens that nobler necessities agitate their soul, they cling with a greedy faith to the formula that the state and the church hold in reserve for such cases. If these unhappy men deserve our compassion, those others deserve our just contempt, who, though set free from those necessities by more fortunate circumstances, yet willingly bend to their yoke. These latter persons prefer this twilight of obscure ideas, where the feelings have more intensity, and the imagination can at will create convenient chimeras, to the rays of truth which put to flight the pleasant illusions of their dreams. They have founded the whole structure of their happiness on these very illusions, which ought to be combated and dissipated by the light of knowledge, and they would think they were paying too dearly for a truth which begins by robbing them of all that has value in their sight. It would be necessary that they should be already sages to love wisdom: a truth that was felt at once by him to whom philosophy owes its name. [The Greek word means, as is known, love of wisdom.]

It is therefore not going far enough to say that the light of the understanding only deserves respect when it reacts on the character; to a certain extent it is from the character that this light proceeds; for the road that terminates in the head must pass through the heart. Accordingly, the most pressing need of the present time is to educate the sensibility, because it is the means, not only to render efficacious in practice the improvement of ideas, but to call this improvement into existence.

LETTER IX.

But perhaps there is a vicious circle in our previous reasoning! Theoretical culture must it seems bring along with it practical culture, and yet the latter must be the condition of the former. All improvement in the political sphere must proceed from the ennobling of the character. But, subject to the influence of a social constitution still barbarous, how can character become ennobled? It would then be necessary to seek for this end an instrument that the state does not furnish, and to open sources that would have preserved themselves pure in the midst of political corruption.

I have now reached the point to which all the considerations tended that have engaged me up to the present time. This instrument is the art of the beautiful; these sources are open to us in its immortal models.

Art, like science, is emancipated from all that is positive, and all that is humanly conventional; both are completely independent of the arbitrary will of man. The political legislator may place their empire under an interdict, but he cannot reign there. He can proscribe the friend of truth, but truth subsists; he can degrade the artist, but he cannot change art. No doubt, nothing is more common than to see science and art bend before the spirit of the age, and creative taste receive its law from critical taste. When the character becomes stiff and hardens itself, we see science severely keeping her limits, and art subject to the harsh restraint of rules; when the character is relaxed and softened, science endeavors to please and art to rejoice. For whole ages philosophers as well as artists show themselves occupied in letting down truth and beauty to the depths of vulgar humanity. They themselves are swallowed up in it; but, thanks to their essential vigor and indestructible life, the true and the beautiful make a victorious fight, and issue triumphant from the abyss.

No doubt the artist is the child of his time, but unhappy for him if he is its disciple or even its favorite! Let a beneficent deity carry off in good time the suckling from the breast of its mother, let it nourish him on the milk of a better age, and suffer him to grow up and arrive at virility under the distant sky of Greece. When he has attained manhood, let him come back, presenting a face strange to his own age; let him come, not to delight it with his apparition, but rather to purify it, terrible as the son of Agamemnon. He will, indeed, receive his matter from the present time, but he will borrow the form from a nobler time and even beyond all time, from the essential, absolute, immutable unity. There, issuing from the pure ether of its heavenly nature, flows the source of all beauty, which was never tainted by the corruptions of generations or of ages, which roll along far beneath it in dark eddies. Its matter may be dishonored as well as ennobled by fancy, but the ever-chaste form escapes from the caprices of imagination. The Roman had already bent his knee for long years to the divinity of the emperors, and yet the statues of the gods stood erect; the temples retained their sanctity for the eye long after the gods had become a theme for mockery, and the noble architecture of the palaces that shielded the infamies of Nero and of Commodus were a protest against them. Humanity has lost its dignity, but art has saved it, and preserves it in marbles full of meaning; truth continues to live in illusion, and the copy will serve to re-establish the model. If the nobility of art has survived the nobility of nature, it also goes before it like an inspiring genius, forming and awakening minds. Before truth causes her triumphant light to penetrate into the depths of the heart, poetry intercepts her rays, and the summits of humanity shine in a bright light, while a dark and humid night still hangs over the valleys.

But how will the artist avoid the corruption of his time which encloses him on all hands? Let him raise his eyes to his own dignity, and to law; let him not lower them to necessity and fortune. Equally exempt from a vain activity which would imprint its trace on the fugitive moment, and from the dreams of an impatient enthusiasm which applies the measure of the absolute to the paltry productions of time, let the artist abandon the real to the understanding, for that is its proper field. But let the artist endeavor to give birth to the ideal by the union of the possible and of the necessary. Let him stamp illusion and truth with the effigy of this ideal; let him apply it to the play of his imagination and his most serious actions, in short, to all sensuous and spiritual forms; then let him quietly launch his work into infinite time.

But the minds set on fire by this ideal have not all received an equal share of calm from the creative genius—that great and patient temper which is required to impress the ideal on the dumb marble, or to spread it over a page of cold, sober letters, and then intrust it to the faithful hands of time. This divine instinct, and creative force, much too ardent to follow this peaceful walk, often throws itself immediately on the present, on active life, and strives to transform the shapeless matter of the moral world. The misfortune of his brothers, of the whole species, appeals loudly to the heart of the man of feeling; their abasement appeals still louder: enthusiasm is inflamed, and in souls endowed with energy the burning desire aspires impatiently to action and facts. But has this innovator examined himself to see if these disorders of the moral world wound his reason, or if they do not rather wound his self-love? If he does not determine this point at once, he will find it from the impulsiveness with which he pursues a prompt and definite end. A pure, moral motive has for its end the absolute; time does not exist for it, and the future becomes the present to it directly; by a necessary development, it has to issue from the present. To a reason having no limits the direction towards an end becomes confounded with the accomplishment of this end, and to enter on a course is to have finished it.

If, then, a young friend of the true and of the beautiful were to ask me how, notwithstanding the resistance of the times, he can satisfy the noble longing of his heart, I should reply: Direct the world on which you act towards that which is good, and the measured and peaceful course of time will bring about the results. You have given it this direction if by your teaching you raise its thoughts towards the necessary and the eternal; if, by your acts or your creations, you make the necessary and the eternal the object of your leanings. The structure of error and of all that is arbitrary must fall, and it has already fallen, as soon as you are sure that it is tottering. But it is important that it should not only totter in the external but also in the internal man. Cherish triumphant truth in the modest sanctuary of your heart; give it an incarnate form through beauty, that it may not only be in the understanding that does homage to it, but that feeling may lovingly grasp its appearance. And that you may not by any chance take from external reality the model which you yourself ought to furnish, do not venture into its dangerous society before you are assured in your own heart that you have a good escort furnished by ideal nature. Live with your age, but be not its creation; labor for your contemporaries, but do for them what they need, and not what they praise. Without having shared their faults, share their punishment with a noble resignation, and bend under the yoke which they find it as painful to dispense with as to bear. By the constancy with which you will despise their good fortune, you will prove to them that it is not through cowardice that you submit to their sufferings. See them in thought such as they ought to be when you must act upon them; but see them as they are when you are tempted to act for them. Seek to owe their suffrage to their dignity; but to make them happy keep an account of their unworthiness: thus, on the one hand, the nobleness of your heart will kindle theirs, and, on the other, your end will not be reduced to nothingness by their unworthiness. The gravity of your principles will keep them off from you, but in play they will still endure them. Their taste is purer than their heart, and it is by their taste you must lay hold of this suspicious fugitive. In vain will you combat their maxims, in vain will you condemn their actions; but you can try your moulding hand on their leisure. Drive away caprice, frivolity, and coarseness from their pleasures, and you will banish them imperceptibly from their acts, and at length from their feelings. Everywhere that you meet them, surround them with great, noble, and ingenious forms; multiply around them the symbols of perfection, till appearance triumphs over reality, and art over nature.

LETTER X.

Convinced by my preceding letters, you agree with me on this point, that man can depart from his destination by two opposite roads, that our epoch is actually moving on these two false roads, and that it has become the prey, in one case, of coarseness, and elsewhere of exhaustion and depravity. It is the beautiful that must bring it back from this twofold departure. But how can the cultivation of the fine arts remedy, at the same time, these opposite defects, and unite in itself two contradictory qualities? Can it bind nature in the savage, and set it free in the barbarian? Can it at once tighten a spring and loose it; and if it cannot produce this double effect, how will it be reasonable to expect from it so important a result as the education of man?

It may be urged that it is almost a proverbial adage that the feeling developed by the beautiful refines manners, and any new proof offered on the subject would appear superfluous. Men base this maxim on daily experience, which shows us almost always clearness of intellect, delicacy of feeling, liberality and even dignity of conduct, associated with a cultivated taste, while an uncultivated taste is almost always accompanied by the opposite qualities. With considerable assurance, the most civilized nation of antiquity is cited as an evidence of this, the Greeks, among whom the perception of the beautiful attained its highest development, and, as a contrast, it is usual to point to nations in a partial savage state, and partly barbarous, who expiate their insensibility to the beautiful by a coarse, or, at all events, a hard, austere character. Nevertheless, some thinkers are tempted occasionally to deny either the fact itself or to dispute the legitimacy of the consequences that are derived from it. They do not entertain so unfavorable an opinion of that savage coarseness which is made a reproach in the case of certain nations; nor do they form so advantageous an opinion of the refinement so highly lauded in the case of cultivated nations. Even as far back as in antiquity there were men who by no means regarded the culture of the liberal arts as a benefit, and who were consequently led to forbid the entrance of their republic to imagination.

I do not speak of those who calumniate art because they have never been favored by it. These persons only appreciate a possession by the trouble it takes to acquire it, and by the profit it brings: and how could they properly appreciate the silent labor of taste in the exterior and interior man? How evident it is that the accidental disadvantages attending liberal culture would make them lose sight of its essential advantages? The man deficient in form despises the grace of diction as a means of corruption, courtesy in the social relations as dissimulation, delicacy and generosity in conduct as an affected exaggeration. He cannot forgive the favorite of the Graces for having enlivened all assemblies as a man of the world, of having directed all men to his views like a statesman, and of giving his impress to the whole century as a writer: while he, the victim of labor, can only obtain with all his learning, the least attention or overcome the least difficulty. As he cannot learn from his fortunate rival the secret of pleasing, the only course open to him is to deplore the corruption of human nature, which adores rather the appearance than the reality.

But there are also opinions deserving respect, that pronounce themselves adverse to the effects of the beautiful, and find formidable arms in experience, with which to wage war against it. "We are free to admit"— such is their language—"that the charms of the beautiful can further honorable ends in pure hands; but it is not repugnant to its nature to produce, in impure hands, a directly contrary effect, and to employ in the service of injustice and error the power that throws the soul of man into chains. It is exactly because taste only attends to the form and never to the substance; it ends by placing the soul on the dangerous incline, leading it to neglect all reality and to sacrifice truth and morality to an attractive envelope. All the real difference of things vanishes, and it is only the appearance that determines the value! How many men of talent"—thus these arguers proceed—"have been turned aside from all effort by the seductive power of the beautiful, or have been led away from all serious exercise of their activity, or have been induced to use it very feebly? How many weak minds have been impelled to quarrel with the organizations of society, simply because it has pleased the imagination of poets to present the image of a world constituted differently, where no propriety chains down opinion and no artifice holds nature in thraldom? What a dangerous logic of the passions they have learned since the poets have painted them in their pictures in the most brilliant colors, and since, in the contest with law and duty, they have commonly remained masters of the battle-field. What has society gained by the relations of society, formerly under the sway of truth, being now subject to the laws of the beautiful, or by the external impression deciding the estimation in which merit is to be held? We admit that all virtues whose appearance produces an agreeable effect are now seen to flourish, and those which, in society, give a value to the man who possesses them. But, as a compensation, all kinds of excesses are seen to prevail, and all vices are in vogue that can be reconciled with a graceful exterior." It is certainly a matter entitled to reflection that, at almost all the periods of history when art flourished and taste held sway, humanity is found in a state of decline; nor can a single instance be cited of the union of a large diffusion of aesthetic culture with political liberty and social virtue, of fine manners associated with good morals, and of politeness fraternizing with truth and loyalty of character and life.

As long as Athens and Sparta preserved their independence, and as long as their institutions were based on respect for the laws, taste did not reach its maturity, art remained in its infancy, and beauty was far from exercising her empire over minds. No doubt, poetry had already taken a sublime flight, but it was on the wings of genius, and we know that genius borders very closely on savage coarseness, that it is a light which shines readily in the midst of darkness, and which therefore often argues against rather than in favor of the taste of time. When the golden age of art appears under Pericles and Alexander, and the sway of taste becomes more general, strength and liberty have abandoned Greece; eloquence corrupts the truth, wisdom offends it on the lips of Socrates, and virtue in the life of Phocion. It is well known that the Romans had to exhaust their energies in civil wars, and, corrupted by Oriental luxury, to bow their heads under the yoke of a fortunate despot, before Grecian art triumphed over the stiffness of their character. The same was the case with the Arabs: civilization only dawned upon them when the vigor of their military spirit became softened under the sceptre of the Abbassides. Art did not appear in modern Italy till the glorious Lombard League was dissolved, Florence submitting to the Medici; and all those brave cities gave up the spirit of independence for an inglorious resignation. It is almost superfluous to call to mind the example of modern nations, with whom refinement has increased in direct proportion to the decline of their liberties. Wherever we direct our eyes in past times, we see taste and freedom mutually avoiding each other. Everywhere we see that the beautiful only founds its sway on the ruins of heroic virtues.

And yet this strength of character, which is commonly sacrificed to establish aesthetic culture, is the most powerful spring of all that is great and excellent in man, and no other advantage, however great, can make up for it. Accordingly, if we only keep to the experiments hitherto made, as to the influence of the beautiful, we cannot certainly be much encouraged in developing feelings so dangerous to the real culture of man. At the risk of being hard and coarse, it will seem preferable to dispense with this dissolving force of the beautiful rather than see human nature a prey to its enervating influence, notwithstanding all its refining advantages. However, experience is perhaps not the proper tribunal at which to decide such a question; before giving so much weight to its testimony, it would be well to inquire if the beauty we have been discussing is the power that is condemned by the previous examples. And the beauty we are discussing seems to assume an idea of the beautiful derived from a source different from experience, for it is this higher notion of the beautiful which has to decide if what is called beauty by experience is entitled to the name.

This pure and rational idea of the beautiful—supposing it can be placed in evidence—cannot be taken from any real and special case, and must, on the contrary, direct and give sanction to our judgment in each special case. It must therefore be sought for by a process of abstraction, and it ought to be deduced from the simple possibility of a nature both sensuous and rational; in short, beauty ought to present itself as a necessary condition of humanity. It is therefore essential that we should rise to the pure idea of humanity, and as experience shows us nothing but individuals, in particular cases, and never humanity at large, we must endeavor to find in their individual and variable mode of being the absolute and the permanent, and to grasp the necessary conditions of their existence, suppressing all accidental limits. No doubt this transcendental procedure will remove us for some time from the familiar circle of phenomena, and the living presence of objects, to keep us on the unproductive ground of abstract idea; but we are engaged in the search after a principle of knowledge solid enough not to be shaken by anything, and the man who does not dare to rise above reality will never conquer this truth.

LETTER XI.

If abstraction rises to as great an elevation as possible, it arrives at two primary ideas, before which it is obliged to stop and to recognize its limits. It distinguishes in man something that continues, and something that changes incessantly. That which continues it names his person; that which changes his position, his condition.

The person and the condition, I and my determinations, which we represent as one and the same thing in the necessary being, are eternally distinct in the finite being. Notwithstanding all continuance in the person, the condition changes; in spite of all change of condition the person remains. We pass from rest to activity, from emotion to indifference, from assent to contradiction, but we are always we ourselves, and what immediately springs from ourselves remains. It is only in the absolute subject that all his determinations continue with his personality. All that Divinity is, it is because it is so; consequently it is eternally what it is, because it is eternal.

As the person and the condition are distinct in man, because he is a finite being, the condition cannot be founded on the person, nor the person on the condition. Admitting the second case, the person would have to change; and in the former case, the condition would have to continue. Thus in either supposition, either the personality or the quality of a finite being would necessarily cease. It is not because we think, feel, and will that we are; it is not because we are that we think, feel, and will. We are because we are. We feel, think, and will because there is out of us something that is not ourselves.

Consequently the person must have its principle of existence in itself, because the permanent cannot be derived from the changeable, and thus we should be at once in possession of the idea of the absolute being, founded on itself; that is to say, of the idea of freedom. The condition must have a foundation, and as it is not through the person, and is not therefore absolute, it must be a sequence and a result; and thus, in the second place, we should have arrived at the condition of every independent being, of everything in the process of becoming something else: that is, of the idea of time. "Time is the necessary condition of all processes, of becoming (Werden);" this is an identical proposition, for it says nothing but this: "That something may follow, there must be a succession."

The person which manifested itself in the eternally continuing Ego, or I myself, and only in him, cannot become something or begin in time, because it is much rather time that must begin with him, because the permanent must serve as basis to the changeable. That change may take place, something must change; this something cannot therefore be the change itself. When we say the flower opens and fades, we make of this flower a permanent being in the midst of this transformation; we lend it, in some sort, a personality, in which these two conditions are manifested. It cannot be objected that man is born, and becomes something; for man is not only a person simply, but he is a person finding himself in a determinate condition. Now our determinate state of condition springs up in time, and it is thus that man, as a phenomenon or appearance, must have a beginning, though in him pure intelligence is eternal. Without time, that is, without a becoming, he would not be a determinate being; his personality would exist virtually no doubt, but not in action. It is not by the succession of its perceptions that the immutable Ego or person manifests himself to himself.

Thus, therefore, the matter of activity, or reality, that the supreme intelligence draws from its own being, must be received by man; and he does, in fact, receive it, through the medium of perception, as something which is outside him in space, and which changes in him in time. This matter which changes in him is always accompanied by the Ego, the personality, that never changes; and the rule prescribed for man by his rational nature is to remain immutably himself in the midst of change, to refer all perceptions to experience, that is, to the unity of knowledge, and to make of each of its manifestations of its modes in time the law of all time. The matter only exists in as far as it changes: he, his personality, only exists in as far as he does not change. Consequently, represented in his perfection, man would be the permanent unity, which remains always the same, among the waves of change.

Now, although an infinite being, a divinity could not become (or be subject to time), still a tendency ought to be named divine which has for its infinite end the most characteristic attribute of the divinity; the absolute manifestation of power—the reality of all the possible—and the absolute unity of the manifestation (the necessity of all reality). It cannot be disputed that man bears within himself, in his personality, a predisposition for divinity. The way to divinity—if the word "way" can be applied to what never leads to its end—is open to him in every direction.

Considered in itself, and independently of all sensuous matter, his personality is nothing but the pure virtuality of a possible infinite manifestation; and so long as there is neither intuition nor feeling, it is nothing more than a form, an empty power. Considered in itself, and independently of all spontaneous activity of the mind, sensuousness can only make a material man; without it, it is a pure form; but it cannot in any way establish a union between matter and it. So long as he only feels, wishes, and acts under the influence of desire, he is nothing more than the world, if by this word we point out only the formless contents of time. Without doubt, it is only his sensuousness that makes his strength pass into efficacious acts, but it is his personality alone that makes this activity his own. Thus, that he may not only be a world, he must give form to matter, and in order not to be a mere form, he must give reality to the virtuality that he bears in him. He gives matter to form by creating time, and by opposing the immutable to change, the diversity of the world to the eternal unity of the Ego. He gives a form to matter by again suppressing time, by maintaining permanence in change, and by placing the diversity of the world under the unity of the Ego.

Now from this source issue for man two opposite exigencies, the two fundamental laws of sensuous-rational nature. The first has for its object absolute reality; it must make a world of what is only form, manifest all that in it is only a force. The second law has for its object absolute formality; it must destroy in him all that is only world, and carry out harmony in all changes. In other terms, he must manifest all that is internal, and give form to all that is external. Considered in its most lofty accomplishment, this twofold labor brings back to the idea of humanity, which was my starting-point.

LETTER XII.

This twofold labor or task, which consists in making the necessary pass into reality in us and in making out of us reality subject to the law of necessity, is urged upon us as a duty by two opposing forces, which are justly styled impulsions or instincts, because they impel us to realize their object. The first of these impulsions, which I shall call the sensuous instinct, issues from the physical existence of man, or from sensuous nature; and it is this instinct which tends to enclose him in the limits of time, and to make of him a material being; I do not say to give him matter, for to do that a certain free activity of the personality would be necessary, which, receiving matter, distinguishes it from the Ego, or what is permanent. By matter I only understand in this place the change or reality that fills time. Consequently the instinct requires that there should be change, and that time should contain something. This simply filled state of time is named sensation, and it is only in this state that physical existence manifests itself.

As all that is in time is successive, it follows by that fact alone that something is: all the remainder is excluded. When one note on an instrument is touched, among all those that it virtually offers, this note alone is real. When man is actually modified, the infinite possibility of all his modifications is limited to this single mode of existence. Thus, then, the exclusive action of sensuous impulsion has for its necessary consequence the narrowest limitation. In this state man is only a unity of magnitude, a complete moment in time; or, to speak more correctly, he is not, for his personality is suppressed as long as sensation holds sway over him and carries time along with it.

This instinct extends its domains over the entire sphere of the finite in man, and as form is only revealed in matter, and the absolute by means of its limits, the total manifestation of human nature is connected on a close analysis with the sensuous instinct. But though it is only this instinct that awakens and develops what exists virtually in man, it is nevertheless this very instinct which renders his perfection impossible. It binds down to the world of sense by indestructible ties the spirit that tends higher, and it calls back to the limits of the present, abstraction which had its free development in the sphere of the infinite. No doubt, thought can escape it for a moment, and a firm will victoriously resist its exigencies: but soon compressed nature resumes her rights to give an imperious reality to our existence, to give it contents, substance, knowledge, and an aim for our activity.

The second impulsion, which may be named the formal instinct, issues from the absolute existence of man, or from his rational nature, and tends to set free, and bring harmony into the diversity of its manifestations, and to maintain personality notwithstanding all the changes of state. As this personality, being an absolute and indivisible unity, can never be in contradiction with itself, as we are ourselves forever, this impulsion, which tends to maintain personality, can never exact in one time anything but what it exacts and requires forever. It therefore decides for always what it decides now, and orders now what it orders forever. Hence it embraces the whole series of times, or what comes to the same thing, it suppresses time and change. It wishes the real to be necessary and eternal, and it wishes the eternal and the necessary to be real; in other terms, it tends to truth and justice.

If the sensuous instinct only produces accidents, the formal instinct gives laws, laws for every judgment when it is a question of knowledge, laws for every will when it is a question of action. Whether, therefore, we recognize an object or conceive an objective value to a state of the subject, whether we act in virtue of knowledge or make of the objective the determining principle of our state; in both cases we withdraw this state from the jurisdiction of time, and we attribute to it reality for all men and for all time, that is, universality and necessity. Feeling can only say: "That is true for this subject and at this moment," and there may come another moment, another subject, which withdraws the affirmation from the actual feeling. But when once thought pronounces and says: "That is," it decides forever and ever, and the validity of its decision is guaranteed by the personality itself, which defies all change. Inclination can only say: "That is good for your individuality and present necessity"; but the changing current of affairs will sweep them away, and what you ardently desire to-day will form the object of your aversion to-morrow. But when the moral feeling says: "That ought to be," it decides forever. If you confess the truth because it is the truth, and if you practise justice because it is justice, you have made of a particular case the law of all possible cases, and treated one moment of your life as eternity.

Accordingly, when the formal impulse holds sway and the pure object acts in us, the being attains its highest expansion, all barriers disappear, and from the unity of magnitude in which man was enclosed by a narrow sensuousness, he rises to the unity of idea, which embraces and keeps subject the entire sphere of phenomena. During this operation we are no longer in time, but time is in us with its infinite succession. We are no longer individuals but a species; the judgment of all spirits is expressed by our own, and the choice of all hearts is represented by our own act.

LETTER XIII.

On a first survey, nothing appears more opposed than these two impulsions; one having for its object change, the other immutability, and yet it is these two notions that exhaust the notion of humanity, and a third fundamental impulsion, holding a medium between them, is quite inconceivable. How then shall we re-establish the unity of human nature, a unity that appears completely destroyed by this primitive and radical opposition?

I admit these two tendencies are contradictory, but it should be noticed that they are not so in the same objects. But things that do not meet cannot come into collision. No doubt the sensuous impulsion desires change; but it does not wish that it should extend to personality and its field, nor that there should be a change of principles. The formal impulsion seeks unity and permanence, but it does not wish the condition to remain fixed with the person, that there should be identity of feeling. Therefore these two impulsions are not divided by nature, and if, nevertheless, they appear so, it is because they have become divided by transgressing nature freely, by ignoring themselves, and by confounding their spheres. The office of culture is to watch over them and to secure to each one its proper limits; therefore culture has to give equal justice to both, and to defend not only the rational impulsion against the sensuous, but also the latter against the former. Hence she has to act a twofold part: first, to protect sense against the attacks of freedom; secondly, to secure personality against the power of sensations. One of these ends is attained by the cultivation of the sensuous, the other by that of reason.

Since the world is developed in time, or change, the perfection of the faculty that places men in relation with the world will necessarily be the greatest possible mutability and extensiveness. Since personality is permanence in change, the perfection of this faculty, which must be opposed to change, will be the greatest possible freedom of action (autonomy) and intensity. The more the receptivity is developed under manifold aspects, the more it is movable and offers surfaces to phenomena, the larger is the part of the world seized upon by man, and the more virtualities he develops in himself. Again, in proportion as man gains strength and depth, and depth and reason gain in freedom, in that proportion man takes in a larger share of the world, and throws out forms outside himself. Therefore his culture will consist, first, in placing his receptivity in contact with the world in the greatest number of points possible, and in raising passivity, to the highest exponent on the side of feeling; secondly, in procuring for the determining faculty the greatest possible amount of independence, in relation to the receptive power, and in raising activity to the highest degree on the side of reason. By the union of these two qualities man will associate the highest degree of self-spontaneity (autonomy) and of freedom with the fullest plenitude of existence, and instead of abandoning himself to the world so as to get lost in it, he will rather absorb it in himself, with all the infinitude of its phenomena, and subject it to the unity of his reason.

But man can invert this relation, and thus fail in attaining his destination in two ways. He can hand over to the passive force the intensity demanded by the active force; he can encroach by material impulsion on the formal impulsion, and convert the receptive into the determining power. He can attribute to the active force the extensiveness belonging to the passive force, he can encroach by the formal impulsion on the material impulsion, and substitute the determining for the receptive power. In the former case, he will never be an Ego, a personality; in the second case, he will never be a Non-Ego, and hence in both cases he will be neither the one nor the other, consequently he will be nothing.

In fact, if the sensuous impulsion becomes determining, if the senses become lawgivers, and if the world stifles personality, he loses as object what he gains in force. It may be said of man that when he is only the contents of time, he is not and consequently he has no other contents. His condition is destroyed at the same time as his personality, because these are two correlative ideas, because change presupposes permanence, and a limited reality implies an infinite reality. If the formal impulsion becomes receptive, that is, if thought anticipates sensation, and the person substitutes itself in the place of the world, it loses as a subject and autonomous force what it gains as object, because immutability implies change, and that to manifest itself also absolute reality requires limits. As soon as man is only form, he has no form, and the personality vanishes with the condition. In a word, it is only inasmuch as he is spontaneous, autonomous, that there is reality out of him, that he is also receptive; and it is only inasmuch as he is receptive that there is reality in him, that he is a thinking force.

Consequently these two impulsions require limits, and looked upon as forces, they need tempering; the former that it may not encroach on the field of legislation, the latter that it may not invade the ground of feeling. But this tempering and moderating the sensuous impulsion ought not to be the effect of physical impotence or of a blunting of sensations, which is always a matter for contempt. It must be a free act, an activity of the person, which by its moral intensity moderates the sensuous intensity, and by the sway of impressions takes from them in depth what it gives them in surface or breadth. The character must place limits to temperament, for the senses have only the right to lose elements if it be to the advantage of the mind. In its turn, the tempering of the formal impulsion must not result from moral impotence, from a relaxation of thought and will, which would degrade humanity. It is necessary that the glorious source of this second tempering should be the fulness of sensations; it is necessary that sensuousness itself should defend its field with a victorious arm and resist the violence that the invading activity of the mind would do to it. In a word, it is necessary that the material impulsion should be contained in the limits of propriety by personality, and the formal impulsion by receptivity or nature.

LETTER XIV.

We have been brought to the idea of such a correlation between the two impulsions that the action of the one establishes and limits at the same time the action of the other, and that each of them, taken in isolation, does arrive at its highest manifestation just because the other is active.

No doubt this correlation of the two impulsions is simply a problem advanced by reason, and which man will only be able to solve in the perfection of his being. It is in the strictest signification of the term: the idea of his humanity; accordingly, it is an infinite to which he can approach nearer and nearer in the course of time, but without ever reaching it. "He ought not to aim at form to the injury of reality, nor to reality to the detriment of the form. He must rather seek the absolute being by means of a determinate being, and the determinate being by means of an infinite being. He must set the world before him because he is a person, and he must be a person because he has the world before him. He must feel because he has a consciousness of himself, and he must have a consciousness of himself because he feels." It is only in conformity with this idea that he is a man in the full sense of the word; but he cannot be convinced of this so long as he gives himself up exclusively to one of these two impulsions, or only satisfies them one after the other. For as long as he only feels, his absolute personality and existence remain a mystery to him, and as long as he only thinks, his condition or existence in time escapes him. But if there were cases in which he could have at once this twofold experience in which he would have the consciousness of his freedom and the feeling of his existence together, in which he would simultaneously feel as matter and know himself as spirit, in such cases, and in such only, would he have a complete intuition of his humanity, and the object that would procure him this intuition would be a symbol of his accomplished destiny and consequently serve to express the infinite to him—since this destination can only be fulfilled in the fulness of time.

Presuming that cases of this kind could present themselves in experience, they would awake in him a new impulsion, which, precisely because the other two impulsions would co-operate in it, would be opposed to each of them taken in isolation, and might, with good grounds, be taken for a new impulsion. The sensuous impulsion requires that there should be change, that time should have contents; the formal impulsion requires that time should be suppressed, that there should be no change. Consequently, the impulsion in which both of the others act in concert—allow me to call it the instinct of play, till I explain the term—the instinct of play would have as its object to suppress time in time, to conciliate the state of transition or becoming with the absolute being, change with identity.

The sensuous instinct wishes to be determined, it wishes to receive an object; the formal instinct wishes to determine itself, it wishes to produce an object. Therefore the instinct of play will endeavor to receive as it would itself have produced, and to produce as it aspires to receive.

The sensuous impulsion excludes from its subject all autonomy and freedom; the formal impulsion excludes all dependence and passivity. But the exclusion of freedom is physical necessity; the exclusion of passivity is moral necessity. Thus the two impulsions subdue the mind: the former to the laws of nature, the latter to the laws of reason. It results from this that the instinct of play, which unites the double action of the two other instincts, will content the mind at once morally and physically. Hence, as it suppresses all that is contingent, it will also suppress all coercion, and will set man free physically and morally. When we welcome with effusion some one who deserves our contempt, we feel painfully that nature is constrained. When we have a hostile feeling against a person who commands our esteem, we feel painfully the constraint of reason. But if this person inspires us with interest, and also wins our esteem, the constraint of feeling vanishes together with the constraint of reason, and we begin to love him, that is to say, to play, to take recreation, at once with our inclination and our esteem.

Moreover, as the sensuous impulsion controls us physically, and the formal impulsion morally, the former makes our formal constitution contingent, and the latter makes our material constitution contingent, that is to say, there is contingence in the agreement of our happiness with our perfection, and reciprocally. The instinct of play, in which both act in concert, will render both our formal and our material constitution contingent; accordingly, our perfection and our happiness in like manner. And on the other hand, exactly because it makes both of them contingent, and because the contingent disappears with necessity, it will suppress this contingence in both, and will thus give form to matter and reality to form. In proportion that it will lessen the dynamic influence of feeling and passion, it will place them in harmony with rational ideas, and by taking from the laws of reason their moral constraint, it will reconcile them with the interest of the senses.

LETTER XV.

I approach continually nearer to the end to which I lead you, by a path offering few attractions. Be pleased to follow me a few steps further, and a large horizon will open up to you, and a delightful prospect will reward you for the labor of the way.

The object of the sensuous instinct, expressed in a universal conception, is named Life in the widest acceptation; a conception that expresses all material existence and all that is immediately present in the senses. The object of the formal instinct, expressed in a universal conception, is called shape or form, as well in an exact as in an inexact acceptation; a conception that embraces all formal qualities of things and all relations of the same to the thinking powers. The object of the play instinct, represented in a general statement, may therefore bear the name of living form; a term that serves to describe all aesthetic qualities of phenomena, and what people style, in the widest sense, beauty.

Beauty is neither extended to the whole field of all living things nor merely enclosed in this field. A marble block, though it is and remains lifeless, can nevertheless become a living form by the architect and sculptor; a man, though he lives and has a form, is far from being a living form on that account. For this to be the case, it is necessary that his form should be life, and that his life should be a form. As long as we only think of his form, it is lifeless, a mere abstraction; as long as we only feel his life, it is without form, a mere impression. It is only when his form lives in our feeling, and his life in our understanding, he is the living form, and this will everywhere be the case where we judge him to be beautiful.

But the genesis of beauty is by no means declared because we know how to point out the component parts, which in their combination produce beauty. For to this end it would be necessary to comprehend that combination itself, which continues to defy our exploration, as well as all mutual operation between the finite and the infinite. The reason, on transcendental grounds, makes the following demand: There shall be a communion between the formal impulse and the material impulse—that is, there shall be a play instinct—because it is only the unity of reality with the form, of the accidental with the necessary, of the passive state with freedom, that the conception of humanity is completed. Reason is obliged to make this demand, because her nature impels her to completeness and to the removal of all bounds; while every exclusive activity of one or the other impulse leaves human nature incomplete and places a limit in it. Accordingly, as soon as reason issues the mandate, "a humanity shall exist," it proclaims at the same time the law, "there shall be a beauty." Experience can answer us if there is a beauty, and we shall know it as soon as she has taught us if a humanity can exist. But neither reason nor experience can tell us how beauty can be and how a humanity is possible.

We know that man is neither exclusively matter nor exclusively spirit. Accordingly, beauty as the consummation of humanity, can neither be exclusively mere life, as has been asserted by sharp-sighted observers, who kept too close to the testimony of experience, and to which the taste of the time would gladly degrade it; Nor can beauty be merely form, as has been judged by speculative sophists, who departed too far from experience, and by philosophic artists, who were led too much by the necessity of art in explaining beauty; it is rather the common object of both impulses, that is of the play instinct. The use of language completely justifies this name, as it is wont to qualify with the word play what is neither subjectively nor objectively accidental, and yet does not impose necessity either externally or internally. As the mind in the intuition of the beautiful finds itself in a happy medium between law and necessity, it is, because it divides itself between both, emancipated from the pressure of both. The formal impulse and the material impulse are equally earnest in their demands, because one relates in its cognition to things in their reality and the other to their necessity; because in action the first is directed to the preservation of life, the second to the preservation of dignity, and therefore both to truth and perfection. But life becomes more indifferent when dignity is mixed up with it, and duty no longer coerces when inclination attracts. In like manner the mind takes in the reality of things, material truth, more freely and tranquilly as soon as it encounters formal truth, the law of necessity; nor does the mind find itself strung by abstraction as soon as immediate intuition can accompany it. In one word, when the mind comes into communion with ideas, all reality loses its serious value because it becomes small; and as it comes in contact with feeling, necessity parts also with its serious value because it is easy.

But perhaps the objection has for some time occurred to you, Is not the beautiful degraded by this, that it is made a mere play? and is it not reduced to the level of frivolous objects which have for ages passed under that name? Does it not contradict the conception of the reason and the dignity of beauty, which is nevertheless regarded as an instrument of culture, to confine it to the work of being a mere play? and does it not contradict the empirical conception of play, which can coexist with the exclusion of all taste, to confine it merely to beauty?

But what is meant by a mere play, when we know that in all conditions of humanity that very thing is play, and only that is play which makes man complete and develops simultaneously his twofold nature? What you style limitation, according to your representation of the matter, according to my views, which I have justified by proofs, I name enlargement. Consequently I should have said exactly the reverse: man is serious only with the agreeable, with the good, and with the perfect, but he plays with beauty. In saying this we must not indeed think of the plays that are in vogue in real life, and which commonly refer only to his material state. But in real life we should also seek in vain for the beauty of which we are here speaking. The actually present beauty is worthy of the really, of the actually present play-impulse; but by the ideal of beauty, which is set up by the reason, an ideal of the play-instinct is also presented, which man ought to have before his eyes in all his plays.

Therefore, no error will ever be incurred if we seek the ideal of beauty on the same road on which we satisfy our play-impulse. We can immediately understand why the ideal form of a Venus, of a Juno, and of an Apollo, is to be sought not at Rome, but in Greece, if we contrast the Greek population, delighting in the bloodless athletic contests of boxing, racing, and intellectual rivalry at Olympia, with the Roman people gloating over the agony of a gladiator. Now the reason pronounces that the beautiful must not only be life and form, but a living form, that is, beauty, inasmuch as it dictates to man the twofold law of absolute formality and absolute reality. Reason also utters the decision that man shall only play with beauty, and he shall only play with beauty.

For, to speak out once for all, man only plays when in the full meaning of the word he is a man, and he is only completely a man when he plays. This proposition, which at this moment perhaps appears paradoxical, will receive a great and deep meaning if we have advanced far enough to apply it to the twofold seriousness of duty and of destiny. I promise you that the whole edifice of aesthetic art and the still more difficult art of life will be supported by this principle. But this proposition is only unexpected in science; long ago it lived and worked in art and in the feeling of the Greeks, her most accomplished masters; only they removed to Olympus what ought to have been preserved on earth. Influenced by the truth of this principle, they effaced from the brow of their gods the earnestness and labor which furrow the cheeks of mortals, and also the hollow lust that smoothes the empty face. They set free the ever serene from the chains of every purpose, of every duty, of every care, and they made indolence and indifference the envied condition of the godlike race; merely human appellations for the freest and highest mind. As well the material pressure of natural laws as the spiritual pressure of moral laws lost itself in its higher idea of necessity, which embraced at the same time both worlds, and out of the union of these two necessities issued true freedom. Inspired by this spirit the Greeks also effaced from the features of their ideal, together with desire or inclination, all traces of volition, or, better still, they made both unrecognizable, because they knew how to wed them both in the closest alliance. It is neither charm, nor is it dignity, which speaks from the glorious face of Juno Ludovici; it is neither of these, for it is both at once. While the female god challenges our veneration, the godlike woman at the same time kindles our love. But while in ecstacy we give ourselves up to the heavenly beauty, the heavenly self-repose awes us back. The whole form rests and dwells in itself—a fully complete creation in itself—and as if she were out of space, without advance or resistance; it shows no force contending with force, no opening through which time could break in. Irresistibly carried away and attracted by her womanly charm, kept off at a distance by her godly dignity, we also find ourselves at length in the state of the greatest repose, and the result is a wonderful impression for which the understanding has no idea and language no name.

LETTER XVI.

From the antagonism of the two impulsions, and from the association of two opposite principles, we have seen beauty to result, of which the highest ideal must therefore be sought in the most perfect union and equilibrium possible of the reality and of the form. But this equilibrium remains always an idea that reality can never completely reach. In reality, there will always remain a preponderance of one of these elements over the other, and the highest point to which experience can reach will consist in an oscillation between two principles, when sometimes reality and at others form will have the advantage. Ideal beauty is therefore eternally one and indivisible, because there can only be one single equilibrium; on the contrary, experimental beauty will be eternally double, because in the oscillation the equilibrium may be destroyed in two ways—this side and that.

I have called attention in the foregoing letters to a fact that can also be rigorously deduced from the considerations that have engaged our attention to the present point; this fact is that an exciting and also a moderating action may be expected from the beautiful. The tempering action is directed to keep within proper limits the sensuous and the formal impulsions; the exciting, to maintain both of them in their full force. But these two modes of action of beauty ought to be completely identified in the idea. The beautiful ought to temper while uniformly exciting the two natures, and it ought also to excite while uniformly moderating them. This result flows at once from the idea of a correlation, in virtue of which the two terms mutually imply each other, and are the reciprocal condition one of the other, a correlation of which the purest product is beauty. But experience does not offer an example of so perfect a correlation. In the field of experience it will always happen more or less that excess on the one side will give rise to deficiency on the other, and deficiency will give birth to excess. It results from this that what in the beau-ideal is only distinct in the idea is different in reality in empirical beauty. The beau-ideal, though simple and indivisible, discloses, when viewed in two different aspects, on the one hand, a property of gentleness and grace, and on the other, an energetic property; in experience there is a gentle and graceful beauty and there is an energetic beauty. It is so, and it will be always so, so long as the absolute is enclosed in the limits of time, and the ideas of reason have to be realized in humanity. For example, the intellectual man has the ideal of virtue, of truth, and of happiness; but the active man will only practise virtues, will only grasp truths, and enjoy happy days. The business of physical and moral education is to bring back this multiplicity to unity, to put morality in the place of manners, science in the place of knowledge; the business of aesthetic education is to make out of beauties the beautiful.

Energetic beauty can no more preserve a man from a certain residue of savage violence and harshness than graceful beauty can secure him against a certain degree of effeminacy and weakness. As it is the effect of the energetic beauty to elevate the mind in a physical and moral point of view and to augment its momentum, it only too often happens that the resistance of the temperament and of the character diminishes the aptitude to receive impressions, that the delicate part of humanity suffers an oppression which ought only to affect its grosser part, and that this coarse nature participates in an increase of force that ought only to turn to the account of free personality. It is for this reason that, at the periods when we find much strength and abundant sap in humanity, true greatness of thought is seen associated with what is gigantic and extravagant, and the sublimest feeling is found coupled with the most horrible excess of passion. It is also the reason why, in the periods distinguished for regularity and form, nature is as often oppressed as it is governed, as often outraged as it is surpassed. And as the action of gentle and graceful beauty is to relax the mind in the moral sphere as well as the physical, it happens quite as easily that the energy of feelings is extinguished with the violence of desires, and that character shares in the loss of strength which ought only to affect the passions. This is the reason why, in ages assumed to be refined, it is not a rare thing to see gentleness degenerate into effeminacy, politeness into platitude, correctness into empty sterility, liberal ways into arbitrary caprice, ease into frivolity, calm into apathy, and, lastly, a most miserable caricature treads on the heels of the noblest, the most beautiful type of humanity. Gentle and graceful beauty is therefore a want to the man who suffers the constraint of manner and of forms, for he is moved by grandeur and strength long before he becomes sensible to harmony and grace. Energetic beauty is a necessity to the man who is under the indulgent sway of taste, for in his state of refinement he is only too much disposed to make light of the strength that he retained in his state of rude savagism.

I think I have now answered and also cleared up the contradiction commonly met in the judgments of men respecting the influence of the beautiful, and the appreciation of aesthetic culture. This contradiction is explained directly we remember that there are two sorts of experimental beauty, and that on both hands an affirmation is extended to the entire race, when it can only be proved of one of the species. This contradiction disappears the moment we distinguish a twofold want in humanity to which two kinds of beauty correspond. It is therefore probable that both sides would make good their claims if they come to an understanding respecting the kind of beauty and the form of humanity that they have in view.

Consequently in the sequel of my researches I shall adopt the course that nature herself follows with man considered from the point of view of aesthetics, and setting out from the two kinds of beauty, I shall rise to the idea of the genus. I shall examine the effects produced on man by the gentle and graceful beauty when its springs of action are in full play, and also those produced by energetic beauty when they are relaxed. I shall do this to confound these two sorts of beauty in the unity of the beau-ideal, in the same way that the two opposite forms and modes of being of humanity are absorbed in the unity of the ideal man.

LETTER XVII.

While we were only engaged in deducing the universal idea of beauty from the conception of human nature in general, we had only to consider in the latter the limits established essentially in itself, and inseparable from the notion of the finite. Without attending to the contingent restrictions that human nature may undergo in the real world of phenomena, we have drawn the conception of this nature directly from reason, as a source of every necessity, and the ideal of beauty has been given us at the same time with the ideal of humanity.

But now we are coming down from the region of ideas to the scene of reality, to find man in a determinate state, and consequently in limits which are not derived from the pure conception of humanity, but from external circumstances and from an accidental use of his freedom. But, although the limitation of the idea of humanity may be very manifold in the individual, the contents of this idea suffice to teach us that we can only depart from it by two opposite roads. For if the perfection of man consist in the harmonious energy of his sensuous and spiritual forces, he can only lack this perfection through the want of harmony and the want of energy. Thus, then, before having received on this point the testimony of experience, reason suffices to assure us that we shall find the real and consequently limited man in a state of tension or relaxation, according as the exclusive activity of isolated forces troubles the harmony of his being, or as the unity of his nature is based on the uniform relaxation of his physical and spiritual forces. These opposite limits are, as we have now to prove, suppressed by the beautiful, which re-establishes harmony in man when excited, and energy in man when relaxed; and which, in this way, in conformity with the nature of the beautiful, restores the state of limitation to an absolute state, and makes of man a whole, complete in himself.

Thus the beautiful by no means belies in reality the idea which we have made of it in speculation; only its action is much less free in it than in the field of theory, where we were able to apply it to the pure conception of humanity. In man, as experience shows him to us, the beautiful finds a matter, already damaged and resisting, which robs him in ideal perfection of what it communicates to him of its individual mode of being. Accordingly in reality the beautiful will always appear a peculiar and limited species, and not as the pure genus; in excited minds in a state of tension it will lose its freedom and variety; in relaxed minds, it will lose its vivifying force; but we, who have become familiar with the true character of this contradictory phenomenon, cannot be led astray by it. We shall not follow the great crowd of critics, in determining their conception by separate experiences, and to make them answerable for the deficiencies which man shows under their influence. We know rather that it is man who transfers the imperfections of his individuality over to them, who stands perpetually in the way of their perfection by his subjective limitation, and lowers their absolute ideal to two limited forms of phenomena.

It was advanced that soft beauty is for an unstrung mind, and the energetic beauty for the tightly strung mind. But I apply the term unstrung to a man when he is rather under the pressure of feelings than under the pressure of conceptions. Every exclusive sway of one of his two fundamental impulses is for man a state of compulsion and violence, and freedom only exists in the co-operation of his two natures. Accordingly, the man governed preponderately by feelings, or sensuously unstrung, is emancipated and set free by matter. The soft and graceful beauty, to satisfy this twofold problem, must therefore show herself under two aspects—in two distinct forms. First, as a form in repose, she will tone down savage life, and pave the way from feeling to thought. She will, secondly, as a living image, equip the abstract form with sensuous power, and lead back the conception to intuition and law to feeling. The former service she does to the man of nature, the second to the man of art. But because she does not in both cases hold complete sway over her matter, but depends on that which is furnished either by formless nature or unnatural art, she will in both cases bear traces of her origin, and lose herself in one place in material life and in another in mere abstract form.

To be able to arrive at a conception how beauty can become a means to remove this twofold relaxation, we must explore its source in the human mind. Accordingly, make up your mind to dwell a little longer in the region of speculation, in order then to leave it forever, and to advance with securer footing on the ground of experience.

LETTER XVIII.

By beauty the sensuous man is led to form and to thought; by beauty the spiritual man is brought back to matter and restored to the world of sense.

From this statement it would appear to follow that between matter and form, between passivity and activity, there must be a middle state, and that beauty plants us in this state. It actually happens that the greater part of mankind really form this conception of beauty as soon as they begin to reflect on its operations, and all experience seems to point to this conclusion. But, on the other hand, nothing is more unwarrantable and contradictory than such a conception, because the aversion of matter and form, the passive and the active, feeling and thought, is eternal, and cannot be mediated in any way. How can we remove this contradiction? Beauty weds the two opposed conditions of feeling and thinking, and yet there is absolutely no medium between them. The former is immediately certain through experience, the other through the reason.

This is the point to which the whole question of beauty leads, and if we succeed in settling this point in a satisfactory way, we have at length found the clue that will conduct us through the whole labyrinth of aesthetics.

But this requires two very different operations, which must necessarily support each other in this inquiry. Beauty, it is said, weds two conditions with one another which are opposite to each other, and can never be one. We must start from this opposition; we must grasp and recognize them in their entire purity and strictness, so that both conditions are separated in the most definite manner; otherwise we mix, but we do not unite them. Secondly, it is usual to say, beauty unites those two opposed conditions, and therefore removes the opposition. But because both conditions remain eternally opposed to one another, they cannot be united in any other way than by being suppressed. Our second business is therefore to make this connection perfect, to carry them out with such purity and perfection that both conditions disappear entirely in a third one, and no trace of separation remains in the whole; otherwise we segregate, but do not unite. All the disputes that have ever prevailed and still prevail in the philosophical world respecting the conception of beauty have no other origin than their commencing without a sufficiently strict distinction, or that it is not carried out fully to a pure union. Those philosophers who blindly follow their feeling in reflecting on this topic can obtain no other conception of beauty, because they distinguish nothing separate in the totality of the sensuous impression. Other philosophers, who take the understanding as their exclusive guide, can never obtain a conception of beauty, because they never see anything else in the whole than the parts; and spirit and matter remain eternally separate, even in their most perfect unity. The first fear to suppress beauty dynamically, that is, as a working power, if they must separate what is united in the feeling. The others fear to suppress beauty logically, that is, as a conception, when they have to hold together what in the understanding is separate. The former wish to think of beauty as it works; the latter wish it to work as it is thought. Both therefore must miss the truth; the former, because they try to follow infinite nature with their limited thinking power; the others, because they wish to limit unlimited nature according to their laws of thought. The first fear to rob beauty of its freedom by a too strict dissection, the others fear to destroy the distinctness of the conception by a too violent union. But the former do not reflect that the freedom in which they very properly place the essence of beauty is not lawlessness, but harmony of laws; not caprice, but the highest internal necessity. The others do not remember that distinctness, which they with equal right demand from beauty, does not consist in the exclusion of certain realities, but the absolute including of all; that is not therefore limitation but infinitude. We shall avoid the quicksands on which both have made shipwreck if we begin from the two elements in which beauty divides itself before the understanding, but then afterwards rise to a pure aesthetic unity by which it works on feeling, and in which both those conditions completely disappear.

LETTER XIX.

Two principal and different states of passive and active capacity of being determined [Bestimmbarkeit] can be distinguished in man; in like manner two states of passive and active determination [Bestimmung]. The explanation of this proposition leads us most readily to our end.

The condition of the state of man before destination or direction is given him by the impression of the senses is an unlimited capacity of being determined. The infinite of time and space is given to his imagination for its free use; and, because nothing is settled in this kingdom of the possible, and therefore nothing is excluded from it, this state of absence of determination can be named an empty infiniteness, which must not by any means be confounded with an infinite void.

Now it is necessary that his sensuous nature should be modified, and that in the indefinite series of possible determinations one alone should become real. One perception must spring up in it. That which, in the previous state of determinableness, was only an empty potency becomes now an active force, and receives contents; but, at the same time, as an active force it receives a limit, after having been, as a simple power, unlimited. Reality exists now, but the infinite has disappeared. To describe a figure in space, we are obliged to limit infinite space; to represent to ourselves a change in time, we are obliged to divide the totality of time. Thus we only arrive at reality by limitation, at the positive, at a real position, by negation or exclusion; to determination, by the suppression of our free determinableness.

But mere exclusion would never beget a reality, nor would a mere sensuous impression ever give birth to a perception, if there were not something from which it was excluded, if by an absolute act of the mind the negation were not referred to something positive, and if opposition did not issue out of non-position. This act of the mind is styled judging or thinking, and the result is named thought.

Before we determine a place in space, there is no space for us; but without absolute space we could never determine a place. The same is the case with time. Before we have an instant, there is no time to us: but without infinite time—eternity—we should never have a representation of the instant. Thus, therefore, we can only arrive at the whole by the part, to the unlimited through limitation; but reciprocally we only arrive at the part through the whole, at limitation through the unlimited.

It follows from this, that when it is affirmed of beauty that it mediates for man, the transition from feeling to thought, this must not be understood to mean that beauty can fill up the gap that separates feeling from thought, the passive from the active. This gap is infinite; and, without the interposition of a new and independent faculty, it is impossible for the general to issue from the individual, the necessary from the contingent. Thought is the immediate act of this absolute power, which, I admit, can only be manifested in connection with sensuous impressions, but which in this manifestation depends so little on the sensuous that it reveals itself specially in an opposition to it. The spontaneity or autonomy with which it acts excludes every foreign influence; and it is not in as far as it helps thought—which comprehends a manifest contradiction but only in as far as it procures for the intellectual faculties the freedom to manifest themselves in conformity with their proper laws. It does it only because the beautiful can become a means of leading man from matter to form, from feeling to laws, from a limited existence to an absolute existence.

But this assumes that the freedom of the intellectual faculties can be balked, which appears contradictory to the conception of an autonomous power. For a power which only receives the matter of its activity from without can only be hindered in its action by the privation of this matter, and consequently by way of negation; it is therefore a misconception of the nature of the mind to attribute to the sensuous passions the power of oppressing positively the freedom of the mind. Experience does indeed present numerous examples where the rational forces appear compressed in proportion to the violence of the sensuous forces. But instead of deducing this spiritual weakness from the energy of passion, this passionate energy must rather be explained by the weakness of the human mind. For the sense can only have a sway such as this over man when the mind has spontaneously neglected to assert its power.

Yet in trying by these explanations to move one objection, I appear to have exposed myself to another, and I have only saved the autonomy of the mind at the cost of its unity. For how can the mind derive at the same time from itself the principles of inactivity and of activity, if it is not itself divided, and if it is not in opposition with itself?

Here we must remember that we have before us, not the infinite mind, but the finite. The finite mind is that which only becomes active through the passive, only arrives at the absolute through limitation, and only acts and fashions in as far as it receives matter. Accordingly, a mind of this nature must associate with the impulse towards form or the absolute, an impulse towards matter or limitation, conditions without which it could not have the former impulse nor satisfy it. How can two such opposite tendencies exist together in the same being? This is a problem that can no doubt embarrass the metaphysician, but not the transcendental philosopher. The latter does not presume to explain the possibility of things, but he is satisfied with giving a solid basis to the knowledge that makes us understand the possibility of experience. And as experience would be equally impossible without this autonomy in the mind, and without the absolute unity of the mind, it lays down these two conceptions as two conditions of experience equally necessary without troubling itself any more to reconcile them. Moreover, this immanence of two fundamental impulses does not in any degree contradict the absolute unity of the mind, as soon as the mind itself, its selfhood, is distinguished from those two motors. No doubt, these two impulses exist and act in it, but itself is neither matter nor form, nor the sensuous nor reason, and this is a point that does not seem always to have occurred to those who only look upon the mind as itself acting when its acts are in harmony with reason, and who declare it passive when its acts contradict reason.

Arrived at its development, each of these two fundamental impulsions tends of necessity and by its nature to satisfy itself; but precisely because each of them has a necessary tendency, and both nevertheless have an opposite tendency, this twofold constraint mutually destroys itself, and the will preserves an entire freedom between them both. It is therefore the will that conducts itself like a power—as the basis of reality—with respect to both these impulses; but neither of them can by itself act as a power with respect to the other. A violent man, by his positive tendency to justice, which never fails in him, is turned away from injustice; nor can a temptation of pleasure, however strong, make a strong character violate its principles. There is in man no other power than his will; and death alone, which destroys man, or some privation of self-consciousness, is the only thing that can rob man of his internal freedom.

An external necessity determines our condition, our existence in time, by means of the sensuous. The latter is quite involuntary, and directly it is produced in us we are necessarily passive. In the same manner an internal necessity awakens our personality in connection with sensations, and by its antagonism with them; for consciousness cannot depend on the will, which presupposes it. This primitive manifestation of personality is no more a merit to us than its privation is a defect in us. Reason can only be required in a being who is self-conscious, for reason is an absolute consecutiveness and universality of consciousness; before this is the case he is not a man, nor can any act of humanity be expected from him. The metaphysician can no more explain the limitation imposed by sensation on a free and autonomous mind than the natural philosopher can understand the infinite, which is revealed in consciousness in connection with these limits. Neither abstraction nor experience can bring us back to the source whence issue our ideas of necessity and of universality: this source is concealed in its origin in time from the observer, and its super-sensuous origin from the researches of the metaphysician. But, to sum up in a few words, consciousness is there, and, together with its immutable unity, the law of all that is for man is established, as well as of all that is to be by man, for his understanding and his activity. The ideas of truth and of right present themselves inevitable, incorruptible, immeasurable, even in the age of sensuousness; and without our being able to say why or how, we see eternity in time, the necessary following the contingent. It is thus that, without any share on the part of the subject, the sensation and self-consciousness arise, and the origin of both is beyond our volition, as it is out of the sphere of our knowledge.

But as soon as these two faculties have passed into action, and man has verified by his experience, through the medium of sensation, a determinate existence, and through the medium of consciousness its absolute existence, the two fundamental impulses exert their influence directly their object is given. The sensuous impulse is awakened with the experience of life—with the beginning of the individual; the rational impulsion with the experience of law —with the beginning of his personality; and it is only when these two inclinations have come into existence that the human type is realized. Up to that time, everything takes place in man according to the law of necessity; but now the hand of nature lets him go, and it is for him to keep upright humanity, which nature places as a germ in his heart. And thus we see that directly the two opposite and fundamental impulses exercise their influence in him, both lose their constraint, and the autonomy of two necessities gives birth to freedom.

LETTER XX.

That freedom is an active and not a passive principle results from its very conception; but that liberty itself should be an effect of nature (taking this word in its widest sense), and not the work of man, and therefore that it can be favored or thwarted by natural means, is the necessary consequence of that which precedes. It begins only when man is complete, and when these two fundamental impulsions have been developed. It will then be wanting whilst he is incomplete, and while one of these impulsions is excluded, and it will be re-established by all that gives back to man his integrity.

Thus it is possible, both with regard to the entire species as to the individual, to remark the moment when man is yet incomplete, and when one of the two exclusions acts solely in him. We know that man commences by life simply, to end by form; that he is more of an individual than a person, and that he starts from the limited or finite to approach the infinite. The sensuous impulsion comes into play therefore before the rational impulsion, because sensation precedes consciousness; and in this priority of sensuous impulsion we find the key of the history of the whole of human liberty.

There is a moment, in fact, when the instinct of life, not yet opposed to the instinct of form, acts as nature and as necessity; when the sensuous is a power because man has not begun; for even in man there can be no other power than his will. But when man shall have attained to the power of thought, reason, on the contrary, will be a power, and moral or logical necessity will take the place of physical necessity. Sensuous power must then be annihilated before the law which must govern it can be established. It is not enough that something shall begin which as yet was not; previously something must end which had begun. Man cannot pass immediately from sensuousness to thought. He must step backwards, for it is only when one determination is suppressed that the contrary determination can take place. Consequently, in order to exchange passive against active liberty, a passive determination against an active, he must be momentarily free from all determination, and must traverse a state of pure determinability. He has then to return in some degree to that state of pure negative indetermination in which he was before his senses were affected by anything. But this state was absolutely empty of all contents, and now the question is to reconcile an equal determination and a determinability equally without limit, with the greatest possible fulness, because from this situation something positive must immediately follow. The determination which man received by sensation must be preserved, because he should not lose the reality; but at the same time, in so far as finite, it should be suppressed, because a determinability without limit would take place. The problem consists then in annihilating the determination of the mode of existence, and yet at the same time in preserving it, which is only possible in one way: in opposing to it another. The two sides of a balance are in equilibrium when empty; they are also in equilibrium when their contents are of equal weight.

Thus, to pass from sensation to thought, the soul traverses a medium position, in which sensibility and reason are at the same time active, and thus they mutually destroy their determinant power, and by their antagonism produce a negation. This medium situation in which the soul is neither physically nor morally constrained, and yet is in both ways active, merits essentially the name of a free situation; and if we call the state of sensuous determination physical, and the state of rational determination logical or moral, that state of real and active determination should be called the aesthetic.

LETTER XXI.

I have remarked in the beginning of the foregoing letter that there is a twofold condition of determinableness and a twofold condition of determination. And now I can clear up this proposition.

The mind can be determined—is determinable—only in as far as it is not determined; it is, however, determinable also, in as far as it is not exclusively determined; that is, if it is not confined in its determination. The former is only a want of determination—it is without limits, because it is without reality; but the latter, the aesthetic determinableness, has no limits, because it unites all reality.

The mind is determined, inasmuch as it is only limited; but it is also determined because it limits itself of its own absolute capacity. It is situated in the former position when it feels, in the second when it thinks. Accordingly the aesthetic constitution is in relation to determinableness what thought is in relation to determination. The latter is a negative from internal and infinite completeness, the former a limitation from internal infinite power. Feeling and thought come into contact in one single point, the mind is determined in both conditions, the man becomes something and exists—either as individual or person—by exclusion; in other cases these two faculties stand infinitely apart. Just in the same manner the aesthetic determinableness comes in contact with the mere want of determination in a single point, by both excluding every distinct determined existence, by thus being in all other points nothing and all, and hence by being infinitely different. Therefore if the latter, in the absence of determination from deficiency, is represented as an empty infiniteness, the aesthetic freedom of determination, which forms the proper counterpart to the former, can be considered as a completed infiniteness; a representation which exactly agrees with the teachings of the previous investigations.

Man is therefore nothing in the aesthetic state, if attention is given to the single result, and not to the whole faculty, and if we regard only the absence or want of every special determination. We must therefore do justice to those who pronounce the beautiful, and the disposition in which it places the mind, as entirely indifferent and unprofitable, in relation to knowledge and feeling. They are perfectly right; for it is certain that beauty gives no separate, single result, either for the understanding or for the will; it does not carry out a single intellectual or moral object; it discovers no truth, does not help us to fulfil a single duty, and, in one word, is equally unfit to found the character or to clear the head. Accordingly, the personal worth of a man, or his dignity, as far as this can only depend on himself, remains entirely undetermined by aesthetic culture, and nothing further is attained than that, on the part of nature, it is made profitable for him to make of himself what he will; that the freedom to be what he ought to be is restored perfectly to him.

But by this something infinite is attained. But as soon as we remember that freedom is taken from man by the one-sided compulsion of nature in feeling, and by the exclusive legislation of the reason in thinking, we must consider the capacity restored to him by the aesthetical disposition, as the highest of all gifts, as the gift of humanity. I admit that he possesses this capacity for humanity, before every definite determination in which he may be placed. But, as a matter of fact, he loses it with every determined condition into which he may come; and if he is to pass over to an opposite condition, humanity must be in every case restored to him by the aesthetic life.

It is therefore not only a poetical license, but also philosophically correct, when beauty is named our second creator. Nor is this inconsistent with the fact that she only makes it possible for us to attain and realize humanity, leaving this to our free will. For in this she acts in common with our original creator, nature, which has imparted to us nothing further than this capacity for humanity, but leaves the use of it to our own determination of will.

LETTER XXII.

Accordingly, if the aesthetic disposition of the mind must be looked upon in one respect as nothing—that is, when we confine our view to separate and determined operations—it must be looked upon in another respect as a state of the highest reality, in as far as we attend to the absence of all limits and the sum of powers which are commonly active in it. Accordingly we cannot pronounce them, again, to be wrong who describe the aesthetic state to be the most productive in relation to knowledge and morality. They are perfectly right, for a state of mind which comprises the whole of humanity in itself must of necessity include in itself also — necessarily and potentially—every separate expression of it. Again, a disposition of mind that removes all limitation from the totality of human nature must also remove it from every special expression of the same. Exactly because its "aesthetic disposition" does not exclusively shelter any separate function of humanity, it is favorable to all without distinction; nor does it favor any particular functions, precisely because it is the foundation of the possibility of all. All other exercises give to the mind some special aptitude, but for that very reason give it some definite limits; only the aesthetical leads him to the unlimited. Every other condition in which we can live refers us to a previous condition, and requires for its solution a following condition; only the aesthetic is a complete whole in itself, for it unites in itself all conditions of its source and of its duration. Here alone we feel ourselves swept out of time, and our humanity expresses itself with purity and integrity as if it had not yet received any impression or interruption from the operation of external powers.

That which flatters our senses in immediate sensation opens our weak and volatile spirit to every impression, but makes us in the same degree less apt for exertion. That which stretches our thinking power and invites to abstract conceptions strengthens our mind for every kind of resistance, but hardens it also in the same proportion, and deprives us of susceptibility in the same ratio that it helps us to greater mental activity. For this very reason, one as well as the other brings us at length to exhaustion, because matter cannot long do without the shaping, constructive force, and the force cannot do without the constructible material. But on the other hand, if we have resigned ourselves to the enjoyment of genuine beauty, we are at such a moment of our passive and active powers in the same degree master, and we shall turn with ease from grave to gay, from rest to movement, from submission to resistance, to abstract thinking and intuition.

This high indifference and freedom of mind, united with power and elasticity, is the disposition in which a true work of art ought to dismiss us, and there is no better test of true aesthetic excellence. If after an enjoyment of this kind we find ourselves specially impelled to a particular mode of feeling or action, and unfit for other modes, this serves as an infallible proof that we have not experienced any pure aesthetic effect, whether this is owing to the object, to our own mode of feeling—as generally happens—or to both together.

As in reality no purely aesthetical effect can be met with—for man can never leave his dependence on material forces—the excellence of a work of art can only consist in its greater approximation to its ideal of aesthetic purity, and however high we may raise the freedom of this effect, we shall always leave it with a particular disposition and a particular bias. Any class of productions or separate work in the world of art is noble and excellent in proportion to the universality of the disposition and the unlimited character of the bias thereby presented to our mind. This truth can be applied to works in various branches of art, and also to different works in the same branch. We leave a grand musical performance with our feelings excited, the reading of a noble poem with a quickened imagination, a beautiful statue or building with an awakened understanding; but a man would not choose an opportune moment who attempted to invite us to abstract thinking after a high musical enjoyment, or to attend to a prosaic affair of common life after a high poetical enjoyment, or to kindle our imagination and astonish our feelings directly after inspecting a fine statue or edifice. The reason of this is, that music, by its matter, even when most spiritual, presents a greater affinity with the senses than is permitted by aesthetic liberty; it is because even the most happy poetry, having for its medium the arbitrary and contingent play of the imagination, always shares in it more than the intimate necessity of the really beautiful allows; it is because the best sculpture touches on severe science by what is determinate in its conception. However, these particular affinities are lost in proportion as the works of these three kinds of art rise to a greater elevation, and it is a natural and necessary consequence of their perfection, that, without confounding their objective limits, the different arts come to resemble each other more and more, in the action which they exercise on the mind. At its highest degree of ennobling, music ought to become a form, and act on us with the calm power of an antique statue; in its most elevated perfection, the plastic art ought to become music and move us by the immediate action exercised on the mind by the senses; in its most complete development, poetry ought both to stir us powerfully like music and like plastic art to surround us with a peaceful light. In each art, the perfect style consists exactly in knowing how to remove specific limits, while sacrificing at the same time the particular advantages of the art, and to give it by a wise use of what belongs to it specially a more general character.

Nor is it only the limits inherent in the specific character of each kind of art that the artist ought to overstep in putting his hand to the work; he must also triumph over those which are inherent in the particular subject of which he treats. In a really beautiful work of art, the substance ought to be inoperative, the form should do everything; for by the form the whole man is acted on; the substance acts on nothing but isolated forces. Thus, however vast and sublime it may be, the substance always exercises a restrictive action on the mind, and true aesthetic liberty can only be expected from the form. Consequently the true search of the matter consists in destroying matter by the form; and the triumph of art is great in proportion as it overcomes matter and maintains its sway over those who enjoy its work. It is great particularly in destroying matter when most imposing, ambitious, and attractive, when therefore matter has most power to produce the effect proper to it, or, again, when it leads those who consider it more closely to enter directly into relation with it. The mind of the spectator and of the hearer must remain perfectly free and intact; it must issue pure and entire from the magic circle of the artist, as from the hands of the Creator. The most frivolous subject ought to be treated in such a way that we preserve the faculty to exchange it immediately for the most serious work. The arts which have passion for their object, as a tragedy for example, do not present a difficulty here; for, in the first place, these arts are not entirely free, because they are in the service of a particular end (the pathetic), and then no connoisseur will deny that even in this class a work is perfect in proportion as amidst the most violent storms of passion it respects the liberty of the soul. There is a fine art of passion, but an impassioned fine art is a contradiction in terms, for the infallible effect of the beautiful is emancipation from the passions. The idea of an instructive fine art (didactic art) or improving (moral) art is no less contradictory, for nothing agrees less with the idea of the beautiful than to give a determinate tendency to the mind.

However, from the fact that a work produces effects only by its substance, it must not always be inferred that there is a want of form in this work; this conclusion may quite as well testify to a want of form in the observer. If his mind is too stretched or too relaxed, if it is only accustomed to receive things either by the senses or the intelligence, even in the most perfect combination, it will only stop to look at the parts, and it will only see matter in the most beautiful form. Only sensible of the coarse elements, he must first destroy the aesthetic organization of a work to find enjoyment in it, and carefully disinter the details which genius has caused to vanish, with infinite art, in the harmony of the whole. The interest he takes in the work is either solely moral or exclusively physical; the only thing wanting to it is to be exactly what it ought to be—aesthetical. The readers of this class enjoy a serious and pathetic poem as they do a sermon: a simple and playful work, as an inebriating draught; and if on the one hand they have so little taste as to demand edification from a tragedy or from an epos, even such as the "Messias," on the other hand they will be infallibly scandalized by a piece after the fashion of Anacreon and Catullus.

LETTER XXIII.

I take up the thread of my researches, which I broke off only to apply the principles I laid down to practical art and the appreciation of its works.

The transition from the passivity of sensuousness to the activity of thought and of will can be effected only by the intermediary state of aesthetic liberty; and though in itself this state decides nothing respecting our opinions and our sentiments, and therefore it leaves our intellectual and moral value entirely problematical, it is, however, the necessary condition without which we should never attain to an opinion or a sentiment. In a word, there is no other way to make a reasonable being out of a sensuous man than by making him first aesthetic.

But, you might object: Is this mediation absolutely indispensable? Could not truth and duty, one or the other, in themselves and by themselves, find access to the sensuous man? To this I reply: Not only is it possible but it is absolutely necessary that they owe solely to themselves their determining force, and nothing would be more contradictory to our preceding affirmations than to appear to defend the contrary opinion. It has been expressly proved that the beautiful furnishes no result, either for the comprehension or for the will; that it mingles with no operations, either of thought or of resolution; and that it confers this double power without determining anything with regard to the real exercise of this power. Here all foreign help disappears, and the pure logical form, the idea, would speak immediately to the intelligence, as the pure moral form, the law, immediately to the will.

But that the pure form should be capable of it, and that there is in general a pure form for sensuous man, is that, I maintain, which should be rendered possible by the aesthetic disposition of the soul. Truth is not a thing which can be received from without like reality or the visible existence of objects. It is the thinking force, in his own liberty and activity, which produces it, and it is just this liberty proper to it, this liberty which we seek in vain in sensuous man. The sensuous man is already determined physically, and thenceforth he has no longer his free determinability; he must necessarily first enter into possession of this lost determinability before he can exchange the passive against an active determination. Therefore, in order to recover it, he must either lose the passive determination that he had, or he should enclose already in himself the active determination to which he should pass. If he confined himself to lose passive determination, he would at the same time lose with it the possibility of an active determination, because thought needs a body, and form can only be realized through matter. He must therefore contain already in himself the active determination, that he may be at once both actively and passively determined, that is to say, he becomes necessarily aesthetic.

Consequently, by the aesthetic disposition of the soul the proper activity of reason is already revealed in the sphere of sensuousness, the power of sense is already broken within its own boundaries, and the ennobling of physical man carried far enough, for spiritual man has only to develop himself according to the laws of liberty. The transition from an aesthetic state to a logical and moral state (from the beautiful to truth and duty) is then infinitely more easy than the transition from the physical state to the aesthetic state (from life pure and blind to form).

This transition man can effectuate alone by his liberty, whilst he has only to enter into possession of himself not to give it himself; but to separate the elements of his nature, and not to enlarge it. Having attained to the aesthetic disposition, man will give to his judgments and to his actions a universal value as soon as he desires it. This passage from brute nature to beauty, in which an entirely new faculty would awaken in him, nature would render easier, and his will has no power over a disposition which, we know, itself gives birth to the will. To bring the aesthetic man to profound views, to elevated sentiments, he requires nothing more than important occasions: to obtain the same thing from the sensuous man, his nature must at first be changed. To make of the former a hero, a sage, it is often only necessary to meet with a sublime situation, which exercises upon the faculty of the will the more immediate action; for the second, it must first be transplanted under another sky.

One of the most important tasks of culture, then, is to submit man to form, even in a purely physical life, and to render it aesthetic as far as the domain of the beautiful can be extended, for it is alone in the aesthetic state, and not in the physical state, that the moral state can be developed. If in each particular case man ought to possess the power to make his judgment and his will the judgment of the entire species; if he ought to find in each limited existence the transition to an infinite existence; if, lastly, he ought from every dependent situation to take his flight to rise to autonomy and to liberty, it must be observed that at no moment he is only individual and solely obeys the laws of nature. To be apt and ready to raise himself from the narrow circle of the ends of nature, to rational ends, in the sphere of the former he must already have exercised himself in the second; he must already have realized his physical destiny with a certain liberty that belongs only to spiritual nature, that is to say according to the laws of the beautiful.

And that he can effect without thwarting in the least degree his physical aim. The exigencies of nature with regard to him turn only upon what he does—upon the substance of his acts; but the ends of nature in no degree determine the way in which he acts, the form of his actions. On the contrary, the exigencies of reason have rigorously the form of his activity for its object. Thus, so much as it is necessary for the moral destination of man, that he be purely moral, that he shows an absolute personal activity, so much is he indifferent that his physical destination be entirely physical, that he acts in a manner entirely passive. Henceforth with regard to this last destination, it entirely depends on him to fulfil it solely as a sensuous being and natural force (as a force which acts only as it diminishes) or, at the same time, as absolute force, as a rational being. To which of these does his dignity best respond? Of this there can be no question. It is as disgraceful and contemptible for him to do under sensuous impulsion that which he ought to have determined merely by the motive of duty, as it is noble and honorable for him to incline towards conformity with laws, harmony, independence; there even where the vulgar man only satisfies a legitimate want. In a word, in the domain of truth and morality, sensuousness must have nothing to determine; but in the sphere of happiness, form may find a place, and the instinct of play prevail.

Thus then, in the indifferent sphere of physical life, man ought to already commence his moral life; his own proper activity ought already to make way in passivity, and his rational liberty beyond the limits of sense; he ought already to impose the law of his will upon his inclinations; he ought—if you will permit me the expression—to carry into the domain of matter the war against matter, in order to be dispensed from combating this redoubtable enemy upon the sacred field of liberty; he ought to learn to have nobler desires, not to be forced to have sublime volitions. This is the fruit of aesthetic culture, which submits to the laws of the beautiful, in which neither the laws of nature nor those of reason suffer, which does not force the will of man, and which by the form it gives to exterior life already opens internal life.

LETTER XXIV.

Accordingly three different moments or stages of development can be distinguished, which the individual man, as well as the whole race, must of necessity traverse in a determinate order if they are to fulfil the circle of their determination. No doubt, the separate periods can be lengthened or shortened, through accidental causes which are inherent either in the influence of external things or under the free caprice of men: but neither of them can be overstepped, and the order of their sequence cannot be inverted either by nature or by the will. Man, in his physical condition, suffers only the power of nature; he gets rid of this power in the aesthetical condition, and he rules them in the moral state.

What is man before beauty liberates him from free pleasure, and the serenity of form tames down the savageness of life? Eternally uniform in his aims, eternally changing in his judgments, self-seeking without being himself, unfettered without being free, a slave without serving any rule. At this period, the world is to him only destiny, not yet an object; all has existence for him only in as far as it procures existence to him; a thing that neither seeks from nor gives to him is non-existent. Every phenomenon stands out before him separate and cut off, as he finds himself in the series of beings. All that is, is to him through the bias of the moment; every change is to him an entirely fresh creation, because with the necessary in him, the necessary out of him is wanting, which binds together all the changing forms in the universe, and which holds fast the law on the theatre of his action, while the individual departs. It is in vain that nature lets the rich variety of her forms pass before him; he sees in her glorious fulness nothing but his prey, in her power and greatness nothing but his enemy. Either he encounters objects, and wishes to draw them to himself in desire, or the objects press in a destructive manner upon him, and he thrusts them away in dismay and terror. In both cases his relation to the world of sense is immediate contact; and perpetually anxious through its pressure, restless and plagued by imperious wants, he nowhere finds rest except in enervation, and nowhere limits save in exhausted desire.

"True, his is the powerful breast, and the mighty hand

  of the Titans. . . .

 A certain inheritance; yet the god welded

 Round his forehead a brazen band;

Advice, moderation, wisdom, and patience,—

Hid it from his shy, sinister look.

Every desire is with him a rage,

And his rage prowls around limitless."—Iphigenia in Tauris.

Ignorant of his own human dignity, he is far removed from honoring it in others, and conscious of his own savage greed, he fears it in every creature that he sees like himself. He never sees others in himself, only himself in others, and human society, instead of enlarging him to the race, only shuts him up continually closer in his individuality. Thus limited, he wanders through his sunless life, till favoring nature rolls away the load of matter from his darkened senses, reflection separates him from things, and objects show themselves at length in the afterglow of the consciousness.

It is true we cannot point out this state of rude nature as we have here portrayed it in any definite people and age. It is only an idea, but an idea with which experience agrees most closely in special features. It may be said that man was never in this animal condition, but he has not, on the other hand, ever entirely escaped from it. Even in the rudest subjects, unmistakable traces of rational freedom can be found, and even in the most cultivated, features are not wanting that remind us of that dismal natural condition. It is possible for man, at one and the same time, to unite the highest and the lowest in his nature; and if his dignity depends on a strict separation of one from the other, his happiness depends on a skilful removal of this separation. The culture which is to bring his dignity into agreement with his happiness will therefore have to provide for the greatest purity of these two principles in their most intimate combination.

Consequently the first appearance of reason in man is not the beginning of humanity. This is first decided by his freedom, and reason begins first by making his sensuous dependence boundless; a phenomenon that does not appear to me to have been sufficiently elucidated, considering its importance and universality. We know that the reason makes itself known to man by the demand for the absolute—the self-dependent and necessary. But as this want of the reason cannot be satisfied in any separate or single state of his physical life, he is obliged to leave the physical entirely and to rise from a limited reality to ideas. But although the true meaning of that demand of the reason is to withdraw him from the limits of time and to lead him from the world of sense to an ideal world, yet this same demand of reason, by misapplication—scarcely to be avoided in this life, prone to sensuousness—can direct him to physical life, and, instead of making man free, plunge him in the most terrible slavery.

Facts verify this supposition. Man raised on the wings of imagination leaves the narrow limits of the present, in which mere animality is enclosed, in order to strive on to an unlimited future. But while the limitless is unfolded to his dazed imagination, his heart has not ceased to live in the separate, and to serve the moment. The impulse towards the absolute seizes him suddenly in the midst of his animality, and as in this cloddish condition all his efforts aim only at the material and temporal, and are limited by his individuality, he is only led by that demand of the reason to extend his individuality into the infinite, instead of to abstract from it. He will be led to seek instead of form an inexhaustible matter, instead of the unchangeable an everlasting change and an absolute securing of his temporal existence. The same impulse which, directed to his thought and action, ought to lead to truth and morality, now directed to his passion and emotional state, produces nothing but an unlimited desire and an absolute want. The first fruits, therefore, that he reaps in the world of spirits are cares and fear—both operations of the reason; not of sensuousness, but of a reason that mistakes its object and applies its categorical imperative to matter. All unconditional systems of happiness are fruits of this tree, whether they have for their object the present day or the whole of life, or what does not make them any more respectable, the whole of eternity, for their object. An unlimited duration of existence and of well-being is only an ideal of the desires; hence a demand which can only be put forth by an animality striving up to the absolute. Man, therefore, without gaining anything for his humanity by a rational expression of this sort, loses the happy limitation of the animal, over which he now only possesses the unenviable superiority of losing the present for an endeavor after what is remote, yet without seeking in the limitless future anything but the present.

But even if the reason does not go astray in its object, or err in the question, sensuousness will continue to falsify the answer for a long time. As soon as man has begun to use his understanding and to knit together phenomena in cause and effect, the reason, according to its conception, presses on to an absolute knitting together and to an unconditional basis. In order, merely, to be able to put forward this demand, man must already have stepped beyond the sensuous, but the sensuous uses this very demand to bring back the fugitive.

In fact, it is now that he ought to abandon entirely the world of sense in order to take his flight into the realm of ideas; for the intelligence remains eternally shut up in the finite and in the contingent, and does not cease putting questions without reaching the last link of the chain. But as the man with whom we are engaged is not yet capable of such an abstraction, and does not find it in the sphere of sensuous knowledge, and because he does not look for it in pure reason, he will seek for it below in the region of sentiment, and will appear to find it. No doubt the sensuous shows him nothing that has its foundation in itself, and that legislates for itself, but it shows him something that does not care for foundation or law; therefore, thus not being able to quiet the intelligence by showing it a final cause, he reduces it to silence by the conception which desires no cause; and being incapable of understanding the sublime necessity of reason, he keeps to the blind constraint of matter. As sensuousness knows no other end than its interest, and is determined by nothing except blind chance, it makes the former the motive of its actions, and the latter the master of the world.

Even the divine part in man, the moral law, in its first manifestation in the sensuous cannot avoid this perversion. As this moral law is only prohibited, and combats in man the interest of sensuous egotism, it must appear to him as something strange until he has come to consider this self-love as the stranger, and the voice of reason as his true self. Therefore he confines himself to feeling the fetters which the latter imposes on him, without having the consciousness of the infinite emancipation which it procures for him. Without suspecting in himself the dignity of lawgiver, he only experiences the constraint and the impotent revolt of a subject fretting under the yoke, because in this experience the sensuous impulsion precedes the moral impulsion, he gives to the law of necessity a beginning in him, a positive origin, and by the most unfortunate of all mistakes he converts the immutable and the eternal in himself into a transitory accident. He makes up his mind to consider the notions of the just and the unjust as statutes which have been introduced by a will, and not as having in themselves an eternal value. Just as in the explanation of certain natural phenomena he goes beyond nature and seeks out of her what can only be found in her, in her own laws; so also in the explanation of moral phenomena he goes beyond reason and makes light of his humanity, seeking a god in this way. It is not wonderful that a religion which he has purchased at the cost of his humanity shows itself worthy of this origin, and that he only considers as absolute and eternally binding laws that have never been binding from all eternity. He has placed himself in relation with, not a holy being, but a powerful. Therefore the spirit of his religion, of the homage that he gives to God, is a fear that abases him, and not a veneration that elevates him in his own esteem.

Though these different aberrations by which man departs from the ideal of his destination cannot all take place at the same time, because several degrees have to be passed over in the transition from the obscure of thought to error, and from the obscure of will to the corruption of the will; these degrees are all, without exception, the consequence of his physical state, because in all the vital impulsion sways the formal impulsion. Now, two cases may happen: either reason may not yet have spoken in man, and the physical may reign over him with a blind necessity, or reason may not be sufficiently purified from sensuous impressions, and the moral may still be subject to the physical; in both cases the only principle that has a real power over him is a material principle, and man, at least as regards his ultimate tendency, is a sensuous being. The only difference is, that in the former case he is an animal without reason, and in the second case a rational animal. But he ought to be neither one nor the other: he ought to be a man. Nature ought not to rule him exclusively; nor reason conditionally. The two legislations ought to be completely independent, and yet mutually complementary.

LETTER XXV.

Whilst man, in his first physical condition, is only passively affected by the world of sense, he is still entirely identified with it; and for this reason the external world, as yet, has no objective existence for him. When he begins in his aesthetic state of mind to regard the world objectively, then only is his personality severed from it, and the world appears to him an objective reality, for the simple reason that he has ceased to form an identical portion of it.

That which first connects man with the surrounding universe is the power of reflective contemplation. Whereas desire seizes at once its object, reflection removes it to a distance and renders it inalienably her own by saving it from the greed of passion. The necessity of sense which he obeyed during the period of mere sensations, lessens during the period of reflection; the senses are for the time in abeyance; even ever-fleeting time stands still whilst the scattered rays of consciousness are gathering and shape themselves; an image of the infinite is reflected upon the perishable ground. As soon as light dawns in man, there is no, longer night outside of him; as soon as there is peace within him the storm lulls throughout the universe, and the contending forces of nature find rest within prescribed limits. Hence we cannot wonder if ancient traditions allude to these great changes in the inner man as to a revolution in surrounding nature, and symbolize thought triumphing over the laws of time, by the figure of Zeus, which terminates the reign of Saturn.

As long as man derives sensations from a contact with nature, he is her slave; but as soon as he begins to reflect upon her objects and laws he becomes her lawgiver. Nature, which previously ruled him as a power, now expands before him as an object. What is objective to him can have no power over him, for in order to become objective it has to experience his own power. As far and as long as he impresses a form upon matter, he cannot be injured by its effect; for a spirit can only be injured by that which deprives it of its freedom. Whereas he proves his own freedom by giving a form to the formless; where the mass rules heavily and without shape, and its undefined outlines are for ever fluctuating between uncertain boundaries, fear takes up its abode; but man rises above any natural terror as soon as he knows how to mould it, and transform it into an object of his art. As soon as he upholds his independence towards phenomenal natures he maintains his dignity toward her as a thing of power, and with a noble freedom he rises against his gods. They throw aside the mask with which they had kept him in awe during his infancy, and to his surprise his mind perceives the reflection of his own image. The divine monster of the Oriental, which roams about changing the world with the blind force of a beast of prey, dwindles to the charming outline of humanity in Greek fable; the empire of the Titans is crushed, and boundless force is tamed by infinite form.

But whilst I have been merely searching for an issue from the material world, and a passage into the world of mind, the bold flight of my imagination has already taken me into the very midst of the latter world. The beauty of which we are in search we have left behind by passing from the life of mere sensations to the pure form and to the pure object. Such a leap exceeds the condition of human nature; in order to keep pace with the latter we must return to the world of sense.

Beauty is indeed the sphere of unfettered contemplation and reflection; beauty conducts us into the world of ideas, without however taking us from the world of sense, as occurs when a truth is perceived and acknowledged. This is the pure product of a process of abstraction from everything material and accidental, a pure object free from every subjective barrier, a pure state of self-activity without any admixture of passive sensations. There is indeed a way back to sensation from the highest abstraction; for thought teaches the inner sensation, and the idea of logical or moral unity passes into a sensation of sensual accord. But if we delight in knowledge we separate very accurately our own conceptions from our sensations; we look upon the latter as something accidental, which might have been omitted without the knowledge being impaired thereby, without truth being less true. It would, however, be a vain attempt to suppress this connection of the faculty of feeling with the idea of beauty, consequently, we shall not succeed in representing to ourselves one as the effect of the other, but we must look upon them both together and reciprocally as cause and effect. In the pleasure which we derive from knowledge we readily distinguish the passage from the active to the passive state, and we clearly perceive that the first ends when the second begins. On the contrary, from the pleasure which we take in beauty, this transition from the active to the passive is not perceivable, and reflection is so intimately blended with feeling that we believe we feel the form immediately. Beauty is then an object to us, it is true, because reflection is the condition of the feeling which we have of it; but it is also a state of our personality (our Ego) because the feeling is the condition of the idea we conceive of it: beauty is therefore doubtless form, because we contemplate it, but it is equally life because we feel it. In a word, it is at once our state and our act. And precisely because it is at the same time both a state and an act, it triumphantly proves to us that the passive does not exclude the active, neither matter nor form, neither the finite nor the infinite; and that consequently the physical dependence to which man is necessarily devoted does not in any way destroy his moral liberty. This is the proof of beauty, and I ought to add that this alone can prove it. In fact, as in the possession of truth or of logical unity, feeling is not necessarily one with the thought, but follows it accidentally; it is a fact which only proves that a sensitive nature can succeed a rational nature, and vice versa; not that they co-exist, that they exercise a reciprocal action one over the other; and, lastly, that they ought to be united in an absolute and necessary manner. From this exclusion of feeling as long as there is thought, and of thought so long as there is feeling, we should on the contrary conclude that the two natures are incompatible, so that in order to demonstrate that pure reason is to be realized in humanity, the best proof given by the analysis is that this realization is demanded. But, as in the realization of beauty or of aesthetic unity, there is a real union, mutual substitution of matter and of form, of passive and of active, by this alone is proved the compatibility of the two natures, the possible realization of the infinite in the finite, and consequently also the possibility of the most sublime humanity.

Henceforth we need no longer be embarrassed to find a transition from dependent feeling to moral liberty, because beauty reveals to us the fact that they can perfectly coexist, and that to show himself a spirit, man need not escape from matter. But if on one side he is free, even in his relation with a visible world, as the fact of beauty teaches, and if on the other side freedom is something absolute and supersensuous, as its idea necessarily implies, the question is no longer how man succeeds in raising himself from the finite to the absolute, and opposing himself in his thought and will to sensuality, as this has already been produced in the fact of beauty. In a word, we have no longer to ask how he passes from virtue to truth which is already included in the former, but how he opens a way for himself from vulgar reality to aesthetic reality, and from the ordinary feelings of life to the perception of the beautiful.

LETTER XXVI.

I have shown in the previous letters that it is only the aesthetic disposition of the soul that gives birth to liberty, it cannot therefore be derived from liberty nor have a moral origin. It must be a gift of nature; the favor of chance alone can break the bonds of the physical state and bring the savage to duty. The germ of the beautiful will find an equal difficulty in developing itself in countries where a severe nature forbids man to enjoy himself, and in those where a prodigal nature dispenses him from all effort; where the blunted senses experience no want, and where violent desire can never be satisfied. The delightful flower of the beautiful will never unfold itself in the case of the Troglodyte hid in his cavern always alone, and never finding humanity outside himself; nor among nomads, who, travelling in great troops, only consist of a multitude, and have no individual humanity. It will only flourish in places where man converses peacefully with himself in his cottage, and with the whole race when he issues from it. In those climates where a limpid ether opens the senses to the lightest impression, whilst a life-giving warmth develops a luxuriant nature, where even in the inanimate creation the sway of inert matter is overthrown, and the victorious form ennobles even the most abject natures; in this joyful state and fortunate zone, where activity alone leads to enjoyment, and enjoyment to activity, from life itself issues a holy harmony, and the laws of order develop life, a different result takes place. When imagination incessantly escapes from reality, and does not abandon the simplicity of nature in its wanderings: then and there only the mind and the senses, the receptive force and the plastic force, are developed in that happy equilibrium which is the soul of the beautiful and the condition of humanity.

What phenomenon accompanies the initiation of the savage into humanity? However far we look back into history the phenomenon is identical among all people who have shaken off the slavery of the animal state: the love of appearance, the inclination for dress and for games.

Extreme stupidity and extreme intelligence have a certain affinity in only seeking the real and being completely insensible to mere appearance. The former is only drawn forth by the immediate presence of an object in the senses, and the second is reduced to a quiescent state only by referring conceptions to the facts of experience. In short, stupidity cannot rise above reality, nor the intelligence descend below truth. Thus, in as far as the want of reality and attachment to the real are only the consequence of a want and a defect, indifference to the real and an interest taken in appearances are a real enlargement of humanity and a decisive step towards culture. In the first place it is the proof of an exterior liberty, for as long as necessity commands and want solicits, the fancy is strictly chained down to the real: it is only when want is satisfied that it develops without hinderance. But it is also the proof of an internal liberty, because it reveals to us a force which, independent of an external substratum, sets itself in motion, and has sufficient energy to remove from itself the solicitations of nature. The reality of things is effected by things, the appearance of things is the work of man, and a soul that takes pleasure in appearance does not take pleasure in what it receives but in what it makes.

It is self-evident that I am speaking of aesthetical evidence different from reality and truth, and not of logical appearance identical with them. Therefore if it is liked it is because it is an appearance, and not because it is held to be something better than it is: the first principle alone is a play, whilst the second is a deception. To give a value to the appearance of the first kind can never injure truth, because it is never to be feared that it will supplant it—the only way in which truth can be injured. To despise this appearance is to despise in general all the fine arts of which it is the essence. Nevertheless, it happens sometimes that the understanding carries its zeal for reality as far as this intolerance, and strikes with a sentence of ostracism all the arts relating to beauty in appearance, because it is only an appearance. However, the intelligence only shows this vigorous spirit when it calls to mind the affinity pointed out further back. I shall find some day the occasion to treat specially of the limits of beauty in its appearance.

It is nature herself which raises man from reality to appearance by endowing him with two senses which only lead him to the knowledge of the real through appearance. In the eye and the ear the organs of the senses are already freed from the persecutions of nature, and the object with which we are immediately in contact through the animal senses is remoter from us. What we see by the eye differs from what we feel; for the understanding to reach objects overleaps the light which separates us from them. In truth, we are passive to an object: in sight and hearing the object is a form we create. While still a savage, man only enjoys through touch merely aided by sight and sound. He either does not rise to perception through sight, or does not rest there. As soon as he begins to enjoy through sight, vision has an independent value, he is aesthetically free, and the instinct of play is developed.

The instinct of play likes appearance, and directly it is awakened it is followed by the formal imitative instinct which treats appearance as an independent thing. Directly man has come to distinguish the appearance from the reality, the form from the body, he can separate, in fact he has already done so. Thus the faculty of the art of imitation is given with the faculty of form in general. The inclination that draws us to it reposes on another tendency I have not to notice here. The exact period when the aesthetic instinct, or that of art, develops, depends entirely on the attraction that mere appearance has for men.

As every real existence proceeds from nature as a foreign power, whilst every appearance comes in the first place from man as a percipient subject, he only uses his absolute sight in separating semblance from essence, and arranging according to subjective law. With an unbridled liberty he can unite what nature has severed, provided he can imagine his union, and he can separate what nature has united, provided this separation can take place in his intelligence. Here nothing can be sacred to him but his own law: the only condition imposed upon him is to respect the border which separates his own sphere from the existence of things or from the realm of nature.

This human right of ruling is exercised by man in the art of appearance; and his success in extending the empire of the beautiful, and guarding the frontiers of truth, will be in proportion with the strictness with which he separates form from substance: for if he frees appearance from reality, he must also do the converse.

But man possesses sovereign power only in the world of appearance, in the unsubstantial realm of imagination, only by abstaining from giving being to appearance in theory, and by giving it being in practice. It follows that the poet transgresses his proper limits when he attributes being to his ideal, and when he gives this ideal aim as a determined existence. For he can only reach this result by exceeding his right as a poet, that of encroaching by the ideal on the field of experience, and by pretending to determine real existence in virtue of a simple possibility, or else he renounces his right as a poet by letting experience encroach on the sphere of the ideal, and by restricting possibility to the conditions of reality.

It is only by being frank or disclaiming all reality, and by being independent or doing without reality, that the appearance is aesthetical. Directly it apes reality or needs reality for effect, it is nothing more than a vile instrument for material ends, and can prove nothing for the freedom of the mind. Moreover, the object in which we find beauty need not be unreal if our judgment disregards this reality; for if it regards this the judgment is no longer aesthetical. A beautiful woman, if living, would no doubt please us as much and rather more than an equally beautiful woman seen in painting; but what makes the former please men is not her being an independent appearance; she no longer pleases the pure aesthetic feeling. In the painting, life must only attract as an appearance, and reality as an idea. But it is certain that to feel in a living object only the pure appearance requires a greatly higher aesthetic culture than to do without life in the appearance.

When the frank and independent appearance is found in man separately, or in a whole people, it may be inferred they have mind, taste, and all prerogatives connected with them. In this case the ideal will be seen to govern real life, honor triumphing over fortune, thought over enjoyment, the dream of immortality over a transitory existence.

In this case public opinion will no longer be feared, and an olive crown will be more valued than a purple mantle. Impotence and perversity alone have recourse to false and paltry semblance, and individuals as well as nations who lend to reality the support of appearance, or to the aesthetic appearance the support of reality, show their moral unworthiness and their aesthetical impotence. Therefore, a short and conclusive answer can be given to this question— how far will appearance be permitted in the moral world? It will run thus in proportion as this appearance will be aesthetical, that is, an appearance that does not try to make up for reality, nor requires to be made up for by it. The aesthetical appearance can never endanger the truth of morals: wherever it seems to do so the appearance is not aesthetical. Only a stranger to the fashionable world can take the polite assurances, which are only a form, for proofs of affection, and say he has been deceived; but only a clumsy fellow in good society calls in the aid of duplicity and flatters to become amiable. The former lacks the pure sense for independent appearance; therefore he can only give a value to appearance by truth. The second lacks reality, and wishes to replace it by appearance. Nothing is more common than to hear depreciators of the times utter these paltry complaints—that all solidity has disappeared from the world, and that essence is neglected for semblance. Though I feel by no means called upon to defend this age against these reproaches, I must say that the wide application of these criticisms shows that they attach blame to the age, not only on the score of the false, but also of the frank appearance. And even the exceptions they admit in favor of the beautiful have for their object less the independent appearance than the needy appearance. Not only do they attack the artificial coloring that hides truth and replaces reality, but also the beneficent appearance that fills a vacuum and clothes poverty; and they even attack the ideal appearance that ennobles a vulgar reality. Their strict sense of truth is rightly offended by the falsity of manners; unfortunately, they class politeness in this category. It displeases them that the noisy and showy so often eclipse true merit, but they are no less shocked that appearance is also demanded from merit, and that a real substance does not dispense with an agreeable form. They regret the cordiality, the energy, and solidity of ancient times; they would restore with them ancient coarseness, heaviness, and the old Gothic profusion. By judgments of this kind they show an esteem for the matter itself unworthy of humanity, which ought only to value the matter inasmuch as it can receive a form and enlarge the empire of ideas. Accordingly, the taste of the age need not much fear these criticisms if it can clear itself before better judges. Our defect is not to grant a value to aesthetic appearance (we do not do this enough): a severe judge of the beautiful might rather reproach us with not having arrived at pure appearance, with not having separated clearly enough existence from the phenomenon, and thus established their limits. We shall deserve this reproach so long as we cannot enjoy the beautiful in living nature without desiring it; as long as we cannot admire the beautiful in the imitative arts without having an end in view; as long as we do not grant to imagination an absolute legislation of its own; and as long as we do not inspire it with care for its dignity by the esteem we testify for its works.

LETTER XXVII.

Do not fear for reality and truth. Even if the elevated idea of aesthetic appearance become general, it would not become so, as long as man remains so little cultivated as to abuse it; and if it became general, this would result from a culture that would prevent all abuse of it. The pursuit of independent appearance requires more power of abstraction, freedom of heart, and energy of will than man requires to shut himself up in reality; and he must have left the latter behind him if he wishes to attain to aesthetic appearance. Therefore, a man would calculate very badly who took the road of the ideal to save himself that of reality. Thus, reality would not have much to fear from appearance, as we understand it; but, on the other hand, appearance would have more to fear from reality. Chained to matter, man uses appearance for his purposes before he allows it a proper personality in the art of the ideal: to come to that point a complete revolution must take place in his mode of feeling, otherwise, he would not be even on the way to the ideal. Consequently, when we find in man the signs of a pure and disinterested esteem, we can infer that this revolution has taken place in his nature, and that humanity has really begun in him. Signs of this kind are found even in the first and rude attempts that he makes to embellish his existence, even at the risk of making it worse in its material conditions. As soon as he begins to prefer form to substance and to risk reality for appearance (known by him to be such), the barriers of animal life fall, and he finds himself on a track that has no end.

Not satisfied with the needs of nature, he demands the superfluous. First, only the superfluous of matter, to secure his enjoyment beyond the present necessity; but afterward; he wishes a superabundance in matter, an aesthetical supplement to satisfy the impulse for the formal, to extend enjoyment beyond necessity. By piling up provisions simply for a future use, and anticipating their enjoyment in the imagination, he outsteps the limits of the present moment, but not those of time in general. He enjoys more; he does not enjoy differently. But as soon as he makes form enter into his enjoyment, and he keeps in view the forms of the objects which satisfy his desires, he has not only increased his pleasure in extent and intensity, but he has also ennobled it in mode and species.

No doubt nature has given more than is necessary to unreasoning beings; she has caused a gleam of freedom to shine even in the darkness of animal life. When the lion is not tormented by hunger, and when no wild beast challenges him to fight, his unemployed energy creates an object for himself; full of ardor, he fills the re-echoing desert with his terrible roars, and his exuberant force rejoices in itself, showing itself without an object. The insect flits about rejoicing in life in the sunlight, and it is certainly not the cry of want that makes itself heard in the melodious song of the bird; there is undeniably freedom in these movements, though it is not emancipation from want in general, but from a determinate external necessity.

The animal works, when a privation is the motor of its activity, and it plays when the plenitude of force is this motor, when an exuberant life is excited to action. Even in inanimate nature a luxury of strength and a latitude of determination are shown, which in this material sense might be styled play. The tree produces numberless germs that are abortive without developing, and it sends forth more roots, branches, and leaves, organs of nutrition, than are used for the preservation of the species. Whatever this tree restores to the elements of its exuberant life, without using it or enjoying it, may be expended by life in free and joyful movements. It is thus that nature offers in her material sphere a sort of prelude to the limitless, and that even there she suppresses partially the chains from which she will be completely emancipated in the realm of form. The constraint of superabundance or physical play answers as a transition from the constraint of necessity, or of physical seriousness, to aesthetical play; and before shaking off, in the supreme freedom of the beautiful, the yoke of any special aim, nature already approaches, at least remotely, this independence, by the free movement which is itself its own end and means.

The imagination, like the bodily organs, has in man its free movement and its material play, a play in which, without any reference to form, it simply takes pleasure in its arbitrary power and in the absence of all hinderance. These plays of fancy, inasmuch as form is not mixed up with them, and because a free succession of images makes all their charm, though confined to man, belong exclusively to animal life, and only prove one thing—that he is delivered from all external sensuous constraint without our being entitled to infer that there is in it an independent plastic force.

From this play of free association of ideas, which is still quite material in nature and is explained by simple natural laws, the imagination, by making the attempt of creating a free form, passes at length at a jump to the aesthetic play: I say at one leap, for quite a new force enters into action here; for here, for the first time, the legislative mind is mixed with the acts of a blind instinct, subjects the arbitrary march of the imagination to its eternal and immutable unity, causes its independent permanence to enter in that which is transitory, and its infinity in the sensuous. Nevertheless, as long as rude nature, which knows of no other law than running incessantly from change to change, will yet retain too much strength, it will oppose itself by its different caprices to this necessity; by its agitation to this permanence; by its manifold needs to this independence, and by its insatiability to this sublime simplicity. It will be also troublesome to recognize the instinct of play in its first trials, seeing that the sensuous impulsion, with its capricious humor and its violent appetites, constantly crosses. It is on that account that we see the taste, still coarse, seize that which is new and startling, the disordered, the adventurous and the strange, the violent and the savage, and fly from nothing so much as from calm and simplicity. It invents grotesque figures, it likes rapid transitions, luxurious forms, sharply-marked changes, acute tones, a pathetic song. That which man calls beautiful at this time is that which excites him, that which gives him matter; but that which excites him to give his personality to the object, that which gives matter to a possible plastic operation, for otherwise it would not be the beautiful for him. A remarkable change has therefore taken place in the form of his judgments; he searches for these objects, not because they affect him, but because they furnish him with the occasion of acting; they please him, not because they answer to a want, but because they satisfy a law which speaks in his breast, although quite low as yet.

Soon it will not be sufficient for things to please him; he will wish to please: in the first place, it is true, only by that which belongs to him; afterwards by that which he is. That which he possesses, that which he produces, ought not merely to bear any more the traces of servitude, nor to mark out the end, simply and scrupulously, by the form. Independently of the use to which it is destined, the object ought also to reflect the enlightened intelligence which imagines it, the hand which shaped it with affection, the mind free and serene which chose it and exposed it to view. Now, the ancient German searches for more magnificent furs, for more splendid antlers of the stag, for more elegant drinking-horns; and the Caledonian chooses the prettiest shells for his festivals. The arms themselves ought to be no longer only objects of terror, but also of pleasure; and the skilfully-worked scabbard will not attract less attention than the homicidal edge of the sword. The instinct of play, not satisfied with bringing into the sphere of the necessary an aesthetic superabundance for the future more free, is at last completely emancipated from the bonds of duty, and the beautiful becomes of itself an object of man's exertions. He adorns himself. The free pleasure comes to take a place among his wants, and the useless soon becomes the best part of his joys. Form, which from the outside gradually approaches him, in his dwelling, his furniture, his clothing, begins at last to take possession of the man himself, to transform him, at first exteriorly, and afterwards in the interior. The disordered leaps of joy become the dance, the formless gesture is changed into an amiable and harmonious pantomime, the confused accents of feeling are developed, and begin to obey measures and adapt themselves to song. When, like the flight of cranes, the Trojan army rushes on to the field of battle with thrilling cries, the Greek army approaches in silence and with a noble and measured step. On the one side we see but the exuberance of a blind force, on the other the triumph of form, and the simple majesty of law.

Now, a nobler necessity binds the two sexes mutually, and the interests of the heart contribute in rendering durable an alliance which was at first capricious and changing like the desire that knits it. Delivered from the heavy fetters of desire, the eye, now calmer, attends to the form, the soul contemplates the soul, and the interested exchange of pleasure becomes a generous exchange of mutual inclination. Desire enlarges and rises to love, in proportion as it sees humanity dawn in its object; and, despising the vile triumphs gained by the senses, man tries to win a nobler victory over the will. The necessity of pleasing subjects the powerful nature to the gentle laws of taste; pleasure may be stolen, but love must be a gift. To obtain this higher recompense, it is only through the form and not through matter that it can carry on the contest. It must cease to act on feeling as a force, to appear in the intelligence as a simple phenomenon; it must respect liberty, as it is liberty it wishes to please. The beautiful reconciles the contrast of different natures in its simplest and purest expression. It also reconciles the eternal contrast of the two sexes in the whole complex framework of society, or at all events it seeks to do so; and, taking as its model the free alliance it has knit between manly strength and womanly gentleness, it strives to place in harmony, in the moral world, all the elements of gentleness and of violence. Now, at length, weakness becomes sacred, and an unbridled strength disgraces; the injustice of nature is corrected by the generosity of chivalrous manners. The being whom no power can make tremble, is disarmed by the amiable blush of modesty, and tears extinguish a vengeance that blood could not have quenched. Hatred itself hears the delicate voice of honor, the conqueror's sword spares the disarmed enemy, and a hospitable hearth smokes for the stranger on the dreaded hillside where murder alone awaited him before.

In the midst of the formidable realm of forces, and of the sacred empire of laws, the aesthetic impulse of form creates by degrees a third and a joyous realm, that of play and of the appearance, where she emancipates man from fetters, in all his relations, and from all that is named constraint, whether physical or moral.

If in the dynamic state of rights men mutually move and come into collision as forces, in the moral (ethical) state of duties, man opposes to man the majesty of the laws, and chains down his will. In this realm of the beautiful or the aesthetic state, man ought to appear to man only as a form, and an object of free play. To give freedom through freedom is the fundamental law of this realm.

The dynamic state can only make society simple possibly by subduing nature through nature; the moral (ethical) state can only make it morally necessary by submitting the will of the individual to the general will.

The aesthetic state alone can make it real, because it carries out the will of all through the nature of the individual. If necessity alone forces man to enter into society, and if his reason engraves on his soul social principles, it is beauty only that can give him a social character; taste alone brings harmony into society, because it creates harmony in the individual. All other forms of perception divide the man, because they are based exclusively either in the sensuous or in the spiritual part of his being. It is only the perception of beauty that makes of him an entirety, because it demands the co-operation of his two natures. All other forms of communication divide society, because they apply exclusively either to the receptivity or to the private activity of its members, and therefore to what distinguishes men one from the other. The aesthetic communication alone unites society because it applies to what is common to all its members. We only enjoy the pleasures of sense as individuals, without the nature of the race in us sharing in it; accordingly, we cannot generalize our individual pleasures, because we cannot generalize our individuality. We enjoy the pleasures of knowledge as a race, dropping the individual in our judgment; but we cannot generalize the pleasures of the understanding, because we cannot eliminate individuality from the judgments of others as we do from our own. Beauty alone can we enjoy both as individuals and as a race, that is, as representing a race. Good appertaining to sense can only make one person happy, because it is founded on inclination, which is always exclusive; and it can only make a man partially happy, because his real personality does not share in it. Absolute good can only render a man happy conditionally, for truth is only the reward of abnegation, and a pure heart alone has faith in a pure will. Beauty alone confers happiness on all, and under its influence every being forgets that he is limited.

Taste does not suffer any superior or absolute authority, and the sway of beauty is extended over appearance. It extends up to the seat of reason's supremacy, suppressing all that is material. It extends down to where sensuous impulse rules with blind compulsion, and form is undeveloped. Taste ever maintains its power on these remote borders, where legislation is taken from it. Particular desires must renounce their egotism, and the agreeable, otherwise tempting the senses, must in matters of taste adorn the mind with the attractions of grace.

Duty and stern necessity must change their forbidding tone, only excused by resistance, and do homage to nature by a nobler trust in her. Taste leads our knowledge from the mysteries of science into the open expanse of common sense, and changes a narrow scholasticism into the common property of the human race. Here the highest genius must leave its particular elevation, and make itself familiar to the comprehension even of a child. Strength must let the Graces bind it, and the arbitrary lion must yield to the reins of love. For this purpose taste throws a veil over physical necessity, offending a free mind by its coarse nudity, and dissimulating our degrading parentage with matter by a delightful illusion of freedom. Mercenary art itself rises from the dust; and the bondage of the bodily, at its magic touch, falls off from the inanimate and animate. In the aesthetic state the most slavish tool is a free citizen, having the same rights as the noblest; and the intellect which shapes the mass to its intent must consult it concerning its destination. Consequently, in the realm of aesthetic appearance, the idea of equality is realized, which the political zealot would gladly see carried out socially. It has often been said that perfect politeness is only found near a throne. If thus restricted in the material, man has, as elsewhere appears, to find compensation in the ideal world.

Does such a state of beauty in appearance exist, and where? It must be in every finely-harmonized soul; but as a fact, only in select circles, like the pure ideal of the church and state —in circles where manners are not formed by the empty imitations of the foreign, but by the very beauty of nature; where man passes through all sorts of complications in all simplicity and innocence, neither forced to trench on another's freedom to preserve his own, nor to show grace at the cost of dignity.

AESTHETICAL ESSAYS.

THE MORAL UTILITY OF AESTHETIC MANNERS.

The author of the article which appeared in the eleventh number of "The Hours," of 1795, upon "The Danger of Aesthetic Manners," was right to hold as doubtful a morality founded only on a feeling for the beautiful, and which has no other warrant than taste; but it is evident that a strong and pure feeling for the beautiful ought to exercise a salutary influence upon the moral life; and this is the question of which I am about to treat.

When I attribute to taste the merit of contributing to moral progress, it is not in the least my intention to pretend that the interest that good taste takes in an action suffices to make an action moral; morality could never have any other foundation than her own. Taste can be favorable to morality in the conduct, as I hope to point out in the present essay; but alone, and by its unaided influence, it could never produce anything moral.

It is absolutely the same with respect to internal liberty as with external physical liberty. I act freely in a physical sense only when, independently of all external influence, I simply obey my will. But for the possibility of thus obeying without hinderance my own will, it is probable, ultimately, that I am indebted to a principle beyond or distinct from myself immediately it is admitted that this principle would hamper my will. The same also with regard to the possibility of accomplishing such action in conformity with duty—it may be that I owe it, ultimately, to a principle distinct from my reason; that is possible, the moment the idea of this principle is recognized as a force which could have constrained my independence. Thus the same as we can say of a man, that he holds his liberty from another man, although liberty in its proper sense consists in not being forced to be regulated by another—in like manner we can also say that taste here obeys virtue, although virtue herself expressly carries this idea, that in the practice of virtue she makes use of no other foreign help. An action does not in any degree cease to be free, because he who could hamper its accomplishment should fortunately abstain from putting any obstacle in the way; it suffices to know that this agent has been moved by his own will without any consideration of another will. In the same way, an action of the moral order does not lose its right to be qualified as a moral action, because the temptations which might have turned it in another direction did not present themselves; it suffices to admit that the agent obeyed solely the decree of his reason to the exclusion of all foreign springs of action. The liberty of an external act is established as soon as it directly proceeds from the will of a person; the morality of an interior action is established from the moment that the will of the agent is at once determined to it by the laws of reason.

It may be rendered easier or more difficult to act as free men according as we meet or not in our path forces adverse to our will that must be overcome. In this sense liberty is more or less susceptible. It is greater, or at least more visible, when we enable it to prevail over the opposing forces, however energetic their opposition; but it is not suspended because our will should have met with no resistance, or that a foreign succor coming to our aid should have destroyed this resistance, without any help from ourselves.

The same with respect to morality; we might have more or less resistance to offer in order on the instant to obey our reason, according as it awakens or not in us those instincts which struggle against its precepts, and which must be put aside. In this sense morality is susceptible of more or of less. Our morality is greater, or at least more in relief, when we immediately obey reason, however powerful the instincts are which push us in a contrary direction; but it is not suspended because we have had no temptation to disobey, or that this force had been paralyzed by some other force other than our will. We are incited to an action solely because it is moral, without previously asking ourselves if it is the most agreeable. It is enough that such an action is morally good, and it would preserve this character even if there were cause to believe that we should have acted differently if the action had cost us any trouble, or had deprived us of a pleasure.

It can be admitted, for the honor of humanity, that no man could fall so low as to prefer evil solely because it is evil, but rather that every man, without exception, would prefer the good because it is the good, if by some accidental circumstance the good did not exclude the agreeable, or did not entail trouble. Thus in reality all moral action seems to have no other principle than a conflict between the good and the agreeable; or, that which comes to the same thing, between desire and reason; the force of our sensuous instincts on one side, and, on the other side, the feebleness of will, the moral faculty: such apparently is the source of all our faults.

There may be, therefore, two different ways of favoring morality, the same as there are two kinds of obstacles which thwart it: either we must strengthen the side of reason, and the power of the good will, so that no temptation can overcome it; or we must break the force of temptation, in order that the reason and the will, although feebler, should yet be in a state to surmount it.

It might be said, without doubt, that true morality gains little by this second proceeding, because it happens without any modification of the will, and yet that it is the nature of the will that alone give to actions their moral character. But I say also, in the case in question, a change of will is not at all necessary; because we do not suppose a bad will which should require to be changed, but only a will turned to good, but which is feeble. Therefore, this will, inclined to good, but too feeble, does not fail to attain by this route to good actions, which might not have happened if a stronger impulse had drawn it in a contrary sense. But every time that a strong will towards good becomes the principle of an action, we are really in presence of a moral action. I have therefore no scruple in advancing this proposition—that all which neutralizes the resistance offered to the law of duty really favors morality.

Morality has within us a natural enemy, the sensuous instinct; this, as soon as some object solicits its desires, aspires at once to gratify it, and, as soon as reason requires from it anything repugnant, it does not fail to rebel against its precepts. This sensuous instinct is constantly occupied in gaining the will on its side. The will is nevertheless under the jurisdiction of the moral law, and it is under an obligation never to be in contradiction with that which reason demands.

But the sensuous instinct does not recognize the moral law; it wishes to enjoy its object and to induce the will to realize it also, notwithstanding what the reason may advance. This tendency of the faculty of our appetites, of immediately directing the will without troubling itself about superior laws, is perpetually in conflict with our moral destination, and it is the most powerful adversary that man has to combat in his moral conduct. The coarse soul, without either moral or aesthetic education, receives directly the law of appetite, and acts only according to the good pleasure of the senses. The moral soul, but which wants aesthetic culture, receives in a direct manner the law of reason, and it is only out of respect for duty that it triumphs over temptation. In the purified aesthetic soul, there is moreover another motive, another force, which frequently takes the place of virtue when virtue is absent, and which renders it easier when it is present—that is, taste.

Taste demands of us moderation and dignity; it has a horror of everything sharp, hard and violent; it likes all that shapes itself with ease and harmony. To listen to the voice of reason amidst the tempest of the senses, and to know where to place a limit to nature in its most brutified explosions, is, as we are aware, required by good breeding, which is no other than an aesthetic law; this is required of every civilized man. Well, then, this constraint imposed upon civilized man in the expression of his feelings, confers upon him already a certain degree of authority over them, or at least develops in him a certain aptitude to rise above the purely passive state of the soul, to interrupt this state by an initiative act, and to stop by reflection the petulance of the feelings, ever ready to pass from affections to acts. Therefore everything that interrupts the blind impetuosity of these movements of the affections does not as yet, however, produce, I own, a virtue (for virtue ought never to have any other active principle than itself), but that at least opens the road to the will, in order to turn it on the side of virtue. Still, this victory of taste over brutish affections is by no means a moral action, and the freedom which the will acquires by the intervention of taste is as yet in no way a moral liberty. Taste delivers the soul from the yoke of instinct, only to impose upon it chains of its own; and in discerning the first enemy, the declared enemy of moral liberty, it remains itself, too often, as a second enemy, perhaps even the more dangerous as it assumes the aspect of a friend. Taste effectively governs the soul itself only by the attraction of pleasure; it is true of a nobler type, because its principle is reason, but still as long as the will is determined by pleasure there is not yet morality.

Notwithstanding this, a great point is gained already by the intervention of taste in the operations of the will. All those material inclinations and brutal appetites, which oppose with so much obstinacy and vehemence the practice of good, the soul is freed from through the aesthetic taste; and in their place, it implants in us nobler and gentler inclinations, which draw nearer to order, to harmony, and to perfection; and although these inclinations are not by themselves virtues, they have at least something in common with virtue; it is their object. Thenceforth, if it is the appetite that speaks, it will have to undergo a rigorous control before the sense of the beautiful; if it is the reason which speaks, and which commands in its acts conformity with order, harmony, and perfection, not only will it no longer meet with an adversary on the side of inclination, but it will find the most active competition. If we survey all the forms under which morality can be produced, we shall see that all these forms can be reduced to two; either it is sensuous nature which moves the soul either to do this thing or not to do the other, and the will finally decides after the law of the reason; or it is the reason itself which impels the motion, and the will obeys it without seeking counsel of the senses.

The Greek princess, Anna Comnena, speaks of a rebel prisoner, whom her father Alexis, then a simple general of his predecessor, had been charged to conduct to Constantinople. During the journey, as they were riding side by side, Alexis desired to halt under the shade of a tree to refresh himself during the great heat of the day. It was not long before he fell asleep, whilst his companion, who felt no inclination to repose with the fear of death awaiting him before his eyes, remained awake. Alexis slumbered profoundly, with his sword hanging upon a branch above his head; the prisoner perceived the sword, and immediately conceived the idea of killing his guardian and thus of regaining his freedom. Anna Comnena gives us to understand that she knows not what might have been the result had not Alexis fortunately awoke at that instant. In this there is a moral of the highest kind, in which the sensuous instinct first raised its voice, and of which the reason had only afterwards taken cognizance in quality of judge. But suppose that the prisoner had triumphed over the temptation only out of respect for justice, there could be no doubt the action would have been a moral action.

When the late Duke Leopold of Brunswick, standing upon the banks of the raging waters of the Oder, asked himself if at the peril of his life he ought to venture into the impetuous flood in order to save some unfortunates who without his aid were sure to perish; and when—I suppose a case—simply under the influence of duty, he throws himself into the boat into which none other dares to enter, no one will contest doubtless that he acted morally. The duke was here in a contrary position to that of the preceding one. The idea of duty, in this circumstance, was the first which presented itself, and afterwards only the instinct of self-preservation was roused to oppose itself to that prescribed by reason, But in both cases the will acted in the same way; it obeyed unhesitatingly the reason, yet both of them are moral actions.

But would the action have continued moral in both cases, if we suppose the aesthetic taste to have taken part in it? For example, suppose that the first, who was tempted to commit a bad action, and who gave it up from respect for justice, had the taste sufficiently cultivated to feel an invincible horror aroused in him against all disgraceful or violent action, the aesthetic sense alone will suffice to turn him from it; there is no longer any deliberation before the moral tribunal, before the conscience; another motive, another jurisdiction has already pronounced. But the aesthetic sense governs the will by the feeling and not by laws. Thus this man refuses to enjoy the agreeable sensation of a life saved, because he cannot support his odious feelings of having committed a baseness. Therefore all, in this, took place before the feelings alone, and the conduct of this man, although in conformity with the law, is morally indifferent; it is simply a fine effect of nature.

Now let us suppose that the second, he to whom his reason prescribed to do a thing against which natural instinct protested; suppose that this man had to the same extent a susceptibility for the beautiful, so that all which is great and perfect enraptured him; at the same moment, when reason gave the order, the feelings would place themselves on the same side, and he would do willingly that which without the inclination for the beautiful he would have had to do contrary to inclination. But would this be a reason for us to find it less perfect? Assuredly not, because in principle it acts out of pure respect for the prescriptions of reason; and if it follows these injunctions with joy, that can take nothing away from the moral purity of the act. Thus, this man will be quite as perfect in the moral sense; and, on the contrary, he will be incomparably more perfect in the physical sense, because he is infinitely more capable of making a virtuous subject.

Thus, taste gives a direction to the soul which disposes it to virtue, in keeping away such inclinations as are contrary to it, and in rousing those which are favorable. Taste could not injure true virtue, although in every case where natural instinct speaks first, taste commences by deciding for its chief that which conscience otherwise ought to have known; in consequence it is the cause that, amongst the actions of those whom it governs, there are many more actions morally indifferent than actions truly moral. It thus happens that the excellency of the man does not consist in the least degree in producing a larger sum of vigorously moral particular actions, but by evincing as a whole a greater conformity of all his natural dispositions with the moral law; and it is not a thing to give people a very high idea of their country or of their age to hear morality so often spoken of and particular acts boasted of as traits of virtue. Let us hope that the day when civilization shall have consummated its work (if we can realize this term in the mind) there will no longer be any question of this. But, on the other side, taste can become of possible utility to true virtue, in all cases when, the first instigations issuing from reason, its voice incurs the risk of being stifled by the more powerful solicitations of natural instinct. Thus, taste determines our feelings to take the part of duty, and in this manner renders a mediocre moral force of will sufficient for the practice of virtue.

In this light, if the taste never injures true morality, and if in many cases it is of evident use—and this circumstance is very important—then it is supremely favorable to the legality of our conduct. Suppose that aesthetic education contributes in no degree to the improvement of our feelings, at least it renders us better able to act, although without true moral disposition, as we should have acted if our soul had been truly moral. Therefore, it is quite true that, before the tribunal of the conscience, our acts have absolutely no importance but as the expression of our feelings: but it is precisely the contrary in the physical order and in the plan of nature: there it is no longer our sentiments that are of importance; they are only important so far as they give occasion to acts which conduce to the aims of nature. But the physical order which is governed by forces, and the moral order which governs itself by laws, are so exactly made one for the other, and are so intimately blended, that the actions which are by their form morally suitable, necessarily contain also a physical suitability; and as the entire edifice of nature seems to exist only to render possible the highest of all aims, which is the good, in the same manner the good can in its turn be employed as the means of preserving the edifice. Thus, the natural order has been rendered dependent upon the morality of our souls, and we cannot go against the moral laws of the world without at the same time provoking a perturbation in the physical world.

If, then, it is impossible to expect that human nature, as long as it is only human nature, should act without interruption or feebleness, uniformly and constantly as pure reason, and that it never offend the laws of moral order; if fully persuaded, as we are, both of the necessity and the possibility of pure virtue, we are forced to avow how subject to accident is the exercise of it, and how little we ought to reckon upon the steadfastness of our best principles; if with this conviction of human fragility we bear in mind that each of the infractions of the moral law attacks the edifice of nature, if we recall all these considerations to our memory, it would be assuredly the most criminal boldness to place the interests of the entire world at the mercy of the uncertainty of our virtue. Let us rather draw from it the following conclusion, that it is for us an obligation to satisfy at the very least the physical order by the object of our acts, even when we do not satisfy the exigencies of the moral order by the form of these acts; to pay, at least, as perfect instruments the aims of nature, that which we owe as imperfect persons to reason, in order not to appear shamefaced before both tribunals. For if we refused to make any effort to conform our acts to it because simple legality is without moral merit, the order of the world might in the meanwhile be dissolved, and before we had succeeded in establishing our principles all the links of society might be broken. No, the more our morality is subjected to chance, the more is it necessary to take measures in order to assure its legality; to neglect, either from levity or pride, this legality is a fault for which we shall have to answer before morality. When a maniac believes himself threatened with a fit of madness, he leaves no knife within reach of his hands, and he puts himself under constraint, in order to avoid responsibility in a state of sanity for the crimes which his troubled brain might lead him to commit. In a similar manner it is an obligation for us to seek the salutary bonds which religion and the aesthetic laws present to us, in order that during the crisis when our passion is dominant it shall not injure the physical order.

It is not unintentionally that I have placed religion and taste in one and the same class; the reason is that both one and the other have the merit, similar in effect, although dissimilar in principle and in value, to take the place of virtue properly so called, and to assure legality where there is no possibility to hope for morality. Doubtless that would hold an incontestably higher rank in the order of pure spirits, as they would need neither the attraction of the beautiful nor the perspective of eternal life, to conform on every occasion to the demands of reason; but we know man is short-sighted, and his feebleness forces the most rigid moralist to temper in some degree the rigidity of his system in practice, although he will yield nothing in theory; it obliges him, in order to insure the welfare of the human race, which would be ill protected by a virtue subjected to chance, to have further recourse to two strong anchors—those of religion and taste.

ON THE SUBLIME.

"Man is never obliged to say, I must—must," says the Jew Nathan [Lessing's play, "Nathan the Wise," act i. scene 3.] to the dervish; and this expression is true in a wider sense than man might be tempted to suppose. The will is the specific character of man, and reason itself is only the eternal rule of his will. All nature acts reasonably; all our prerogative is to act reasonably, with consciousness and with will. All other objects obey necessity; man is the being who wills.

It is exactly for this reason that there is nothing more inconsistent with the dignity of man than to suffer violence, for violence effaces him. He who does violence to us disputes nothing less than our humanity; he who submits in a cowardly spirit to the violence abdicates his quality of man. But this pretension to remain absolutely free from all that is violence seems to imply a being in possession of a force sufficiently great to keep off all other forces. But if this pretension is found in a being who, in the order of forces, cannot claim the first rank, the result is an unfortunate contradiction between his instinct and his power.

Man is precisely in this case. Surrounded by numberless forces, which are all superior to him and hold sway over him, he aspires by his nature not to have to suffer any injury at their hands. It is true that by his intelligence he adds artificially to his natural forces, and that up to a certain point he actually succeeds in reigning physically over everything that is physical. The proverb says, "there is a remedy for everything except death;" but this exception, if it is one in the strictest acceptation of the term, would suffice to entirely ruin the very idea of our nature. Never will man be the cause that wills, if there is a case, a single case, in which, with or without his consent, he is forced to what he does not wish. This single terrible exception, to be or to do what is necessary and not what he wishes, this idea will pursue him as a phantom; and as we see in fact among the greater part of men, it will give him up a prey to the blind terrors of imagination. His boasted liberty is nothing, if there is a single point where he is under constraint and bound. It is education that must give back liberty to man, and help him to complete the whole idea of his nature. It ought, therefore, to make him capable of making his will prevail, for, I repeat it, man is the being who wills.

It is possible to reach this end in two ways: either really, by opposing force to force, by commanding nature, as nature yourself; or by the idea, issuing from nature, and by thus destroying in relation to self the very idea of violence. All that helps man really to hold sway over nature is what is styled physical education. Man cultivates his understanding and develops his physical force, either to convert the forces of nature, according to their proper laws, into the instruments of his will, or to secure himself against their effects when he cannot direct them. But the forces of nature can only be directed or turned aside up to a certain point; beyond that point they withdraw from the influence of man and place him under theirs.

Thus beyond the point in question his freedom would be lost, were he only susceptible of physical education. But he must be man in the full sense of the term, and consequently he must have nothing to endure, in any case, contrary to his will. Accordingly, when he can no longer oppose to the physical forces any proportional physical force, only one resource remains to him to avoid suffering any violence: that is, to cause to cease entirely that relation which is so fatal to him. It is, in short, to annihilate as an idea the violence he is obliged to suffer in fact. The education that fits man for this is called moral education.

The man fashioned by moral education, and he only, is entirely free. He is either superior to nature as a power, or he is in harmony with her. None of the actions that she brings to bear upon him is violence, for before reaching him it has become an act of his own will, and dynamic nature could never touch him, because he spontaneously keeps away from all to which she can reach. But to attain to this state of mind, which morality designates as resignation to necessary things, and religion styles absolute submission to the counsels of Providence, to reach this by an effort of his free will and with reflection, a certain clearness is required in thought, and a certain energy in the will, superior to what man commonly possesses in active life. Happily for him, man finds here not only in his rational nature a moral aptitude that can be developed by the understanding, but also in his reasonable and sensible nature—that is, in his human nature—an aesthetic tendency which seems to have been placed there expressly: a faculty awakens of itself in the presence of certain sensuous objects, and which, after our feelings are purified, can be cultivated to such a point as to become a powerful ideal development. This aptitude, I grant, is idealistic in its principle and in its essence, but one which even the realist allows to be seen clearly enough in his conduct, though he does not acknowledge this in theory. I am now about to discuss this faculty.

I admit that the sense of the beautiful, when it is developed by culture, suffices of itself even to make us, in a certain sense, independent of nature as far as it is a force. A mind that has ennobled itself sufficiently to be more sensible of the form than of the matter of things, contains in itself a plenitude of existence that nothing could make it lose, especially as it does not trouble itself about the possession of the things in question, and finds a very liberal pleasure in the mere contemplation of the phenomenon. As this mind has no want to appropriate the objects in the midst of which it lives, it has no fear of being deprived of them. But it is nevertheless necessary that these phenomena should have a body, through which they manifest themselves; and, consequently, as long as we feel the want even only of finding a beautiful appearance or a beautiful phenomenon, this want implies that of the existence of certain objects; and it follows that our satisfaction still depends on nature, considered as a force, because it is nature who disposes of all existence in a sovereign manner. It is a different thing, in fact, to feel in yourself the want of objects endowed with beauty and goodness, or simply to require that the objects which surround us are good and beautiful. This last desire is compatible with the most perfect freedom of the soul; but it is not so with the other. We are entitled to require that the object before us should be beautiful and good, but we can only wish that the beautiful and the good should be realized objectively before us. Now the disposition of mind is, par excellence, called grand and sublime, in which no attention is given to the question of knowing if the beautiful, the good, and the perfect exist; but when it is rigorously required that that which exists should be good, beautiful and perfect, this character of mind is called sublime, because it contains in it positively all the characteristics of a fine mind without sharing its negative features. A sign by which beautiful and good minds, but having weaknesses, are recognized, is the aspiring always to find their moral ideal realized in the world of facts, and their being painfully affected by all that places an obstacle to it. A mind thus constituted is reduced to a sad state of dependence in relation to chance, and it may always be predicted of it, without fear of deception, that it will give too large a share to the matter in moral and aesthetical things, and that it will not sustain the more critical trials of character and taste. Moral imperfections ought not to be to us a cause of suffering and of pain: suffering and pain bespeak rather an ungratified wish than an unsatisfied moral want. An unsatisfied moral want ought to be accompanied by a more manly feeling, and fortify our mind and confirm it in its energy rather than make us unhappy and pusillanimous.

Nature has given to us two genii as companions in our life in this lower world. The one, amiable and of good companionship, shortens the troubles of the journey by the gayety of its plays. It makes the chains of necessity light to us, and leads us amidst joy and laughter, to the most perilous spots, where we must act as pure spirits and strip ourselves of all that is body, on the knowledge of the true and the practice of duty. Once when we are there, it abandons us, for its realm is limited to the world of sense; its earthly wings could not carry it beyond. But at this moment the other companion steps upon the stage, silent and grave, and with his powerful arm carries us beyond the precipice that made us giddy.

In the former of these genii we recognize the feeling of the beautiful, in the other the feeling of the sublime. No doubt the beautiful itself is already an expression of liberty. This liberty is not the kind that raises us above the power of nature, and that sets us free from all bodily influence, but it is only the liberty which we enjoy as men, without issuing from the limits of nature. In the presence of beauty we feel ourselves free, because the sensuous instincts are in harmony with the laws of reason. In presence of the sublime we feel ourselves sublime, because the sensuous instincts have no influence over the jurisdiction of reason, because it is then the pure spirit that acts in us as if it were not absolutely subject to any other laws than its own.

The feeling of the sublime is a mixed feeling. It is at once a painful state, which in its paroxysm is manifested by a kind of shudder, and a joyous state, that may rise to rapture, and which, without being properly a pleasure, is greatly preferred to every kind of pleasure by delicate souls. This union of two contrary sensations in one and the same feeling proves in a peremptory manner our moral independence. For as it is absolutely impossible that the same object should be with us in two opposite relations, it follows that it is we ourselves who sustain two different relations with the object. It follows that these two opposed natures should be united in us, which, on the idea of this object, are brought into play in two perfectly opposite ways. Thus we experience by the feeling of the beautiful that the state of our spiritual nature is not necessarily determined by the state of our sensuous nature; that the laws of nature are not necessarily our laws; and that there is in us an autonomous principle independent of all sensuous impressions.

The sublime object may be considered in two lights. We either represent it to our comprehension, and we try in vain to make an image or idea of it, or we refer it to our vital force, and we consider it as a power before which ours is nothing. But though in both cases we experience in connection with this object the painful feeling of our limits, yet we do not seek to avoid it; on the contrary we are attracted to it by an irresistible force. Could this be the case if the limits of our imagination were at the same time those of our comprehension? Should we be willingly called back to the feeling of the omnipotence of the forces of nature if we had not in us something that cannot be a prey of these forces. We are pleased with the spectacle of the sensuous infinite, because we are able to attain by thought what the senses can no longer embrace and what the understanding cannot grasp. The sight of a terrible object transports us with enthusiasm, because we are capable of willing what the instincts reject with horror, and of rejecting what they desire. We willingly allow our imagination to find something in the world of phenomena that passes beyond it; because, after all, it is only one sensuous force that triumphs over another sensuous force, but nature, notwithstanding all her infinity, cannot attain to the absolute grandeur which is in ourselves. We submit willingly to physical necessity both our well-being and our existence. This is because the very power reminds us that there are in us principles that escape its empire. Man is in the hands of nature, but the will of man is in his own hands.

Nature herself has actually used a sensuous means to teach us that we are something more than mere sensuous natures. She has even known how to make use of our sensations to put us on the track of this discovery—that we are by no means subject as slaves to the violence of the sensations. And this is quite a different effect from that which can be produced by the beautiful; I mean the beautiful of the real world, for the sublime itself is surpassed by the ideal. In the presence of beauty, reason and sense are in harmony, and it is only on account of this harmony that the beautiful has attraction for us. Consequently, beauty alone could never teach us that our destination is to act as pure intelligences, and that we are capable of showing ourselves such. In the presence of the sublime, on the contrary, reason and the sensuous are not in harmony, and it is precisely this contradiction between the two which makes the charm of the sublime—its irresistible action on our minds. Here the physical man and the moral man separate in the most marked manner; for it is exactly in the presence of objects that make us feel at once how limited the former is that the other makes the experience of its force. The very thing that lowers one to the earth is precisely that which raises the other to the infinite.

Let us imagine a man endowed with all the virtues of which the union constitutes a fine character. Let us suppose a man who finds his delight in practising justice, beneficence, moderation, constancy, and good faith. All the duties whose accomplishment is prescribed to him by circumstances are only a play to him, and I admit that fortune favors him in such wise that none of the actions which his good heart may demand of him will be hard to him. Who would not be charmed with such a delightful harmony between the instincts of nature and the prescriptions of reason? and who could help admiring such a man? Nevertheless, though he may inspire us with affection, are we quite sure that he is really virtuous? Or in general that he has anything that corresponds to the idea of virtue? If this man had only in view to obtain agreeable sensations, unless he were mad he could not act in any other possible way; and he would have to be his own enemy to wish to be vicious. Perhaps the principle of his actions is pure, but this is a question to be discussed between himself and his conscience. For our part, we see nothing of it; we do not see him do anything more than a simply clever man would do who had no other god than pleasure. Thus all his virtue is a phenomenon that is explained by reasons derived from the sensuous order, and we are by no means driven to seek for reasons beyond the world of sense.

Let us suppose that this same man falls suddenly under misfortune. He is deprived of his possessions; his reputation is destroyed; he is chained to his bed by sickness and suffering; he is robbed by death of all those he loves; he is forsaken in his distress by all in whom he had trusted. Let us under these circumstances again seek him, and demand the practice of the same virtues under trial as he formerly had practised during the period of his prosperity. If he is found to be absolutely the same as before, if his poverty has not deteriorated his benevolence, or ingratitude his kindly offices of good-will, or bodily suffering his equanimity, or adversity his joy in the happiness of others; if his change of fortune is perceptible in externals, but not in his habits, in the matter, but not in the form of his conduct; then, doubtless, his virtue could not be explained by any reason drawn from the physical order; the idea of nature—which always necessarily supposes that actual phenomena rest upon some anterior phenomenon, as effects upon cause—this idea no longer suffices to enable us to comprehend this man; because there is nothing more contradictory than to admit that effect can remain the same when the cause has changed to its contrary. We must then give up all natural explanation or thought of finding the reason of his acts in his condition; we must of necessity go beyond the physical order, and seek the principle of his conduct in quite another world, to which the reason can indeed raise itself with its ideas, but which the understanding cannot grasp by its conceptions. It is this revelation of the absolute moral power which is subjected to no condition of nature, it is this which gives to the melancholy feeling that seizes our heart at the sight of such a man that peculiar, inexpressible charm, which no delight of the senses, however refined, could arouse in us to the same extent as the sublime.

Thus the sublime opens to us a road to overstep the limits of the world of sense, in which the feeling of the beautiful would forever imprison us. It is not little by little (for between absolute dependence and absolute liberty there is no possible transition), it is suddenly and by a shock that the sublime wrenches our spiritual and independent nature away from the net which feeling has spun round us, and which enchains the soul the more tightly because of its subtle texture. Whatever may be the extent to which feeling has gained a mastery over men by the latent influence of a softening taste, when even it should have succeeded in penetrating into the most secret recesses of moral jurisdiction under the deceptive envelope of spiritual beauty, and there poisoning the holiness of principle at its source—one single sublime emotion often suffices to break all this tissue of imposture, at one blow to give freedom to the fettered elasticity of spiritual nature, to reveal its true destination, and to oblige it to conceive, for one instant at least, the feeling of its liberty. Beauty, under the shape of the divine Calypso, bewitched the virtuous son of Ulysses, and the power of her charms held him long a prisoner in her island. For long he believed he was obeying an immortal divinity, whilst he was only the slave of sense; but suddenly an impression of the sublime in the form of Mentor seizes him; he remembers that he is called to a higher destiny—he throws himself into the waves, and is free.

The sublime, like the beautiful, is spread profusely throughout nature, and the faculty to feel both one and the other has been given to all men; but the germ does not develop equally; it is necessary that art should lend its aid. The aim of nature supposes already that we ought spontaneously to advance towards the beautiful, although we still avoid the sublime: for the beautiful is like the nurse of our childhood, and it is for her to refine our soul in withdrawing it from the rude state of nature. But though she is our first affection, and our faculty of feeling is first developed for her, nature has so provided, nevertheless, that this faculty ripens slowly and awaits its full development until the understanding and the heart are formed. If taste attains its full maturity before truth and morality have been established in our heart by a better road than that which taste would take, the sensuous world would remain the limit of our aspirations. We should not know, either in our ideas or in our feelings, how to pass beyond the world of sense, and all that imagination failed to represent would be without reality to us. But happily it enters into the plan of nature, that taste, although it first comes into bloom, is the last to ripen of all the faculties of the mind. During this interval, man has time to store up in his mind a provision of ideas, a treasure of principles in his heart, and then to develop especially, in drawing from reason, his feeling for the great and the sublime.

As long as man was only the slave of physical necessity, while he had found no issue to escape from the narrow circle of his appetites, and while he as yet felt none of that superior liberty which connects him with the angels, nature, so far as she is incomprehensible, could not fail to impress him with the insufficiency of his imagination, and again, as far as she is a destructive force, to recall his physical powerlessness. He is forced then to pass timidly towards one, and to turn away with affright from the other. But scarcely has free contemplation assured him against the blind oppression of the forces of nature—scarcely has he recognized amidst the tide of phenomena something permanent in his own being—than at once the coarse agglomeration of nature that surrounds him begins to speak in another language to his heart, and the relative grandeur which is without becomes for him a mirror in which he contemplates the absolute greatness which is within himself. He approaches without fear, and with a thrill of pleasure, those pictures which terrified his imagination, and intentionally makes an appeal to the whole strength of that faculty by which we represent the infinite perceived by the senses, in order if she fails in this attempt, to feel all the more vividly how much these ideas are superior to all that the highest sensuous faculty can give. The sight of a distant infinity—of heights beyond vision, this vast ocean which is at his feet, that other ocean still more vast which stretches above his head, transport and ravish his mind beyond the narrow circle of the real, beyond this narrow and oppressive prison of physical life. The simple majesty of nature offers him a less circumscribed measure for estimating its grandeur, and, surrounded by the grand outlines which it presents to him, he can no longer bear anything mean in his way of thinking. Who can tell how many luminous ideas, how many heroic resolutions, which would never have been conceived in the dark study of the imprisoned man of science, nor in the saloons where the people of society elbow each other, have been inspired on a sudden during a walk, only by the contact and the generous struggle of the soul with the great spirit of nature? Who knows if it is not owing to a less frequent intercourse with this sublime spirit that we must partially attribute the narrowness of mind so common to the dwellers in towns, always bent under the minutiae which dwarf and wither their soul, whilst the soul of the nomad remains open and free as the firmament beneath which he pitches his tent?

But it is not only the unimaginable or the sublime in quantity, it is also the incomprehensible, that which escapes the understanding and that which troubles it, which can serve to give us an idea of the super-sensuous infinity. As soon as this element attains the grandiose and announces itself to us as the work of nature (for otherwise it is only despicable), it then aids the soul to represent to itself the ideal, and imprints upon it a noble development. Who does not love the eloquent disorder of natural scenery to the insipid regularity of a French garden? Who does not admire in the plains of Sicily the marvellous combat of nature with herself—of her creative force and her destructive power? Who does not prefer to feast his eyes upon the wild streams and waterfalls of Scotland, upon its misty mountains, upon that romantic nature from which Ossian drew his inspiration—rather than to grow enthusiastic in this stiff Holland, before the laborious triumph of patience over the most stubborn of elements? No one will deny that in the rich grazing-grounds of Holland, things are not better ordered for the wants of physical man than upon the perfid crater of Vesuvius, and that the understanding which likes to comprehend and arrange all things, does not find its requirements rather in the regularly planted farm-garden than in the uncultivated beauty of natural scenery. But man has requirements which go beyond those of natural life and comfort or well-being; he has another destiny than merely to comprehend the phenomena which surround him.

In the same manner as for the observant traveller, the strange wildness of nature is so attractive in physical nature—thus, and for the same reason, every soul capable of enthusiasm finds even in the regrettable anarchy found in the moral world a source of singular pleasure. Without doubt he who sees the grand economy of nature only from the impoverished light of the understanding; he who has never any other thought than to reform its defiant disorder and to substitute harmony, such a one could not find pleasure in a world which seems given up to the caprice of chance rather than governed according to a wise ordination, and where merit and fortune are for the most part in opposition. He desires that the whole world throughout its vast space should be ruled like a house well regulated; and when this much-desired regularity is not found, he has no other resource than to defer to a future life, and to another and better nature, the satisfaction which is his due, but which neither the present nor the past afford him. On the contrary, he renounces willingly the pretension of restoring this chaos of phenomena to one single notion; he regains on another side, and with interest, what he loses on this side. Just this want of connection, this anarchy, in the phenomena, making them useless to the understanding, is what makes them valuable to reason. The more they are disorderly the more they represent the freedom of nature. In a sense, if you suppress all connection, you have independence. Thus, under the idea of liberty, reason brings back to unity of thought that which the understanding could not bring to unity of notion. It thus shows its superiority over the understanding, as a faculty subject to the conditions of a sensuous order. When we consider of what value it is to a rational being to be independent of natural laws, we see how much man finds in the liberty of sublime objects as a set-off against the checks of his cognitive faculty. Liberty, with all its drawbacks, is everywhere vastly more attractive to a noble soul than good social order without it—than society like a flock of sheep, or a machine working like a watch. This mechanism makes of man only a product; liberty makes him the citizen of a better world.

It is only thus viewed that history is sublime to me. The world, as a historic object, is only the strife of natural forces; with one another and with man's freedom. History registers more actions referable to nature than to free will; it is only in a few cases, like Cato and Phocion, that reason has made its power felt. If we expect a treasury of knowledge in history how we are deceived! All attempts of philosophy to reconcile what the moral world demands with what the real world gives is belied by experience, and nature seems as illogical in history as she is logical in the organic kingdoms.

But if we give up explanation it is different. Nature, in being capricious and defying logic, in pulling down great and little, in crushing the noblest works of man, taking centuries to form— nature, by deviating from intellectual laws, proves that you cannot explain nature by nature's laws themselves, and this sight drives the mind to the world of ideas, to the absolute.

But though nature as a sensuous activity drives us to the ideal, it throws us still more into the world of ideas by the terrible. Our highest aspiration is to be in good relations with physical nature, without violating morality. But it is not always convenient to serve two masters; and though duty and the appetites should never be at strife, physical necessity is peremptory, and nothing can save men from evil destiny. Happy is he who learns to bear what he cannot change! There are cases where fate overpowers all ramparts, and where the only resistance is, like a pure spirit, to throw freely off all interest of sense, and strip yourself of your body. Now this force comes from sublime emotions, and a frequent commerce with destructive nature. Pathos is a sort of artificial misfortune, and brings us to the spiritual law that commands our soul. Real misfortune does not always choose its time opportunely, while pathos finds us armed at all points. By frequently renewing this exercise of its own activity the mind controls the sensuous, so that when real misfortune comes, it can treat it as an artificial suffering, and make it a sublime emotion. Thus pathos takes away some of the malignity of destiny, and wards off its blows.

Away then with that false theory which supposes falsely a harmony binding well being and well doing. Let evil destiny show its face. Our safety is not in blindness, but in facing our dangers. What can do so better than familiarity with the splendid and terrible evolution of events, or than pictures showing man in conflict with chance; evil triumphant, security deceived— pictures shown us throughout history, and placed before us by tragedy? Whoever passes in review the terrible fate of Mithridates, of Syracuse, and Carthage, cannot help keeping his appetite in check, at least for a time, and, seeing the vanity of things, strive after that which is permanent. The capacity of the sublime is one of the noblest aptitudes of man. Beauty is useful, but does not go beyond man. The sublime applies to the pure spirit. The sublime must be joined to the beautiful to complete the aesthetic education, and to enlarge man's heart beyond the sensuous world.

Without the beautiful there would be an eternal strife between our natural and rational destiny. If we only thought of our vocation as spirits we should be strangers to this sphere of life. Without the sublime, beauty would make us forget our dignity. Enervated—wedded to this transient state, we should lose sight of our true country. We are only perfect citizens of nature when the sublime is wedded to the beautiful.

Many things in nature offer man the beautiful and sublime. But here again he is better served at second-hand. He prefers to have them ready-made in art rather than seek them painfully in nature. This instinct for imitation in art has the advantage of being able to make those points essential that nature has made secondary. While nature suffers violence in the organic world, or exercises violence, working with power upon man, though she can only be aesthetical as an object of pure contemplation, art, plastic art, is fully free, because it throws off all accidental restrictions and leaves the mind free, because it imitates the appearance, not the reality of objects. As all sublimity and beauty consists in the appearance, and not in the value of the object, it follows that art has all the advantages of nature without her shackles.

THE PATHETIC.

The depicting of suffering, in the shape of simple suffering, is never the end of art, but it is of the greatest importance as a means of attaining its end. The highest aim of art is to represent the super-sensuous, and this is effected in particular by tragic art, because it represents by sensible marks the moral man, maintaining himself in a state of passion, independently of the laws of nature. The principle of freedom in man becomes conscious of itself only by the resistance it offers to the violence of the feelings. Now the resistance can only be measured by the strength of the attack. In order, therefore, that the intelligence may reveal itself in man as a force independent of nature, it is necessary that nature should have first displayed all her power before our eyes. The sensuous being must be profoundly and strongly affected, passion must be in play, that the reasonable being may be able to testify his independence and manifest himself in action.

It is impossible to know if the empire which man has over his affections is the effect of a moral force, till we have acquired the certainty that it is not an effect of insensibility. There is no merit in mastering the feelings which only lightly and transitorily skim over the surface of the soul. But to resist a tempest which stirs up the whole of sensuous nature, and to preserve in it the freedom of the soul, a faculty of resistance is required infinitely superior to the act of natural force. Accordingly it will not be possible to represent moral freedom, except by expressing passion, or suffering nature, with the greatest vividness; and the hero of tragedy must first have justified his claim to be a sensuous being before aspiring to our homage as a reasonable being, and making us believe in his strength of mind.

Therefore the pathetic is the first condition required most strictly in a tragic author, and he is allowed to carry his description of suffering as far as possible, without prejudice to the highest end of his art, that is, without moral freedom being oppressed by it. He must give in some sort to his hero, as to his reader, their full load of suffering, without which the question will always be put whether the resistance opposed to suffering is an act of the soul, something positive, or whether it is not rather a purely negative thing, a simple deficiency.

The latter case is offered in the purer French tragedy, where it is very rare, or perhaps unexampled, for the author to place before the reader suffering nature, and where generally, on the contrary, it is only the poet who warms up and declaims, or the comedian who struts about on stilts. The icy tone of declamation extinguishes all nature here, and the French tragedians, with their superstitious worship of decorum, make it quite impossible for them to paint human nature truly. Decorum, wherever it is, even in its proper place, always falsifies the expression of nature, and yet this expression is rigorously required by art. In a French tragedy, it is difficult for us to believe that the hero ever suffers, for he explains the state of his soul, as the coolest man would do, and always thinking of the effect he is making on others, he never lets nature pour forth freely. The kings, the princesses, and the heroes of Corneille or Voltaire never forget their rank even in the most violent excess of passion; and they part with their humanity much sooner than with their dignity. They are like those kings and emperors of our old picture-books, who go to bed with their crowns on.

What a difference from the Greeks and those of the moderns who have been inspired with their spirit in poetry! Never does the Greek poet blush at nature; he leaves to the sensuous all its rights, and yet he is quite certain never to be subdued by it. He has too much depth and too much rectitude in his mind not to distinguish the accidental, which is the principal point with false taste, from the really necessary; but all that is not humanity itself is accidental in man. The Greek artist who has to represent a Laocoon, a Niobe, and a Philoctetes, does not care for the king, the princess, or the king's son; he keeps to the man. Accordingly the skilful statuary sets aside the drapery, and shows us nude figures, though he knows quite well it is not so in real life. This is because drapery is to him an accidental thing, and because the necessary ought never to be sacrificed to the accidental. It is also because, if decency and physical necessities have their laws, these laws are not those of art. The statuary ought to show us, and wishes to show us, the man himself; drapery conceals him, therefore he sets that aside, and with reason.

The Greek sculptor rejects drapery as a useless and embarrassing load, to make way for human nature; and in like manner the Greek poet emancipates the human personages he brings forward from the equally useless constraint of decorum, and all those icy laws of propriety, which put nothing but what is artificial in man, and conceal nature in it. Take Homer and the tragedians; suffering nature speaks the language of truth and ingenuousness in their pages, and in a way to penetrate to the depths of our hearts. All the passions play their part freely, nor do the rules of propriety compress any feeling with the Greeks. The heroes are just as much under the influence of suffering as other men, and what makes them heroes is the very fact that they feel suffering strongly and deeply, without suffering overcoming them. They love life as ardently as others; but they are not so ruled by this feeling as to be unable to give up life when the duties of honor or humanity call on them to do so. Philoctetes filled the Greek stage with his lamentations; Hercules himself, when in fury, does not keep under his grief. Iphigenia, on the point of being sacrificed, confesses with a touching ingenuousness that she grieves to part with the light of the sun. Never does the Greek place his glory in being insensible or indifferent to suffering, but rather in supporting it, though feeling it in its fulness. The very gods of the Greeks must pay their tribute to nature, when the poet wishes to make them approximate to humanity. Mars, when wounded, roars like ten thousand men together, and Venus, scratched by an iron lance, mounts again to Olympus, weeping, and cursing all battles.

This lively susceptibility on the score of suffering, this warm, ingenuous nature, showing itself uncovered and in all truth in the monuments of Greek art, and filling us with such deep and lively emotions—this is a model presented for the imitation of all artists; it is a law which Greek genius has laid down for the fine arts. It is always and eternally nature which has the first rights over man; she ought never to be fettered, because man, before being anything else, is a sensuous creature. After the rights of nature come those of reason, because man is a rational, sensuous being, a moral person, and because it is a duty for this person not to let himself be ruled by nature, but to rule her. It is only after satisfaction has been given in the first place to nature, and after reason in the second place has made its rights acknowledged, that it is permitted for decorum in the third place to make good its claims, to impose on man, in the expression of his moral feelings and of his sensations, considerations towards society, and to show in it the social being, the civilized man. The first law of the tragic art was to represent suffering nature. The second law is to represent the resistance of morality opposed to suffering.

Affection, as affection, is an unimportant thing; and the portraiture of affection, considered in itself, would be without any aesthetic value; for, I repeat it, nothing that only interests sensuous nature is worthy of being represented by art. Thus not only the affections that do nothing but enervate and soften man, but in general all affections, even those that are exalted, ecstatic, whatever may be their nature, are beneath the dignity of tragic art.

The soft emotions, only producing tenderness, are of the nature of the agreeable, with which the fine arts are not concerned. They only caress the senses, while relaxing and creating languidness, and only relate to external nature, not at all to the inner nature of man. A good number of our romances and of our tragedies, particularly those that bear the name of dramas —a sort of compromise between tragedy and comedy—a good number also of those highly-appreciated family portraits, belong to this class. The only effect of these works is to empty the lachrymal duct, and soothe the overflowing feelings; but the mind comes back from them empty, and the moral being, the noblest part of our nature, gathers no new strength whatever from them. "It is thus," says Kant, "that many persons feel themselves edified by a sermon that has nothing edifying in it." It seems also that modern music only aims at interesting the sensuous, and in this it flatters the taste of the day, which seeks to be agreeably tickled, but not to be startled, nor strongly moved and elevated. Accordingly we see music prefer all that is tender; and whatever be the noise in a concert-room, silence is immediately restored, and every one is all ears directly a sentimental passage is performed. Then an expression of sensibility common to animalism shows itself commonly on all faces; the eyes are swimming with intoxication, the open mouth is all desire, a voluptuous trembling takes hold of the entire body, the breath is quick and full, in short, all the symptoms of intoxication appear. This is an evident proof that the senses swim in delight, but that the mind or the principle of freedom in man has become a prey to the violence of the sensuous impression. Real taste, that of noble and manly minds, rejects all these emotions as unworthy of art, because they only please the senses, with which art has nothing in common.

But, on the other hand, real taste excludes all extreme affections, which only put sensuousness to the torture, without giving the mind any compensation. These affections oppress moral liberty by pain, as the others by voluptuousness; consequently they can excite aversion, and not the emotion that would alone be worthy of art. Art ought to charm the mind and give satisfaction to the feeling of moral freedom. This man who is a prey to his pain is to me simply a tortured animate being, and not a man tried by suffering. For a moral resistance to painful affections is already required of man—a resistance which can alone allow the principle of moral freedom, the intelligence, to make itself known in it.

If it is so, the poets and the artists are poor adepts in their art when they seek to reach the pathetic only by the sensuous force of affection and by representing suffering in the most vivid manner. They forget that suffering in itself can never be the last end of imitation, nor the immediate source of the pleasure we experience in tragedy. The pathetic only has aesthetic value in as far as it is sublime. Now, effects that only allow us to infer a purely sensuous cause, and that are founded only on the affection experienced by the faculty of sense, are never sublime, whatever energy they may display, for everything sublime proceeds exclusively from the reason.

I imply by passion the affections of pleasure as well as the painful affections, and to represent passion only, without coupling with it the expression of the super-sensuous faculty which resists it, is to fall into what is properly called vulgarity; and the opposite is called nobility. Vulgarity and nobility are two ideas which, wherever they are applied, have more or less relation with the super-sensuous share a man takes in a work. There is nothing noble but what has its source in the reason; all that issues from sensuousness alone is vulgar or common. We say of a man that he acts in a vulgar manner when he is satisfied with obeying the suggestions of his sensuous instinct; that he acts suitably when he only obeys his instinct in conformity with the laws; that he acts nobly when he obeys reason only, without having regard to his instincts. We say of a physiognomy that it is common when it does not show any trace of the spiritual man, the intelligence; we say it has expression when it is the mind which has determined its features: and that it is noble when a pure spirit has determined them. If an architectural work is in question we qualify it as common if it aims at nothing but a physical end; we name it noble if, independently of all physical aim, we find in it at the same time the expression of a conception.

Accordingly, I repeat it, correct taste disallows all painting of the affections, however energetic, which rests satisfied with expressing physical suffering and the physical resistance opposed to it by the subject, without making visible at the same time the superior principle of the nature of man, the presence of a super-sensuous faculty. It does this in virtue of the principle developed farther back, namely, that it is not suffering in itself, but only the resistance opposed to suffering, that is pathetic and deserving of being represented. It is for this reason that all the absolutely extreme degrees of the affections are forbidden to the artist as well as to the poet. All of these, in fact, oppress the force that resists from within or rather, all betray of themselves, and without any necessity of other symptoms, the oppression of this force, because no affection can reach this last degree of intensity as long as the intelligence in man makes any resistance.

Then another question presents itself. How is this principle of resistance, this super-sensuous force, manifested in the phenomenon of the affections? Only in one way, by mastering or, more commonly, by combating affection. I say affection, for sensuousness can also fight, but this combat of sensuousness is not carried on with the affection, but with the cause that produces it; a contest which has no moral character, but is all physical, the same combat that the earthworm, trodden under foot, and the wounded bull engage in, without thereby exciting the pathetic. When suffering man seeks to give an expression to his feelings, to remove his enemy, to shelter the suffering limb, he does all this in common with the animals, and instinct alone takes the initiative here, without the will being applied to. Therefore, this is not an act that emanates from the man himself, nor does it show him as an intelligence. Sensuous nature will always fight the enemy that makes it suffer, but it will never fight against itself.

On the other hand, the contest with affection is a contest with sensuousness, and consequently presupposes something that is distinct from sensuous nature. Man can defend himself with the help of common sense and his muscular strength against the object that makes him suffer; against suffering itself he has no other arms than those of reason.

These ideas must present themselves to the eye in the portraiture of the affections, or be awakened by this portraiture in order that the pathetic may exist. But it is impossible to represent ideas, in the proper sense of the word, and positively, as nothing corresponds to pure ideas in the world of sense. But they can be always represented negatively and in an indirect way if the sensuous phenomenon by which they are manifested has some character of which you would seek in vain the conditions in physical nature. All phenomena of which the ultimate principle cannot be derived from the world of sense are an indirect representation of the upper-sensuous element.

And how does one succeed in representing something that is above nature without having recourse to supernatural means? What can this phenomenon be which is accomplished by natural forces—otherwise it would not be a phenomenon—and yet which cannot be derived from physical causes without a contradiction? This is the problem; how can the artist solve it?

It must be remembered that the phenomena observable in a man in a state of passion are of two kinds. They are either phenomena connected simply with animal nature, and which, therefore, only obey the physical law, without the will being able to master them, or the independent force in him being able to exercise an immediate influence over them. It is the instinct which immediately produces these phenomena, and they obey blindly the laws of instinct. To this kind belong, for example, the organs of the circulation of the blood, of respiration, and all the surface of the skin. But, moreover, the other organs, and those subject to the will, do not always await the decision of the will; and often instinct itself sets them immediately in play, especially when the physical state is threatened with pain or with danger. Thus, the movements of my arm depend, it is true, on my will; but if I place my hand, without knowing it, on a burning body, the movement by which I draw it back is certainly not a voluntary act, but a purely instinctive phenomenon. Nay more, speech is assuredly subject to the empire of the will, and yet instinct can also dispose of this organ according to its whim, and even of this and of the mind, without consulting beforehand the will, directly a sharp pain, or even an energetic affection, takes us by surprise. Take the most impassible stoic and make him see suddenly something very wonderful, or a terrible and unexpected object. Fancy him, for example, present when a man slips and falls to the bottom of an abyss. A shout, a resounding cry, and not only inarticulate, but a distinct word will escape his lips, and nature will have acted in him before the will: a certain proof that there are in man phenomena which cannot be referred to his person as an intelligence, but only to his instinct as a natural force.

But there is also in man a second order of phenomena, which are subject to the influence and empire of the will, or which may be considered at all events as being of such a kind that will might always have prevented them, consequently phenomena for which the person and not instinct is responsible. It is the office of instinct to watch with a blind zeal over the interests of the senses; but it is the office of the person to hold instinct in proper bounds, out of respect for the moral law. Instinct in itself does not hold account of any law; but the person ought to watch that instinct may not infringe in any way on the decrees of reason. It is therefore evident that it is not for instinct alone to determine unconditionally all the phenomena that take place in man in the state of affection, and that on the contrary the will of man can place limits to instinct. When instinct only determines all phenomena in man, there is nothing more that can recall the person; there is only a physical creature before you, and consequently an animal; for every physical creature subject to the sway of instinct is nothing else. Therefore, if you wish to represent the person itself, you must propose to yourself in man certain phenomena that have been determined in opposition to instinct, or at least that have not been determined by instinct. That they have not been determined by instinct is sufficient to refer them to a higher source, the moment we see that instinct would no doubt have determined them in another way if its force had not been broken by some obstacle.

We are now in a position to point out in what way the super-sensuous element, the moral and independent force of man, his Ego in short, can be represented in the phenomena of the affections. I understand that this is possible if the parts which only obey physical nature, those where will either disposes nothing at all, or only under certain circumstances, betray the presence of suffering; and if those, on the contrary, that escape the blind sway of instinct, that only obey physical nature, show no trace, or only a very feeble trace, of suffering, and consequently appear to have a certain degree of freedom. Now this want of harmony between the features imprinted on animal nature in virtue of the laws of physical necessity, and those determined with the spiritual and independent faculty of man, is precisely the point by which that super-sensuous principle is discovered in man capable of placing limits to the effects produced by physical nature, and therefore distinct from the latter. The purely animal part of man obeys the physical law, and consequently may show itself oppressed by the affection. It is, therefore, in this part that all the strength of passion shows itself, and it answers in some degree as a measure to estimate the resistance— that is to say, of the energy of the moral faculty in man—which can only be judged according to the force of the attack. Thus in proportion as the affection manifests itself with decision and violence in the field of animal nature, without being able to exercise the same power in the field of human nature, so in proportion the latter makes itself manifestly known—in the same proportion the moral independence of man shows itself gloriously: the portraiture becomes pathetic and the pathetic sublime.

The statues of the ancients make this principle of aesthetics sensible to us; but it is difficult to reduce to conceptions and express in words what the very inspection of ancient statues makes the senses feel in so lively a manner. The group of Laocoon and his children can give to a great extent the measure of what the plastic art of the ancients was capable of producing in the matter of pathos. Winckelmann, in his "History of Art,", says: "Laocoon is nature seized in the highest degree of suffering, under the features of a man who seeks to gather up against pain all the strength of which the mind is conscious. Hence while his suffering swells his muscles and stretches his nerves, the mind, armed with an interior force shows itself on his contracted brow, and the breast rises, because the breathing is broken, and because there is an internal struggle to keep in the expression of pain, and press it back into his heart. The sigh of anguish he wishes to keep in, his very breath which he smothers, exhaust the lower part of his trunk, and works into his flanks, which make us judge in some degree of the palpitations of his visceral organs. But his own suffering appears to occasion less anguish than the pain of his children, who turn their faces toward their father, and implore him, crying for help. His father's heart shows itself in his eyes, full of sadness, and where pity seems to swim in a troubled cloud. His face expresses lament, but he does not cry; his eyes are turned to heaven, and implore help from on high. His mouth also marks a supreme sadness, which depresses the lower lip and seems to weigh upon it, while the upper lip, contracted from the top to the bottom, expresses at once both physical suffering and that of the soul. Under the mouth there is an expression of indignation that seems to protest against an undeserved suffering, and is revealed in the nostrils, which swell out and enlarge and draw upwards. Under the forehead, the struggle between pain and moral strength, united as it were in a single point, is represented with great truth, for, while pain contracts and raises the eyebrows, the effort opposed to it by the will draws down towards the upper eyelid all the muscles above it, so that the eyelid is almost covered by them. The artist, not being able to embellish nature, has sought at least to develop its means, to increase its effect and power. Where is the greatest amount of pain is also the highest beauty. The left side, which the serpent besets with his furious bites, and where he instils his poison, is that which appears to suffer the most intensely, because sensation is there nearest to the heart. The legs strive to raise themselves as if to shun the evil; the whole body is nothing but movement, and even the traces of the chisel contribute to the illusion; we seem to see the shuddering and icy-cold skin."

How great is the truth and acuteness of this analysis! In what a superior style is this struggle between spirit and the suffering of nature developed! How correctly the author has seized each of the phenomena in which the animal element and the human element manifest themselves, the constraint of nature and the independence of reason! It is well known that Virgil has described this same scene in his "Aeneid," but it did not enter into the plan of the epic poet to pause as the sculptor did, and describe the moral nature of Laocoon; for this recital is in Virgil only an episode; and the object he proposes is sufficiently attained by the simple description of the physical phenomenon, without the necessity on his part of looking into the soul of the unhappy sufferer, as his aim is less to inspire us with pity than to fill us with terror. The duty of the poet from this point of view was purely negative; I mean he had only to avoid carrying the picture of physical suffering to such a degree that all expression of human dignity or of moral resistance would cease, for if he had done this indignation and disgust would certainly be felt. He, therefore, preferred to confine himself to the representation of the least of the suffering, and he found it advisable to dwell at length on the formidable nature of the two serpents, and on the rage with which they attack their victims, rather than on the feelings of Laocoon. He only skims over those feelings, because his first object was to represent a chastisement sent by the gods, and to produce an impression of terror that nothing could diminish. If he had, on the contrary, detained our looks on the person of Laocoon himself with as much perseverance as the statuary, instead of on the chastizing deity, the suffering man would have become the hero of the scene, and the episode would have lost its propriety in connection with the whole piece.

The narrative of Virgil is well known through the excellent commentary of Lessing. But Lessing only proposed to make evident by this example the limits that separate partial description from painting, and not to make the notion of the pathetic issue from it. Yet the passage of Virgil does not appear to me less valuable for this latter object, and I crave permission to bring it forward again under this point of view:—

Ecce autem gemini Tenedo tranquilla per alta

(Horresco referens) immensis orbibus angues

Incumbunt pelago, pariterque ad litora tendunt;

Pectora quorum inter fluctus arrecta jubaeque

Sanguineae exsuperant undas; pars caetera pontum

Pone legit, sinuatque immensa volumine terga.

Fit sonitus spumante salo, jamque arva tenebant,

Ardentes oculos suffecti sanguine et igni,

Sibila lambebant linguis vibrantibus ora!

      Aeneid, ii. 203-211.

We find here realized the first of the three conditions of the sublime that have been mentioned further back,—a very powerful natural force, armed for destruction, and ridiculing all resistance. But that this strong element may at the same time be terrible, and thereby sublime, two distinct operations of the mind are wanted; I mean two representations that we produce in ourselves by our own activity. First, we recognize this irresistible natural force as terrible by comparing it with the weakness of the faculty of resistance that the physical man can oppose to it; and, secondly, it is by referring it to our will, and recalling to our consciousness that the will is absolutely independent of all influence of physical nature, that this force becomes to us a sublime object. But it is we ourselves who represent these two relations; the poet has only given us an object armed with a great force seeking to manifest itself. If this object makes us tremble, it is only because we in thought suppose ourselves, or some one like us, engaged with this force. And if trembling in this way, we experience the feeling of the sublime, it is because our consciousness tells us that, if we are the victims of this force, we should have nothing to fear, from the freedom of our Ego, for the autonomy of the determinations of our will. In short the description up to here is sublime, but quite a contemplative, intuitive sublimity:—

Diffugimus visu exsangues, illi agmine certo

Laocoonta petunt . . .—Aeneid, ii. 212-213.

Here the force is presented to us as terrible also; and contemplative sublimity passes into the pathetic. We see that force enter really into strife with man's impotence. Whether it concerns Laocoon or ourselves is only a question of degree. The instinct of sympathy excites and frightens in us the instinct of preservation: there are the monsters, they are darting—on ourselves; there is no more safety, flight is vain.

It is no more in our power to measure this force with ours, and to refer it or not to our own existence. This happens without our co-operation, and is given us by the object itself. Accordingly our fear has not, as in the preceding moment, a purely subjective ground, residing in our soul; it has an objective ground, residing in the object. For, even if we recognize in this entire scene a simple fiction of the imagination, we nevertheless distinguish in this fiction a conception communicated to us from without, from another conception that we produce spontaneously in ourselves.

Thus the mind loses a part of her freedom, inasmuch as she receives now from without that which she produced before her own activity. The idea of danger puts on an appearance of objective reality, and affection becomes now a serious affair.

If we were only sensuous creatures, obeying no other instinct than that of self-preservation, we should stop here, and we should remain in a state of mere and pure affection. But there is something in us which takes no part in the affections of sensuous nature, and whose activity is not directed according to physical conditions. According, then, as this independently acting principle (the disposition, the moral faculty) has become to a degree developed in the soul, there is left more or less space for passive nature, and there remains more or less of the independent principle in the affection.

In the truly moral soul the terrible trial (of the imagination) passes quickly and readily into the sublime. In proportion as imagination loses its liberty, reason makes its own prevail, and the soul ceases not to enlarge within when it thus finds outward limits. Driven from all the intrenchments which would give physical protection to sensuous creatures, we seek refuge in the stronghold of our moral liberty, and we arrive by that means at an absolute and unlimited safety, at the very moment when we seem to be deprived in the world of phenomena of a relative and precarious rampart. But precisely because it was necessary to have arrived at the physical oppression before having recourse to the assistance of our moral nature, we can only buy this high sentiment of our liberty through suffering. An ordinary soul confines itself entirely to this suffering, and never comprehends in the sublime or the pathetic anything beyond the terrible. An independent soul, on the contrary, precisely seizes this occasion to rise to the feeling of his moral force, in all that is most magnificent in this force, and from every terrible object knows how to draw out the sublime.

The moral man (the father) [see Aeneid, ii. 213-215] is here attacked before the physical man, and that has a grand effect. All the affections become more aesthetic when we receive them second-hand; there is no stronger sympathy than that we feel for sympathy.

The moment [see Aeneid, ii. 216-217] had arrived when the hero himself had to be recommended to our respect as a moral personage, and the poet seized upon that moment. We already know by his description all the force, all the rage of the two monsters who menace

Laocoon, and we know how all resistance would be in vain. If Laocoon were only a common man he would better understand his own interests, and, like the rest of the Trojans, he would find safety in rapid flight. But there is a heart in that breast; the danger to his children holds him back, and decides him to meet his fate. This trait alone renders him worthy of our pity. At whatever moment the serpents had assailed him, we should have always been touched and troubled. But because it happens just at the moment when as father he shows himself so worthy of respect, his fate appears to us as the result of having fulfilled his duty as parent, of his tender disquietude for his children. It is this which calls forth our sympathy in the highest degree. It appears, in fact, as if he deliberately devoted himself to destruction, and his death becomes an act of the will.

Thus there are two conditions in every kind of the pathetic: 1st. Suffering, to interest our sensuous nature; 2d. Moral liberty, to interest our spiritual nature. All portraiture in which the expression of suffering nature is wanting remains without aesthetic action, and our heart is untouched. All portraiture in which the expression of moral aptitude is wanting, even did it possess all the sensuous force possible, could not attain to the pathetic, and would infallibly revolt our feelings. Throughout moral liberty we require the human being who suffers; throughout all the sufferings of human nature we always desire to perceive the independent spirit, or the capacity for independence.

But the independence of the spiritual being in the state of suffering can manifest itself in two ways. Either negatively, when the moral man does not receive the law from the physical man, and his state exercises no influence over his manner of feeling; or positively, when the moral man is a ruler over the physical being, and his manner of feeling exercises an influence upon his state. In the first case, it is the sublime of disposition; in the second, it is the sublime of action.

The sublime of disposition is seen in all character independent of the accidents of fate. "A noble heart struggling against adversity," says Seneca, "is a spectacle full of attraction even for the gods." Such for example is that which the Roman Senate offered after the disaster of Cannae. Lucifer even, in Milton, when for the first time he contemplates hell—which is to be his future abode—penetrates us with a sentiment of admiration by the force of soul he displays:—

"Hail, horrors, hail.

Infernal world, and thou, profoundest Hell;

Receive thy new possessor!—one who brings

A mind not to be changed by place or time;

The mind is its own place, and in itself

Can make a Heaven of Hell. . . .

Here at least

We shall be free," etc.

The reply of Medea in the tragedy belongs also to this order of the sublime.

The sublime of disposition makes itself seen, it is visible to the spectator, because it rests upon co-existence, the simultaneous; the sublime action, on the contrary, is conceived only by the thought, because the impression and the act are successive, and the intervention of the mind is necessary to infer from a free determination the idea of previous suffering.

It follows that the first alone can be expressed by the plastic arts, because these arts give but that which is simultaneous; but the poet can extend his domain over one and the other. Even more; when the plastic art has to represent a sublime action, it must necessarily bring it back to sublimity.

In order that the sublimity of action should take place, not only must the suffering of man have no influence upon the moral constitution, but rather the opposite must be the case. The affection is the work of his moral character. This can happen in two ways: either mediately, or according to the law of liberty, when out of respect for such and such a duty it decides from free choice to suffer—in this case, the idea of duty determines as a motive, and its suffering is a voluntary act—or immediately, and according to the necessity of nature, when he expiates by a moral suffering the violation of duty; in this second case, the idea of duty determines him as a force, and his suffering is no longer an effect. Regulus offers us an example of the first kind, when, to keep his word, he gives himself up to the vengeance of the Carthaginians; and he would serve as an example of the second class, if, having betrayed his trust, the consciousness of this crime would have made him miserable. In both cases suffering has a moral course, but with this difference, that on the one part Regulus shows us its moral character, and that, on the other, he only shows us that he was made to have such a character. In the first case he is in our eyes a morally great person; in the second he is only aesthetically great.

This last distinction is important for the tragic art; it consequently deserves to be examined more closely.

Man is already a sublime object, but only in the aesthetic sense, when the state in which he is gives us an idea of his human destination, even though we might not find this destination realized in his person. He only becomes sublime to us in a moral point of view, when he acts, moreover, as a person, in a manner conformable with this destination; if our respect bears not only on his moral faculty, but on the use he makes of this faculty; if dignity, in his case, is due, not only to his moral aptitude; but to the real morality of his conduct. It is quite a different thing to direct our judgment and attention to the moral faculty generally, and to the possibility of a will absolutely free, and to be directing it to the use of this faculty, and to the reality of this absolute freedom of willing.

It is, I repeat, quite a different thing; and this difference is connected not only with the objects to which we may have to direct our judgment, but to the very criterion of our judgment. The same object can displease us if we appreciate it in a moral point of view, and be very attractive to us in the aesthetical point of view. But even if the moral judgment and the aesthetical judgment were both satisfied, this object would produce this effect on one and the other in quite a different way. It is not morally satisfactory because it has an aesthetical value, nor has it an aesthetical value because it satisfies us morally. Let us take, as example, Leonidas and his devotion at Thermopylae. Judged from the moral point of view, this action represents to me the moral law carried out notwithstanding all the repugnance of instinct. Judged from the aesthetic point of view, it gives me the idea of the moral faculty, independent of every constraint of instinct. The act of Leonidas satisfies the moral sense, the reason; it enraptures the aesthetical sense, the imagination.

Whence comes this difference in the feelings in connection with the same object? I account for it thus:—

In the same way that our being consists of two principles and natures, so also and consequently our feelings are divided into two kinds, entirely different. As reasonable beings we experience a feeling of approbation or of disapprobation; as sensuous creatures we experience pleasure or displeasure. The two feelings, approbation and pleasure, repose on satisfaction: one on a satisfaction given to a requirement of reason— reason has only requirements, and not wants. The other depends on a satisfaction given to a sensuous want—sense only knows of wants, and cannot prescribe anything. These two terms—requirements of reason, wants of the senses—are mutually related, as absolute necessity and the necessity of nature. Accordingly, both are included in the idea of necessity, but with this difference, that the necessity of reason is unconditional, and the necessity of sense only takes place under conditions. But, for both, satisfaction is a purely contingent thing. Accordingly every feeling, whether of pleasure or approbation, rests definitively on an agreement between the contingent and the necessary. If the necessary has thus an imperative character, the feeling experienced will be that of approbation. If necessity has the character of a want, the feeling experienced will be that of pleasure, and both will be strong in proportion as the satisfaction will be contingent. Now, underlying every moral judgment there is a requirement of reason which requires us to act conformably with the moral law, and it is an absolute necessity that we should wish what is good. But as the will is free, it is physically an accidental thing that we should do in fact what is good. If we actually do it, this agreement between the contingent in the use of free will and the imperative demand of reason gives rise to our assent or approbation, which will be greater in proportion as the resistance of the inclinations made this use that we make of our free will more accidental and more doubtful. Every aesthetic judgment, on the contrary, refers the object to the necessity which cannot help willing imperatively, but only desires that there should be an agreement between the accidental and its own interest. Now what is the interest of imagination? It is to emancipate itself from all laws, and to play its part freely. The obligation imposed on the will by the moral law, which prescribes its object in the strictest manner, is by no means favorable to this need of independence. And as the moral obligation of the will is the object of the moral judgment, it is clear that in this mode of judging, the imagination could not find its interest. But a moral obligation imposed on the will cannot be conceived, except by supposing this same will absolutely independent of the moral instincts and from their constraint. Accordingly the possibility of the moral act requires liberty, and therefore agrees here in the most perfect manner with the interest of imagination. But as imagination, through the medium of its wants, cannot give orders to the will of the individual, as reason does by its imperative character, it follows that the faculty of freedom, in relation to imagination, is something accidental, and consequently that the agreement between the accidental and the necessary (conditionally necessary) must excite pleasure. Therefore, if we bring to bear a moral judgment on this act of Leonidas, we shall consider it from a point of view where its accidental character strikes the eye less than its necessary side. If, on the other hand, we apply the aesthetical judgment to it, this is another point of view, where its character of necessity strikes us less forcibly than its accidental character. It is a duty for every will to act thus, directly it is a free will; but the fact that there is a free will that makes this act possible is a favor of nature in regard to this faculty, to which freedom is a necessity. Thus an act of virtue judged by the moral sense—by reason—will give us as its only satisfaction the feeling of approbation, because reason can never find more, and seldom finds as much as it requires. This same act, judged, on the contrary, by the aesthetic sense—by imagination—will give us a positive pleasure, because the imagination, never requiring the end to agree with the demand, must be surprised, enraptured, at the real satisfaction of this demand as at a happy chance. Our reason will merely approve, and only approve, of Leonidas actually taking this heroic resolution; but that he could take this resolution is what delights and enraptures us.

This distinction between the two sorts of judgments becomes more evident still, if we take an example where the moral sense and the aesthetic sense pronounce a different verdict. Suppose we take the act of Perigrinus Proteus burning himself at Olympia. Judging this act morally, I cannot give it my approbation, inasmuch as I see it determined by impure motives, to which Proteus sacrifices the duty of respecting his own existence. But in the aesthetic judgment this same act delights me; it delights me precisely because it testifies to a power of will capable of resisting even the most potent of instincts, that of self-preservation. Was it a moral feeling, or only a more powerful sensuous attraction, that silenced the instinct of self-preservation in this enthusiast. It matters little, when I appreciate the act from an aesthetic point of view. I then drop the individual, I take away the relation of his will to the law that ought to govern him; I think of human will in general, considered as a common faculty of the race, and I regard it in connection with all the forces of nature. We have seen that in a moral point of view, the preservation of our being seemed to us a duty, and therefore we were offended at seeing Proteus violate this duty. In an aesthetic point of view the self-preservation only appears as an interest, and therefore the sacrifice of this interest pleases us. Thus the operation that we perform in the judgments of the second kind is precisely the inverse of that which we perform in those of the first. In the former we oppose the individual, a sensuous and limited being, and his personal will, which can be effected pathologically, to the absolute law of the will in general, and of unconditional duty which binds every spiritual being; in the second case, on the contrary, we oppose the faculty of willing, absolute volition, and the spiritual force as an infinite thing, to the solicitations of nature and the impediments of sense. This is the reason why the aesthetical judgment leaves us free, and delights and enraptures us. It is because the mere conception of this faculty of willing in an absolute manner, the mere idea of this moral aptitude, gives us in itself a consciousness of a manifest advantage over the sensuous. It is because the mere possibility of emancipating ourselves from the impediments of nature is in itself a satisfaction that flatters our thirst for freedom. This is the reason why moral judgment, on the contrary, makes us experience a feeling of constraint that humbles us. It is because in connection with each voluntary act we appreciate in this manner, we feel, as regards the absolute law that ought to rule the will in general, in a position of inferiority more or less decided, and because the constraint of the will thus limited to a single determination, which duty requires of it at all costs, contradicts the instinct of freedom which is the property of imagination. In the former case we soared from the real to the possible, and from the individual to the species; in the latter, on the contrary, we descend from the possible to the real, and we shut up the species in the narrow limits of the individual. We cannot therefore be surprised if the aesthetical judgment enlarges the heart, while the moral judgment constrains and straitens it.

It results, therefore, from all that which precedes, that the moral judgment and the aesthetic, far from mutually corroborating each other, impede and hinder each other, because they impress on the soul two directions entirely opposite. In fact, this observance of rule which reason requires of us as moral judge is incompatible with the independence which the imagination calls for as aesthetic judge. It follows that an object will have so much the less aesthetic value the more it has the character of a moral object, and if the poet were obliged notwithstanding that to choose it, he would do well in treating of it, not to call the attention of our reason to the rule of the will, but that of our imagination to the power of the will. In his own interest it is necessary for the poet to enter on this path, for with our liberty his empire finishes. We belong to him only inasmuch as we look beyond ourselves; we escape from him the moment we re-enter into our innermost selves, and that is what infallibly takes place the moment an object ceases to be a phenomenon in our consideration, and takes the character of a law which judges us.

Even in the manifestation of the most sublime virtue, the poet can only employ for his own views that which in those acts belongs to force. As to the direction of the force, he has no reason to be anxious. The poet, even when he places before our eyes the most perfect models of morality, has not, and ought not to have, any other end than that of rejoicing our soul by the contemplation of this spectacle. Moreover, nothing can rejoice our soul except that which improves our personality, and nothing can give us a spiritual joy except that which elevates the spiritual faculty. But in what way can the morality of another improve our own personality, and raise our spiritual force? That this other one accomplishes really his duty results from an accidental use which he makes of his liberty, and which for that very reason can prove nothing to us. We only have in common with him the faculty to conform ourselves equally to duty; the moral power which he exhibits reminds us also of our own, and that is why we then feel something which upraises our spiritual force. Thus it is only the idea of the possibility of an absolutely free will which makes the real exercise of this will in us charming to the aesthetic feeling.

We shall be still more convinced when we think how little the poetic force of impression which is awakened in us by an act or a moral character is dependent on their historic reality. The pleasure which we take in considering an ideal character will in no way be lessened when we come to think that this character is nothing more than a poetic fiction; for it is on the poetic truth, and not on historic truth, that every aesthetic impression of the feelings rest. Moreover, poetic truth does not consist in that this or that thing has effectually taken place, but in that it may have happened, that is to say, that the thing is in itself possible. Thus the aesthetic force is necessarily obliged to rest in the first place in the idea of possibility.

Even in real subjects, for which the actors are borrowed from history, it is not the reality of the simple possibility of the fact, but that which is guaranteed to us by its very reality which constitutes the poetic element. That these personages have indeed existed, and that these events have in truth taken place, is a circumstance which can, it is true, in many cases add to our pleasure, but that which it adds to it is like a foreign addition, much rather unfavorable than advantageous to the poetical impression.

It was long thought that a great service was rendered to German poetry by recommending German poets to treat of national themes. Why, it was asked, did Greek poetry have so much power over the mind? Because it brought forward national events and immortalized domestic exploits. No doubt the poetry of the ancients may have been indebted to this circumstance for certain effects of which modern poetry cannot boast; but do these effects belong to art and the poet? It is small glory for the Greek genius if it had only this accidental advantage over modern genius; still more if it were necessary for the poets, in order to gain this advantage, to obtain it by this conformity of their invention with real history! It is only a barbarous taste that requires this stimulant of a national interest to be captivated by beautiful things; and it is only a scribbler who borrows from matter a force to which he despairs of giving a form.

Poetry ought not to take its course through the frigid region of memory; it ought never to convert learning into its interpreter, nor private interest its advocate with the popular mind. It ought to go straight to the heart, because it has come from the heart; and aim at the man in the citizen, not the citizen in the man.

Happily, true genius does not make much account of all these counsels that people are so anxious to give her with better intentions than competence. Otherwise, Sulzer and his school might have made German poetry adopt a very equivocal style. It is no doubt a very honorable aim in a poet to moralize the man, and excite the patriotism of the citizen, and the Muses know better than any one how well the arts of the sublime and of the beautiful are adapted to exercise this influence. But that which poetry obtains excellently by indirect means it would accomplish very badly as an immediate end. Poetry is not made to serve in man for the accomplishment of a particular matter, nor could any instrument be selected less fitted to cause a particular object to succeed, or to carry out special projects and details. Poetry acts on the whole of human nature, and it is only by its general influence on the character of a man that it can influence particular acts. Poetry can be for man what love is for the hero. It can neither counsel him, nor strike for him, nor do anything for him in short; but it can form a hero in him, call him to great deeds, and arm him with a strength to be all that he ought to be.

Thus the degree of aesthetical energy with which sublime feelings and sublime acts take possession of our souls, does not rest at all on the interest of reason, which requires every action to be really conformable with the idea of good. But it rests on the interest of the imagination, which requires conformity with good should be possible, or, in other terms, that no feeling, however strong, should oppress the freedom of the soul. Now this possibility is found in every act that testifies with energy to liberty, and to the force of the will; and if the poet meets with an action of this kind, it matters little where, he has a subject suitable for his art. To him, and to the interest we have in him, it is quite the same, to take his hero in one class of characters or in another, among the good or the wicked, as it often requires as much strength of character to do evil conscientiously and persistently as to do good. If a proof be required that in our aesthetic judgments we attend more to the force than to its direction, to its freedom than to its lawfulness, this is sufficient for our evidence. We prefer to see force and freedom manifest themselves at the cost of moral regularity, rather than regularity at the cost of freedom and strength. For directly one of those cases offers itself, in which the general law agrees with the instincts which by their strength threaten to carry away the will, the aesthetic value of the character is increased, if he be capable of resisting these instincts. A vicious person begins to interest us as soon as he must risk his happiness and life to carry out his perverse designs; on the contrary, a virtuous person loses in proportion as he finds it useful to be virtuous. Vengeance, for instance, is certainly an ignoble and a vile affection, but this does not prevent it from becoming aesthetical, if to satisfy it we must endure painful sacrifice. Medea slaying her children aims at the heart of Jason, but at the same time she strikes a heavy blow at her own heart, and her vengeance aesthetically becomes sublime directly we see in her a tender mother.

In this sense the aesthetic judgment has more of truth than is ordinarily believed. The vices which show a great force of will evidently announce a greater aptitude for real moral liberty than do virtues which borrow support from inclination; seeing that it only requires of the man who persistently does evil to gain a single victory over himself, one simple upset of his maxims, to gain ever after to the service of virtue his whole plan of life, and all the force of will which he lavished on evil. And why is it we receive with dislike medium characters, whilst we at times follow with trembling admiration one which is altogether wicked? It is evident, that with regard to the former, we renounce all hope, we cannot even conceive the possibility of finding absolute liberty of the will; whilst with the other, on the contrary, each time he displays his faculties, we feel that one single act of the will would suffice to raise him up to the fullest height of human dignity.

Thus, in the aesthetic judgment, that which excites our interest is not morality itself, but liberty alone; and moral purity can only please our imagination when it places in relief the forces of the will. It is then manifestly to confound two very distinct orders of ideas, to require in aesthetic things so exact a morality, and, in order to stretch the domain of reason, to exclude the imagination from its own legitimate sphere.

Either it would be necessary to subject it entirely, then there would be an end to all aesthetic effect; or it would share the realm of reason, then morality would not gain much. For if we pretend to pursue at the same time two different ends, there would be risk of missing both one and the other. The liberty of the imagination would be fettered by too great respect for the moral law; and violence would be done to the character of necessity which is in the reason, in missing the liberty which belongs to the imagination.

ON GRACE AND DIGNITY.

The Greek fable attributes to the goddess of beauty a wonderful girdle which has the quality of lending grace and of gaining hearts in all who wear it. This same divinity is accompanied by the Graces, or goddesses of grace. From this we see that the Greeks distinguished from beauty grace and the divinities styled the Graces, as they expressed the ideas by proper attributes, separable from the goddess of beauty. All that is graceful is beautiful, for the girdle of love winning attractions is the property of the goddess of Cnidus; but all beauty is not of necessity grace, for Venus, even without this girdle, does not cease to be what she is.

However, according to this allegory, the goddess of beauty is the only one who wears and who lends to others the girdle of attractions. Juno, the powerful queen of Olympus, must begin by borrowing this girdle from Venus, when she seeks to charm Jupiter on Mount Ida [Pope's "Iliad," Book XIV. v. 220]. Thus greatness, even clothed with a certain degree of beauty, which is by no means disputed in the spouse of Jupiter, is never sure of pleasing without the grace, since the august queen of the gods, to subdue the heart of her consort, expects the victory not from her own charms but from the girdle of Venus.

But we see, moreover, that the goddess of beauty can part with this girdle, and grant it, with its quality and effects, to a being less endowed with beauty. Thus grace is not the exclusive privilege of the beautiful; it can also be handed over, but only by beauty, to an object less beautiful, or even to an object deprived of beauty.

If these same Greeks saw a man gifted in other respects with all the advantages of mind, but lacking grace, they advised him to sacrifice to the Graces. If, therefore, they conceived these deities as forming an escort to the beauty of the other sex, they also thought that they would be favorable to man, and that to please he absolutely required their help.

But what then is grace, if it be true that it prefers to unite with beauty, yet not in an exclusive manner? What is grace if it proceeds from beauty, but yet produces the effects of beauty, even when beauty is absent. What is it, if beauty can exist indeed without it, and yet has no attraction except with it? The delicate feeling of the Greek people had marked at an early date this distinction between grace and beauty, whereof the reason was not then able to give an account; and, seeking the means to express it, it borrowed images from the imagination, because the understanding could not offer notions to this end. On this score, the myth of the girdle deserves to fix the attention of the philosopher, who, however, ought to be satisfied to seek ideas corresponding with these pictures when the pure instinctive feeling throws out its discoveries, or, in other words, with explaining the hieroglyphs of sensation. If we strip off its allegorical veil from this conception of the Greeks, the following appears the only meaning it admits.

Grace is a kind of movable beauty, I mean a beauty which does not belong essentially to its subject, but which may be produced accidentally in it, as it may also disappear from it. It is in this that grace is distinguished from beauty properly so called, or fixed beauty, which is necessarily inherent in the subject itself. Venus can no doubt take off her girdle and give it up for the moment to Juno, but she could only give up her beauty with her very person. Venus, without a girdle, is no longer the charming Venus, without beauty she is no longer Venus.

But this girdle as a symbol of movable beauty has this particular feature, that the person adorned with it not only appears more graceful, but actually becomes so. The girdle communicates objectively this property of grace, in this contrasting with other articles of dress, which have only subjective effects, and without modifying the person herself, only modify the impression produced on the imagination of others. Such is the express meaning of the Greek myth; grace becomes the property of the person who puts on this girdle; she does more than appear amiable, it is so in fact.

No doubt it may be thought that a girdle, which after all is only an outward, artificial ornament, does not prove a perfectly correct emblem to express grace as a personal quality. But a personal quality that is conceived at the same time as separable from the subject, could only be represented to the senses by an accidental ornament which can be detached from the person, without the essence of the latter being affected by it.

Thus the girdle of charms operates not by a natural effect (for then it would not change anything in the person itself) but by a magical effect; that is to say, its virtue extends beyond all natural conditions. By this means, which is nothing more, I admit, than an expedient, it has been attempted to avoid the contradiction to which the mind, as regards its representative faculty, is unavoidably reduced, every time it asks an expression from nature herself, for an object foreign to nature and which belongs to the free field of the ideal. If this magic girdle is the symbol of an objective property which can be separated from its subject without modifying in any degree its nature, this myth can only express one thing—the beauty of movement, because movement is the only modification that can affect an object without changing its identity.

The beauty of movement is an idea that satisfies the two conditions contained in the myth which now occupies us. In the first place, it is an objective beauty, not entirely depending upon the impression that we receive from the object, but belonging to the object itself. In the second place, this beauty has in itself something accidental, and the object remains identical even when we conceive it to be deprived of this property. The girdle of attractions does not lose its magic virtue in passing to an object of less beauty, or even to that which is without beauty; that is to say, that a being less beautiful, or even one which is not beautiful, may also lay claim to the beauty of movement. The myth tells us that grace is something accidental in the subject in which we suppose it to be. It follows that we can attribute this property only to accidental movements. In an ideal of beauty the necessary movements must be beautiful, because inasmuch as necessary they form an integral part of its nature; the idea of Venus once given, the idea of this beauty of necessary movements is that implicitly comprised in it; but it is not the same with the beauty of accidental movements; this is an extension of the former; there can be a grace in the voice, there is none in respiration.

But all this beauty in accidental movements—is it necessarily grace? It is scarcely necessary to notice that the Greek fable attributes grace exclusively to humanity. It goes still further, for even the beauty of form it restricts within the limits of the human species, in which, as we know, the Greeks included also their gods. But if grace is the exclusive privilege of the human form, none of the movements which are common to man with the rest of nature can evidently pretend to it. Thus, for example, if it were admitted that the ringlets of hair on a beautiful head undulate with grace, there would also be no reason to deny a grace of movement to the branches of trees, to the waves of the stream, to the ears of a field of corn, or to the limbs of animals. No, the goddess of Cnidus represents exclusively the human species; therefore, as soon as you see only a physical creature in man, a purely sensuous object, she is no longer concerned with him. Thus, grace can only be met with in voluntary movements, and then in those only which express some sentiment of the moral order. Those which have as principle only animal sensuousness belong only, however voluntary we may suppose them to be, to physical nature, which never reaches of itself to grace. If it were possible to have grace in the manifestations of the physical appetites and instincts, grace would no longer be either capable or worthy to serve as the expression of humanity. Yet it is humanity alone which to the Greek contains all the idea of beauty and of perfection. He never consents to see separated from the soul the purely sensuous part, and such is with him that which might be called man's sensuous nature, which it is equally impossible for him to isolate either from his lower nature or from his intelligence. In the same way that no idea presents itself to his mind without taking at once a visible form, and without his endeavoring to give a bodily envelope even to his intellectual conceptions, so he desires in man that all his instinctive acts should express at the same time his moral destination. Never for the Greek is nature purely physical nature, and for that reason he does not blush to honor it; never for him is reason purely reason, and for that reason he has not to tremble in submitting to its rule. The physical nature and moral sentiments, matter and mind, earth and heaven, melt together with a marvellous beauty in his poetry. Free activity, which is truly at home only in Olympus, was introduced by him even into the domain of sense, and it is a further reason for not attaching blame to him if reciprocally he transported the affections of the sense into Olympus. Thus, this delicate sense of the Greeks, which never suffered the material element unless accompanied by the spiritual principle, recognizes in man no voluntary movement belonging only to sense which did not at the same time manifest the moral sentiment of the soul. It follows that for them grace is one of the manifestations of the soul, revealed through beauty in voluntary movements; therefore, wherever there is grace, it is the soul which is the mobile, and it is in her that beauty of movement has its principle. The mythological allegory thus expresses the thought, "Grace is a beauty not given by nature, but produced by the subject itself."

Up to the present time I have confined myself to unfolding the idea of grace from the Greek myth, and I hope I have not forced the sense: may I now be permitted to try to what result a philosophical investigation on this point will lead us, and to see if this subject, as so many others, will confirm this truth, that the spirit of philosophy can hardly flatter itself that it can discover anything which has not already been vaguely perceived by sentiment and revealed in poetry?

Without her girdle, and without the Graces, Venus represents the ideal of beauty, such as she could have come forth from the hands of nature, and such as she is made without the intervention of mind endowed with sentiment and by the virtue alone of plastic forces. It is not without reason that the fable created a particular divinity to represent this sort of beauty, because it suffices to see and to feel in order to distinguish it very distinctly from the other, from that which derives its origin from the influence of a mind endowed with sentiments.

This first beauty, thus formed by nature solely and in virtue of the laws of necessity, I shall distinguish from that which is regulated upon conditions of liberty, in calling it, if allowed, beauty of structure (architectonic beauty). It is agreed, therefore, to designate under this name that portion of human beauty which not only has as efficient principle the forces and agents of physical nature (for we can say as much for every phenomenon), but which also is determined, so far as it is beauty solely, by the forces of this nature.

Well-proportioned limbs, rounded contours, an agreeable complexion, delicacy of skin, an easy and graceful figure, a harmonious tone of voice, etc., are advantages which are gifts of nature and fortune: of nature, which predisposed to this, and developed it herself; of fortune, which protects against all influence adverse to the work of nature.

Venus came forth perfect and complete from the foam of the sea. Why perfect? because she is the finished and exactly determined work of necessity, and on that account she is neither susceptible of variety nor of progress. In other terms, as she is only a beautiful representation of the various ends which nature had in view in forming man, and thence each of her properties is perfectly determined by the idea that she realizes; hence it follows that we can consider her as definitive and determined (with regard to its connection with the first conception) although this conception is subject, in its development, to the conditions of time.

The architectonic beauty of the human form and its technical perfection are two ideas, which we must take good care not to confound. By the latter, the ensemble of particular ends must be understood, such as they co-ordinate between themselves towards a general and higher end; by the other, on the contrary, a character suited to the representation of these ends, as far as these are revealed, under a visible form, to our faculty of seeing and observing. When, then, we speak of beauty, we neither take into consideration the justness of the aims of nature in themselves, nor formally, the degree of adaptation to the principles of art which their combination could offer. Our contemplative faculties hold to the manner in which the object appears to them, without taking heed to its logical constitution. Thus, although the architectonic beauty, in the structure of man, be determined by the idea which has presided at this structure, and by the ends that nature proposes for it, the aesthetic judgment, making abstraction of these ends, considers this beauty in itself; and in the idea which we form of it, nothing enters which does not immediately and properly belong to the exterior appearance.

We are, then, not obliged to say that the dignity of man and of his condition heightens the beauty of his structure. The idea we have of his dignity may influence, it is true, the judgment that we form on the beauty of his structure; but then this judgment ceases to be purely aesthetic. Doubtless, the technical constitution of the human form is an expression of its destiny, and, as such, it ought to excite our admiration; but this technical constitution is represented to the understanding and not to sense; it is a conception and not a phenomenon.

The architectonic beauty, on the contrary, could never be an expression of the destiny of man, because it addresses itself to quite a different faculty from that to which it belongs to pronounce upon his destiny.

If, then, man is, amongst all the technical forces created by nature, that to whom more especially we attribute beauty, this is exact and true only under one condition, which is, that at once and upon the simple appearance he justifies this superiority, without the necessity, in order to appreciate it, that we bring to mind his humanity. For, to recall this, we must pass through a conception; and then it would no longer be the sense, but the understanding, that would become the judge of beauty, which would imply contradiction. Man, therefore, cannot put forward the dignity of his moral destiny, nor give prominence to his superiority as intelligence, to increase the price of his beauty. Man, here, is but a being thrown like others into space—a phenomenon amongst other phenomena. In the world of sense no account is made of the rank he holds in the world of ideas; and if he desires in that to hold the first place, he can only owe it to that in him which belongs to the physical order.

But his physical nature is determined, we know, by the idea of his humanity; from which it follows that his architectonic beauty is so also mediately. If, then he is distinguished by superior beauty from all other creatures of the sensuous world, it is incontestable that he owes this advantage to his destiny as man, because it is in it that the reason is of the differences which in general separate him from the rest of the sensuous world. But the beauty of the human form is not due to its being the expression of this superior destiny, for if it were so, this form would necessarily cease to be beautiful, from the moment it began to express a less high destiny, and the contrary to this form would be beautiful as soon as it could be admitted that it expresses this higher destination. However, suppose that at the sight of a fine human face we could completely forget that which it expresses, and put in its place, without chancing anything of its outside, the savage instincts of the tiger, the judgment of the eyesight would remain absolutely the same, and the tiger would be for it the chef-d'oeuvre of the Creator.

The destiny of man as intelligence contributes, then, to the beauty of his structure only so far as the form that represents this destiny, the expression that makes it felt, satisfies at the same time the conditions which are prescribed in the world of sense to the manifestations of the beautiful; which signifies that beauty ought always to remain a pure effect of physical nature, and that the rational conception which had determined the technical utility of the human structure cannot confer beauty, but simply be compatible with beauty.

It could be objected, it is true, that in general all which is manifested by a sensuous representation is produced by the forces of nature, and that consequently this character cannot be exclusively an indication of the beautiful. Certainly, and without doubt, all technical creations are the work of nature; but it is not by the fact of nature that they are technical, or at least that they are so judged to be. They are technical only through the understanding, and thus their technical perfection has already its existence in the understanding, before passing into the world of sense, and becoming a sensible phenomenon. Beauty, on the contrary, has the peculiarity, that the sensuous world is not only its theatre, but the first source from whence it derives its birth, and that it owes to nature not only its expression, but also its creation.

Beauty is absolutely but a property of the world of sense; and the artist, who has the beautiful in view, would not attain to it but inasmuch as he entertains this illusion, that his work is the work of nature.

In order to appreciate the technical perfection of the human body, we must bear in mind the ends to which it is appropriated; this being quite unnecessary for the appreciation of its beauty. Here the senses require no aid, and of themselves judge with full competence; however they would not be competent judges of the beautiful, if the world of sense (the senses have no other object) did not contain all the conditions of beauty and was therefore competent to produce it. The beauty of man, it is true, has for mediate reason the idea of his humanity, because all his physical nature is founded on this idea; but the senses, we know, hold to immediate phenomena, and for them it is exactly the same as if this beauty were a simple effect of nature, perfectly independent.

From what we have said, up to the present time, it would appear that the beautiful can offer absolutely no interest to the understanding, because its principle belongs solely to the world of sense, and amongst all our faculties of knowledge it addresses itself only to our senses. And in fact, the moment that we sever from the idea of the beautiful, as a foreign element, all that is mixed with the idea of technical perfection, almost inevitably, in the judgment of beauty, it appears that nothing remains to it by which it can become the object of an intellectual pleasure. And nevertheless, it is quite as incontestable that the beautiful pleases the understanding, as it is beyond doubt that the beautiful rests upon no property of the object that could not be discovered but by the understanding.

To solve this apparent contradiction, it must be remembered that the phenomena can in two different ways pass to the state of objects of the understanding and express ideas. It is not always necessary that the understanding draws these ideas from phenomena; it can also put them into them. In the two cases, the phenomena will be adequate to a rational conception, with this simple difference, that, in the first case, the understanding finds it objectively given, and to a certain extent only receives it from the object because it is necessary that the idea should be given to explain the nature and often even the possibility of the object; whilst in the second case, on the contrary, it is the understanding which of itself interprets, in a manner to make of it the expression of its idea, that which the phenomenon offers us, without any connection with this idea, and thus treats by a metaphysical process that which in reality is purely physical. There, then, in the association of the idea with the object there is an objective necessity; here, on the contrary, a subjective necessity at the utmost. It is unnecessary to say that, in my mind, the first of these two connections ought to be understood of technical perfection, the second, of the beautiful.

As then in the second case it is a thing quite contingent for the sensuous object that there should or should not be outside of it an object which perceives it—an understanding that associates one of its own ideas with it, consequently, the ensemble of these objective properties ought to be considered as fully independent of this idea; we have perfectly the right to reduce the beautiful, objectively, to the simple conditions of physical nature, and to see nothing more in beauty than effect belonging purely to the world of sense. But as, on the other side, the understanding makes of this simple fact of the world of sense a transcendent usage, and in lending it a higher signification inasmuch as he marks it, as it were, with his image, we have equally the right to transport the beautiful, subjectively, into the world of intelligence. It is in this manner that beauty belongs at the same time to the two worlds—to one by the right of birth, to the other by adoption; it takes its being in the world of sense, it acquires the rights of citizenship in the world of understanding. It is that which explains how it can be that taste, as the faculty for appreciating the beautiful, holds at once the spiritual element and that of sense; and that these two natures, incompatible one with the other, approach in order to form in it a happy union. It is this that explains how taste can conciliate respect for the understanding with the material element, and with the rational principle the favor and the sympathy of the senses, how it can ennoble the perceptions of the senses so as to make ideas of them, and, in a certain measure, transform the physical world itself into a domain of the ideal.

At all events, if it is accidental with regard to the object, that the understanding associates, at the representation of this object, one of its own ideas with it, it is not the less necessary for the subject which represents it to attach to such a representation such an idea. This idea, and the sensuous indication which corresponds to it in the object, ought to be one with the other in such relation, that the understanding be forced to this association by its own immutable laws; the understanding then must have in itself the reason which leads it to associate exclusively a certain phenomenon with a certain determined idea, and, reciprocally, the object should have in itself the reason for which it exclusively provokes that idea and not another. As to knowing what the idea can be which the understanding carries into the beautiful, and by what objective property the object gifted with beauty can be capable of serving as symbol to this idea, is then a question much too grave to be solved here in passing, and I reserve this examination for an analytical theory of the beautiful.

The architectonic beauty of man is then, in the way I have explained it, the visible expression of a rational conception, but it is so only in the same sense and the same title as are in general all the beautiful creations of nature. As to the degree, I agree that it surpasses all the other beauties; but with regard to kind, it is upon the same rank as they are, because it also manifests that which alone is perceptible of its subject, and it is only when we represent it to ourselves that it receives a super-sensuous value.

If the ends of creation are marked in man with more of success and of beauty than in the organic beings, it is to some extent a favor which the intelligence, inasmuch as it dictated the laws of the human structure, has shown to nature charged to execute those laws. The intelligence, it is true, pursues its end in the technique of man with a rigorous necessity, but happily its exigencies meet and accord with the necessary laws of nature so well, that one executes the order of the other whilst acting according to its own inclination.

But this can only be true respecting the architectonic beauty of man, where the necessary laws of physical nature are sustained by another necessity, that of the teleological principle which determines them. It is here only that the beautiful could be calculated by relation to the technique of the structure, which can no longer take place when the necessity is on one side alone, and the super-sensuous cause which determines the phenomenon takes a contingent character. Thus, it is nature alone who takes upon herself the architectonic beauty of man, because here, from the first design, she had been charged once for all by the creating intelligence with the execution of all that man needs in order to arrive at the ends for which he is destined, and she has in consequence no change to fear in this organic work which she accomplishes.

But man is moreover a person—that is to say, a being whose different states can have their cause in himself, and absolutely their last cause; a being who can be modified by reason that he draws from himself. The manner in which he appears in the world of sense depends upon the manner in which he feels and wills, and, consequently, upon certain states which are freely determined by himself, and not fatally by nature.

If man were only a physical creature, nature, at the same time that she establishes the general laws of his being, would determine also the various causes of application. But here she divides her empire with free arbitration; and, although its laws are fixed, it is the mind that pronounces upon particular cases.

The domain of mind extends as far as living nature goes, and it finishes only at the point at which organic life loses itself in unformed matter, at the point at which the animal forces cease to act. It is known that all the motive forces in man are connected one with the other, and this makes us understand how the mind, even considered as principle of voluntary movement, can propagate its action through all organisms. It is not only the instruments of the will, but the organs themselves upon which the will does not immediately exercise its empire, that undergo, indirectly at least, the influence of mind; the mind determines then, not only designedly when it acts, but again, without design, when it feels.

From nature in herself (this result is clearly perceived from what precedes) we must ask nothing but a fixed beauty, that of the phenomena that she alone has determined according to the law of necessity. But with free arbitration, chance (the accidental), interferes in the work of nature, and the modifications that affect it thus under the empire of free will are no longer, although all behave according to its own laws, determined by these laws. From thence it is to the mind to decide the use it will make of its instruments, and with regard to that part of beauty which depends on this use, nature has nothing further to command, nor, consequently, to incur any responsibility.

And thus man by reason that, making use of his liberty, he raises himself into the sphere of pure intelligences, would find himself in danger of sinking, inasmuch as he is a creature of sense, and of losing in the judgment of taste that which he gains at the tribunal of reason. This moral destiny, therefore, accomplished by the moral action of man, would cost him a privilege which was assured to him by this same moral destiny when only indicated in his structure; a purely sensuous privilege, it is true, but one which receives, as we have seen, a signification and a higher value from the understanding. No; nature is too much enamored with harmony to be guilty of so gross a contradiction, and that which is harmonious in the world of the understanding could not be rendered by a discord in the world of sense.

As soon, then, as in man the person, the moral and free agent, takes upon himself to determine the play of phenomena, and by his intervention takes from nature the power to protect the beauty of her work, he then, as it were, substitutes himself for nature, and assumes in a certain measure, with the rights of nature, a part of the obligations incumbent on her. When the mind, taking possession of the sensuous matter subservient to it, implicates it in his destiny and makes it depend on its own modifications, it transforms itself to a certain point into a sensuous phenomenon, and, as such, is obliged to recognize the law which regulates in general all the phenomena. In its own interest it engages to permit that nature in its service, placed under its dependence, shall still preserve its character of nature, and never act in a manner contrary to its anterior obligations. I call the beautiful an obligation of phenomena, because the want which corresponds to it in the subject has its reason in the understanding itself, and thus it is consequently universal and necessary. I call it an anterior obligation because the senses, in the matter of beauty, have given their judgment before the understanding commences to perform its office.

Thus it is now free arbitration which rules the beautiful. If nature has furnished the architectonic beauty, the soul in its turn determines the beauty of the play, and now also we know what we must understand by charm and grace. Grace is the beauty of the form under the influence of free will; it is the beauty of this kind of phenomena that the person himself determines. The architectonic beauty does honor to the author of nature; grace does honor to him who possesses it. That is a gift, this is a personal merit.

Grace can be found only in movement, for a modification which takes place in the soul can only be manifested in the sensuous world as movement. But this does not prevent features fixed and in repose also from possessing grace. There immobility is, in its origin, movement which, from being frequently repeated, at length becomes habitual, leaving durable traces.

But all the movements of man are not capable of grace. Grace is never otherwise than beauty of form animated into movement by free will; and the movements which belong only to physical nature could not merit the name. It is true that an intellectual man, if he be keen, ends by rendering himself master of almost all the movements of the body; but when the chain which links a fine lineament to a moral sentiment lengthens much, this lineament becomes the property of the structure, and can no longer be counted as a grace. It happens, ultimately, that the mind moulds the body, and that the structure is forced to modify itself according to the play that the soul imprints upon the organs, so entirely, that grace finally is transformed—and the examples are not rare—into architectonic beauty. As at one time an antagonistic mind which is ill at ease with itself alters and destroys the most perfect beauty of structure, until at last it becomes impossible to recognize this magnificent chef-d'oeuvre of nature in the state to which it is reduced under the unworthy hands of free will, so at other times the serenity and perfect harmony of the soul come to the aid of the hampered technique, unloose nature and develop with divine splendor the beauty of form, enveloped until then, and oppressed.

The plastic nature of man has in it an infinity of resources to retrieve the negligencies and repair the faults that she may have committed. To this end it is sufficient that the mind, the moral agent, sustain it, or even withhold from troubling it in the labor of rebuilding.

Since the movements become fixed (gestures pass to a state of lineament), are themselves capable of grace, it would perhaps appear to be rational to comprehend equally under this idea of beauty some apparent or imitative movements (the flamboyant lines for example, undulations). It is this which Mendelssohn upholds. But then the idea of grace would be confounded with the ideal of beauty in general, for all beauty is definitively but a property of true or apparent movement (objective or subjective), as I hope to demonstrate in an analysis of beauty. With regard to grace, the only movements which can offer any are those which respond at the same time to a sentiment.

The person (it is known what I mean by the expression) prescribes the movements of the body, either through the will, when he desires to realize in the world of sense an effect of which he has proposed the idea, and in that case the movements are said to be voluntary or intentional; or, on the other hand, they take place without its will taking any part in it—in virtue of a fatal law of the organism—but on the occasion of a sentiment, in the latter case, I say that the movements are sympathetic. The sympathetic movement, though it may be involuntary and provoked by a sentiment, ought not to be confounded with those purely instinctive movements that proceed from physical sensibility. Physical instinct is not a free agent, and that which it executes is not an act of the person; I understand then here exclusively, by sympathetic movements, those which accompany a sentiment, a disposition of the moral order.

The question that now presents itself is this: Of these two kinds of movement, having their principle in the person, which is capable of grace?

That which we are rigorously forced to distinguish in philosophic analysis is not always separated also in the real. Thus it is rare that we meet intentional movements without sympathetic movements, because the will determines the intentional movements only after being decided itself by the moral sentiments which are the principle of the sympathetic movements. When a person speaks, we see his looks, his lineaments, his hands, often the whole person all together speaks to us; and it is not rare that this mimic part of the discourse is the most eloquent. Still more there are cases where an intentional movement can be considered at the same time as sympathetic; and it is that which happens when something involuntary mingles with the voluntary act which determines this movement.

I will explain: the mode, the manner in which a voluntary movement is executed, is not a thing so exactly determined by the intention which is proposed by it that it cannot be executed in several different ways. Well, then, that which the will or intention leaves undetermined can be sympathetically determined by the state of moral sensibility in which the person is found to be, and consequently can express this state. When I extend the arm to seize an object, I execute, in truth, an intention, and the movement I make is determined in general by the end that I have in view; but in what way does my arm approach the object? how far do the other parts of my body follow this impulsion? What will be the degree of slowness or of the rapidity of the movement? What amount of force shall I employ? This is a calculation of which my will, at the instant, takes no account, and in consequence there is a something left to the discretion of nature.

But nevertheless, though that part of the movement is not determined by the intention itself, it must be decided at length in one way or the other, and the reason is that the manner in which my moral sensibility is affected can have here decisive influence: it is this which will give the tone, and which thus determines the mode and the manner of the movement. Therefore this influence, which exercises upon the voluntary movement the state of moral sensibility in which the subject is found, represents precisely the involuntary part of this movement, and it is there then that we must seek for grace.

A voluntary movement, if it is not linked to any sympathetic movement—or that which comes to the same thing, if there is nothing involuntary mixed up with it having for principle the moral state of sensibility in which the subject happens to be—could not in any manner present grace, for grace always supposes as a cause a disposition of the soul. Voluntary movement is produced after an operation of the soul, which in consequence is already completed at the moment in which the movement takes place.

The sympathetic movement, on the contrary, accompanies this operation of the soul, and the moral state of sensibility which decides it to this operation. So that this movement ought to be considered as simultaneous with regard to both one and the other.

From that alone it results that voluntary movement not proceeding immediately from the disposition of the subject could not be an expression of this disposition also. For between the disposition and the movement itself the volition has intervened, which, considered in itself, is something perfectly indifferent. This movement is the work of the volition, it is determined by the aim that is proposed; it is not the work of the person, nor the product of the sentiments that affect it.

The voluntary movement is united but accidentally with the disposition which precedes it; the concomitant movement, on the contrary, is necessarily linked to it. The first is to the soul that which the conventional signs of speech are to the thoughts which they express. The second, on the contrary, the sympathetic movement or concomitant, is to the soul that which the cry of passion is to the passion itself. The involuntary movement is, then, an expression of the mind, not by its nature, but only by its use. And in consequence we are not authorized to say that the mind is revealed in a voluntary movement; this movement never expresses more than the substance of the will (the aim), and not the form of the will (the disposition). The disposition can only manifest itself to us by concomitant movements.

It follows that we can infer from the words of a man the kind of character he desires to have attributed to him; but if we desire to know what is in reality his character we must seek to divine it in the mimic expression which accompanies his words, and in his gestures, that is to say, in the movements which he did not desire. If we perceive that this man wills even the expression of his features, from the instant we have made this discovery we cease to believe in his physiognomy and to see in it an indication of his sentiments.

It is true that a man, by dint of art and of study, can at last arrive at this result, to subdue to his will even the concomitant movements; and, like a clever juggler, to shape according to his pleasure such or such a physiognomy upon the mirror from which his soul is reflected through mimic action. But then, with such a man all is dissembling, and art entirely absorbs nature. The true grace, on the contrary, ought always to be pure nature, that is to say, involuntary (or at least appear to be so), to be graceful. The subject even ought not to appear to know that it possesses grace.

By which we can also see incidentally what we must think of grace, either imitated or learned (I would willingly call it theatrical grace, or the grace of the dancing-master). It is the pendant of that sort of beauty which a woman seeks from her toilet-table, reinforced with rouge, white paint, false ringlets, pads, and whalebone. Imitative grace is to true grace what beauty of toilet is to architectonic beauty. One and the other could act in absolutely the same manner upon the senses badly exercised, as the original of which they wish to be the imitation; and at times even, if much art is put into it, they might create an illusion to the connoisseur. But there will be always some indication through which the intention and constraint will betray it in the end, and this discovery will lead inevitably to indifference, if not even to contempt and disgust. If we are warned that the architectonic beauty is factitious, at once, the more it has borrowed from a nature which is not its own, the more it loses in our eyes of that which belongs to humanity (so far as it is phenomenal), and then we, who forbid the renunciation lightly of an accidental advantage, how can we see with pleasure or even with indifference an exchange through which man sacrifices a part of his proper nature in order to substitute elements taken from inferior nature? How, even supposing we could forgive the illusion produced, how could we avoid despising the deception? If we are told that grace is artificial, our heart at once closes; our soul, which at first advanced with so much vivacity to meet the graceful object, shrinks back. That which was mind has suddenly become matter. Juno and her celestial beauty has vanished, and in her place there is nothing but a phantom of vapour.

Although grace ought to be, or at least ought to appear, something involuntary, still we seek it only in the movements that depend more or less on the will. I know also that grace is attributed to a certain mimic language, and we say a pleasing smile, a charming blush, though the smile and the blush are sympathetic movements, not determined by the will, but by moral sensibility. But besides that, the first of these movements is, after all, in our power, and that it is not shown that in the second there is, properly speaking, any grace, it is right to say, in general, that most frequently when grace appears it is on the occasion of a voluntary movement. Grace is desired both in language and in song; it is asked for in the play of the eyes and of the mouth, in the movements of the hands and the arms whenever these movements are free and voluntary; it is required in the walk, in the bearing, and attitude, in a word, in all exterior demonstrations of man, so far as they depend on his will. As to the movements which the instinct of nature produces in us, or which an overpowering affection excites, or, so to speak, is lord over; that which we ask of these movements, in origin purely physical, is, as we shall see presently, quite another thing than grace. These kinds of movements belong to nature, and not to the person, but it is from the person alone, as we have seen, that all grace issues.

If, then, grace is a property that we demand only from voluntary movements, and if, on the other hand, all voluntary element should be rigorously excluded from grace, we have no longer to seek it but in that portion of the intentional movements to which the intention of the subject is unknown, but which, however, does not cease to answer in the soul to a moral cause.

We now know in what kind of movements he must ask for grace; but we know nothing more, and a movement can have these different characters, without on that account being graceful; it is as yet only speaking (or mimic).

I call speaking (in the widest sense of the word) every physical phenomenon which accompanies and expresses a certain state of the soul; thus, in this acceptation, all the sympathetic movements are speaking, including those which accompany the simple affections of the animal sensibility.

The aspect, even, under which the animals present themselves, can be speaking, as soon as they outwardly show their inward dispositions. But, with them, it is nature alone which speaks, and NOT LIBERTY. By the permanent configuration of animals through their fixed and architectonic features, nature expresses the aim she proposed in creating them; by their mimic traits she expresses the want awakened and the want satisfied. Necessity reigns in the animal as well as in the plant, without meeting the obstacle of a person. The animals have no individuality farther than each of them is a specimen by itself of a general type of nature, and the aspect under which they present themselves at such or such an instant of their duration is only a particular example of the accomplishment of the views of nature under determined natural conditions.

To take the word in a more restricted sense, the configuration of man alone is speaking, and it is itself so only in those of the phenomena that accompany and express the state of its moral sensibility.

I say it is only in this sort of phenomena; for, in all the others, man is in the same rank as the rest of sensible beings. By the permanent configuration of man, by his architectonic features, nature only expresses, just as in the animals and other organic beings, her own intention. It is true the intention of nature may go here much further, and the means she employs to reach her end may offer in their combination more of art and complication; but all that ought to be placed solely to the account of nature, and can confer no advantage on man himself.

In the animal, and in the plant, nature gives not only the destination; she acts herself and acts alone in the accomplishment of her ends. In man, nature limits herself in marking her views; she leaves to himself their accomplishment, it is this alone that makes of him a man.

Alone of all known beings—man, in his quality of person, has the privilege to break the chain of necessity by his will, and to determine in himself an entire series of fresh spontaneous phenomena. The act by which he thus determines himself is properly that which we call an action, and the things that result from this sort of action are what we exclusively name his acts. Thus man can only show his personality by his own acts.

The configuration of the animal not only expresses the idea of his destination, but also the relation of his present state with this destination. And as in the animal it is nature which determines and at the same time accomplishes its destiny, the configuration of the animal can never express anything else than the work of nature.

If then nature, whilst determining the destiny of man, abandons to the will of man himself the care to accomplish it, the relation of his present state with his destiny cannot be a work of nature, but ought to be the work of the person; it follows, that all in the configuration which expresses this relation will belong, not to nature, but to the person, that is to say, will be considered as a personal expression; if then, the architectonic part of his configuration tells us the views that nature proposed to herself in creating him, the mimic part of his face reveals what he has himself done for the accomplishment of these views.

It is not then enough for us, when there is question of the form of man, to find in it the expression of humanity in general, or even of that which nature has herself contributed to the individual in particular, in order to realize the human type in it; for he would have that in common with every kind of technical configuration. We expect something more of his face; we desire that it reveal to us at the same time, up to what point man himself, in his liberty, has contributed towards the aim of nature; in other words, we desire that his face bear witness to his character. In the first case we see that nature proposed to create in him a man; but it is in the second case only that we can judge if he has become so in reality.

Thus, the face of a man is truly his own only inasmuch as his face is mimic; but also all that is mimic in his face is entirely his own. For, if we suppose the case in which the greatest part, and even the totality, of these mimic features express nothing more than animal sensations or instincts, and, in consequence, would show nothing more than the animal in him, it would still remain that it was in his destiny and in his power to limit, by his liberty, his sensuous nature. The presence of these kinds of traits clearly witness that he has not made use of this faculty. We see by that he has not accomplished his destiny, and in this sense his face is speaking; it is still a moral expression, the same as the non-accomplishment of an act commanded by duty is likewise a sort of action.

We must distinguish from these speaking features which are always an expression of the soul, the features non-speaking or dumb, which are exclusively the work of plastic nature, and which it impresses on the human face when it acts independently of all influence of the soul. I call them dumb, because, like incomprehensible figures put there by nature, they are silent upon the character. They mark only distinctive properties attributed by nature to all the kind; and if at times they are sufficient to distinguish the individual, they at least never express anything of the person.

These features are by no means devoid of signification for the physiognomies, because the physiognomies not only studies that which man has made of his being, but also that which nature has done for him and against him.

It is not also easy to determine with precision where the dumb traits or features end, where the speaking traits commence. The plastic forces on one side, with their uniform action, and, on the other, the affections which depend on no law, dispute incessantly the ground; and that which nature, in its dumb and indefatigable activity, has succeeded in raising up, often is overturned by liberty, as a river that overflows and spreads over its banks: the mind when it is gifted with vivacity acquires influence over all the movements of the body, and arrives at last indirectly to modify by force the sympathetic play as far as the architectonic and fixed forms of nature, upon which the will has no hold. In a man thus constituted it becomes at last characteristic; and it is that which we can often observe upon certain heads which a long life, strange accidents, and an active mind have moulded and worked. In these kinds of faces there is only the generic character which belongs to plastic nature; all which here forms individuality is the act of the person himself, and it is this which causes it to be said, with much reason, that those faces are all soul.

Look at that man, on the contrary, who has made for himself a mechanical existence, those disciples of the rule. The rule can well calm the sensuous nature, but not awaken human nature, the superior faculties: look at those flat and inexpressive physiognomies; the finger of nature has alone left there its impression; a soul inhabits these bodies, but it is a sluggish soul, a discreet guest, and, as a peaceful and silent neighbour who does not disturb the plastic force at its work, left to itself. Never a thought which requires an effort, never a movement of passion, hurries the calm cadence of physical life. There is no danger that the architectonic features ever become changed by the play of voluntary movements, and never would liberty trouble the functions of vegetative life. As the profound calm of the mind does not bring about a notable degeneracy of forces, the expense would never surpass the receipts; it is rather the animal economy which would always be in excess. In exchange for a certain sum of well-being which it throws as bait, the mind makes itself the servant, the punctual major-domo of physical nature, and places all his glory in keeping his books in order. Thus will be accomplished that which organic nature can accomplish; thus will the work of nutrition and of reproduction prosper. So happy a concord between animal nature and the will cannot but be favorable to architectonic beauty, and it is there that we can observe this beauty in all its purity. But the general forces of nature, as every one knows, are eternally at warfare with the particular or organic forces, and, however cleverly balanced is the technique of a body, the cohesion and the weight end always by getting the upper hand. Also architectonic beauty, so far as it is a simple production of nature, has its fixed periods, its blossoming, its maturity, and its decline—periods the revolution of which can easily be accelerated, but not retarded in any case, by the play of the will, and this is the way in which it most frequently finishes; little by little matter takes the upper hand over form, and the plastic principle, which vivified the being, prepares for itself its tomb under the accumulation of matter.

However, although no dumb trait, considered in an isolated point of view, can be an expression of the mind, a face composed entirely of these kinds of features can be characterized in its entirety by precisely the same reason as a face which is speaking only as an expression of sensuous nature can be nevertheless characteristic. I mean to say that the mind is obliged to exercise its activity and to feel conformably to its moral nature, and it accuses itself and betrays its fault when the face which it animates shows no trace of this moral activity. If, therefore, the pure and beautiful expression of the destination of man, which is marked in his architectonic structure, penetrates us with satisfaction and respect for the sovereign, reason, who is the author of it, at all events these two sentiments will not be for us without mixture but in as far as we see in man a simple creation of nature. But if we consider in him the moral person, we have a right to demand of his face an expression of the person, and if this expectation is deceived contempt will infallibly follow. Simply organic beings have a right to our respect as creatures; man cannot pretend to it but in the capacity of creator, that is to say, as being himself the determiner of his own condition. He ought not only, as the other sensuous creatures, to reflect the rays of a foreign intelligence, were it even the divine intelligence; man ought, as a sun, to shine by his own light.

Thus we require of man a speaking expression as soon as he becomes conscious of his moral destiny; but we desire at the same time that this expression speak to his advantage, that is to say, it marks in him sentiments conformable to his moral destiny, and a superior moral aptitude. This is what reason requires in the human face.

But, on the other side, man, as far as he is a phenomenon, is an object of sense; there, where the moral sentiment is satisfied, the aesthetic sentiment does not understand its being made a sacrifice, and the conformity with an idea ought not to lessen the beauty of the phenomenon. Thus, as much as reason requires an expression of the morality of the subject in the human face, so much, and with no less rigor, does the eye demand beauty. As these two requirements, although coming from the principles of the appreciation of different degrees, address themselves to the same object, also both one and the other must be given satisfaction by one and the same cause. The disposition of the soul which places man in the best state for accomplishing his moral destiny ought to give place to an expression that will be at the same time the most advantageous to his beauty as phenomenon; in other terms, his moral exercise ought to be revealed by grace.

But a great difficulty now presents itself from the idea alone of the expressive movements which bear witness to the morality of the subject: it appears that the cause of these movements is necessarily a moral cause, a principle which resides beyond the world of sense; and from the sole idea of beauty it is not less evident that its principle is purely sensuous, and that it ought to be a simple effect of nature, or at the least appear to be such. But if the ultimate reason of the movements which offer a moral expression is necessarily without, and the ultimate reason of the beautiful necessarily within, the sensuous world, it appears that grace, which ought to unite both of them, contains a manifest contradiction.

To avoid this contradiction we must admit that the moral cause, which in our soul is the foundation of grace, brings, in a necessary manner, in the sensibility which depends on that cause, precisely that state which contains in itself the natural conditions of beauty. I will explain. The beautiful, as each sensuous phenomenon, supposes certain conditions, and, in as far as it is beautiful, these are purely conditions of the senses; well, then, in that the mind (in virtue of a law that we cannot fathom), from the state in which it is, itself prescribes to physical nature which accompanies it, its own state, and in that the state of moral perfection is precisely in it the most favorable for the accomplishment of the physical conditions of beauty, it follows that it is the mind which renders beauty possible; and there its action ends. But whether real beauty comes forth from it, that depends upon the physical conditions alluded to, and is consequently a free effect of nature. Therefore, as it cannot be said that nature is properly free in the voluntary movements, in which it is employed but as a means to attain an end, and as, on the other side, it cannot be said that it is free in its involuntary movements, which express the moral, the liberty with which it manifests itself, dependent as it is on the will of the subject, must be a concession that the mind makes to nature; and, consequently, it can be said that grace is a favor in which the moral has desired to gratify the sensuous element; the same as the architectonic beauty may be considered as nature acquiescing to the technical form.

May I be permitted a comparison to clear up this point? Let us suppose a monarchical state administered in such a way that, although all goes on according to the will of one person, each citizen could persuade himself that he governs and obeys only his own inclination, we should call that government a liberal government.

But we should look twice before we should thus qualify a government in which the chief makes his will outweigh the wishes of the citizens, or a government in which the will of the citizens outweighs that of the chief. In the first case, the government would be no more liberal; in the second, it would not be a government at all.

It is not difficult to make application of these examples to what the human face could be under the government of the mind. If the mind is manifested in such a way through the sensuous nature subject to its empire that it executes its behests with the most faithful exactitude, or expresses its sentiments in the most perfectly speaking manner, without going in the least against that which the aesthetic sense demands from it as a phenomenon, then we shall see produced that which we call grace. But this is far from being grace, if mind is manifested in a constrained manner by the sensuous nature, or if sensuous nature acting alone in all liberty the expression of moral nature was absent. In the first case there would not be beauty; in the second the beauty would be devoid of play.

The super-sensuous cause, therefore, the cause of which the principle is in the soul, can alone render grace speaking, and it is the purely sensuous cause having its principle in nature which alone can render it beautiful. We are not more authorized in asserting that mind engenders beauty than we should be, in the former example, in maintaining that the chief of the state produces liberty; because we can indeed leave a man in his liberty, but not give it to him.

But just as when a people feels itself free under the constraint of a foreign will, it is in a great degree due to the sentiments animating the prince; and as this liberty would run great risks if the prince took opposite sentiments, so also it is in the moral dispositions of the mind which suggests them that we must seek the beauty of free movements. And now the question which is presented is this one: What then are the conditions of personal morality which assure the utmost amount of liberty to the sensuous instruments of the will? and what are the moral sentiments which agree the best in their expression with the beautiful?

That which is evident is that neither the will, in the intentional movement, nor the passion, in the sympathetic movement, ought to act as a force with regard to the physical nature which is subject to it, in order that this, in obeying it, may have beauty. In truth, without going further, common sense considers ease to be the first requisite of grace. It is not less evident that, on another side, nature ought not to act as a force with regard to mind, in order to give occasion for a fine moral expression; for there, where physical nature commands alone, it is absolutely necessary that the character of the man should vanish.

We can conceive three sorts of relation of man with himself: I mean the sensuous part of man with the reasonable part. From these three relations we have to seek which is that one which best suits him in the sensuous world, and the expression of which constitutes the beautiful. Either man enforces silence upon the exigencies of his sensuous nature, to govern himself conformably with the superior exigencies of his reasonable nature; or else, on the contrary, he subjects the reasonable portion of his being to the sensuous part, reducing himself thus to obey only the impulses which the necessity of nature imprints upon him, as well as upon the other phenomena; or lastly, harmony is established between the impulsions of the one and the laws of the other, and man is in perfect accord with himself.

If he has the consciousness of his spiritual person, of his pure autonomy, man rejects all that is sensuous, and it is only when thus isolated from matter that he feels to the full his moral liberty. But for that, as his sensuous nature opposes an obstinate and vigorous resistance to him, he must, on his side, exercise upon it a notable pressure and a strong effort, without which he could neither put aside the appetites nor reduce to silence the energetic voice of instinct. A mind of this quality makes the physical nature which depends on him feel that it has a master in him, whether it fulfils the orders of the will or endeavors to anticipate them. Under its stern discipline sensuousness appears then repressed, and interior resistance will betray itself exteriorly by the constraint. This moral state cannot, then, be favorable to beauty, because nature cannot produce the beautiful but as far as it is free, and consequently that which betrays to us the struggles of moral liberty against matter cannot either be grace.

If, on the contrary, subdued by its wants, man allows himself to be governed without reserve by the instinct of nature, it is his interior autonomy that vanishes, and with it all trace of this autonomy is exteriorly effaced. The animal nature is alone visible upon his visage; the eye is watery and languishing, the mouth rapaciously open, the voice trembling and muffled, the breathing short and rapid, the limbs trembling with nervous agitation: the whole body by its languor betrays its moral degradation. Moral force has renounced all resistance, and physical nature, with such a man, is placed in full liberty. But precisely this complete abandonment of moral independence, which occurs ordinarily at the moment of sensuous desire, and more still at the moment of enjoyment, sets suddenly brute matter at liberty which until then had been kept in equilibrium by the active and passive forces. The inert forces of nature commence from thence to gain the upper hand over the living forces of the organism; the form is oppressed by matter, humanity by common nature. The eye, in which the soul shone forth, becomes dull, or it protrudes from its socket with I know not what glassy haggardness; the delicate pink of the cheeks thickens, and spreads as a coarse pigment in uniform layers. The mouth is no longer anything but a simple opening, because its form no longer depends upon the action of forces, but on their non-resistance; the gasping voice and breathing are no more than an effort to ease the laborious and oppressed lungs, and which show a simple mechanical want, with nothing that reveals a soul. In a word, in that state of liberty which physical nature arrogates to itself from its chief, we must not think of beauty. Under the empire of the moral agent, the liberty of form was only restrained, here it is crushed by brutal matter, which gains as much ground as is abstracted from the will. Man in this state not only revolts the moral sense, which incessantly claims of the face an expression of human dignity, but the aesthetic sense, which is not content with simple matter, and which finds in the form an unfettered pleasure—the aesthetic sense will turn away with disgust from such a spectacle, where concupiscence could alone find its gratification.

Of these two relations between the moral nature of man and his physical nature, the first makes us think of a monarchy, where strict surveillance of the prince holds in hand all free movement; the second is an ochlocracy, where the citizen, in refusing to obey his legitimate sovereign, finds he has liberty quite as little as the human face has beauty when the moral autonomy is oppressed; nay, on the contrary, just as the citizens are given over to the brutal despotism of the lowest classes, so the form is given over here to the despotism of matter. Just as liberty finds itself between the two extremes of legal oppression and anarchy, so also we shall find the beautiful between two extremes, between the expression of dignity which bears witness to the domination exercised by the mind, and the voluptuous expression which reveals the domination exercised by instinct.

In other terms, if the beauty of expression is incompatible with the absolute government of reason over sensuous nature, and with the government of sensuous nature over the reason, it follows that the third state (for one could not conceive a fourth)—that in which the reason and the senses, duty and inclination, are in harmony—will be that in which the beauty of play is produced. In order that obedience to reason may become an object of inclination, it must represent for us the principle of pleasure; for pleasure and pain are the only springs which set the instincts in motion. It is true that in life it is the reverse that takes place, and pleasure is ordinarily the motive for which we act according to reason. If morality itself has at last ceased to hold this language, it is to the immortal author of the "Critique" to whom we must offer our thanks; it is to him to whom the glory is due of having restored the healthy reason in separating it from all systems. But in the manner in which the principles of this philosopher are ordinarily expressed by himself and also by others, it appears that the inclination can never be for the moral sense otherwise than a very suspicious companion, and pleasure a dangerous auxiliary for moral determinations. In admitting that the instinct of happiness does not exercise a blind domination over man, it does not the less desire to interfere in the moral actions which depend on free arbitration, and by that it changes the pure action of the will, which ought always to obey the law alone, never the instinct. Thus, to be altogether sure that the inclination has not interfered with the demonstrations of the will, we prefer to see it in opposition rather than in accord with the law of reason; because it may happen too easily, when the inclination speaks in favor of duty, that duty draws from the recommendation all its credit over the will. And in fact, as in practical morals, it is not the conformity of the acts with the law, but only the conformity of the sentiments with duty, which is important. We do not attach, and with reason, any value to this consideration, that it is ordinarily more favorable to the conformity of acts with the law that inclination is on the side of duty. As a consequence, this much appears evident: that the assent of sense, if it does not render suspicious the conformity of the will with duty, at least does not guarantee it. Thus the sensuous expression of this assent, expression that grace offers to us, could never bear a sufficient available witness to the morality of the act in which it is met; and it is not from that which an action or a sentiment manifests to the eyes by graceful expression that we must judge of the moral merit of that sentiment or of that action.

Up to the present time I believe I have been in perfect accord with the rigorists in morals. I shall not become, I hope, a relaxed moralist in endeavoring to maintain in the world of phenomena and in the real fulfilment of the law of duty those rights of sensuous nature which, upon the ground of pure reason and in the jurisdiction of the moral law, are completely set aside and excluded.

I will explain. Convinced as I am, and precisely because I am convinced, that the inclination in associating itself to an act of the will offers no witness to the pure conformity of this act with the duty, I believe that we are able to infer from this that the moral perfection of man cannot shine forth except from this very association of his inclination with his moral conduct. In fact, the destiny of man is not to accomplish isolated moral acts, but to be a moral being. That which is prescribed to him does not consist of virtues, but of virtue, and virtue is not anything else "than an inclination for duty." Whatever, then, in the objective sense, may be the opposition which separates the acts suggested by the inclination from those which duty determines, we cannot say it is the same in the subjective sense; and not only is it permitted to man to accord duty with pleasure, but he ought to establish between them this accord, he ought to obey his reason with a sentiment of joy. It is not to throw it off as a burden, nor to cast it off as a too coarse skin. No, it is to unite it, by a union the most intimate, with his Ego, with the most noble part of his being, that a sensuous nature has been associated in him to his purely spiritual nature. By the fact that nature has made of him a being both at once reasonable and sensuous, that is to say, a man, it has prescribed to him the obligation not to separate that which she has united; not to sacrifice in him the sensuous being, were it in the most pure manifestations of the divine part; and never to found the triumph of one over the oppression and the ruin of the other. It is only when he gathers, so to speak, his entire humanity together, and his way of thinking in morals becomes the result of the united action of the two principles, when morality has become to him a second nature, it is then only that it is secure; for, as far as the mind and the duty are obliged to employ violence, it is necessary that the instinct shall have force to resist them. The enemy which only is overturned can rise up again, but the enemy reconciled is truly vanquished. In the moral philosophy of Kant the idea of duty is proposed with a harshness enough to ruffle the Graces, and one which could easily tempt a feeble mind to seek for moral perfection in the sombre paths of an ascetic and monastic life. Whatever precautions the great philosopher has been able to take in order to shelter himself against this false interpretation, which must be repugnant more than all else to the serenity of the free mind, he has lent it a strong impulse, it seems to me, in opposing to each other by a harsh contrast the two principles which act upon the human will. Perhaps it was hardly possible, from the point of view in which he was placed, to avoid this mistake; but he has exposed himself seriously to it. Upon the basis of the question there is no longer, after the demonstration he has given, any discussion possible, at least for the heads which think and which are quite willing to be persuaded; and I am not at all sure if it would not be better to renounce at once all the attributes of the human being than to be willing to reach on this point, by reason, a different result. But although he began to work without any prejudice when he searched for the truth, and though all is here explained by purely objective reasons, it appears that when he put forward the truth once found he had been guided by a more subjective maxim, which is not difficult, I believe, to be accounted for by the time and circumstances.

What, in fact, was the moral of his time, either in theory or in its application? On one side, a gross materialism, of which the shameless maxims would revolt his soul; impure resting-places offered to the bastard characters of a century by the unworthy complacency of philosophers; on the other side, a pretended system of perfectibility, not less suspicious, which, to realize the chimera of a general perfection common to the whole universe, would not be embarrassed for a choice of means. This is what would meet his attention. So he carried there, where the most pressing danger lay and reform was the most urgent, the strongest forces of his principles, and made it a law to pursue sensualism without pity, whether it walks with a bold face, impudently insulting morality, or dissimulates under the imposing veil of a moral, praiseworthy end, under which a certain fanatical kind of order know how to disguise it. He had not to disguise ignorance, but to reform perversion; for such a cure a violent blow, and not persuasion or flattery, was necessary; and the more the contrast would be violent between the true principles and the dominant maxims, the more he would hope to provoke reflection upon this point. He was the Draco of his time, because his time seemed to him as yet unworthy to possess a Solon, neither capable of receiving him. From the sanctuary of pure reason he drew forth the moral law, unknown then, and yet, in another way, so known; he made it appear in all its saintliness before a degraded century, and troubled himself little to know whether there were eyes too enfeebled to bear the brightness.

But what had the children of the house done for him to have occupied himself only with the valets? Because strongly impure inclinations often usurp the name of virtue, was it a reason for disinterested inclinations in the noblest heart to be also rendered suspicious? Because the moral epicurean had willingly relaxed the law of reason, in order to fit it as a plaything to his customs, was it a reason to thus exaggerate harshness, and to make the fulfilment of duty, which is the most powerful manifestation of moral freedom, another kind of decorated servitude of a more specious name? And, in fact, between the esteem and the contempt of himself has the truly moral man a more free choice than the slave of sense between pleasure and pain? Is there less of constraint there for a pure will than here for a depraved will? Must one, by this imperative form given to the moral law, accuse man and humble him, and make of this law, which is the most sublime witness of our grandeur, the most crushing argument for our fragility? Was it possible with this imperative force to avoid that a prescription which man imposes on himself, as a reasonable being, and which is obligatory only for him on that account, and which is conciliatory with the sentiment of his liberty only—that this prescription, say I, took the appearance of a foreign law, a positive law, an appearance which could hardly lessen the radical tendency which we impute to man to react against the law?

It is certainly not an advantage for moral truth to have against itself sentiments which man can avow without shame. Thus, how can the sentiment of the beautiful, the sentiment of liberty, accord with the austere mind of a legislation which governs man rather through fear than trust, which tends constantly to separate that which nature has united, and which is reduced to hold us in defiance against a part of our being, to assure its empire over the rest? Human nature forms a whole more united in reality than it is permitted to the philosopher, who can only analyze, to allow it to appear. The reason can never reject as unworthy of it the affections which the heart recognizes with joy; and there, where man would be morally fallen, he can hardly rise in his own esteem. If in the moral order the sensuous nature were only the oppressed party and not an ally, how could it associate with all the ardor of its sentiments in a triumph which would be celebrated only over itself? how could it be so keen a participator in the satisfaction of a pure spirit having consciousness of itself, if in the end it could not attach itself to the pure spirit with such closeness that it is not possible even to intellectual analysis to separate it without violence.

The will, besides, is in more immediate relation with the faculty of feeling than with the cognitive faculties, and it would be regrettable in many circumstances if it were obliged, in order to guide itself, to take advice of pure reason. I prejudge nothing good of a man who dares so little trust to the voice of instinct that he is obliged each time to make it appear first before the moral law; he is much more estimable who abandons himself with a certain security to inclination, without having to fear being led astray by her. That proves in fact that with him the two principles are already in harmony—in that harmony which places a seat upon the perfection of the human being, and which constitutes that which we understand by a noble soul.

It is said of a man that he has a great soul when the moral sense has finished assuring itself of all the affections, to the extent of abandoning without fear the direction of the senses to the will, and never incurring the risk of finding himself in discord with its decisions. It follows that in a noble soul it is not this or that particular action, it is the entire character which is moral. Thus we can make a merit of none of its actions because the satisfaction of an instinct could not be meritorious. A noble soul has no other merit than to be a noble soul. With as great a facility as if the instinct alone were acting, it accomplishes the most painful duties of humanity, and the most heroic sacrifice that she obtains over the instinct of nature seems the effect of the free action of the instinct itself. Also, it has no idea of the beauty of its act, and it never occurs to it that any other way of acting could be possible; on the contrary, the moralist formed by the school and by rule, is always ready at the first question of the master to give an account with the most rigorous precision of the conformity of its acts with the moral law. The life of this one is like a drawing where the pencil has indicated by harsh and stiff lines all that the rule demands, and which could, if necessary, serve for a student to learn the elements of art. The life of a noble soul, on the contrary, is like a painting of Titian; all the harsh outlines are effaced, which does not prevent the whole face being more true, lifelike and harmonious.

It is then in a noble soul that is found the true harmony between reason and sense, between inclination and duty, and grace is the expression of this harmony in the sensuous world. It is only in the service of a noble soul that nature can at the same time be in possession of its liberty, and preserve from all alteration the beauty of its forms; for the one, its liberty would be compromised under the tyranny of an austere soul, the other, under the anarchical regimen of sensuousness. A noble soul spreads even over a face in which the architectonic beauty is wanting an irresistible grace, and often even triumphs over the natural disfavor. All the movements which proceed from a noble soul are easy, sweet, and yet animated. The eye beams with serenity as with liberty, and with the brightness of sentiment; gentleness of heart would naturally give to the mouth a grace that no affectation, no art, could attain. You trace there no effort in the varied play of the physiognomy, no constraint in the voluntary movements—a noble soul knows not constraint; the voice becomes music, and the limpid stream of its modulations touches the heart. The beauty of structure can excite pleasure, admiration, astonishment; grace alone can charm. Beauty has its adorers; grace alone has its lovers: for we pay our homage to the Creator, and we love man. As a whole, grace would be met with especially amongst women; beauty, on the contrary, is met with more frequently in man, and we need not go far without finding the reason. For grace we require the union of bodily structure, as well as that of character: the body, by its suppleness, by its promptitude to receive impressions and to bring them into action; the character, by the moral harmony of the sentiments. Upon these two points nature has been more favorable to the woman than to man.

The more delicate structure of the woman receives more rapidly each impression and allows it to escape as rapidly. It requires a storm to shake a strong constitution, and when vigorous muscles begin to move we should not find the ease which is one of the conditions of grace. That which upon the face of woman is still a beautiful sensation would express suffering already upon the face of man. Woman has the more tender nerves; it is a reed which bends under the gentlest breath of passion. The soul glides in soft and amiable ripples upon her expressive face, which soon regains the calm and smooth surface of the mirror.

The same also for the character: for that necessary union of the soul with grace the woman is more happily gifted than man. The character of woman rises rarely to the supreme ideal of moral purity, and would rarely go beyond acts of affection; her character would often resist sensuousness with heroic force. Precisely because the moral nature of woman is generally on the side of inclination, the effect becomes the same, in that which touches the sensuous expression of this moral state, as if the inclination were on the side of duty. Thus grace would be the expression of feminine virtue, and this expression would often be wanting in manly virtue.

ON DIGNITY.

As grace is the expression of a noble soul, so is dignity the expression of elevated feeling.

It has been prescribed to man, it is true, to establish between his two natures a unison, to form always an harmonious whole, and to act as in union with his entire humanity. But this beauty of character, this last fruit of human maturity, is but an ideal to which he ought to force his conformity with a constant vigilance, but to which, with all his efforts, he can never attain.

He cannot attain to it because his nature is thus made and it will not change; the physical conditions of his existence themselves are opposed to it.

In fact, his existence, so far as he is a sensuous creature, depends on certain physical conditions; and in order to insure this existence man ought—because, in his quality of a free being, capable of determining his modifications by his own will—to watch over his own preservation himself. Man ought to be made capable of certain acts in order to fulfil these physical conditions of his existence, and when these conditions are out of order to re-establish them.

But although nature had to give up to him this care which she reserves exclusively to herself in those creatures which have only a vegetative life, still it was necessary that the satisfaction of so essential a want, in which even the existence of the individual and of the species is interested, should not be absolutely left to the discretion of man, and his doubtful foresight. It has then provided for this interest, which in the foundation concerns it, and it has also interfered with regard to the form in placing in the determination of free arbitration a principle of necessity. From that arises natural instinct, which is nothing else than a principle of physical necessity which acts upon free arbitration by the means of sensation.

The natural instinct solicits the sensuous faculty through the combined force of pain and of pleasure: by pain when it asks satisfaction, and by pleasure when it has found what it asks.

As there is no bargaining possible with physical necessity, man must also, in spite of his liberty, feel what nature desires him to feel. According as it awakens in him a painful or an agreeable sensation, there will infallibly result in him either aversion or desire. Upon this point man quite resembles the brute; and the stoic, whatever his power of soul, is not less sensible of hunger, and has no less aversion to it, than the worm that crawls at his feet.

But here begins the great difference: with the lower creature action succeeds to desire or aversion quite as of necessity, as the desire to the sensation, and the expression to the external impression. It is here a perpetual circle, a chain, the links of which necessarily join one to the other. With man there is one more force—the will, which, as a super-sensuous faculty, is not so subject to the law of nature, nor that of reason, that he remains without freedom to choose, and to guide himself according to this or to that. The animal cannot do otherwise than seek to free itself from pain; man can decide to suffer.

The will of man is a privilege, a sublime idea, even when we do not consider the moral use that he can make of it. But firstly, the animal nature must be in abeyance before approaching the other, and from that cause it is always a considerable step towards reaching the moral emancipation of the will to have conquered in us the necessity of nature, even in indifferent things, by the exercise in us of the simple will.

The jurisdiction of nature extends as far as the will, but there it stops, and the empire of reason commences. Placed between these two jurisdictions, the will is absolutely free to receive the law from one and the other; but it is not in the same relation with one and the other. Inasmuch as it is a natural force it is equally free with regard to nature and with respect to reason; I mean to say it is not forced to pass either on the side of one or of the other: but as far as it is a moral faculty it is not free; I mean that it ought to choose the law of reason. It is not chained to one or the other, but it is obliged towards the law of reason. The will really then makes use of its liberty even whilst it acts contrary to reason: but it makes use of it unworthily, because, notwithstanding its liberty, it is no less under the jurisdiction of nature, and adds no real action to the operation of pure instinct; for to will by virtue of desire is only to desire in a different way.

There may be conflict between the law of nature, which works in us through the instinct, and the law of reason, which comes out of principles, when the instinct, to satisfy itself, demands of us an action which disgusts our moral sense. It is, then, the duty of the will to make the exigencies of the instinct give way to reason. Whilst the laws of nature oblige the will only conditionally, the laws of reason oblige absolutely and without conditions.

But nature obstinately maintains her rights, and as it is never by the result of free choice that she solicits us, she also does not withdraw any of her exigencies as long as she has not been satisfied. Since, from the first cause which gave the impulsion to the threshold of the will where its jurisdiction ends, all in her is rigorously necessary, consequently she can neither give way nor go back, but must always go forward and press more and more the will on which depends the satisfaction of her wants. Sometimes, it is true, we could say that nature shortens her road and acts immediately as a cause for the satisfaction of her needs without having in the first instance carried her request before the will. In such a case, that is to say, if man not simply allowed instinct to follow a free course, but if instinct took this course of itself, man would be no more than the brute. But it is very doubtful whether this case would ever present itself, and if ever it were really presented it would remain to be seen whether we should not blame the will itself for this blind power which the instinct would have usurped.

Thus the appetitive faculty claims with persistence the satisfaction of its wants, and the will is solicited to procure it; but the will should receive from the reason the motives by which she determines. What does the reason permit? What does she prescribe? This is what the will should decide upon. Well, then, if the will turns towards the reason before consenting to the request of the instinct, it is properly a moral act; but if it immediately decides, without consulting the reason, it is a physical act.

Every time, then, that nature manifests an exigence and seeks to draw the will along with it by the blind violence of affective movement, it is the duty of the will to order nature to halt until reason has pronounced. The sentence which reason pronounces, will it be favorable or the contrary to the interest of sensuousness? This is, up to the present time, what the will does not know. Also it should observe this conduct for all the affective movements without exception, and when it is nature which has spoken the first, never allow it to act as an immediate cause. Man would testify only by that to his independence. It is when, by an act of his will, he breaks the violence of his desires, which hasten towards the object which should satisfy them, and would dispense entirely with the co-operation of the will,—it is only then that he reveals himself in quality of a moral being, that is to say, as a free agent, which does not only allow itself to experience either aversion or desire, but which at all times must will his aversions and his desires.

But this act of taking previously the advice of reason is already an attempt against nature, who is a competent judge in her own cause, and who will not allow her sentences to be submitted to a new and strange jurisdiction; this act of the will which thus brings the appetitive faculty before the tribunal of reason is then, in the proper acceptation of the word, an act against nature, in that it renders accidental that which is necessary, in that it attributes to the laws of reason the right to decide in a cause where the laws of nature can alone pronounce, and where they have pronounced effectively. Just, in fact, as the reason in the exercise of its moral jurisdiction is little troubled to know if the decisions it can come to will satisfy or not the sensuous nature, so the sensuous in the exercise of the right which is proper to it does not trouble itself whether its decisions would satisfy pure reason or not. Each is equally necessary, though different in necessity, and this character of necessity would be destroyed if it were permitted for one to modify arbitrarily the decisions of the other. This is why the man who has the most moral energy cannot, whatever resistance he opposes to instinct, free himself from sensuousness, or stifle desire, but can only deny it an influence upon the decisions of his will; he can disarm instinct by moral means, but he cannot appease it but by natural means. By his independent force he may prevent the laws of nature from exercising any constraint over his will, but he can absolutely change nothing of the laws themselves.

Thus in the affective movements in which nature (instinct) acts the first and seeks to do without the will, or to draw it violently to its side, the morality of character cannot manifest itself but by its resistance, and there is but one means of preventing the instinct from restraining the liberty of the will: it is to restrain the instinct itself. Thus we can only have agreement between the law of reason and the affective phenomena, under the condition of putting both in discord with the exigencies of instinct. And as nature never gives way to moral reasons, and recalls her claims, and as on her side, consequently, all remains in the same state, in whatever manner the will acts towards her, it results that there is no possible accord between the inclination and duty, between reason and sense; and that here man cannot act at the same time with all his being and with all the harmony of his nature, but exclusively with his reasonable nature. Thus in these sorts of actions we could not find moral beauty, because an action is morally good only as far as inclination has taken part in it, and here the inclination protests against much more than it concurs with it. But these actions have moral grandeur, because all that testifies to a preponderating authority exercised over the sensuous nature has grandeur, and grandeur is found only there.

It is, then, in the affective movements that this great soul of which we speak transforms itself and becomes sublime; and it is the touchstone to distinguish the soul truly great from what is called a good heart, or from the virtue of temperament. When in man the inclination is ranged on the side of morality only because morality itself is happily on the side of inclination, it will happen that the instinct of nature in the affective movements will exercise upon the will a full empire, and if a sacrifice is necessary it is the moral nature, and not the sensuous nature, that will make it. If, on the contrary, it is reason itself which has made the inclination pass to the side of duty (which is the case in the fine character), and which has only confided the rudder to the sensuous nature, it will be always able to retake it as soon as the instinct should misuse its full powers. Thus the virtue of temperament in the affective movements falls back to the state of simple production of nature, whilst the noble soul passes to heroism and rises to the rank of pure intelligence.

The rule over the instincts by moral force is the emancipation of mind, and the expression by which this independence presents itself to the eyes in the world of phenomena is what is called dignity.

To consider this rigorously: the moral force in man is susceptible of no representation, for the super-sensuous could not explain itself by a phenomenon that falls under the sense; but it can be represented indirectly to the mind by sensuous signs, and this is actually the case with dignity in the configuration of man.

When the instinct of nature is excited, it is accompanied just as the heart in its moral emotions is, by certain movements of the body, which sometimes go before the will, sometimes, even as movements purely sympathetic, escape altogether its empire. In fact, as neither sensation, nor the desire, nor aversion, are subject to the free arbitration of man, man has no right over the physical movements which immediately depend on it. But the instinct does not confine itself to simple desire; it presses, it advances, it endeavors to realize its object; and if it does not meet in the autonomy of the mind an energetic resistance, it will even anticipate it, it will itself take the initiative of those sorts of acts over which the will alone has the right to pronounce. For the instinct of conservation tends without ceasing to usurp the legislative powers in the domain of the will, and its efforts go to exercise over man a domination as absolute as over the beast. There are, then, two sorts of distinct movements, which, in themselves and by their origin, in each affective phenomenon, arise in man by the instinct of conservation: those firstly which immediately proceed from sensation, and which, consequently, are quite involuntary; then those which in principle could and would be voluntary, but from which the blind instinct of nature takes all freedom. The first refer to the affection itself, and are united necessarily with it; the others respond rather to the cause and to the object of the affections, and are thus accidental and susceptible of modification, and cannot be mistaken for infallible signs of the affective phenomena. But as both one and the other, when once the object is determined, are equally necessary to the instinct of nature, so they assist, both one and the other, the expression of affective phenomena; a necessary competition, in order that the expression should be complete and form a harmonious whole.

If, then, the will is sufficiently independent to repress the aggressions of instinct and to maintain its rights against this blind force, all the phenomena which the instinct of nature, once excited, produce, in its proper domain, will preserve, it is true, their force; but those of the second kind, those which came out of a foreign jurisdiction, and which it pretended to subject arbitrarily to its power, these phenomena would not take place. Thus the phenomena are no longer in harmony; but it is precisely in their opposition that consists the expression of the moral force. Suppose that we see a man a prey to the most poignant affection, manifested by movements of the first kind, by quite involuntary movements. His veins swell, his muscles contract convulsively, his voice is stifled, his chest is raised and projects, whilst the lower portion of the torso is sunken and compressed; but at the same time the voluntary movements are soft, the features of the face free, and serenity beams forth from the brow and in the look. If man were only a physical being, all his traits, being determined only by one and the same principle, would be in unison one with the other, and would have a similar expression. Here, for example, they would unite in expressing exclusively suffering; but as those traits which express calmness are mixed up with those which express suffering, and as similar causes do not produce opposite effects, we must recognize in this contrast the presence and the action of a moral force, independent of the passive affections, and superior to the impressions beneath which we see sensuous nature give way. And this is why calmness under suffering, in which properly consists dignity, becomes—indirectly, it is true, and by means of reasoning—a representation of the pure intelligence which is in man, and an expression of his moral liberty. But it is not only under suffering, in the restricted sense of the word, in the sense in which it marks only the painful affections, but generally in all the cases in which the appetitive faculty is strongly interested, that mind ought to show its liberty, and that dignity ought to be the dominant expression. Dignity is not less required in the agreeable affections than in the painful affections, because in both cases nature would willingly play the part of master, and has to be held in check by the will. Dignity relates to the form and not to the nature of the affection, and this is why it can be possible that often an affection, praiseworthy in the main, but one to which we blindly commit ourselves, degenerates, from the want of dignity, into vulgarity and baseness; and, on the contrary, a condemnable affection, as soon as it testifies by its form to the empire of the mind over the senses, changes often its character and approaches even towards the sublime.

Thus in dignity the mind reigns over the body and bears itself as ruler: here it has its independence to defend against imperious impulse, always ready to do without it, to act and shake off its yoke. But in grace, on the contrary, the mind governs with a liberal government, for here the mind itself causes sensuous nature to act, and it finds no resistance to overcome. But obedience only merits forbearance, and severity is only justifiable when provoked by opposition.

Thus grace is nothing else than the liberty of voluntary movements, and dignity consists in mastering involuntary movements. Grace leaves to sensuous nature, where it obeys the orders of the mind, a certain air of independence; dignity, on the contrary, submits the sensuous nature to mind where it would make the pretensions to rule; wherever instinct takes the initiative and allows itself to trespass upon the attributes of the will, the will must show it no indulgence, but it must testify to its own independence (autonomy), in opposing to it the most energetic resistance. If, on the contrary, it is the will that commences, and if instinct does but follow it, the free arbitration has no longer to display any rigor, now it must show indulgence. Such is in a few words the law which ought to regulate the relation of the two natures of man in what regards the expression of this relation in the world of phenomena.

It follows that dignity is required, and is seen particularly in passive affection, whilst grace is shown in the conduct, for it is only in suffering that the liberty of the soul can be manifested, and only in action that the liberty of the body can be displayed.

If dignity is an expression of resistance opposed to instinct by moral liberty, and if the instinct consequently ought to be considered as a force that renders resistance necessary, it follows that dignity is ridiculous where you have no force of this kind to resist, and contemptible where there ought not to be any such force to combat. We laugh at a comedian, whatever rank or condition he may occupy, who even in indifferent actions affects dignity. We despise those small souls who, for having accomplished an ordinary action, and often for having simply abstained from a base one, plume themselves on their dignity.

Generally, what is demanded of virtue is not properly speaking dignity, but grace. Dignity is implicitly contained in the idea of virtue, which even by its nature supposes already the rule of man over his instincts. It is rather sensuous nature that, in the fulfilment of moral duties, is found in a state of oppression and constraint, particularly when it consummates in a painful sacrifice. But as the ideal of perfection in man does not require a struggle, but harmony between the moral and physical nature, this ideal is little compatible with dignity, which is only the expression of a struggle between the two natures, and as such renders visible either the particular impotence of the individual, or the impotence common to the species. In the first case, when the want of harmony between inclination and duty, with regard to a moral act, belongs to the particular powerlessness of the subject, the act would always lose its moral value, in as far as that combat is necessary, and, in consequence, proportionally as there would be dignity in the exterior expression of this act; for our moral judgment connects each individual with the common measure of the species, and we do not allow man to be stopped by other limits than those of human nature.

In the second case, when the action commanded by duty cannot be placed in harmony with the exigencies of instinct without going against the idea of human nature, the resistance of the inclination is necessary, and then only the sight of the combat can convince us of the possibility of victory. Thus we ask here of the features and attitudes an expression of this interior struggle, not being able to take upon ourselves to believe in virtue where there is no trace of humanity. Where then the moral law commands of us an action which necessarily makes the sensuous nature suffer, there the matter is serious, and ought not to be treated as play; ease and lightness in accomplishing this act would be much more likely to revolt us than to satisfy us; and thus, in consequence, expression is no longer grace, but dignity. In general, the law which prevails here is, that man ought to accomplish with grace all the acts that he can execute in the sphere of human nature; and with dignity all those for the accomplishment of which he is obliged to go beyond his nature.

In like manner as we ask of virtue to have grace, we ask of inclination to have dignity. Grace is not less natural to inclination than dignity to virtue, and that is evident from the idea of grace, which is all sensuous and favorable to the liberty of physical nature, and which is repugnant to all idea of constraint. The man without cultivation lacks not by himself a certain degree of grace, when love or any other affection of this kind animates him; and where do we find more grace than in children, who are nevertheless entirely under the direction of instinct. The danger is rather that inclination should end by making the state of passion the dominant one, stifling the independence of mind, and bringing about a general relaxation. Therefore in order to conciliate the esteem of a noble sentiment—esteem can only be inspired by that which proceeds from a moral source—the inclination must always be accompanied by dignity. It is for that reason a person in love desires to find dignity in the object of this passion. Dignity alone is the warrant that it is not need which has forced, but free choice which has chosen, that he is not desired as a thing, but esteemed as a person.

We require grace of him who obliges, dignity of the person obliged: the first, to set aside an advantage which he has over the other, and which might wound, ought to give to his actions, though his decision may have been disinterested, the character of an affective movement, that thus, from the part which he allows inclination to take, he may have the appearance of being the one who gains the most: the second, not to compromise by the dependence in which he put himself the honor of humanity, of which liberty is the saintly palladium, ought to raise what is only a pure movement of instinct to the height of an act of the will, and in this manner, at the moment when he receives a favor, return in a certain sense another favor.

We must censure with grace, and own our faults with dignity: to put dignity into our remonstrances is to have the air of a man too penetrated by his own advantage: to put grace into our confessions is to forget the inferiority in which our fault has placed us. Do the powerful desire to conciliate affection? Their superiority must be tempered by grace. The feeble, do they desire to conciliate esteem? They must through dignity rise above their powerlessness. Generally it is thought that dignity is suitable to the throne, and every one knows that those seated upon it desire to find in their councillors, their confessors, and in their parliaments—grace. But that which may be good and praiseworthy in a kingdom is not so always in the domain of taste. The prince himself enters into this domain as soon as he descends from his throne (for thrones have their privileges), and the crouching courtier places himself under the saintly and free probation of this law as soon as he stands erect and becomes again a man. The first we would counsel to supplement from the superfluity of the second that which he himself needs, and to give him as much of his dignity as he requires to borrow grace from him.

Although dignity and grace have each their proper domain in which they are manifest, they do not exclude each other. They can be met with in the same person, and even in the same state of that person. Further, it is grace alone which guarantees and accredits dignity, and dignity alone can give value to grace.

Dignity alone, wherever met with, testifies that the desires and inclinations are restrained within certain limits. But what we take for a force which moderates and rules, may it not be rather an obliteration of the faculty of feeling (hardness)? Is it really the moral autonomy, and may it not be rather the preponderance of another affection, and in consequence a voluntary interested effort that restrains the outburst of the present affection? This is what grace alone can put out of doubt in joining itself to dignity. It is grace, I mean to say, that testifies to a peaceful soul in harmony with itself and a feeling heart.

In like manner grace by itself shows a certain susceptibility of the feeling faculty, and a certain harmony of sentiment. But may this not be a certain relaxation of the mind which allows so much liberty to sensuous nature and which opens the heart to all impressions? Is it indeed the moral which has established this harmony between the sentiments? It is dignity alone which can in its turn guarantee this to us in joining itself to grace; I mean it is dignity alone which attests in the subject an independent force, and at the moment when the will represses the license of involuntary movement, it is by dignity that it makes known that the liberty of voluntary movements is a simple concession on its part.

If grace and dignity, still supported, the one by architectonic beauty and the other by force, were united in the same person, the expression of human nature would be accomplished in him: such a person would be justified in the spiritual world and set at liberty in the sensuous world. Here the two domains touch so closely that their limits are indistinguishable. The smile that plays on the lips; this sweetly animated look; that serenity spread over the brow—it is the liberty of the reason which gleams forth in a softened light. This noble majesty impressed on the face is the sublime adieu of the necessity of nature, which disappears before the mind. Such is the ideal of human beauty according to which the antique conceptions were formed, and we see it in the divine forms of a Niobe, of the Apollo Belvedere, in the winged Genius of the Borghese, and in the Muse of the Barberini palace. There, where grace and dignity are united, we experience by turns attraction and repulsion; attraction as spiritual creatures, and repulsion as being sensuous creatures.

Dignity offers to us an example of subordination of sensuous nature to moral nature—an example which we are bound to imitate, but which at the same time goes beyond the measure of our sensuous faculty. This opposition between the instincts of nature and the exigencies of the moral law, exigencies, however, that we recognize as legitimate, brings our feelings into play and awakens a sentiment that we name esteem, which is inseparable from dignity.

With grace, on the contrary, as with beauty in general, reason finds its demands satisfied in the world of sense, and sees with surprise one of its own ideas presented to it, realized in the world of phenomena. This unexpected encounter between the accident of nature and the necessity of reason awakens in us a sentiment of joyous approval (contentment) which calms the senses, but which animates and occupies the mind, and it results necessarily that we are attracted by a charm towards the sensuous object. It is this attraction which we call kindliness, or love—a sentiment inseparable from grace and beauty.

The attraction—I mean the attraction (stimulus) not of love but of voluptuousness—proposes to the senses a sensuous object that promises to these the satisfaction of a want, that is to say a pleasure; the senses are consequently solicited towards this sensuous object, and from that springs desire, a sentiment which increases and excites the sensuous nature, but which, on the contrary, relaxes the spiritual nature.

We can say of esteem that it inclines towards its object; of love, that it approaches with inclination towards its object; of desire, that it precipitates itself upon its object; with esteem, the object is reason, and the subject is sensuous nature; with love, the object is sensuous, and the subject is moral nature; with desire, the object and the subject are purely sensuous.

With love alone is sentiment free, because it is pure in its principle, and because it draws its source from the seat of liberty, from the breast of our divine nature. Here, it is not the weak and base part of our nature that measures itself with the greater and more noble part; it is not the sensibility, a prey to vertigo, which gazes up at the law of reason. It is absolute greatness which is reflected in beauty and in grace, and satisfied in morality; it becomes the legislator even, the god in us who plays with his own image in the world of sense. Thus love consoles and dilates the heart, whilst esteem strains it; because here there is nothing which could limit the heart and compress its impulses, there being nothing higher than absolute greatness; and sensibility, from which alone hinderance could come, is reconciled, in the breast of beauty and of grace, with the ideas even of the mind. Love has but to descend; esteem aspires with effort towards an object placed above it. This is the reason that the wicked love nothing, though they are obliged to esteem many things. This is why the well-disposed man can hardly esteem without at once feeling love for the object. Pure spirit can only love, but not esteem; the senses know only esteem, but not love.

The culpable man is perpetually a prey to fear, that he may meet in the world of sense the legislator within himself; and sees an enemy in all that bears the stamp of greatness, of beauty, and of perfection: the man, on the contrary, in whom a noble soul breathes, knows no greater pleasure than to meet out of himself the image or realization of the divine that is in him; and to embrace in the world of sense a symbol of the immortal friend he loves. Love is at the same time the most generous and the most egotistical thing in nature; the most generous, because it receives nothing and gives all—pure mind being only able to give and not receive; the most egotistical, for that which he seeks in the subject, that which he enjoys in it, is himself and never anything else.

But precisely because he who loves receives from the beloved object nothing but that which he has himself given, it often happens that he gives more than he has received.

The exterior senses believe to have discovered in the object that which the internal sense alone contemplates in it, in the end believing what is desired with ardor, and the riches belonging to the one who loves hide the poverty of the object loved. This is the reason why love is subject to illusion, whilst esteem and desire are never deceived. As long as the super-excitement of the internal senses overcomes the internal senses, the soul remains under the charm of this Platonic love, which gives place only in duration to the delights enjoyed by the immortals. But as soon as internal sense ceases to share its visions with the exterior sense, these take possession of their rights and imperiously demand that which is its due—matter. It is the terrestrial Venus who profits by the fire kindled by the celestial Venus, and it is not rare to find the physical instinct, so long sacrificed, revenge itself by a rule all the more absolute. As external sense is never a dupe to illusion, it makes this advantage felt with a brutal insolence over its noble rival; and it possesses audacity to the point of asserting that it has settled an account that the spiritual nature had left under sufferance.

Dignity prevents love from degenerating into desire, and grace, from esteem turning into fear. True beauty, true grace, ought never to cause desire. Where desire is mingled, either the object wants dignity, or he who considers it wants morality in his sentiments. True greatness ought never to cause fear. If fear finds a place, you may hold for certain either that the object is wanting in taste and grace, or that he who considers it is not at peace with his conscience.

Attraction, charm, grace: words commonly employed as synonyms, but which are not, or ought not to be so, the idea they express being capable of many determinations, requiring different designations.

There is a kind of grace which animates, and another which calms the heart. One touches nearly the sphere of the senses, and the pleasure which is found in these, if not restrained by dignity, would easily degenerate into concupiscence; we may use the word attraction [Reiz] to designate this grace. A man with whom the feelings have little elasticity does not find in himself the necessary force to awaken his affections: he needs to borrow it from without and to seek from impressions which easily exercise the phantasy, by rapid transition from sentiment to action, in order to establish in himself the elasticity he had lost. It is the advantage that he will find in the society of an attractive person, who by conversation and look would stir his imagination and agitate this stagnant water.

The calming grace approaches more nearly to dignity, inasmuch as it manifests itself through the moderation which it imposes upon the impetuosity of the movements. It is to this the man addresses himself whose imagination is over-excited; it is in this peaceful atmosphere that the heart seeks repose after the violence of the storm. It is to this that I reserve especially the appellation of grace. Attraction is not incompatible with laughter, jest, or the sting of raillery; grace agrees only with sympathy and love.

Dignity has also its degrees and its shades. If it approaches grace and beauty, it takes the name of nobleness; if, on the contrary, it inclines towards the side of fear, it becomes haughtiness.

The utmost degree of grace is ravishing charm. Dignity, in its highest form, is called majesty. In the ravishing we love our Ego, and we feel our being fused with the object. Liberty in its plenitude and in its highest enjoyment tends to the complete destruction of liberty, and the excitement of the mind to the delirium of the voluptuousness of the senses. Majesty, on the contrary, proposes to us a law, a moral ideal, which constrains us to turn back our looks upon ourselves. God is there, and the sentiment we have of His presence makes us bend our eyes upon the ground. We forget all that is without ourselves, and we feel but the heavy burden of our own existence.

Majesty belongs to what is holy. A man capable of giving us an idea of holiness possesses majesty, and if we do not go so far as to kneel, our mind at least prostrates itself before him. But the mind recoils at once upon the slightest trace of human imperfection which he discovers in the object of his adoration, because that which is only comparatively great cannot subdue the heart.

Power alone, however terrible or without limit we may suppose it to be, can never confer majesty. Power imposes only upon the sensuous being; majesty should act upon the mind itself, and rob it of its liberty. A man who can pronounce upon me a sentence of death has neither more nor less of majesty for me the moment I am what I ought to be. His advantage over me ceases as soon as I insist on it. But he who offers to me in his person the image of pure will, before him I would prostrate myself, if it is possible, for all eternity.

Grace and dignity are too high in value for vanity and stupidity not to be excited to appropriate them by imitation. There is only one means of attaining this: it is to imitate the moral state of which they are the expression. All other imitation is but to ape them, and would be recognized directly through exaggeration.

Just as exaggeration of the sublime leads to inflation, and affectation of nobleness to preciosity, in the same manner affectation of grace ends in coquetry, and that of dignity to stiff solemnity, false gravity.

There where true grace simply used ease and provenance, affected grace becomes effeminacy. One is content to use discreetly the voluntary movements, and not thwart unnecessarily the liberty of nature; the other has not even the heart to use properly the organs of will, and, not to fall into hardness and heaviness, it prefers to sacrifice something of the aim of movement, or else it seeks to reach it by cross ways and indirect means. An awkward and stiff dancer expends as much force as if he had to work a windmill; with his feet and arms he describes lines as angular as if he were tracing figures with geometrical precision; the affected dancer, on the other hand, glides with an excess of delicacy, as if he feared to injure himself on coming in contact with the ground, and his feet and hands describe only lines in sinuous curves. The other sex, which is essentially in possession of true grace, is also that one which is more frequently culpable of affected grace, but this affectation is never more distasteful than when used as a bait to desire. The smile of true grace thus gives place to the most repulsive grimace; the fine play of look, so ravishing when it displays a true sentiment, is only contortion; the melodious inflections of the voice, an irresistible attraction from candid lips, are only a vain cadence, a tremulousness which savors of study: in a word, all the harmonious charms of woman become only deception, an artifice of the toilet.

If we have many occasions to observe the affected grace in the theatre and in the ball-room, there is also often occasion of studying the affected dignity in the cabinet of ministers and in the study-rooms of men of science (notably at universities). True dignity is content to prevent the domination of the affections, to keep the instinct within just limits, but there only where it pretends to be master in the involuntary movements; false dignity regulates with an iron sceptre even the voluntary movements, it oppresses the moral movements, which were sacred to true dignity, as well as the sensual movements, and destroys all the mimic play of the features by which the soul gleams forth upon the face. It arms itself not only against rebel nature, but against submissive nature, and ridiculously seeks its greatness in subjecting nature to its yoke, or, if this does not succeed, in hiding it. As if it had vowed hatred to all that is called nature, it swathes the body in long, heavy-plaited garments, which hide the human structure; it paralyzes the limbs in surcharging them with vain ornaments, and goes even the length of cutting the hair to replace this gift of nature by an artificial production. True dignity does not blush for nature, but only for brute nature; it always has an open and frank air; feeling gleams in its look; calm and serenity of mind is legible upon the brow in eloquent traits. False gravity, on the contrary, places its dignity in the lines of its visage; it is close, mysterious, and guards its features with the care of an actor; all the muscles of its face are tormented, all natural and true expression disappears, and the entire man is like a sealed letter.

But false dignity is not always wrong to keep the mimic play of its features under sharp discipline, because it might betray more than would be desired, a precaution true dignity has not to consider. True dignity wishes only to rule, not to conceal nature; in false dignity, on the contrary, nature rules the more powerfully within because it is controlled outwardly. [Art can make use of a proper solemnity. Its object is only to prepare the mind for something important. When the poet is anxious to produce a great impression he tunes the mind to receive it.]

ON THE NECESSARY LIMITATIONS IN THE USE OF BEAUTY OF FORM.

The abuse of the beautiful and the encroachments of imagination, when, having only the casting vote, it seeks to grasp the law-giving sceptre, has done great injury alike in life and in science. It is therefore highly expedient to examine very closely the bounds that have been assigned to the use of beautiful forms. These limits are embodied in the very nature of the beautiful, and we have only to call to mind how taste expresses its influence to be able to determine how far it ought to extend it.

The following are the principal operations of taste; to bring the sensuous and spiritual powers of man into harmony, and to unite them in a close alliance. Consequently, whenever such an intimate alliance between reason and the senses is suitable and legitimate, taste may be allowed influence. But taste reaches the bounds which it is not permitted to pass without defeating its end or removing us from our duty, in all cases where the bond between mind and matter is given up for a time, where we must act for the time as purely creatures of reason, whether it be to attain an end or to perform a duty. Cases of this kind do really occur, and they are even incumbent on us in carrying out our destiny.

For we are destined to obtain knowledge and to act from knowledge. In both cases a certain readiness is required to exclude the senses from that which the spirit does, because feelings must be abstracted from knowledge, and passion or desire from every moral act of the will.

When we know, we take up an active attitude, and our attention is directed to an object, to a relation between different representations. When we feel, we have a passive attitude, and our attention—if we may call that so, which is no conscious operation of the mind—is only directed to our own condition, as far as it is modified by the impression received. Now, as we only feel and do not know the beautiful, we do not distinguish any relation between it and other objects, we do not refer its representation to other representations, but to ourselves who have experienced the impression. We learn or experience nothing in the beautiful object, but we perceive a change occasioned by it in our own condition, of which the impression produced is the expression. Accordingly our knowledge is not enlarged by judgments of taste, and no knowledge, not even that of beauty, is obtained by the feeling of beauty. Therefore, when knowledge is the object, taste can give us no help, at least directly and immediately; on the contrary, knowledge is shut out as long as we are occupied with beauty.

But it may be objected, What is the use then of a graceful embodiment of conceptions, if the object of the discussion or treatise, which is simply and solely to produce knowledge, is rather hindered than benefited by ornament? To convince the understanding this gracefulness of clothing can certainly avail as little as the tasteful arrangement of a banquet can satisfy the appetite of the guests, or the outward elegance of a person can give a clue to his intrinsic worth. But just as the appetite is excited by the beautiful arrangement of the table, and attention is directed to the elegant person in question, by the attractiveness of the exterior, so also we are placed in a favorable attitude to receive truth by the charming representation given of it; we are led to open our souls to its reception, and the obstacles are removed from our minds which would have otherwise opposed the difficult pursuit of a long and strict concatenation of thought. It is never the contents, the substance, that gains by the beauty of form; nor is it the understanding that is helped by taste in the act of knowing. The substance, the contents, must commend themselves to the understanding directly, of themselves; whilst the beautiful form speaks to the imagination, and flatters it with an appearance of freedom.

But even further limitations are necessary in this innocent subserviency to the senses, which is only allowed in the form, without changing anything in the substance. Great moderation must be always used, and sometimes the end in view may be completely defeated according to the kind of knowledge and degree of conviction aimed at in imparting our views to others. There is a scientific knowledge, which is based on clear conceptions and known principles; and a popular knowledge, which is founded on feelings more or less developed. What may be very useful to the latter is quite possibly adverse to the former.

When the object in view is to produce a strict conviction on principles, it is not sufficient to present the truth only in respect to its contents or subject; the test of the truth must at the same time be contained in the manner of its presentation. But this can mean nothing else than that not only the contents, but also the mode of stating them, must be according to the laws of thought. They must be connected in the presentation with the same strict logical sequence with which they are chained together in the seasonings of the understanding; the stability of the representation must guarantee that of the ideas. But the strict necessity with which the understanding links together reasonings and conclusions, is quite antagonistic to the freedom granted to imagination in matters of knowledge. By its very nature, the imagination strives after perceptions, that is, after complete and completely determinate representations, and is indefatigably active to represent the universal in one single case, to limit it in time and space, to make of every conception an individual, and to give a body to abstractions. Moreover, the imagination likes freedom in its combinations, and admits no other law in them than the accidental connection with time and space; for this is the only connection that remains to our representations, if we separate from them in thought all that is conception, all that binds them internally and substantially together. The understanding, following a diametrically opposite course, only occupies itself with part representations or conceptions, and its effort is directed to distinguish features in the living unity of a perception. The understanding proceeds on the same principles in putting together and taking to pieces, but it can only combine things by part-representations, just as it can separate them; for it only unites, according to their inner relations, things that first disclosed themselves in their separation.

The understanding observes a strict necessity and conformity with laws in its combinations, and it is only the consistent connection of ideas that satisfies it. But this connection is destroyed as often as the imagination insinuates entire representations (individual cases) in this chain of abstractions, and mixes up the accidents of time with the strict necessity of a chain of circumstances. Accordingly, in every case where it is essential to carry out a rigidly accurate sequence of reasoning, imagination must forego its capricious character; and its endeavor to obtain all possible sensuousness in conceptions, and all freedom in their combination, must be made subordinate and sacrificed to the necessity of the understanding. From this it follows that the exposition must be so fashioned as to overthrow this effort of the imagination by the exclusion of all that is individual and sensuous. The poetic impulse of imagination must be curbed by distinctness of expression, and its capricious tendency to combine must be limited by a strictly legitimate course of procedure. I grant that it will not bend to this yoke without resistance; but in this matter reliance is properly placed on a certain amount of self-denial, and on an earnest determination of the hearer or reader not to be deterred by the difficulties accompanying the form, for the sake of the subject-matter. But in all cases where no sufficient dependence can be placed on this self-denial, or where the interest felt in the subject-matter is insufficient to inspire courage for such an amount of exertion, it is necessary to resign the idea of imparting strictly scientific knowledge; and to gain instead greater latitude in the form of its presentation. In such a case it is expedient to abandon the form of science, which exercises too great violence over the imagination, and can only be made acceptable through the importance of the object in view. Instead of this, it is proper to choose the form of beauty, which, independent of the contents or subject, recommends itself by its very appearance. As the matter cannot excuse the form in this case, the form must trespass on the matter.

Popular instruction is compatible with this freedom. By the term popular speakers or popular writers I imply all those who do not direct their remarks exclusively to the learned. Now, as these persons do not address any carefully trained body of hearers or readers, but take them as they find them, they must only assume the existence of the general conditions of thought, only the universal impulses that call attention, but no special gift of thinking, no acquaintance with distinct conceptions, nor any interest in special subjects. These lecturers and authors must not be too particular as to whether their audience or readers assign by their imagination a proper meaning to their abstractions, or whether they will furnish a proper subject-matter for the universal conceptions to which the scientific discourse is limited. In order to pursue a safer, easier course, these persons will present along with their ideas the perceptions and separate cases to which they relate, and they leave it to the understanding of the reader to form a proper conception impromptu. Accordingly, the faculty of imagination is much more mixed up with a popular discourse, but only to reproduce, to renew previously received representations, and not to produce, to express its own self-creating power. Those special cases or perceptions are much too certainly calculated for the object on hand, and much too closely applied to the use that is to be made of them, to allow the imagination ever to forget that it only acts in the service of the understanding. It is true that a discourse of this popular kind holds somewhat closer to life and the world of sense, but it does not become lost in it. The mode of presenting the subject is still didactic; for in order to be beautiful it is still wanting in the two most distinguished features of beauty, sensuousness of expression and freedom of movement.

The mode of presenting a theme may be called free when the understanding, while determining the connection of ideas, does so with so little prominence that the imagination appears to act quite capriciously in the matter, and to follow only the accident of time. The presentation of a subject becomes sensuous when it conceals the general in the particular, and when the fancy gives the living image (the whole representation), where attention is merely concerned with the conception (the part representation). Accordingly, sensuous presentation is, viewed in one aspect, rich, for in cases where only one condition is desired, a complete picture, an entirety of conditions, an individual is offered. But viewed in another aspect it is limited and poor, because it only confines to a single individual and a single case what ought to be understood of a whole sphere. It therefore curtails the understanding in the same proportion that it grants preponderance to the imagination; for the completer a representation is in substance, the smaller it is in compass.

It is the interest of the imagination to change objects according to its caprice; the interest of the understanding is to unite its representations with strict logical necessity.

To satisfy the imagination, a discourse must have a material part, a body; and these are formed by the perceptions, from which the understanding separates distinct features or conceptions. For though we may attempt to obtain the highest pitch of abstraction, something sensuous always lies at the ground of the thought. But imagination strives to pass unfettered and lawless from one conception to another conception, and seeks not to be bound by any other connection than that of time. So when the perceptions that constitute the bodily part of a discourse have no concatenation as things, when they appear rather to stand apart as independent limbs and separate unities, when they betray the utter disorder of a sportive imagination, obedient to itself alone, then the clothing has aesthetic freedom and the wants of the fancy are satisfied. A mode of presentation such as this might be styled an organic product, in which not only the whole lives, but also each part has its individual life. A merely scientific presentation is a mechanical work, when the parts, lifeless in themselves, impart by their connection an artificial life to the whole.

On the other hand, a discourse, in order to satisfy the understanding and to produce knowledge, must have a spiritual part, it must have significance, and it receives this through the conceptions, by means of which those perceptions are referred to one another and united into a whole. The problem of satisfying the understanding by conformity with law, while the imagination is flattered by being set free from restrictions, is solved thus: by obtaining the closest connection between the conceptions forming the spiritual part of the discourse, while the perceptions, corresponding to them and forming the sensuous part of the discourse, appear to cohere merely through an arbitrary play of the fancy.

If an inquiry be instituted into the magic influence of a beautiful diction, it will always be found that it consists in this happy relation between external freedom and internal necessity. The principal features that contribute to this freedom of the imagination are the individualizing of objects and the figurative or inexact expression of a thing; the former employed to give force to its sensuousness, the latter to produce it where it does not exist. When we express a species or kind by an individual, and portray a conception in a single case, we remove from fancy the chains which the understanding has placed upon her and give her the power to act as a creator. Always grasping at completely determinate images, the imagination obtains and exercises the right to complete according to her wish the image afforded to her, to animate it, to fashion it, to follow it in all the associations and transformations of which it is capable. She may forget for a moment her subordinate position, and act as an independent power, only self-directing, because the strictness of the inner concatenation has sufficiently guarded against her breaking loose from the control of the understanding. An inexact or figurative expression adds to the liberty, by associating ideas which in their nature differ essentially from one another, but which unite in subordination to the higher idea. The imagination adheres to the concrete object, the understanding to this higher idea, and thus the former finds movement and variety even where the other verifies a most perfect continuity. The conceptions are developed according to the law of necessity, but they pass before the imagination according to the law of liberty.

Thought remains the same; the medium that represents it is the only thing that changes. It is thus that an eloquent writer knows how to extract the most splendid order from the very centre of anarchy, and that he succeeds in erecting a solid structure on a constantly moving ground, on the very torrent of imagination.

If we compare together scientific statement or address, popular address, and fine language, it is seen directly that all three express the idea with an equal faithfulness as regards the matter, and consequently that all three help us to acquire knowledge, but that as regards the mode and degree of this knowledge a very marked difference exists between them. The writer who uses the language of the beautiful rather represents the matter of which he treats as possible and desirable than indulges in attempts to convince us of its reality, and still less of its necessity. His thought does in fact only present itself as an arbitrary creation of the imagination, which is never qualified, in itself, to guarantee the reality of what it represents. No doubt the popular writer leads us to believe that the matter really is as he describes it, but does not require anything more firm; for, though he may make the truth of a proposition credible to our feelings, he does not make it absolutely certain. Now, feeling may always teach us what is, but not what must be. The philosophical writer raises this belief to a conviction, for he proves by undeniable reasons that the matter is necessarily so.

Starting from the principle that we have just established, it will not be difficult to assign its proper part and sphere to each of the three forms of diction. Generally it may be laid down as a rule that preference ought to be given to the scientific style whenever the chief consideration is not only the result, but also the proofs. But when the result merely is of the most essential importance the advantage must be given to popular elocution and fine language. But it may be asked in what cases ought popular elocution to rise to a fine, a noble style? This depends on the degree of interest in the reader, or which you wish to excite in his mind.

The purely scientific statement may incline either to popular discourse or to philosophic language, and according to this bias it places us more or less in possession of some branch of knowledge. All that popular elocution does is to lend us this knowledge for a momentary pleasure or enjoyment. The first, if I may be allowed the comparison, gives us a tree with its roots, though with the condition that we wait patiently for it to blossom and bear fruit. The other, or fine diction, is satisfied with gathering its flowers and fruits, but the tree that bore them does not become our property, and when once the flowers are faded and the fruit is consumed our riches depart. It would therefore be equally unreasonable to give only the flower and fruit to a man who wishes the whole tree to be transplanted into his garden, and to offer the whole tree with its fruit in the germ to a man who only looks for the ripe fruit. The application of the comparison is self-evident, and I now only remark that a fine ornate style is as little suited to the professor's chair as the scholastic style to a drawing-room, the pulpit, or the bar.

The student accumulates in view of an ulterior end and for a future use; accordingly the professor ought to endeavor to transmit the full and entire property of the knowledge that he communicates to him. Now, nothing belongs to us as our own but what has been communicated to the understanding. The orator, on the other hand, has in view an immediate end, and his voice must correspond with an immediate want of the public. His interest is to make his knowledge practically available as soon as possible; and the surest way is to hand it over to the senses, and to prepare it for the use of sensation. The professor, who only admits hearers on certain conditions, and who is entitled to suppose in his hearers the dispositions of mind in which a man ought to be to receive the truth, has only in view in his lecture the object of which he is treating; while the orator, who cannot make any conditions with his audience, and who needs above everything sympathy, to secure it on his side, must regulate his action and treatment according to the subjects on which he turns his discourse. The hearers of the professor have already attended his lectures, and will attend them again; they only want fragments that will form a whole after having been linked to the preceding lectures. The audience of the orator is continually renewed; it comes unprepared, and perhaps will not return; accordingly in every address the orator must finish what he wishes to do; each of his harangues must form a whole and contain expressly and entirely his conclusion.

It is not therefore surprising that a dogmatic composition or address, however solid, should not have any success either in conversation or in the pulpit, nor that a fine diction, whatever wit it may contain, should not bear fruit in a professor's chair. It is not surprising that the fashionable world should not read writings that stand out in relief in the scientific world, and that the scholar and the man of science are ignorant of works belonging to the school of worldly people that are devoured greedily by all lovers of the beautiful. Each of these works may be entitled to admiration in the circle to which it belongs; and more than this, both, fundamentally, may be quite of equal value; but it would be requiring an impossibility to expect that the work which demands all the application of the thinker should at the same time offer an easy recreation to the man who is only a fine wit.

For the same reason I consider that it is hurtful to choose for the instruction of youth books in which scientific matters are clothed in an attractive style. I do not speak here of those in which the substance is sacrificed to the form, but of certain writings really excellent, which are sufficiently well digested to stand the strictest examination, but which do not offer their proofs by their very form. No doubt books of this kind attain their end, they are read; but this is always at the cost of a more important end, the end for which they ought to be read. In this sort of reading the understanding is never exercised save in as far as it agrees with the fancy; it does not learn to distinguish the form from the substance, nor to act alone as pure understanding. And yet the exercise of the pure understanding is in itself an essential and capital point in the instruction of youth; and very often the exercise itself of thought is much more important than the object on which it is exercised. If you wish for a matter to be done seriously, be very careful not to announce it as a diversion. It is preferable, on the contrary, to secure attention and effort by the very form that is employed, and to use a kind of violence to draw minds over from the passive to an active state. The professor ought never to hide from his pupil the exact regularity of the method; he ought rather to fix his attention on it, and if possible to make him desire this strictness. The student ought to learn to pursue an end, and in the interest of that end to put up with a difficult process. He ought early to aspire to that loftier satisfaction which is the reward of exertion. In a scientific lecture the senses are altogether set aside; in an aesthetic address it is wished to interest them. What is the result? A writing or conversation of the aesthetic class is devoured with interest; but questions are put as to its conclusions; the hearer is scarcely able to give an answer. And this is quite natural, as here the conceptions reach the mind only in entire masses, and the understanding only knows what it analyzes. The mind during a lecture of this kind is more passive than active, and the intellect only possesses what it has produced by its own activity.

However, all this applies only to the vulgarly beautiful, and to a vulgar fashion of perceiving beauty. True beauty reposes on the strictest limitation, on the most exact definition, on the highest and most intimate necessity. Only this limitation ought rather to let itself be sought for than be imposed violently. It requires the most perfect conformity to law, but this must appear quite natural. A product that unites these conditions will fully satisfy the understanding as soon as study is made of it. But exactly because this result is really beautiful, its conformity is not expressed; it does not take the understanding apart to address it exclusively; it is a harmonious unity which addresses the entire man—all his faculties together; it is nature speaking to nature.

A vulgar criticism may perhaps find it empty, paltry, and too little determined. He who has no other knowledge than that of distinguishing, and no other sense than that for the particular, is actually pained by what is precisely the triumph of art, this harmonious unity where the parts are blended in a pure entirety. No doubt it is necessary, in a philosophical discourse, that the understanding, as a faculty of analysis, find what will satisfy it; it must obtain single concrete results; this is the essential that must not by any means be lost sight of. But if the writer, while giving all possible precision to the substance of his conceptions, has taken the necessary measures to enable the understanding, as soon as it will take the trouble, to find of necessity these truths, I do not see that he is a less good writer because he has approached more to the highest perfection. Nature always acts as a harmonious unity, and when she loses this in her efforts after abstraction, nothing appears more urgent to her than to re-establish it, and the writer we are speaking of is not less commendable if he obeys nature by attaching to the understanding what had been separated by abstraction, and when, by appealing at the same time to the sensuous and to the spiritual faculties, he addresses altogether the entire man. No doubt the vulgar critic will give very scant thanks to this writer for having given him a double task. For vulgar criticism has not the feeling for this harmony, it only runs after details, and even in the Basilica of St. Peter would exclusively attend to the pillars on which the ethereal edifice reposes. The fact is that this critic must begin by translating it to understand it—in the same way that the pure understanding, left to itself, if it meets beauty and harmony, either in nature or in art, must begin by transferring them into its own language—and by decomposing it, by doing in fact what the pupil does who spells before reading. But it is not from the narrow mind of his readers that the writer who expresses his conceptions in the language of the beautiful receives his laws. The ideal which he carries in himself is the goal at which he aims without troubling himself as to who follows and who remains behind. Many will stay behind; for if it be a rare thing to find readers simply capable of thinking, it is infinitely more rare to meet any who can think with imagination. Thus our writer, by the force of circumstances, will fall out, on the one hand, with those who have only intuitive ideas and feelings, for he imposes on them a painful task by forcing them to think; and, on the other hand, he aggravates those who only know how to think, for he asks of them what is absolutely impossible—to give a living, animated form to conception. But as both only represent true humanity very imperfectly—that normal humanity which requires the absolute harmony of these two operations—their contradictory objections have no weight, and if their judgments prove anything, it is rather that the author has succeeded in attaining his end. The abstract thinker finds that the substance of the work is solidly thought; the reader of intuitive ideas finds his style lively and animated; both consequently find and approve in him what they are able to understand, and that alone is wanting which exceeds their capacity.

But precisely for this very reason a writer of this class is not adapted to make known to an ignorant reader the object of what he treats, or, in the most proper sense of the word, to teach. Happily also, he is not required for that, for means will not be wanting for the teaching of scholars. The professor in the strictest acceptation is obliged to bind himself to the needs of his scholars; the first thing he has to presuppose is the ignorance of those who listen to him; the other, on the other hand, demands a certain maturity and culture in his reader or audience. Nor is his office confined to impart to them dead ideas; he grasps the living object with a living energy, and seizes at once on the entire man—his understanding, his heart, and his will.

We have found that it is dangerous for the soundness of knowledge to give free scope to the exigencies of taste in teaching, properly so called. But this does not mean by any means that the culture of this faculty in the student is a premature thing. He must, on the contrary, be encouraged to apply the knowledge that he has appropriated in the school to the field of living development. When once the first point has been observed, and the knowledge acquired, the other point, the exercise of taste, can only have useful results. It is certain that it is necessary to be quite the master of a truth to abandon without danger the form in which it has been found; a great strength of understanding is required not to lose sight of your object while giving free play to the imagination. He who transmits his knowledge under a scholastic form persuades me, I admit, that he has grasped these truths properly and that he knows how to support them. But he who besides this is in a condition to communicate them to me in a beautiful form not only proves that he is adapted to promulgate them, he shows moreover that he has assimilated them and that he is able to make their image pass into his productions and into his acts. There is for the results of thought only one way by which they can penetrate into the will and pass into life; that is, by spontaneous imagination, only what in ourselves was already a living act can become so out of us; and the same thing happens with the creations of the mind as with those of organic nature, that the fruit issues only from the flower. If we consider how many truths were living and active as interior intuitions before philosophy showed their existence, and how many truths most firmly secured by proofs often remain inactive on the will and the feelings, it will be seen how important it is for practical life to follow in this the indications of nature, and when we have acquired a knowledge scientifically to bring it back again to the state of a living intuition. It is the only way to enable those whose nature has forbidden them to follow the artificial path of science to share in the treasures of wisdom. The beautiful renders us here in relation with knowledge what, in morals, it does in relation with conduct; it places men in harmony on results, and on the substance of things, who would never have agreed on the form and principles.

The other sex, by its very nature and fair destiny, cannot and ought not to rival ours in scientific knowledge; but it can share truth with us by the reproduction of things. Man agrees to have his taste offended, provided compensation be given to his understanding by the increased value of its possessions. But women do not forgive negligence in form, whatever be the nature of the conception; and the inner structure of all their being gives them the right to show a strict severity on this point. The fair sex, even if it did not rule by beauty, would still be entitled to its name because it is ruled by beauty, and makes all objects presented to it appear before the tribunal of feeling, and all that does not speak to feeling or belies it is lost in the opinion of women. No doubt through this medium nothing can be made to reach the mind of woman save the matter of truth, and not truth itself, which is inseparable from its proofs. But happily woman only needs the matter of truth to reach her highest perfection, and the few exceptions hitherto seen are not of a nature to make us wish that the exception should become the rule. As, therefore, nature has not only dispensed but cut off the other sex from this task, man must give a double attention to it if he wishes to vie with woman and be equal to her in what is of great interest in human life. Consequently he will try to transfer all that he can from the field of abstraction, where he is master, to that of imagination, of feeling, where woman is at once a model and a judge. The mind of woman being a ground that does not admit of durable cultivation, he will try to make his own ground yield as many flowers and as much fruit as possible, so as to renew as often as possible the quickly-fading produce on the other ground, and to keep up a sort of artificial harvest where natural harvests could not ripen. Taste corrects or hides the natural differences of the two sexes. It nourishes and adorns the mind of woman with the productions of that of man, and allows the fair sex to feel without being previously fatigued by thought, and to enjoy pleasures without having bought them with labors. Thus, save the restrictions I have named, it is to the taste that is intrusted the care of form in every statement by which knowledge is communicated, but under the express condition that it will not encroach on the substance of things. Taste must never forget that it carries out an order emanating elsewhere, and that it is not its own affairs it is treating of. All its parts must be limited to place our minds in a condition favorable to knowledge; over all that concerns knowledge itself it has no right to any authority. For it exceeds its mission, it betrays it, it disfigures the object that it ought faithfully to transmit, it lays claim to authority out of its proper province; if it tries to carry out there, too, its own law, which is nothing but that of pleasing the imagination and making itself agreeable to the intuitive faculties; if it applies this law not only to the operation, but also to the matter itself; if it follows this rule not only to arrange the materials, but also to choose them. When this is the case the first consideration is not the things themselves, but the best mode of presenting them so as to recommend them to the senses. The logical sequence of conceptions of which only the strictness should have been hidden from us is rejected as a disagreeable impediment. Perfection is sacrificed to ornament, the truth of the parts to the beauty of the whole, the inmost nature of things to the exterior impression. Now, directly the substance is subordinated to form, properly speaking it ceases to exist; the statement is empty, and instead of having extended our knowledge we have only indulged in an amusing game.

The writers who have more wit than understanding and more taste than science, are too often guilty of this deception; and readers more accustomed to feel than to think are only too inclined to forgive them. In general it is unsafe to give to the aesthetical sense all its culture before having exercised the understanding as the pure thinking faculty, and before having enriched the head with conceptions; for as taste always looks at the carrying out and not at the basis of things, wherever it becomes the only arbiter, there is an end of the essential difference between things. Men become indifferent to reality, and they finish by giving value to form and appearance only.

Hence arises that superficial and frivolous bel-esprit that we often see hold sway in social conditions and in circles where men pride themselves, and not unreasonably, on the finest culture. It is a fatal thing to introduce a young man into assemblies where the Graces hold sway before the Muses have dismissed him and owned his majority. Moreover, it can hardly be prevented that what completes the external education of a young man whose mind is ripe turns him who is not ripened by study into a fool. I admit that to have a fund of conceptions, and not form, is only a half possession. For the most splendid knowledge in a head incapable of giving them form is like a treasure buried in the earth. But form without substance is a shadow of riches, and all possible cleverness in expression is of no use to him who has nothing to express.

Thus, to avoid the graces of education leading us in a wrong road, taste must be confined to regulating the external form, while reason and experience determine the substance and the essence of conceptions. If the impression made on the senses is converted into a supreme criterion, and if things are exclusively referred to sensation, man will never cease to be in the service of matter; he will never clear a way for his intelligence; in short, reason will lose in freedom in proportion as it allows imagination to usurp undue influence.

The beautiful produces its effect by mere intuition; the truth demands study. Accordingly, the man who among all his faculties has only exercised the sense of the beautiful is satisfied even when study is absolutely required, with a superficial view of things; and he fancies he can make a mere play of wit of that which demands a serious effort. But mere intuition cannot give any result. To produce something great it is necessary to enter into the fundamental nature of things, to distinguish them strictly, to associate them in different manners, and study them with a steady attention. Even the artist and the poet, though both of them labor to procure us only the pleasure of intuition, can only by most laborious and engrossing study succeed in giving us a delightful recreation by their works.

I believe this to be the test to distinguish the mere dilettante from the artist of real genius. The seductive charm exercised by the sublime and the beautiful, the fire which they kindle in the young imagination, the apparent ease with which they place the senses under an illusion, have often persuaded inexperienced minds to take in hand the palette or the harp, and to transform into figures or to pour out in melody what they felt living in their heart. Misty ideas circulate in their heads, like a world in formation, and make them believe that they are inspired. They take obscurity for depth, savage vehemence for strength, the undetermined for the infinite, what has not senses for the super-sensuous. And how they revel in these creations of their brain! But the judgment of the connoisseur does not confirm this testimony of an excited self-love. With his pitiless criticism he dissipates all the prestige of the imagination and of its dreams, and carrying the torch before these novices he leads them into the mysterious depths of science and life, where, far from profane eyes, the source of all true beauty flows ever towards him who is initiated. If now a true genius slumbers in the young aspirant, no doubt his modesty will at first receive a shock; but soon the consciousness of real talent will embolden him for the trial. If nature has endowed him with gifts for plastic art, he will study the structure of man with the scalpel of the anatomist; he will descend into the lowest depths to be true in representing surfaces, and he will question the whole race in order to be just to the individual. If he is born to be a poet, he examines humanity in his own heart to understand the infinite variety of scenes in which it acts on the vast theatre of the world. He subjects imagination and its exuberant fruitfulness to the discipline of taste, and charges the understanding to mark out in its cool wisdom the banks that should confine the raging waters of inspiration. He knows full well that the great is only formed of the little—from the imperceptible. He piles up, grain by grain, the materials of the wonderful structure, which, suddenly disclosed to our eyes, produces a startling effect and turns our head. But if nature has only intended him for a dilettante, difficulties damp his impotent zeal, and one of two things happens: either he abandons, if he is modest, that to which he was diverted by a mistaken notion of his vocation; or, if he has no modesty, he brings back the ideal to the narrow limits of his faculties, for want of being able to enlarge his faculties to the vast proportions of the ideal. Thus the true genius of the artist will be always recognized by this sign—that when most enthusiastic for the whole, he preserves a coolness, a patience defying all obstacles, as regards details. Moreover, in order not to do any injury to perfection, he would rather renounce the enjoyment given by the completion. For the simple amateur, it is the difficulty of means that disgusts him and turns him from his aim; his dreams would be to have no more trouble in producing than he had in conception and intuition.

I have spoken hitherto of the dangers to which we are exposed by an exaggerated sensuousness and susceptibility to the beautiful in the form, and from too extensive aesthetical requirements; and I have considered these dangers in relation to the faculty of thinking and knowing. What, then, will be the result when these pretensions of the aesthetical taste bear on the will? It is one thing to be stopped in your scientific progress by too great a love of the beautiful, another to see this inclination become a cause of degeneracy in character itself, and make us violate the law of duty. In matters of thought the caprices of "taste" are no doubt an evil, and they must of necessity darken the intelligence; but these same caprices applied to the maxims of the will become really pernicious and infallibly deprave the heart. Yet this is the dangerous extreme to which too refined an aesthetic culture brings us directly we abandon ourselves exclusively to the feelings for the beautiful, and directly we raise taste to the part of absolute lawgiver over our will.

The moral destination of man requires that the will should be completely independent of all influence of sensuous instincts, and we know that taste labors incessantly at making the link between reason and the senses continually closer. Now this effort has certainly as its result the ennobling of the appetites, and to make them more conformable with the requirements of reason; but this very point may be a serious danger for morality.

I proceed to explain my meaning. A very refined aesthetical education accustoms the imagination to direct itself according to laws, even in its free exercise, and leads the sensuous not to have any enjoyments without the concurrence of reason; but it soon follows that reason, in its turn, is required to be directed, even in the most serious operations of its legislative power, according to the interests of imagination, and to give no more orders to the will without the consent of the sensuous instincts. The moral obligation of the will, which is, however, an absolute and unconditional law, takes unperceived the character of a simple contract, which only binds each of the contracting parties when the other fulfils its engagement. The purely accidental agreement of duty with inclination ends by being considered a necessary condition, and thus the principle of all morality is quenched in its source.

How does the character become thus gradually depraved? The process may be explained thus: So long as man is only a savage, and his instincts' only bear on material things and a coarse egotism determines his actions, sensuousness can only become a danger to morality by its blind strength, and does not oppose reason except as a force. The voice of justice, moderation, and humanity is stifled by the appetites, which make a stronger appeal. Man is then terrible in his vengeance, because he is terribly sensitive to insults. He robs, he kills, because his desires are still too powerful for the feeble guidance of reason. He is towards others like a wild beast, because the instinct of nature still rules him after the fashion of animals.

But when to the savage state, to that of nature, succeeds civilization; when taste ennobles the instincts, and holds out to them more worthy objects taken from the moral order; when culture moderates the brutal outbursts of the appetites and brings them back under the discipline of the beautiful, it may happen that these same instincts, which were only dangerous before by their blind power, coming to assume an air of dignity and a certain assumed authority, may become more dangerous than before to the morality of the character; and that, under the guise of innocence, nobleness, and purity, they may exercise over the will a tyranny a hundred times worse than the other.

The man of taste willingly escapes the gross thraldom of the appetites. He submits to reason the instinct which impels him to pleasure, and he is willing to take counsel from his spiritual and thinking nature for the choice of the objects he ought to desire. Now, reason is very apt to mistake a spiritualized instinct for one of its own instincts, and at length to give up to it the guidance of the will, and this in proportion as moral judgment and aesthetic judgment, the sense of the good and the sense of the beautiful, meet in the same object and in the same decision.

So long as it remains possible for inclination and duty to meet in the same object and in a common desire, this representation of the moral sense by the aesthetic sense may not draw after it positively evil consequences, though, if the matter be strictly considered, the morality of particular actions does not gain by this agreement. But the consequences will be quite different when sensuousness and reason have each of them a different interest. If, for example, duty commands us to perform an action that revolts our taste, or if taste feels itself drawn towards an object which reason as a moral judge is obliged to condemn, then, in fact, we suddenly encounter the necessity of distinguishing between the requirements of the moral sense and those of the aesthetic sense, which so long an agreement had almost confounded to such a degree that they could not be distinguished. We must now determine their reciprocal rights, and find which of them is the real master in our soul. But such a long representation of the moral sense by the sense of the beautiful has made us forget this master. When we have so long practised this rule of obeying at once the suggestions of taste, and when we have found the result always satisfactory, taste ends by assuming a kind of appearance of right. As taste has shown itself irreproachable in the vigilant watch it has kept over the will, we necessarily come to grant a certain esteem to its decisions; and it is precisely to this esteem that inclination, with captious logic, gives weight against the duties of conscience.

Esteem is a feeling that can only be felt for law, and what corresponds to it. Whatever is entitled to esteem lays claim to an unconditional homage. The ennobled inclination which has succeeded in captivating our esteem will, therefore, no longer be satisfied with being subordinate to reason; it aspires to rank alongside it. It does not wish to be taken for a faithless subject in revolt against his sovereign; it wishes to be regarded as a queen; and, treating reason as its peer, to dictate, like reason, laws to the conscience. Thus, if we listen to her, she would weigh by right equally in the scale; and then have we not good reason to fear that interest will decide?

Of all the inclinations that are decided from the feeling for the beautiful and that are special to refined minds, none commends itself so much to the moral sense as the ennobled instinct of love; none is so fruitful in impressions which correspond to the true dignity of man. To what an elevation does it raise human nature! and often what divine sparks does it kindle in the common soul! It is a sacred fire that consumes every egotistical inclination, and the very principles of morality are scarcely a greater safeguard of the soul's chastity than love is for the nobility of the heart. How often it happens while the moral principles are still struggling that love prevails in their favor, and hastens by its irresistible power the resolutions that duty alone would have vainly demanded from weak human nature! Who, then, would distrust an

155

affection that protects so powerfully what is most excellent in human nature, and which fights so victoriously against the moral foe of all morality, egotism?

But do not follow this guide till you have secured a better. Suppose a loved object be met that is unhappy, and unhappy because of you, and that it depends only on you to make it happy by sacrificing a few moral scruples. You may be disposed to say, "Shall I let this loved being suffer for the pleasure of keeping our conscience pure? Is this resistance required by this generous, devoted affection, always ready to forget itself for its object? I grant it is going against conscience to have recourse to this immoral means to solace the being we love; but can we be said to love if in presence of this being and of its sorrow we continue to think of ourselves? Are we not more taken up with ourselves than with it, since we prefer to see it unhappy rather than consent to be so ourselves by the reproaches of our conscience?" These are the sophisms that the passion of love sets against conscience (whose voice thwarts its interests), making its utterances despicable as suggestions of selfishness, and representing our moral dignity as one of the components of our happiness that we are free to alienate. Then, if the morality of our character is not strongly backed by good principles, we shall surrender, whatever may be the impetus of our exalted imagination, to disgraceful acts; and we shall think that we gain a glorious victory over our self-love, while we are only the despicable victims of this instinct. A well-known French romance, "Les Liaisons Dangereuses," gives us a striking example of this delusion, by which love betrays a soul otherwise pure and beautiful. The Presidente de Tourvel errs by surprise, and seeks to calm her remorse by the idea that she has sacrificed her virtue to her generosity.

Secondary and imperfect duties, as they are styled, are those that the feeling for the beautiful takes most willingly under its patronage, and which it allows to prevail on many occasions over perfect duties. As they assign a much larger place to the arbitrary option of the subject, and at the same time as they have the appearance of merit, which gives them lustre, they commend themselves far more to the aesthetic taste than perfect or necessary duties, which oblige us strictly and unconditionally. How many people allow themselves to be unjust that they may be generous! How many fail in their duties to society that they may do good to an individual, and reciprocally! How many people forgive a lie sooner than a rudeness, a crime against humanity rather than an insult to honor! How many debase their bodies to hasten the perfection of their minds, and degrade their character to adorn their understanding! How many do not scruple to commit a crime when they have a laudable end in view, pursue an ideal of political happiness through all the terrors of anarchy, tread under foot existing laws to make way for better ones, and do not scruple to devote the present generation to misery to secure at this cost the happiness of future generations! The apparent unselfishness of certain virtues gives them a varnish of purity, which makes them rash enough to break and run counter to the moral law; and many people are the dupes of this strange illusion, to rise higher than morality and to endeavor to be more reasonable than reason.

The man of a refined taste is susceptible, in this respect, of a moral corruption, from which the rude child of nature is preserved by his very coarseness. In the latter, the opposite of the demands of sense and the decrees of the moral law is so strongly marked and so manifest, and the spiritual element has so small a share in his desires, that although the appetites exercise a despotic sway over him, they cannot wrest his esteem from him. Thus, when the savage, yielding to the superior attraction of sense, gives way to the committal of an unjust action, he may yield to temptation, but he will not hide from himself that he is committing a fault, and he will do homage to reason even while he violates its mandates. The child of civilization, on the contrary, the man of refinement, will not admit that he commits a fault, and to soothe his conscience he prefers to impose on it by a sophism. No doubt he wishes to obey his appetite, but at the same time without falling in his own esteem. How does he manage this? He begins by overthrowing the superior authority that thwarts his inclination, and before transgressing the law he calls in question the competence of the lawgiver. Could it be expected that a corrupt will should so corrupt the intelligence? The only dignity that an inclination can assume accrues to it from its agreement with reason; yet we find that inclination, independent as well as blind, aspires, at the very moment she enters into contest with reason, to keep this dignity which she owes to reason alone. Nay, inclination even aspires to use this dignity she owes to reason against reason itself.

These are the dangers that threaten the morality of the character when too intimate an association is attempted between sensuous instincts and moral instincts, which can never perfectly agree in real life, but only in the ideal. I admit that the sensuous risks nothing in this association, because it possesses nothing except what it must give up directly duty speaks and reason demands the sacrifice. But reason, as the arbiter of the moral law, will run the more risk from this union if it receives as a gift from inclination what it might enforce; for, under the appearance of freedom, the feeling of obligation may be easily lost, and what reason accepts as a favor may quite well be refused it when the sensuous finds it painful to grant it. It is, therefore, infinitely safer for the morality of the character to suspend, at least for a time, this misrepresentation of the moral sense by the sense of the beautiful. It is best of all that reason should command by itself without mediation, and that it should show to the will its true master. The remark is, therefore, quite justified, that true morality only knows itself in the school of adversity, and that a continual prosperity becomes easily a rock of offence to virtue. I mean here by prosperity the state of a man who, to enjoy the goods of life, need not commit injustice, and who to conform to justice need not renounce any of the goods of life. The man who enjoys a continual prosperity never sees moral duty face to face, because his inclinations, naturally regular and moderate, always anticipate the mandate of reason, and because no temptation to violate the law recalls to his mind the idea of law. Entirely guided by the sense of the beautiful, which represents reason in the world of sense, he will reach the tomb without having known by experience the dignity of his destiny. On the other hand, the unfortunate man, if he be at the same time a virtuous man, enjoys the sublime privilege of being in immediate intercourse with the divine majesty of the moral law; and as his virtue is not seconded by any inclination, he bears witness in this lower world, and as a human being, of the freedom of pure spirits!

REFLECTIONS ON THE USE OF THE VULGAR AND LOW ELEMENTS IN WORKS OF ART.

I call vulgar (common) all that does not speak to the mind, of which all the interest is addressed only to the senses. There are, no doubt, an infinite number of things vulgar in themselves from their material and subject. But as the vulgarity of the material can always be ennobled by the treatment, in respect of art the only question is that relating to the vulgarity in form. A vulgar mind will dishonor the most noble matter by treating it in a common manner. A great and noble mind, on the contrary, will ennoble even a common matter, and it will do so by superadding to it something spiritual and discovering in it some aspect in which this matter has greatness. Thus, for example, a vulgar historian will relate to us the most insignificant actions of a hero with a scrupulousness as great as that bestowed on his sublimest exploit, and will dwell as lengthily on his pedigree, his costume, and his household as on his projects and his enterprises. He will relate those of his actions that have the most grandeur in such wise that no one will perceive that character in them. On the contrary, a historian of genius, himself endowed with nobleness of mind, will give even to the private life and the least considerable actions of his hero an interest and a value that will make them considerable. Thus, again, in the matter of the plastic arts, the Dutch and Flemish painters have given proof of a vulgar taste; the Italians, and still more the ancient Greeks, of a grand and noble taste. The Greeks always went to the ideal; they rejected every vulgar feature, and chose no common subject.

A portrait painter can represent his model in a common manner or with grandeur; in a common manner if he reproduce the merely accidental details with the same care as the essential features, if he neglect the great to carry out the minutiae curiously. He does it grandly if he know how to find out and place in relief what is most interesting, and distinguish the accidental from the necessary; if he be satisfied with indicating what is paltry, reserving all the finish of the execution for what is great. And the only thing that is great is the expression of the soul itself, manifesting itself by actions, gestures, or attitudes.

The poet treats his subject in a common manner when in the execution of his theme he dwells on valueless facts and only skims rapidly over those that are important. He treats his theme with grandeur when he associates with it what is great. For example, Homer treated the shield of Achilles grandly, though the making of a shield, looking merely at the matter, is a very commonplace affair.

One degree below the common or the vulgar is the element of the base or gross, which differs from the common in being not only something negative, a simple lack of inspiration or nobleness, but something positive, marking coarse feelings, bad morals, and contemptible manners. Vulgarity only testifies that an advantage is wanting, whereof the absence is a matter of regret; baseness indicates the want of a quality which we are authorized to require in all. Thus, for example, revenge, considered in itself, in whatever place or way it manifests itself, is something vulgar, because it is the proof of a lack of generosity. But there is, moreover, a base vengeance, when the man, to satisfy it, employs means exposed to contempt. The base always implies something gross, or reminds one of the mob, while the common can be found in a well-born and well-bred man, who may think and act in a common manner if he has only mediocre faculties. A man acts in a common manner when he is only taken up with his own interest, and it is in this that he is in opposition with the really noble man, who, when necessary, knows how to forget himself to procure some enjoyment for others. But the same man would act in a base manner if he consulted his interests at the cost of his honor, and if in such a case he did not even take upon himself to respect the laws of decency. Thus the common is only the contrary of the noble; the base is the contrary both of the noble and the seemly. To give yourself up, unresisting, to all your passions, to satisfy all your impulses, without being checked even by the rules of propriety, still less by those of morality, is to conduct yourself basely, and to betray baseness of the soul.

The artist also may fall into a low style, not only by choosing ignoble subjects, offensive to decency and good taste, but moreover by treating them in a base manner. It is to treat a subject in a base manner if those sides are made prominent which propriety directs us to conceal, or if it is expressed in a manner that incidentally awakens low ideas. The lives of the greater part of men can present particulars of a low kind, but it is only a low imagination that will pick out these for representation.

There are pictures describing sacred history in which the Apostles, the Virgin, and even the Christ, are depicted in such wise that they might be supposed to be taken from the dregs of the populace. This style of execution always betrays a low taste, and might justly lead to the inference that the artist himself thinks coarsely and like the mob.

No doubt there are cases where art itself may be allowed to produce base images: for example, when the aim is to provoke laughter. A man of polished manners may also sometimes, and without betraying a corrupt taste, be amused by certain features when nature expresses herself crudely but with truth, and he may enjoy the contrast between the manners of polished society and those of the lower orders. A man of position appearing intoxicated will always make a disagreeable impression on us; but a drunken driver, sailor, or carter will only be a risible object. Jests that would be insufferable in a man of education amuse us in the mouth of the people. Of this kind are many of the scenes of Aristophanes, who unhappily sometimes exceeds this limit, and becomes absolutely condemnable. This is, moreover, the source of the pleasure we take in parodies, when the feelings, the language, and the mode of action of the common people are fictitiously lent to the same personages whom the poet has treated with all possible dignity and decency. As soon as the poet means only to jest, and seeks only to amuse, we can overlook traits of a low kind, provided he never stirs up indignation or disgust.

He stirs up indignation when he places baseness where it is quite unpardonable, that is in the case of men who are expected to show fine moral sense. In attributing baseness to them he will either outrage truth, for we prefer to think him a liar than to believe that well-trained men can act in a base manner; or his personages will offend our moral sense, and, what is worse, excite our imagination. I do not mean by this to condemn farces; a farce implies between the poet and the spectator a tacit consent that no truth is to be expected in the piece. In a farce we exempt the poet from all faithfulness in his pictures; he has a kind of privilege to tell us untruths. Here, in fact, all the comic consists exactly in its contrast with the truth, and so it cannot possibly be true.

This is not all: even in the serious and the tragic there are certain places where the low element can be brought into play. But in this case the affair must pass into the terrible, and the momentary violation of our good taste must be masked by a strong impression, which brings our passion into play. In other words, the low impression must be absorbed by a superior tragic impression. Theft, for example, is a thing absolutely base, and whatever arguments our heart may suggest to excuse the thief, whatever the pressure of circumstances that led him to the theft, it is always an indelible brand stamped upon him, and, aesthetically speaking, he will always remain a base object. On this point taste is even less forgiving than morality, and its tribunal is more severe; because an aesthetical object is responsible even for the accessory ideas that are awakened in us by such an object, while moral judgment eliminates all that is merely accidental. According to this view a man who robs would always be an object to be rejected by the poet who wishes to present serious pictures. But suppose this man is at the same time a murderer, he is even more to be condemned than before by the moral law. But in the aesthetic judgment he is raised one degree higher and made better adapted to figure in a work of art. Continuing to judge him from the aesthetic point of view, it may be added that he who abases himself by a vile action can to a certain extent be raised by a crime, and can be thus reinstated in our aesthetic estimation. This contradiction between the moral judgment and the aesthetical judgment is a fact entitled to attention and consideration. It may be explained in different ways. First, I have already said that, as the aesthetic judgment depends on the imagination, all the accessory ideas awakened in us by an object and naturally associated with it, must themselves influence this judgment. Now, if these accessory ideas are base, they infallibly stamp this character on the principal object.

In the second place, what we look for in the aesthetic judgment is strength; whilst in a judgment pronounced in the name of the moral sense we consider lawfulness. The lack of strength is something contemptible, and every action from which it may be inferred that the agent lacks strength is, by that very fact, a contemptible action. Every cowardly and underhand action is repugnant to us, because it is a proof of impotence; and, on the contrary, a devilish wickedness can, aesthetically speaking, flatter our taste, as soon as it marks strength. Now, a theft testifies to a vile and grovelling mind: a murder has at least on its side the appearance of strength; the interest we take in it aesthetically is in proportion to the strength that is manifested in it.

A third reason is, because in presence of a deep and horrible crime we no longer think of the quality but the awful consequences of the action. The stronger emotion covers and stifles the weaker one. We do not look back into the mind of the agent; we look onward into his destiny, we think of the effects of his action. Now, directly we begin to tremble all the delicacies of taste are reduced to silence. The principal impression entirely fills our mind: the accessory and accidental ideas, in which chiefly dwell all impressions of baseness, are effaced from it. It is for this reason that the theft committed by young Ruhberg, in the "Crime through Ambition," [a play of Iffland] far from displeasing on the stage, is a real tragic effect. The poet with great skill has managed the circumstances in such wise that we are carried away; we are left almost breathless. The frightful misery of the family, and especially the grief of the father, are objects that attract our attention, turn it aside, from the person of the agent, towards the consequences of his act. We are too much moved to tarry long in representing to our minds the stamp of infamy with which the theft is marked. In a word, the base element disappears in the terrible. It is singular that this theft, really accomplished by young Ruhberg, inspires us with less repugnance than, in another piece, the mere suspicion of a theft, a suspicion which is actually without foundation. In the latter case it is a young officer who is accused without grounds of having abstracted a silver spoon, which is recovered later on. Thus the base element is reduced in this case to a purely imaginary thing, a mere suspicion, and this suffices nevertheless to do an irreparable injury, in our aesthetical appreciation, to the hero of the piece, in spite of his innocence. This is because a man who is supposed capable of a base action did not apparently enjoy a very solid reputation for morality, for the laws of propriety require that a man should be held to be a man of honor as long as he does not show the opposite. If therefore anything contemptible is imputed to him, it seems that by some part of his past conduct he has given rise to a suspicion of this kind, and this does him injury, though all the odious and the base in an undeserved suspicion are on the side of him who accuses. A point that does still greater injury to the hero of the piece of which I am speaking is the fact that he is an officer, and the lover of a lady of condition brought up in a manner suitable to her rank. With these two titles, that of thief makes quite a revolting contrast, and it is impossible for us, when we see him near his lady, not to think that perhaps at that very moment he had the silver spoon in his pocket. Lastly, the most unfortunate part of the business is, that he has no idea of the suspicion weighing over him, for if he had a knowledge of it, in his character of officer, he would exact a sanguinary reparation. In this case the consequences of the suspicion would change to the terrible, and all that is base in the situation would disappear.

We must distinguish, moreover, between the baseness of feeling and that which is connected with the mode of treatment and circumstance. The former in all respects is below aesthetic dignity; the second in many cases may perfectly agree with it. Slavery, for example, is a base thing; but a servile mind in a free man is contemptible. The labors of the slave, on the contrary, are not so when his feelings are not servile. Far from this, a base condition, when joined to elevated feelings, can become a source of the sublime. The master of Epictetus, who beat him, acted basely, and the slave beaten by him showed a sublime soul. True greatness, when it is met in a base condition, is only the more brilliant and splendid on that account: and the artist must not fear to show us his heroes even under a contemptible exterior as soon as he is sure of being able to give them, when he wishes, the expression of moral dignity.

But what can be granted to the poet is not always allowed in the artist. The poet only addresses the imagination; the painter addresses the senses directly. It follows not only that the impression of the picture is more lively than that of the poem, but also that the painter, if he employ only his natural signs, cannot make the minds of his personages as visible as the poet can with the arbitrary signs at his command: yet it is only the sight of the mind that can reconcile us to certain exteriors. When Homer causes his Ulysses to appear in the rags of a beggar ["Odyssey," book xiii. v. 397], we are at liberty to represent his image to our mind more or less fully, and to dwell on it as long as we like. But in no case will it be sufficiently vivid to excite our repugnance or disgust. But if a painter, or even a tragedian, try to reproduce faithfully the Ulysses of Homer, we turn away from the picture with repugnance. It is because in this case the greater or less vividness of the impression no longer depends on our will: we cannot help seeing what the painter places under our eyes; and it is not easy for us to remove the accessory repugnant ideas which the picture recalls to our mind.

DETACHED REFLECTIONS ON DIFFERENT QUESTIONS OF AESTHETICS.

All the properties by which an object can become aesthetic, can be referred to four classes, which, as well according to their objective differences as according to their different relation with the subject, produce on our passive and active faculties pleasures unequal not only in intensity but also in worth; classes which also are of an unequal use for the end of the fine arts: they are the agreeable, the good, the sublime, and the beautiful.

Of these four categories, the sublime and the beautiful only belong properly to art. The agreeable is not worthy of art, and the good is at least not its end; for the aim of art is to please, and the good, whether we consider it in theory or in practice, neither can nor ought to serve as a means of satisfying the wants of sensuousness. The agreeable only satisfies the senses, and is distinguished thereby from the good, which only pleases the reason. The agreeable only pleases by its matter, for it is only matter that can affect the senses, and all that is form can only please the reason. It is true that the beautiful only pleases through the medium of the senses, by which it is distinguished from the good; but it pleases reason, on account of its form, by which it is essentially distinguished from the agreeable. It might be said that the good pleases only by its form being in harmony with reason; the beautiful by its form having some relation of resemblance with reason, and that the agreeable absolutely does not please by its form. The good is perceived by thought, the beautiful by intuition, and the agreeable only by the senses. The first pleases by the conception, the second by the idea, and the third by material sensation.

The distance between the good and the agreeable is that which strikes the eyes the most. The good widens our understanding, because it procures and supposes an idea of its object; the pleasure which it makes us perceive rests on an objective foundation, even when this pleasure itself is but a certain state in which we are situated. The agreeable, on the contrary, produces no notion of its object, and, indeed, reposes on no objective foundation. It is agreeable only inasmuch as it is felt by the subject, and the idea of it completely vanishes the moment an obstruction is placed on the affectibility of the senses, or only when it is modified. For a man who feels the cold the agreeable would be a warm air; but this same man, in the heat of summer, would seek the shade and coolness; but we must agree that in both cases he has judged well.

On the other hand, that which is objective is altogether independent of us, and that which to-day appears to us true, useful, reasonable, ought yet (if this judgment of to-day be admitted as just) to seem to us the same twenty years hence. But our judgment of the agreeable changes as soon as our state, with regard to its object, has changed. The agreeable is therefore not a property of the object; it springs entirely from the relations of such an object with our senses, for the constitution of our senses is a necessary condition thereof.

The good, on the contrary, is good in itself, before being represented to us, and before being felt. The property by which it pleases exists fully in itself without being in want of our subject, although the pleasure which we take in it rests on an aptitude for feeling that which is in us. Thus we can say that the agreeable exists only because it is experienced, and that the good, on the contrary, is experienced because it exists.

The distinction between the beautiful and the agreeable, great as it is, moreover, strikes the eye less. The beautiful approaches the agreeable in this—that it must always be proposed to the senses, inasmuch as it pleases only as a phenomenon. It comes near to it again in as far as it neither procures nor supposes any notion of its object. But, on the other hand, it is widely separated from the agreeable, because it pleases by the form under which it is produced, and not by the fact of the material sensation. No doubt it only pleases the reasonable subject in so far as it is also a sensuous subject; but also it pleases the sensuous subject only inasmuch as it is at the same time a reasonable subject. The beautiful is not only pleasing to the individual but to the whole species; and although it draws its existence but from its relation with creatures at the same time reasonable and sensuous, it is not less independent of all empirical limitations of sensuousness, and it remains identical even when the particular constitution of the individual is modified. The beautiful has exactly in common with the good that by which it differs from the agreeable, and it differs from the good exactly in that in which it approximates to the agreeable.

By the good we must understand that in which reason recognizes a conformity with her theoretical and practical laws. But the same object can be perfectly conformable to the theoretical reason, and not be the less in contradiction in the highest degree with the practical reason. We can disapprove of the end of an enterprise, and yet admire the skill of the means and their relation with the end in view. We can despise the pleasures which the voluptuous man makes the end of his life, and nevertheless praise the skill which he exhibits in the choice of his means, and the logical result with which he carries out his principles. That which pleases us only by its form is good, absolutely good, and without any conditions, when its form is at the same time its matter. The good is also an object of sensuousness, but not of an immediate sensuousness, as the agreeable, nor moreover of a mixed sensuousness, as the beautiful. It does not excite desire as the first, nor inclination as the second. The simple idea of the good inspires only esteem.

The difference separating the agreeable, the good, and the beautiful being thus established, it is evident that the same object can be ugly, defective, even to be morally rejected, and nevertheless be agreeable and pleasing to the senses; that an object can revolt the senses, and yet be good, i.e., please the reason; that an object can from its inmost nature revolt the moral senses, and yet please the imagination which contemplates it, and still be beautiful. It is because each one of these ideas interests different faculties, and interests differently.

But have we exhausted the classification of the aesthetic attributes? No, there are objects at the same time ugly, revolting, and horrifying to the senses, which do not please the understanding, and of no account to the moral judgment, and these objects do not fail to please; certainly to please to such a degree, that we would willingly sacrifice the pleasure of these senses and that of the understanding to procure for us the enjoyment of these objects. There is nothing more attractive in nature than a beautiful landscape, illuminated by the purple light of evening. The rich variety of the objects, the mellow outlines, the play of lights infinitely varying the aspect, the light vapors which envelop distant objects,—all combine in charming the senses; and add to it, to increase our pleasure, the soft murmur of a cascade, the song of the nightingales, an agreeable music. We give ourselves up to a soft sensation of repose, and whilst our senses, touched by the harmony of the colors, the forms, and the sounds, experience the agreeable in the highest, the mind is rejoiced by the easy and rich flow of the ideas, the heart by the sentiments which overflow in it like a torrent. All at once a storm springs up, darkening the sky and all the landscape, surpassing and silencing all other noises, and suddenly taking from us all our pleasures. Black clouds encircle the horizon; the thunder falls with a deafening noise. Flash succeeds flash. Our sight and hearing is affected in the most revolting manner. The lightning only appears to render to us more visible the horrors of the night: we see the electric fluid strike, nay, we begin to fear lest it may strike us. Well, that does not prevent us from believing that we have gained more than lost by the change; I except, of course, those whom fear has bereft of all liberty of judgment. We are, on the one hand, forcibly drawn towards this terrible spectacle, which on the other wounds and repulses our senses, and we pause before it with a feeling which we cannot properly call a pleasure, but one which we often like much more than pleasure. But still, the spectacle that nature then offers to us is in itself rather destructive than good (at all events we in no way need to think of the utility of a storm to take pleasure in this phenomenon), is in itself rather ugly than beautiful, for the darkness, hiding from us all the images which light affords, cannot be in itself a pleasant thing; and those sudden crashes with which the thunder shakes the atmosphere, those sudden flashes when the lightning rends the cloud—all is contrary to one of the essential conditions of the beautiful, which carries with it nothing abrupt, nothing violent. And moreover this phenomenon, if we consider only our senses, is rather painful than agreeable, for the nerves of our sight and those of our hearing are each in their turn painfully strained, then not less violently relaxed, by the alternations of light and darkness, of the explosion of the thunder, and silence. And in spite of all these causes of displeasure, a storm is an attractive phenomenon for whomsoever is not afraid of it.

Another example. In the midst of a green and smiling plain there rises a naked and barren hillock, which hides from the sight a part of the view. Each one would wish that this hillock were removed which disfigures the beauty of all the landscape. Well, let us imagine this hillock rising, rising still, without indeed changing at all its shape, and preserving, although on a greater scale, the same proportions between its width and height. To begin with, our impression of displeasure will but increase with the hillock itself, which will the more strike the sight, and which will be the more repulsive. But continue; raise it up twice as high as a tower, and insensibly the displeasure will efface itself to make way for quite another feeling. The hill has at last become a mountain, so high a mountain that it is quite impossible for our eyes to take it in at one look. There is an object more precocious than all this smiling plain which surrounds it, and the impression that it makes on us is of such a nature that we should regret to exchange it for any other impression, however beautiful it might be. Now, suppose this mountain to be leaning, and of such an inclination that we could expect it every minute to crash down, the previous impression will be complicated with another impression: terror will be joined to it: the object itself will be but still more attractive. But suppose it were possible to prop up this leaning mountain with another mountain, the terror would disappear, and with it a good part of the pleasure we experienced. Suppose that there were beside this mountain four or five other mountains, of which each one was a fourth or a fifth part lower than the one which came immediately after; the first impression with which the height of one mountain inspired us will be notably weakened. Something somewhat analogous would take place if the mountain itself were cut into ten or twelve terraces, uniformly diminishing; or again if it were artificially decorated with plantations. We have at first subjected one mountain to no other operation than that of increasing its size, leaving it otherwise just as it was, and without altering its form; and this simple circumstance has sufficed to make an indifferent or even disagreeable object satisfying to the eyes. By the second operation, this enlarged object has become at the same time an object of terror; and the pleasure which we have found in contemplating it has but been the greater. Finally, by the last operation which we have made, we have diminished the terror which its sight occasioned, and the pleasure has diminished as much. We have diminished subjectively the idea of its height, whether by dividing the attention of the spectator between several objects, or in giving to the eyes, by means of these smaller mountains, placed near to the large one, a measure by which to master the height of the mountain all the more easily. The great and the terrible can therefore be of themselves in certain cases a source of aesthetic pleasure.

There is not in the Greek mythology a more terrible, and at the same time more hideous, picture than the Furies, or Erinyes, quitting the infernal regions to throw themselves in the pursuit of a criminal. Their faces frightfully contracted and grimacing, their fleshless bodies, their heads covered with serpents in the place of hair—revolt our senses as much as they offend our taste. However, when these monsters are represented to us in the pursuit of Orestes, the murderer of his mother, when they are shown to us brandishing the torches in their hands, and chasing their prey, without peace or truce, from country to country, until at last, the anger of justice being appeased, they engulf themselves in the abyss of the infernal regions; then we pause before the picture with a horror mixed with pleasure. But not only the remorse of a criminal which is personified by the Furies, even his unrighteous acts nay, the real perpetration of a crime, are able to please us in a work of art. Medea, in the Greek tragedy; Clytemnestra, who takes the life of her husband; Orestes, who kills his mother, fill our soul with horror and with pleasure. Even in real life, indifferent and even repulsive or frightful objects begin to interest us the moment that they approach the monstrous or the terrible. An altogether vulgar and insignificant man will begin to please us the moment that a violent passion, which indeed in no way upraises his personal value, makes him an object of fear and terror, in the same way that a vulgar, meaningless object becomes to us the source of aesthetic pleasure the instant we have enlarged it to the point where it threatens to overstep our comprehension. An ugly man is made still more ugly by passion, and nevertheless it is in bursts of this passion, provided that it turns to the terrible and not to the ridiculous, that this man will be to us of the most interest. This remark extends even to animals. An ox at the plow, a horse before a carriage, a dog, are common objects; but excite this bull to the combat, enrage this horse who is so peaceable, or represent to yourself this dog a prey to madness; instantly these animals are raised to the rank of aesthetic objects, and we begin to regard them with a feeling which borders on pleasure and esteem. The inclination to the pathetic—an inclination common to all men—the strength of the sympathetic sentiment—this force which in mature makes us wish to see suffering, terror, dismay, which has so many attractions for us in art, which makes us hurry to the theatre, which makes us take so much pleasure in the picturing of great misfortune,—all this bears testimony to a fourth source of aesthetic pleasure, which neither the agreeable, nor the good, nor the beautiful are in a state to produce.

All the examples that I have alleged up to the present have this in common—that the feeling they excite in us rests on something objective. In all these phenomena we receive the idea of something "which oversteps, or which threatens to overstep, the power of comprehension of our senses, or their power of resistance"; but not, however, going so far as to paralyze these two powers, or so far as to render us incapable of striving, either to know the object, or to resist the impression it makes on us. There is in the phenomena a complexity which we cannot retrace to unity without driving the intuitive faculty to its furthest limits.

We have the idea of a force in comparison with which our own vanishes, and which we are nevertheless compelled to compare with our own. Either it is an object which at the same time presents and hides itself from our faculty of intuition, and which urges us to strive to represent it to ourselves, without leaving room to hope that this aspiration will be satisfied; or else it is an object which appears to upraise itself as an enemy, even against our existence—which provokes us, so to say, to combat, and makes us anxious as to the issue. In all the alleged examples there is visible in the same way the same action on the faculty of feeling. All throw our souls into an anxious agitation and strain its springs. A certain gravity which can even raise itself to a solemn rejoicing takes possession of our soul, and whilst our organs betray evident signs of internal anxiety, our mind falls back on itself by reflection, and appears to find a support in a higher consciousness of its independent strength and dignity. This consciousness of ourselves must always dominate in order that the great and the horrible may have for us an aesthetic value. It is because the soul before such sights as these feels itself inspired and lifted above itself that they are designated under the name of sublime, although the things themselves are objectively in no way sublime; and consequently it would be more just to say that they are elevating than to call them in themselves elevated or sublime.

For an object to be called sublime it must be in opposition with our sensuousness. In general it is possible to conceive but two different relations between the objects and our sensuousness, and consequently there ought to be two kinds of resistance. They ought either to be considered as objects from which we wish to draw a knowledge, or else they should be regarded as a force with which we compare our own. According to this division there are two kinds of the sublime, the sublime of knowledge and the sublime of force. Moreover, the sensuous faculties contribute to knowledge only in grasping a given matter, and putting one by the other its complexity in time and in space.

As to dissecting this complex property and assorting it, it is the business of the understanding and not of the imagination. It is for the understanding alone that the diversity exists: for the imagination (considered simply as a sensuous faculty) there is but an uniformity, and consequently it is but the number of the uniform things (the quantity and not the quality) which can give origin to any difference between the sensuous perception of phenomena. Thus, in order that the faculty of picturing things sensuously maybe reduced to impotence before an object, necessarily it is imperative that this object exceeds in its quantity the capacity of our imagination.

ON SIMPLE AND SENTIMENTAL POETRY.

There are moments in life when nature inspires us with a sort of love and respectful emotion, not because she is pleasing to our senses, or because she satisfies our mind or our taste (it is often the very opposite that happens), but merely because she is nature. This feeling is often elicited when nature is considered in her plants, in her mineral kingdom, in rural districts; also in the case of human nature, in the case of children, and in the manners of country people and of the primitive races. Every man of refined feeling, provided he has a soul, experiences this feeling when he walks out under the open sky, when he lives in the country, or when he stops to contemplate the monuments of early ages; in short, when escaping from factitious situations and relations, he finds himself suddenly face to face with nature. This interest, which is often exalted in us so as to become a want, is the explanation of many of our fancies for flowers and for animals, our preference for gardens laid out in the natural style, our love of walks, of the country and those who live there, of a great number of objects proceeding from a remote antiquity, etc. It is taken for granted that no affectation exists in the matter, and moreover that no accidental interest comes into play. But this sort of interest which we take in nature is only possible under two conditions. First the object that inspires us with this feeling must be really nature, or something we take for nature; secondly this object must be in the full sense of the word simple, that is, presenting the entire contrast of nature with art, all the advantage remaining on the side of nature. Directly this second condition is united to the first, but no sooner, nature assumes the character of simplicity.

Considered thus, nature is for us nothing but existence in all its freedom; it is the constitution of things taken in themselves; it is existence itself according to its proper and immutable laws.

It is strictly necessary that we should have this idea of nature to take an interest in phenomena of this kind. If we conceive an artificial flower so perfectly imitated that it has all the appearance of nature and would produce the most complete illusion, or if we imagine the imitation of simplicity carried out to the extremest degree, the instant we discover it is only an imitation, the feeling of which I have been speaking is completely destroyed. It is, therefore, quite evident that this kind of satisfaction which nature causes us to feel is not a satisfaction of the aesthetical taste, but a satisfaction of the moral sense; for it is produced by means of a conception and not immediately by the single fact of intuition: accordingly it is by no means determined by the different degrees of beauty in forms. For, after all, is there anything so specially charming in a flower of common appearance, in a spring, a moss-covered stone, the warbling of birds, or the buzzing of bees, etc.? What is that can give these objects a claim to our love? It is not these objects in themselves; it is an idea represented by them that we love in them. We love in them life and its latent action, the effects peacefully produced by beings of themselves, existence under its proper laws, the inmost necessity of things, the eternal unity of their nature.

These objects which captivate us are what we were, what we must be again some day. We were nature as they are; and culture, following the way of reason and of liberty, must bring us back to nature. Accordingly, these objects are an image of our infancy irrevocably past—of our infancy which will remain eternally very dear to us, and thus they infuse a certain melancholy into us; they are also the image of our highest perfection in the ideal world, whence they excite a sublime emotion in us.

But the perfection of these objects is not a merit that belongs to them, because it is not the effect of their free choice. Accordingly they procure quite a peculiar pleasure for us, by being our models without having anything humiliating for us. It is like a constant manifestation of the divinity surrounding us, which refreshes without dazzling us. The very feature that constitutes their character is precisely what is lacking in ours to make it complete; and what distinguishes us from them is precisely what they lack to be divine. We are free and they are necessary; we change and they remain identical. Now it is only when these two conditions are united, when the will submits freely to the laws of necessity, and when, in the midst of all the changes of which the imagination is susceptible, reason maintains its rule—it is only then that the divine or the ideal is manifested. Thus we perceive eternally in them that which we have not, but which we are continually forced to strive after; that which we can never reach, but which we can hope to approach by continual progress. And we perceive in ourselves an advantage which they lack, but in which some of them—the beings deprived of reason—cannot absolutely share, and in which the others, such as children, can only one day have a share by following our way. Accordingly, they procure us the most delicious feeling of our human nature, as an idea, though in relation to each determinate state of our nature they cannot fail to humble us.

As this interest in nature is based on an idea, it can only manifest itself in a soul capable of ideas, that is, in a moral soul. For the immense majority it is nothing more than pure affectation; and this taste of sentimentality so widely diffused in our day, manifesting itself, especially since the appearance of certain books, by sentimental excursions and journeys, by sentimental gardens, and other fancies akin to these—this taste by no means proves that true refinement of sense has become general. Nevertheless, it is certain that nature will always produce something of this impression, even on the most insensible hearts, because all that is required for this is the moral disposition or aptitude, which is common to all men. For all men, however contrary their acts may be to simplicity and to the truth of nature, are brought back to it in their ideas. This sensibility in connection with nature is specially and most strongly manifested, in the greater part of persons, in connection with those sorts of objects which are closely related to us, and which, causing us to look closer into ourselves, show us more clearly what in us departs from nature; for example, in connection with children, or with nations in a state of infancy. It is an error to suppose that it is only the idea of their weakness that, in certain moments, makes us dwell with our eyes on children with so much emotion. This may be true with those who, in the presence of a feeble being, are used to feel nothing but their own superiority. But the feeling of which I speak is only experienced in a very peculiar moral disposition, nor must it be confounded with the feeling awakened in us by the joyous activity of children. The feeling of which I speak is calculated rather to humble than to flatter our self-love; and if it gives us the idea of some advantage, this advantage is at all events not on our side.

We are moved in the presence of childhood, but it is not because from the height of our strength and of our perfection we drop a look of pity on it; it is, on the contrary, because from the depths of our impotence, of which the feeling is inseparable from that of the real and determinate state to which we have arrived, we raise our eyes to the child's determinableness and pure innocence. The feeling we then experience is too evidently mingled with sadness for us to mistake its source. In the child, all is disposition and destination; in us, all is in the state of a completed, finished thing, and the completion always remains infinitely below the destination. It follows that the child is to us like the representation of the ideal; not, indeed, of the ideal as we have realized it, but such as our destination admitted; and, consequently, it is not at all the idea of its indigence, of its hinderances, that makes us experience emotion in the child's presence; it is, on the contrary, the idea of its pure and free force, of the integrity, the infinity of its being. This is the reason why, in the sight of every moral and sensible man, the child will always be a sacred thing; I mean an object which, by the grandeur of an idea, reduces to nothingness all grandeur realized by experience; an object which, in spite of all it may lose in the judgment of the understanding, regains largely the advantage before the judgment of reason.

Now it is precisely this contradiction between the judgment of reason and that of the understanding which produces in us this quite special phenomenon, this mixed feeling, called forth in us by the sight of the simple—I mean the simple in the manner of thinking. It is at once the idea of a childlike simplicity and of a childish simplicity. By what it has of childish simplicity it exposes a weak side to the understanding, and provokes in us that smile by which we testify our superiority (an entirely speculative superiority). But directly we have reason to think that childish simplicity is at the same time a childlike simplicity—that it is not consequently a want of intelligence, an infirmity in a theoretical point of view, but a superior force (practically), a heart-full of truth and innocence, which is its source, a heart that has despised the help of art because it was conscious of its real and internal greatness—directly this is understood, the understanding no longer seeks to triumph. Then raillery, which was directed against simpleness, makes way for the admiration inspired by noble simplicity. We feel ourselves obliged to esteem this object, which at first made us smile, and directing our eyes to ourselves, to feel ourselves unhappy in not resembling it. Thus is produced that very special phenomenon of a feeling in which good-natured raillery, respect, and sadness are confounded. It is the condition of the simple that nature should triumph over art, either unconsciously to the individual and against his inclination, or with his full and entire cognizance. In the former case it is simplicity as a surprise, and the impression resulting from it is one of gayety; in the second case, it is simplicity of feeling, and we are moved.

With regard to simplicity as a surprise, the person must be morally capable of denying nature. In simplicity of feeling the person may be morally incapable of this, but we must not think him physically incapable, in order that it may make upon us the impression of the simple. This is the reason why the acts and words of children only produce the impression of simplicity upon us when we forget that they are physically incapable of artifice, and in general only when we are exclusively impressed by the contrast between their natural character and what is artificial in us. Simplicity is a childlike ingenuousness which is encountered when it is not expected; and it is for this very reason that, taking the word in its strictest sense, simplicity could not be attributed to childhood properly speaking.

But in both cases, in simplicity as a surprise and simplicity as a feeling, nature must always have the upper hand, and art succumb to her.

Until we have established this distinction we can only form an incomplete idea of simplicity. The affections are also something natural, and the rules of decency are artificial; yet the triumph of the affections over decency is anything but simple. But when affection triumphs over artifice, over false decency, over dissimulation, we shall have no difficulty in applying the word simple to this. Nature must therefore triumph over art, not by its blind and brutal force as a dynamical power, but in virtue of its form as a moral magnitude; in a word, not as a want, but as an internal necessity. It must not be insufficiency, but the inopportune character of the latter that gives nature her victory; for insufficiency is only a want and a defect, and nothing that results from a want or defect could produce esteem. No doubt in the simplicity resulting from surprise, it is always the predominance of affection and a want of reflection that causes us to appear natural. But this want and this predominance do not by any means suffice to constitute simplicity; they merely give occasion to nature to obey without let or hinderance her moral constitution, that is, the law of harmony.

The simplicity resulting from surprise can only be encountered in man and that only in as far as at the moment he ceases to be a pure and innocent nature. This sort of simplicity implies a will that is not in harmony with that which nature does of her own accord. A person simple after this fashion, when recalled to himself, will be the first to be alarmed at what he is; on the other hand, a person in whom simplicity is found as a feeling, will only wonder at one thing, that is, at the way in which men feel astonishment. As it is not the moral subject as a person, but only his natural character set free by affection, that confesses the truth, it follows from this that we shall not attribute this sincerity to man as a merit, and that we shall be entitled to laugh at it, our raillery not being held in check by any personal esteem for his character. Nevertheless, as it is still the sincerity of nature which, even in the simplicity caused by surprise, pierces suddenly through the veil of dissimulation, a satisfaction of a superior order is mixed with the mischievous joy we feel in having caught any one in the act. This is because nature, opposed to affectation, and truth, opposed to deception, must in every case inspire us with esteem. Thus we experience, even in the presence of simplicity originating in surprise, a really moral pleasure, though it be not in connection with a moral object.

I admit that in simplicity proceeding from surprise we always experience a feeling of esteem for nature, because we must esteem truth; whereas in the simplicity of feeling we esteem the person himself, enjoying in this way not only a moral satisfaction, but also a satisfaction of which the object is moral. In both cases nature is right, since she speaks the truth; but in the second case not only is nature right, but there is also an act that does honor to the person. In the first case the sincerity of nature always puts the person to the blush, because it is involuntary; in the second it is always a merit which must be placed to the credit of the person, even when what he confesses is of a nature to cause a blush.

We attribute simplicity of feeling to a man, when, in the judgments he pronounces on things, he passes, without seeing them, over all the factitious and artificial sides of an object, to keep exclusively to simple nature. We require of him all the judgments that can be formed of things without departing from a sound nature; and we only hold him entirely free in what presupposes a departure from nature in his mode of thinking or feeling.

If a father relates to his son that such and such a person is dying of hunger, and if the child goes and carries the purse of his father to this unfortunate being, this is a simple action. It is in fact a healthy nature that acts in the child; and in a world where healthy nature would be the law, he would be perfectly right to act so. He only sees the misery of his neighbor and the speediest means of relieving him. The extension given to the right of property, in consequence of which part of the human race might perish, is not based on mere nature. Thus the act of this child puts to shame real society, and this is acknowledged by our heart in the pleasure it experiences from this action.

If a good-hearted man, inexperienced in the ways of the world, confides his secrets to another, who deceives him, but who is skilful in disguising his perfidy, and if by his very sincerity he furnishes him with the means of doing him injury, we find his conduct simple. We laugh at him, yet we cannot avoid esteeming him, precisely on account of his simplicity. This is because his trust in others proceeds from the rectitude of his own heart; at all events, there is simplicity here only as far as this is the case.

Simplicity in the mode of thinking cannot then ever be the act of a depraved man; this quality only belongs to children, and to men who are children in heart. It often happens to these in the midst of the artificial relations of the great world to act or to think in a simple manner. Being themselves of a truly good and humane nature, they forget that they have to do with a depraved world; and they act, even in the courts of kings, with an ingenuousness and an innocence that are only found in the world of pastoral idyls.

Nor is it always such an easy matter to distinguish exactly childish candor from childlike candor, for there are actions that are on the skirts of both. Is a certain act foolishly simple, and must we laugh at it? or is it nobly simple, and must we esteem the actors the higher on that account? It is difficult to know which side to take in some cases. A very remarkable example of this is found in the history of the government of Pope Adrian VI., related by Mr. Schroeckh with all the solidity and the spirit of practical truth which distinguish him. Adrian, a Netherlander by birth, exerted the pontifical sway at one of the most critical moments for the hierarchy—at a time when an exasperated party laid bare without any scruple all the weak sides of the Roman Church, while the opposite party was interested in the highest degree in covering them over. I do not entertain the question how a man of a truly simple character ought to act in such a case, if such a character were placed in the papal chair. But, we ask, how could this simplicity of feeling be compatible with the part of a pope? This question gave indeed very little embarrassment to the predecessors and successors of Adrian. They followed uniformly the system adopted once for all by the court of Rome, not to make any concessions anywhere. But Adrian had preserved the upright character of his nation and the innocence of his previous condition. Issuing from the humble sphere of literary men to rise to this eminent position, he did not belie at that elevation the primitive simplicity of his character. He was moved by the abuses of the Roman Church, and he was much too sincere to dissimulate publicly what he confessed privately. It was in consequence of this manner of thinking that, in his instruction to his legate in Germany, he allowed himself to be drawn into avowals hitherto unheard of in a sovereign pontiff, and diametrically contrary to the principles of that court "We know well," he said, among other things, "that for many years many abominable things have taken place in this holy chair; it is not therefore astonishing that the evil has been propagated from the head to the members, from the pope to the prelates. We have all gone astray from the good road, and for a long time there is none of us, not one, who has done anything good." Elsewhere he orders his legate to declare in his name "that he, Adrian, cannot be blamed for what other popes have done before him; that he himself, when he occupied a comparatively mediocre position, had always condemned these excesses." It may easily be conceived how such simplicity in a pope must have been received by the Roman clergy. The smallest crime of which he was accused was that of betraying the church and delivering it over to heretics. Now this proceeding, supremely imprudent in a pope, would yet deserve our esteem and admiration if we could believe it was real simplicity; that is, that Adrian, without fear of consequences, had made such an avowal, moved by his natural sincerity, and that he would have persisted in acting thus, though he had understood all the drift of his clumsiness. Unhappily we have some reason to believe that he did not consider his conduct as altogether impolitic, and that in his candor he went so far as to flatter himself that he had served very usefully the interests of his church by his indulgence to his adversaries. He did not even imagine that he ought to act thus in his quality as an honest man; he thought also as a pope to be able to justify himself, and forgetting that the most artificial of structures could only be supported by continuing to deny the truth, he committed the unpardonable fault of having recourse to means of safety, excellent perhaps, in a natural situation, but here applied to entirely contrary circumstances. This necessarily modifies our judgment very much, and although we cannot refuse our esteem for the honesty of heart in which the act originates, this esteem is greatly lessened when we reflect that nature on this occasion was too easily mistress of art, and that the heart too easily overruled the head.

True genius is of necessity simple, or it is not genius. Simplicity alone gives it this character, and it cannot belie in the moral order what it is in the intellectual and aesthetical order. It does not know those rules, the crutches of feebleness, those pedagogues which prop up slippery spirits; it is only guided by nature and instinct, its guardian angel; it walks with a firm, calm step across all the snares of false taste, snares in which the man without genius, if he have not the prudence to avoid them the moment he detects them, remains infallibly imbedded. It is therefore the part only of genius to issue from the known without ceasing to be at home, or to enlarge the circle of nature without overstepping it. It does indeed sometimes happen that a great genius oversteps it; but only because geniuses have their moments of frenzy, when nature, their protector, abandons them, because the force of example impels them, or because the corrupt taste of their age leads them astray.

The most intricate problems must be solved by genius with simplicity, without pretension, with ease; the egg of Christopher Columbus is the emblem of all the discoveries of genius. It only justifies its character as genius by triumphing through simplicity over all the complications of art. It does not proceed according to known principles, but by feelings and inspiration; the sallies of genius are the inspirations of a God (all that healthy nature produces is divine); its feelings are laws for all time, for all human generations.

This childlike character imprinted by genius on its works is also shown by it in its private life and manners. It is modest, because nature is always so; but it is not decent, because corruption alone is decent. It is intelligent, because nature cannot lack intelligence; but it is not cunning, because art only can be cunning. It is faithful to its character and inclinations, but this is not so much because it has principles as because nature, notwithstanding all its oscillations, always returns to its equilibrium, and brings back the same wants. It is modest and even timid, because genius remains always a secret to itself; but it is not anxious, because it does not know the dangers of the road in which it walks. We know little of the private life of the greatest geniuses; but the little that we know of it—what tradition has preserved, for example, of Sophocles, of Archimedes, of Hippocrates, and in modern times of Ariosto, of Dante, of Tasso, of Raphael, of Albert Duerer, of Cervantes, of Shakespeare, of Fielding, of Sterne, etc.— confirms this assertion.

Nay, more; though this admission seems more difficult to support, even the greatest philosophers and great commanders, if great by their genius, have simplicity in their character. Among the ancients I need only name Julius Caesar and Epaminondas; among the moderns Henry IV. in France, Gustavus Adolphus in Sweden, and the Czar Peter the Great. The Duke of Marlborough, Turenne, and Vendome all present this character. With regard to the other sex, nature proposes to it simplicity of character as the supreme perfection to which it should reach. Accordingly, the love of pleasing in women strives after nothing so much as the appearance of simplicity; a sufficient proof, if it were the only one, that the greatest power of the sex reposes in this quality. But, as the principles that prevail in the education of women are perpetually struggling with this character, it is as difficult for them in the moral order to reconcile this magnificent gift of nature with the advantages of a good education as it is difficult for men to preserve them unchanged in the intellectual order: and the woman who knows how to join a knowledge of the world to this sort of simplicity in manners is as deserving of respect as a scholar who joins to the strictness of scholastic rules the freedom and originality of thought.

Simplicity in our mode of thinking brings with it of necessity simplicity in our mode of expression, simplicity in terms as well as movement; and it is in this that grace especially consists. Genius expresses its most sublime and its deepest thoughts with this simple grace; they are the divine oracles that issue from the lips of a child; while the scholastic spirit, always anxious to avoid error, tortures all its words, all its ideas, and makes them pass through the crucible of grammar and logic, hard and rigid, in order to keep from vagueness, and uses few words in order not to say too much, enervates and blunts thought in order not to wound the reader who is not on his guard—genius gives to its expression, with a single and happy stroke of the brush, a precise, firm, and yet perfectly free form. In the case of grammar and logic, the sign and the thing signified are always heterogenous and strangers to each other: with genius, on the contrary, the expression gushes forth spontaneously from the idea, the language and the thought are one and the same; so that even though the expression thus gives it a body the spirit appears as if disclosed in a nude state. This fashion of expression, when the sign disappears entirely in the thing signified, when the tongue, so to speak, leaves the thought it translates naked, whilst the other mode of expression cannot represent thought without veiling it at the same time: this is what is called originality and inspiration in style.

This freedom, this natural mode by which genius expresses itself in works of intellect, is also the expression of the innocence of heart in the intercourse of life. Every one knows that in the world men have departed from simplicity, from the rigorous veracity of language, in the same proportion as they have lost the simplicity of feelings. The guilty conscience easily wounded, the imagination easily seduced, made an anxious decency necessary. Without telling what is false, people often speak differently from what they think; we are obliged to make circumlocutions to say certain things, which however, can never afflict any but a sickly self-love, and that have no danger except for a depraved imagination. The ignorance of these laws of propriety (conventional laws), coupled with a natural sincerity which despises all kinds of bias and all appearance of falsity (sincerity I mean, not coarseness, for coarseness dispenses with forms because it is hampered), gives rise in the intercourse of life to a simplicity of expression that consists in naming things by their proper name without circumlocution. This is done because we do not venture to designate them as they are, or only to do so by artificial means. The ordinary expressions of children are of this kind. They make us smile because they are in opposition to received manners; but men would always agree in the bottom of their hearts that the child is right.

It is true that simplicity of feeling cannot properly be attributed to the child any more than to the man,—that is, to a being not absolutely subject to nature, though there is still no simplicity, except on the condition that it is pure nature that acts through him. But by an effort of the imagination, which likes to poetise things, we often carry over these attributes of a rational being to beings destitute of reason. It is thus that, on seeing an animal, a landscape, a building, and nature in general, from opposition to what is arbitrary and fantastic in the conceptions of man, we often attribute to them a simple character. But that implies always that in our thought we attribute a will to these things that have none, and that we are struck to see it directed rigorously according to the laws of necessity. Discontented as we are that we have ill employed our own moral freedom, and that we no longer find moral harmony in our conduct, we are easily led to a certain disposition of mind, in which we willingly address ourselves to a being destitute of reason, as if it were a person. And we readily view it as if it had really had to struggle against the temptation of acting otherwise, and proceed to make a merit of its eternal uniformity, and to envy its peaceable constancy. We are quite disposed to consider in those moments reason, this prerogative of the human race, as a pernicious gift and as an evil; we feel so vividly all that is imperfect in our conduct that we forget to be just to our destiny and to our aptitudes.

We see, then, in nature, destitute of reason, only a sister who, more fortunate than ourselves, has remained under the maternal roof, while in the intoxication of our freedom we have fled from it to throw ourselves into a stranger world. We regret this place of safety, we earnestly long to come back to it as soon as we have begun to feel the bitter side of civilization, and in the totally artificial life in which we are exiled we hear in deep emotion the voice of our mother. While we were still only children of nature we were happy, we were perfect: we have become free, and we have lost both advantages. Hence a twofold and very unequal longing for nature: the longing for happiness and the longing for the perfection that prevails there. Man, as a sensuous being, deplores sensibly the loss of the former of these goods; it is only the moral man who can be afflicted at the loss of the other.

Therefore, let the man with a sensible heart and a loving nature question himself closely. Is it your indolence that longs for its repose, or your wounded moral sense that longs for its harmony? Ask yourself well, when, disgusted with the artifices, offended by the abuses that you discover in social life, you feel yourself attracted towards inanimate nature, in the midst of solitude ask yourself what impels you to fly the world. Is it the privation from which you suffer, its loads, its troubles? or is it the moral anarchy, the caprice, the disorder that prevail there? Your heart ought to plunge into these troubles with joy, and to find in them the compensation in the liberty of which they are the consequence. You can, I admit, propose as your aim, in a distant future, the calm and the happiness of nature; but only that sort of happiness which is the reward of your dignity. Thus, then, let there be no more complaint about the loads of life, the inequality of conditions, or the hampering of social relations, or the uncertainty of possession, ingratitude, oppression, and persecution. You must submit to all these evils of civilization with a free resignation; it is the natural condition of good, par excellence, of the only good, and you ought to respect it under this head. In all these evils you ought only to deplore what is morally evil in them, and you must do so not with cowardly tears only. Rather watch to remain pure yourself in the midst of these impurities, free amidst this slavery, constant with yourself in the midst of these capricious changes, a faithful observer of the law amidst this anarchy. Be not frightened at the disorder that is without you, but at the disorder which is within; aspire after unity, but seek it not in uniformity; aspire after repose, but through equilibrium, and not by suspending the action of your faculties. This nature which you envy in the being destitute of reason deserves no esteem: it is not worth a wish. You have passed beyond it; it ought to remain for ever behind you. The ladder that carried you having given way under your foot, the only thing for you to do is to seize again on the moral law freely, with a free consciousness, a free will, or else to roll down, hopeless of safety, into a bottomless abyss.

But when you have consoled yourself for having lost the happiness of nature, let its perfection be a model to your heart. If you can issue from the circle in which art keeps you enclosed and find nature again, if it shows itself to you in its greatness and in its calm, in its simple beauty, in its childlike innocence and simplicity, oh! then pause before its image, cultivate this feeling lovingly. It is worthy of you, and of what is noblest in man. Let it no more come into your mind to change with it; rather embrace it, absorb it into your being, and try to associate the infinite advantage it has over you with that infinite prerogative that is peculiar to you, and let the divine issue from this sublime union. Let nature breathe around you like a lovely idyl, where far from artifice and its wanderings you may always find yourself again, where you may go to draw fresh courage, a new confidence, to resume your course, and kindle again in your heart the flame of the ideal, so readily extinguished amidst the tempests of life.

If we think of that beautiful nature which surrounded the ancient Greeks, if we remember how intimately that people, under its blessed sky, could live with that free nature; how their mode of imagining, and of feeling, and their manners, approached far nearer than ours to the simplicity of nature, how faithfully the works of their poets express this; we must necessarily remark, as a strange fact, that so few traces are met among them of that sentimental interest that we moderns ever take in the scenes of nature and in natural characters. I admit that the Greeks are superiorly exact and faithful in their descriptions of nature. They reproduce their details with care, but we see that they take no more interest in them and more heart in them than in describing a vestment, a shield, armor, a piece of furniture, or any production of the mechanical arts. In their love for the object it seems that they make no difference between what exists in itself and what owes its existence to art, to the human will. It seems that nature interests their minds and their curiosity more than moral feeling. They do not attach themselves to it with that depth of feeling, with that gentle melancholy, that characterize the moderns. Nay, more, by personifying nature in its particular phenomena, by deifying it, by representing its effects as the acts of free being, they take from it that character of calm necessity which is precisely what makes it so attractive to us. Their impatient imagination only traverses nature to pass beyond it to the drama of human life. It only takes pleasure in the spectacle of what is living and free; it requires characters, acts, the accidents of fortune and of manners; and whilst it happens with us, at least in certain moral dispositions, to curse our prerogative, this free will, which exposes us to so many combats with ourselves, to so many anxieties and errors, and to wish to exchange it for the condition of beings destitute of reason, for that fatal existence that no longer admits of any choice, but which is so calm in its uniformity;—while we do this, the Greeks, on the contrary, only have their imagination occupied in retracing human nature in the inanimate world, and in giving to the will an influence where blind necessity rules.

Whence can arise this difference between the spirit of the ancients and the modern spirit? How comes it that, being, for all that relates to nature, incomparably below the ancients, we are superior to them precisely on this point, that we render a more complete homage to nature; that we have a closer attachment to it; and that we are capable of embracing even the inanimate world with the most ardent sensibility. It is because nature, in our time, is no longer in man, and that we no longer encounter it in its primitive truth, except out of humanity, in the inanimate world. It is not because we are more conformable to nature—quite the contrary;

it is because in our social relations, in our mode of existence, in our manners, we are in opposition with nature. This is what leads us, when the instinct of truth and of simplicity is awakened—this instinct which, like the moral aptitude from which it proceeds, lives incorruptible and indelible in every human heart—to procure for it in the physical world the satisfaction which there is no hope of finding in the moral order. This is the reason why the feeling that attaches us to nature is connected so closely with that which makes us regret our infancy, forever flown, and our primitive innocence. Our childhood is all that remains of nature in humanity, such as civilization has made it, of untouched, unmutilated nature. It is, therefore, not wonderful, when we meet out of us the impress of nature, that we are always brought back to the idea of our childhood.

It was quite different with the Greeks in antiquity. Civilization with them did not degenerate, nor was it carried to such an excess that it was necessary to break with nature. The entire structure of their social life reposed on feelings, and not on a factitious conception, on a work of art. Their very theology was the inspiration of a simple spirit, the fruit of a joyous imagination, and not, like the ecclesiastical dogmas of modern nations, subtle combinations of the understanding. Since, therefore, the Greeks had not lost sight of nature in humanity, they had no reason, when meeting it out of man, to be surprised at their discovery, and they would not feel very imperiously the need of objects in which nature could be retraced. In accord with themselves, happy in feeling themselves men, they would of necessity keep to humanity as to what was greatest to them, and they must needs try to make all the rest approach it; while we, who are not in accord with ourselves—we who are discontented with the experience we have made of our humanity—have no more pressing interest than to fly out of it and to remove from our sight a so ill-fashioned form. The feeling of which we are treating here is, therefore, not that which was known by the ancients; it approaches far more nearly that which we ourselves experience for the ancients. The ancients felt naturally; we, on our part, feel what is natural. It was certainly a very different inspiration that filled the soul of Homer, when he depicted his divine cowherd [Dios uphorbos, "Odyssey," xiv. 413, etc.] giving hospitality to Ulysses, from that which agitated the soul of the young Werther at the moment when he read the "Odyssey" [Werther, May 26, June 21, August 28, May 9, etc.] on issuing from an assembly in which he had only found tedium. The feeling we experience for nature resembles that of a sick man for health.

As soon as nature gradually vanishes from human life—that is, in proportion as it ceases to be experienced as a subject (active and passive)—we see it dawn and increase in the poetical world in the guise of an idea and as an object. The people who have carried farthest the want of nature, and at the same time the reflections on that matter, must needs have been the people who at the same time were most struck with this phenomenon of the simple, and gave it a name. If I am not mistaken, this people was the French. But the feeling of the simple, and the interest we take in it, must naturally go much farther back, and it dates from the time when the moral sense and the aesthetical sense began to be corrupt. This modification in the manner of feeling is exceedingly striking in Euripides, for example, if compared with his predecessors, especially Aeschylus; and yet Euripides was the favorite poet of his time. The same revolution is perceptible in the ancient historians. Horace, the poet of a cultivated and corrupt epoch, praises, under the shady groves of Tibur, the calm and happiness of the country, and he might be termed the true founder of this sentimental poetry, of which he has remained the unsurpassed model. In Propertius, Virgil, and others, we find also traces of this mode of feeling; less of it is found in Ovid, who would have required for that more abundance of heart, and who in his exile at Tomes sorrowfully regrets the happiness that Horace so readily dispensed with in his villa at Tibur.

It is in the fundamental idea of poetry that the poet is everywhere the guardian of nature. When he can no longer entirely fill this part, and has already in himself suffered the deleterious influence of arbitrary and factitious forms, or has had to struggle against this influence, he presents himself as the witness of nature and as its avenger. The poet will, therefore, be the expression of nature itself, or his part will be to seek it, if men have lost sight of it. Hence arise two kinds of poetry, which embrace and exhaust the entire field of poetry. All poets —I mean those who are really so—will belong, according to the time when they flourish, according to the accidental circumstances that have influenced their education generally, and the different dispositions of mind through which they pass, will belong, I say, to the order of the sentimental poetry or to simple poetry.

The poet of a young world, simple and inspired, as also the poet who at an epoch of artificial civilization approaches nearest to the primitive bards, is austere and prudish, like the virginal Diana in her forests. Wholly unconfiding, he hides himself from the heart that seeks him, from the desire that wishes to embrace him. It is not rare for the dry truth with which he treats his subject to resemble insensibility. The whole object possesses him, and to reach his heart it does not suffice, as with metals of little value, to stir up the surface; as with pure gold, you must go down to the lowest depths. Like the Deity behind this universe, the simple poet hides himself behind his work; he is himself his work, and his work is himself. A man must be no longer worthy of the work, nor understand it, or be tired of it, to be even anxious to learn who is its author.

Such appears to us, for instance, Homer in antiquity, and Shakespeare among moderns: two natures infinitely different and separated in time by an abyss, but perfectly identical as to this trait of character. When, at a very youthful age, I became first acquainted with Shakespeare, I was displeased with his coldness, with his insensibility, which allows him to jest even in the most pathetic moments, to disturb the impression of the most harrowing scenes in "Hamlet," in "King Lear," and in "Macbeth," etc., by mixing with them the buffooneries of a madman. I was revolted by his insensibility, which allowed him to pause sometimes at places where my sensibility would bid me hasten and bear me along, and which sometimes carried him away with indifference when my heart would be so happy to pause. Though I was accustomed, by the practice of modern poets, to seek at once the poet in his works, to meet his heart, to reflect with him in his theme—in a word, to see the object in the subject—I could not bear that the poet could in Shakespeare never be seized, that he would never give me an account of himself. For some years Shakespeare had been the object of my study and of all my respect before I had learned to love his personality. I was not yet able to comprehend nature at first hand. All that my eyes could bear was its image only, reflected by the understanding and arranged by rules:

and on this score the sentimental poetry of the French, or that of the Germans of 1750 to 1780, was what suited me best. For the rest, I do not blush at this childish judgment: adult critics pronounced in that day in the same way, and carried their simplicity so far as to publish their decisions to the world.

The same thing happened to me in the case of Homer, with whom I made acquaintance at a later date. I remember now that remarkable passage of the sixth book of the "Iliad," where Glaucus and Diomed meet each other in the strife, and then, recognizing each other as host and guest, exchange presents. With this touching picture of the piety with which the laws of hospitality were observed even in war, may be compared a picture of chivalrous generosity in Ariosto. The knights, rivals in love, Ferragus and Rinaldo—the former a Saracen, the latter a Christian —after having fought to extremity, all covered with wounds, make peace together, and mount the same horse to go and seek the fugitive Angelica. These two examples, however different in other respects, are very similar with regard to the impression produced on our heart: both represent the noble victory of moral feeling over passion, and touch us by the simplicity of feeling displayed in them. But what a difference in the way in which the two poets go to work to describe two such analogous scenes! Ariosto, who belongs to an advanced epoch, to a world where simplicity of manners no longer existed, in relating this trait, cannot conceal the astonishment, the admiration, he feels at it. He measures the distance from those manners to the manners of his own age, and this feeling of astonishment is too strong for him. He abandons suddenly the painting of the object, and comes himself on the scene in person. This beautiful stanza is well known, and has been always specially admired at all times:—

"Oh nobleness, oh generosity of the ancient manners of chivalry! These were rivals, separated by their faith, suffering bitter pain throughout their frames in consequence of a desperate combat; and, without any suspicion, behold them riding in company along dark and winding paths. Stimulated by four spurs, the horse hastens his pace till they arrive at the place where the road divides." ["Orlando Furioso," canto i., stanza 32.]

Now let us turn to old Homer. Scarcely has Diomed learned by the story of Glaucus, his adversary, that the latter has been, from the time of their fathers, the host and friend of his family, when he drives his lance into the ground, converses familiarly with him, and both agree henceforth to avoid each other in the strife. But let us hear Homer himself:—

"'Thus, then, I am for thee a faithful host in Argos, and thou to me in Lycia, when I shall visit that country. We shall, therefore, avoid our lances meeting in the strife. Are there not for me other Trojans or brave allies to kill when a god shall offer them to me and my steps shall reach them? And for thee, Glaucus, are there not enough Achaeans, that thou mayest immolate whom thou wishest? But let us exchange our arms, in order that others may also see that we boast of having been hosts and guests at the time of our fathers.' Thus they spoke, and, rushing from their chariots, they seized each other's hands, and swore friendship the one to the other." [Pope's "Iliad," vi. 264-287.]

It would have been difficult for a modern poet (at least to one who would be modern in the moral sense of the term) even to wait as long as this before expressing his joy in the presence of

179

such an action. We should pardon this in him the more easily, because we also, in reading it, feel that our heart makes a pause here, and readily turns aside from the object to bring back its thoughts on itself. But there is not the least trace of this in Homer. As if he had been relating something that is seen everyday—nay, more, as if he had no heart beating in his breast—he continues, with his dry truthfulness:—

"Then the son of Saturn blinded Glaucus, who, exchanging his armor with Diomed, gave him golden arms of the value of one hecatomb, for brass arms only worth nine beeves." ["Iliad," vi. 234-236.]

The poets of this order,—the genuinely simple poets, are scarcely any longer in their place in this artificial age. Accordingly they are scarcely possible in it, or at least they are only possible on the condition of traversing their age, like scared persons, at a running pace, and of being preserved by a happy star from the influence of their age, which would mutilate their genius. Never, for ay and forever, will society produce these poets; but out of society they still appear sometimes at intervals, rather, I admit, as strangers, who excite wonder, or as ill-trained children of nature, who give offence. These apparitions, so very comforting for the artist who studies them, and for the real connoisseur, who knows how to appreciate them, are, as a general conclusion, in the age when they are begotten, to a very small degree preposterous. The seal of empire is stamped on their brow, and we,—we ask the Muses to cradle us, to carry us in their arms. The critics, as regular constables of art, detest these poets as disturbers of rules or of limits. Homer himself may have been only indebted to the testimony of ten centuries for the reward these aristarchs are kindly willing to concede him. Moreover, they find it a hard matter to maintain their rules against his example, or his authority against their rules.

SENTIMENTAL POETRY.

I have previously remarked that the poet is nature, or he seeks nature. In the former case, he is a simple poet, in the second case, a sentimental poet.

The poetic spirit is immortal, nor can it disappear from humanity; it can only disappear with humanity itself, or with the aptitude to be a man, a human being. And actually, though man by the freedom of his imagination and of his understanding departs from simplicity, from truth, from the necessity of nature, not only a road always remains open to him to return to it, but, moreover, a powerful and indestructible instinct, the moral instinct, brings him incessantly back to nature; and it is precisely the poetical faculty that is united to this instinct by the ties of the closest relationship. Thus man does not lose the poetic faculty directly he parts with the simplicity of nature; only this faculty acts out of him in another direction.

Even at present nature is the only flame that kindles and warms the poetic soul. From nature alone it obtains all its force; to nature alone it speaks in the artificial culture-seeking man. Any other form of displaying its activity is remote from the poetic spirit. Accordingly it may be remarked that it is incorrect to apply the expression poetic to any of the so-styled productions of wit, though the high credit given to French literature has led people for a long period to class them in that category. I repeat that at present, even in the existing phase of culture, it is still nature that powerfully stirs up the poetic spirit, only its present relation to nature is of a different order from formerly.

As long as man dwells in a state of pure nature (I mean pure and not coarse nature), all his being acts at once like a simple sensuous unity, like a harmonious whole. The senses and reason, the receptive faculty and the spontaneously active faculty, have not been as yet separated in their respective functions: a fortiori they are not yet in contradiction with each other. Then the feelings of man are not the formless play of chance; nor are his thoughts an empty play of the imagination, without any value. His feelings proceed from the law of necessity; his thoughts from reality. But when man enters the state of civilization, and art has fashioned him, this sensuous harmony which was in him disappears, and henceforth he can only manifest himself as a moral unity, that is, as aspiring to unity. The harmony that existed as a fact in the former state, the harmony of feeling and thought, only exists now in an ideal state. It is no longer in him, but out of him; it is a conception of thought which he must begin by realizing in himself; it is no longer a fact, a reality of his life. Well, now let us take the idea of poetry, which is nothing else than expressing humanity as completely as possible, and let us apply this idea to these two states. We shall be brought to infer that, on the one hand, in the state of natural simplicity, when all the faculties of man are exerted together, his being still manifests itself in a harmonious unity, where, consequently, the totality of his nature expresses itself in reality itself, the part of the poet is necessarily to imitate the real as completely as is possible. In the state of civilization, on the contrary, when this harmonious competition of the whole of human nature is no longer anything but an idea, the part of the poet is necessarily to raise reality to the ideal, or, what amounts to the same thing, to represent the ideal. And, actually, these are the only two ways in which, in general, the poetic genius can manifest itself. Their great difference is quite evident, but though there be great opposition between them, a higher idea exists that embraces both, and there is no cause to be astonished if this idea coincides with the very idea of humanity.

This is not the place to pursue this thought any further, as it would require a separate discussion to place it in its full light. But if we only compare the modern and ancient poets together, not according to the accidental forms which they may have employed, but according to their spirit, we shall be easily convinced of the truth of this thought. The thing that touches us in the ancient poets is nature; it is the truth of sense, it is a present and a living reality modern poets touch us through the medium of ideas.

The path followed by modern poets is moreover that necessarily followed by man generally, individuals as well as the species. Nature reconciles man with himself; art divides and disunites him; the ideal brings him back to unity. Now, the ideal being an infinite that he never succeeds in reaching, it follows that civilized man can never become perfect in his kind, while the man of nature can become so in his. Accordingly in relation to perfection one would be infinitely below the other, if we only considered the relation in which they are both to their own kind and to their maximum. If, on the other hand, it is the kinds that are compared together, it is ascertained that the end to which man tends by civilization is infinitely superior to that which he reaches through nature. Thus one has his reward, because having for object a finite magnitude, he completely reaches this object; the merit of the other is to approach an object that is of infinite magnitude. Now, as there are only degrees, and as there is only progress in the second of these evolutions, it follows that the relative merit of the man engaged in the ways of civilization is never determinable in general, though this man, taking the individuals separately, is necessarily at a disadvantage, compared with the man in whom nature acts in all its perfection. But we know also that humanity cannot reach its final end except by progress, and that the man of nature cannot make progress save through culture, and consequently by passing himself through the way of civilization. Accordingly there is no occasion to ask with which of the two the advantage must remain, considering this last end.

All that we say here of the different forms of humanity may be applied equally to the two orders of poets who correspond to them.

Accordingly it would have been desirable not to compare at all the ancient and the modern poets, the simple and the sentimental poets, or only to compare them by referring them to a higher idea (since there is really only one) which embraces both. For, sooth to say, if we begin by forming a specific idea of poetry, merely from the ancient poets, nothing is easier, but also nothing is more vulgar, than to depreciate the moderns by this comparison. If persons wish to confine the name of poetry to that which has in all times produced the same impression in simple nature, this places them in the necessity of contesting the title of poet in the moderns precisely in that which constitutes their highest beauties, their greatest originality and sublimity; for precisely in the points where they excel the most, it is the child of civilization whom they address, and they have nothing to say to the simple child of nature.

To the man who is not disposed beforehand to issue from reality in order to enter the field of the ideal, the richest and most substantial poetry is an empty appearance, and the sublimest flights of poetic inspiration are an exaggeration. Never will a reasonable man think of placing alongside Homer, in his grandest episodes, any of our modern poets; and it has a discordant and ridiculous effect to hear Milton or Klopstock honored with the name of a "new Homer." But take in modern poets what characterizes them, what makes their special merit, and try to compare any ancient poet with them in this point, they will not be able to support the comparison any better, and Homer less than any other. I should express it thus: the power of the ancients consists in compressing objects into the finite, and the moderns excel in the art of the infinite.

What we have said here may be extended to the fine arts in general, except certain restrictions that are self-evident. If, then, the strength of the artists of antiquity consists in determining and limiting objects, we must no longer wonder that in the field of the plastic arts the ancients remain so far superior to the moderns, nor especially that poetry and the plastic arts with the moderns, compared respectively with what they were among the ancients, do not offer the same relative value. This is because an object that addresses itself to the eyes is only perfect in proportion as the object is clearly limited in it; whilst a work that is addressed to the imagination can also reach the perfection which is proper to it by means of the ideal and the infinite. This is why the superiority of the moderns in what relates to ideas is not of great aid to them in the plastic arts, where it is necessary for them to determine in space, with the greatest precision, the image which their imagination has conceived, and where they must therefore measure themselves with the ancient artist just on a point where his superiority cannot be contested. In the matter of poetry it is another affair, and if the advantage is still with the ancients on that ground, as respects the simplicity of forms—all that can be represented by sensuous features, all that is something bodily—yet, on the other hand, the moderns have the advantage over the ancients as regards fundamental wealth, and all that can neither be represented nor translated by sensuous signs, in short, for all that is called mind and idea in the works of art.

From the moment that the simple poet is content to follow simple nature and feeling, that he is contented with the imitation of the real world, he can only be placed, with regard to his subject, in a single relation. And in this respect he has no choice as to the manner of treating it. If simple poetry produces different impressions—I do not, of course, speak of the impressions that are connected with the nature of the subject, but only of those that are dependent on poetic execution—the whole difference is in the degree; there is only one way of feeling, which varies from more to less; even the diversity of external forms changes nothing in the quality of aesthetic impressions. Whether the form be lyric or epic, dramatic or descriptive, we can receive an impression either stronger or weaker, but if we remove what is connected with the nature of the subject, we shall always be affected in the same way. The feeling we experience is absolutely identical; it proceeds entirely from one single and the same element to such a degree that we are unable to make any distinction. The very difference of tongues and that of times does not here occasion any diversity, for their strict unity of origin and of effect is precisely a characteristic of simple poetry.

It is quite different with sentimental poetry. The sentimental poet reflects on the impression produced on him by objects; and it is only on this reflection that his poetic force is based. It follows that the sentimental poet is always concerned with two opposite forces, has two modes of representing objects to himself, and of feeling them; these are, the real or limited, and the ideal or infinite; and the mixed feeling that he will awaken will always testify to this duality of origin. Sentimental poetry thus admitting more than one principle, it remains to know which of the two will be predominant in the poet, both in his fashion of feeling and in that of representing the object; and consequently a difference in the mode of treating it is possible. Here, then, a new subject is presented: shall the poet attach himself to the real or the ideal? to the real as an object of aversion and of disgust, or to the ideal as an object of inclination? The poet will therefore be able to treat the same subject either in its satirical aspect or in its elegiac aspect,—taking these words in a larger sense, which will be explained in the sequel: every sentimental poet will of necessity become attached to one or the other of these two modes of feeling.

SATIRICAL POETRY.

The poet is a satirist when he takes as subject the distance at which things are from nature, and the contrast between reality and the ideal: as regards the impression received by the soul, these two subjects blend into the same. In the execution, he may place earnestness and passion, or jests and levity, according as he takes pleasure in the domain of the will or in that of the understanding. In the former case it is avenging and pathetic satire; in the second case it is sportive, humorous, and mirthful satire.

Properly speaking, the object of poetry is not compatible either with the tone of punishment or that of amusement. The former is too grave for play, which should be the main feature of poetry; the latter is too trifling for seriousness, which should form the basis of all poetic play. Our mind is necessarily interested in moral contradictions, and these deprive the mind of its liberty. Nevertheless, all personal interest, and reference to a personal necessity, should be banished from poetic feeling. But mental contradictions do not touch the heart, nevertheless the poet deals with the highest interests of the heart—nature and the ideal. Accordingly it is a hard matter for him not to violate the poetic form in pathetic satire, because this form consists in the liberty of movement; and in sportive satire he is very apt to miss the true spirit of poetry, which ought to be the infinite. The problem can only be solved in one way: by the pathetic satire assuming the character of the sublime, and the playful satire acquiring poetic substance by enveloping the theme in beauty.

In satire, the real as imperfection is opposed to the ideal, considered as the highest reality. In other respects it is by no means essential that the ideal should be expressly represented, provided the poet knows how to awaken it in our souls, but he must in all cases awaken it, otherwise he will exert absolutely no poetic action. Thus reality is here a necessary object of aversion; but it is also necessary, for the whole question centres here, that this aversion should come necessarily from the ideal, which is opposed to reality. To make this clear—this aversion might proceed from a purely sensuous source, and repose only on a want of which the satisfaction finds obstacles in the real. How often, in fact, we think we feel, against society a moral discontent, while we are simply soured by the obstacles that it opposes to our inclination. It is this entirely material interest that the vulgar satirist brings into play; and as by this road he never fails to call forth in us movements connected with the affections, he fancies that he holds our heart in his hand, and thinks he has graduated in the pathetic. But all pathos derived from this source is unworthy of poetry, which ought only to move us through the medium of ideas, and reach our heart only by passing through the reason. Moreover, this impure and material pathos will never have its effect on minds, except by over-exciting the affective faculties and by occupying our hearts with painful feelings; in this it differs entirely from the truly poetic pathos, which raises in us the feeling of moral independence, and which is recognized by the freedom of our mind persisting in it even while it is in the state of affection. And, in fact, when the emotion emanates from the ideal opposed to the real, the sublime beauty of the ideal corrects all impression of restraint; and the grandeur of the idea with which we are imbued raises us above all the limits of experience. Thus in the representation of some revolting reality, the essential thing is that the necessary be the foundation on which the poet or the narrator places the real: that he know how to dispose our mind for ideas. Provided the point from which we see and judge be elevated, it matters little if the object be low and far beneath us. When the historian Tacitus depicts the profound decadence of the Romans of the first century, it is a great soul which from a loftier position lets his looks drop down on a low object; and the disposition in which he places us is truly poetic, because it is the height where he is himself placed, and where he has succeeded in raising us, which alone renders so perceptible the baseness of the object.

Accordingly the satire of pathos must always issue from a mind deeply imbued with the ideal. It is nothing but an impulsion towards harmony that can give rise to that deep feeling of moral opposition and that ardent indignation against moral obliquity which amounted to the fulness of enthusiasm in Juvenal, Swift, Rousseau, Haller, and others. These same poets would have succeeded equally well in forms of poetry relating to all that is tender and touching in feeling, and it was only the accidents of life in their early days that diverted their minds into other walks. Nay, some amongst them actually tried their hand successfully in these other branches of poetry. The poets whose names have been just mentioned lived either at a period of degeneracy, and had scenes of painful moral obliquity presented to their view, or personal troubles had combined to fill their souls with bitter feelings. The strictly austere spirit in which Rousseau, Haller, and others paint reality is a natural result, moreover, of the philosophical mind, when with rigid adherence to laws of thought it separates the mere phenomenon from the substance of things. Yet these outer and contingent influences, which always put restraint on the mind, should never be allowed to do more than decide the direction taken by enthusiasm, nor should they ever give the material for it. The substance ought always to remain unchanged, emancipated from all external motion or stimulus, and it ought to issue from an ardent impulsion towards the ideal, which forms the only true motive that can be put forth for satirical poetry, and indeed for all sentimental poetry.

While the satire of pathos is only adapted to elevated minds, playful satire can only be adequately represented by a heart imbued with beauty. The former is preserved from triviality by the serious nature of the theme; but the latter, whose proper sphere is confined to the treatment of subjects of morally unimportant nature, would infallibly adopt the form of frivolity, and be deprived of all poetic dignity, were it not that the substance is ennobled by the form, and did not the personal dignity of the poet compensate for the insignificance of the subject. Now, it is only given to mind imbued with beauty to impress its character, its entire image, on each of its manifestations, independently of the object of its manifestations. A sublime soul can only make itself known as such by single victories over the rebellion of the senses, only in certain moments of exaltation, and by efforts of short duration. In a mind imbued with beauty, on the contrary, the ideal acts in the same manner as nature, and therefore continuously; accordingly it can manifest itself in it in a state of repose. The deep sea never appears more sublime than when it is agitated; the true beauty of a clear stream is in its peaceful course.

The question has often been raised as to the comparative preference to be awarded to tragedy or comedy. If the question is confined merely to their respective themes, it is certain that tragedy has the advantage. But if our inquiry be directed to ascertain which has the more important personality, it is probable that a decision may be given in favor of comedy. In tragedy the theme in itself does great things; in comedy the object does nothing and the poet all. Now, as in the judgments of taste no account must be kept of the matter treated of, it follows naturally that the aesthetic value of these two kinds will be in an inverse ratio to the proper importance of their themes.

The tragic poet is supported by the theme, while the comic poet, on the contrary, has to keep up the aesthetic character of his theme by his own individual influence. The former may soar, which is not a very difficult matter, but the latter has to remain one and the same in tone; he has to be in the elevated region of art, where he must be at home, but where the tragic poet has to be projected and elevated by a bound. And this is precisely what distinguishes a soul of beauty from a sublime soul. A soul of beauty bears in itself by anticipation all great ideas; they flow without constraint and without difficulty from its very nature—an infinite nature, at least in potency, at whatever point of its career you seize it. A sublime soul can rise to all kinds of greatness, but by an effort; it can tear itself from all bondage, to all that limits and constrains it, but only by strength of will. Consequently the sublime soul is only free by broken efforts; the other with ease and always.

The noble task of comedy is to produce and keep up in us this freedom of mind, just as the end of tragedy is to re-establish in us this freedom of mind by aesthetic ways, when it has been violently suspended by passion. Consequently it is necessary that in tragedy the poet, as if he made an experiment, should artificially suspend our freedom of mind, since tragedy shows its poetic virtue by re-establishing it; in comedy, on the other hand, care must be taken that things never reach this suspension of freedom.

It is for this reason that the tragic poet invariably treats his theme in a practical manner, and the comic poet in a theoretic manner, even when the former, as happened with Lessing in his "Nathan," should have the curious fancy to select a theoretical, and the latter should have that of choosing a practical subject. A piece is constituted a tragedy or a comedy not by the sphere from which the theme is taken, but by the tribunal before which it is judged. A tragic poet ought never to indulge in tranquil reasoning, and ought always to gain the interest of the heart; but the comic poet ought to shun the pathetic and bring into play the understanding. The former displays his art by creating continual excitement, the latter by perpetually subduing his passion; and it is natural that the art in both cases should acquire magnitude and strength in proportion as the theme of one poet is abstract and that of the other pathetic in character. Accordingly, if tragedy sets out from a more exalted place, it must be allowed, on the other hand, that comedy aims at a more important end; and if this end could be actually attained it would make all tragedy not only unnecessary, but impossible. The aim that comedy has in view is the same as that of the highest destiny of man, and this consists in liberating himself from the influence of violent passions, and taking a calm and lucid survey of all that surrounds him, and also of his own being, and of seeing everywhere occurrence rather than fate or hazard, and ultimately rather smiling at the absurdities than shedding tears and feeling anger at sight of the wickedness of man.

It frequently happens in human life that facility of imagination, agreeable talents, a good-natured mirthfulness are taken for ornaments of the mind. The same fact is discerned in the case of poetical displays.

Now, public taste scarcely if ever soars above the sphere of the agreeable, and authors gifted with this sort of elegance of mind and style do not find it a difficult matter to usurp a glory which is or ought to be the reward of so much real labor. Nevertheless, an infallible text exists to enable us to discriminate a natural facility of manner from ideal gentleness, and qualities that consist in nothing more than natural virtue from genuine moral worth of character. This test is presented by trials such as those presented by difficulty and events offering great opportunities. Placed in positions of this kind, the genius whose essence is elegance is sure infallibly to fall into platitudes, and that virtue which only results from natural causes drops down to a material sphere. But a mind imbued with true and spiritual beauty is in cases of the kind we have supposed sure to be elevated to the highest sphere of character and of feeling. So long as Lucian merely furnishes absurdity, as in his "Wishes," in the "Lapithae," in "Jupiter Tragoedus," etc., he is only a humorist, and gratifies us by his sportive humor; but he changes character in many passages in his "Nigrinus," his "Timon," and his "Alexander," when his satire directs its shafts against moral depravity. Thus he begins in his "Nigrinus" his picture of the degraded corruption of Rome at that time in this way: "Wretch, why didst thou quit Greece, the sunlight, and that free and happy life? Why didst thou come here into this turmoil of splendid slavery, of service and festivals, of sycophants, flatterers, poisoners, orphan-robbers, and false friends?" It is on such occasions that the poet ought to show the lofty earnestness of soul which has to form the basis of all plays, if a poetical character is to be obtained by them. A serious intention may even be detected under the malicious jests with which Lucian and Aristophanes pursue Socrates. Their purpose is to avenge truth against sophistry, and to do combat for an ideal which is not always prominently put forward. There can be no doubt that Lucian has justified this character in his Diogenes and Demonax. Again, among modern writers, how grave and beautiful is the character depicted on all occasions by Cervantes in his Don Quixote! How splendid must have been the ideal that filled the mind of a poet who created a Tom Jones and a Sophonisba! How deeply and strongly our hearts are moved by the jests of Yorick when he pleases! I detect this seriousness also in our own Wieland: even the wanton sportiveness of his humor is elevated and impeded by the goodness of his heart; it has an influence even on his rhythm; nor does he ever lack elastic power, when it is his wish, to raise us up to the most elevated planes of beauty and of thought.

The same judgment cannot be pronounced on the satire of Voltaire. No doubt, also, in his case, it is the truth and simplicity of nature which here and there makes us experience poetic emotions, whether he really encounters nature and depicts it in a simple character, as many times in his "Ingenu;" or whether he seeks it and avenges it as in his "Candide" and elsewhere. But when neither one nor the other takes place, he can doubtless amuse us with his fine wit, but he assuredly never touches us as a poet. There is always rather too little of the serious under his raillery, and this is what makes his vocation as poet justly suspicious. You always meet his intelligence only; never his feelings. No ideal can be detected under this light gauze envelope; scarcely can anything absolutely fixed be found under this perpetual movement. His prodigious diversity of externals and forms, far from proving anything in favor of the inner fulness of his inspiration, rather testifies to the contrary; for he has exhausted all forms without finding a single one on which he has succeeded in impressing his heart. We are almost driven to fear that in the case of his rich talent the poverty of heart alone determined his choice of satire. And how could we otherwise explain the fact that he could pursue so long a road without ever issuing from its narrow rut? Whatever may be the variety of matter and of external forms, we see the inner form return everywhere with its sterile and eternal uniformity, and in spite of his so productive career, he never accomplished in himself the circle of humanity, that circle which we see joyfully traversed throughout by the satirists previously named.

ELEGIAC POETRY.

When the poet opposes nature to art, and the ideal to the real, so that nature and the ideal form the principal object of his pictures, and that the pleasure we take in them is the dominant impression, I call him an elegiac poet. In this kind, as well as in satire, I distinguish two classes. Either nature and the ideal are objects of sadness, when one is represented as lost to man and the other as unattained; or both are objects of joy, being represented to us as reality. In the first case it is elegy in the narrower sense of the term; in the second case it is the idyl in its most extended acceptation.

Indignation in the pathetic and ridicule in mirthful satire are occasioned by an enthusiasm which the ideal has excited; and thus also sadness should issue from the same source in elegy. It is this, and this only, that gives poetic value to elegy, and any other origin for this description of poetical effusion is entirely beneath the dignity of poetry. The elegiac poet seeks after nature, but he strives to find her in her beauty, and not only in her mirth; in her agreement with conception, and not merely in her facile disposition towards the requirements and demands of sense. Melancholy at the privation of joys, complaints at the disappearance of the world's golden age, or at the vanished happiness of youth, affection, etc., can only become the proper themes for elegiac poetry if those conditions implying peace and calm in the sphere of the senses can moreover be portrayed as states of moral harmony. On this account I cannot bring myself to regard as poetry the complaints of Ovid, which he transmitted from his place of exile by the Black Sea; nor would they appear so to me however touching and however full of passages of the highest poetry they might be. His suffering is too devoid of spirit, and nobleness. His lamentations display a want of strength and enthusiasm; though they may not reflect the traces of a vulgar soul, they display a low and sensuous condition of a noble spirit that has been trampled into the dust by its hard destiny. If, indeed, we call to mind that his regrets are directed to Rome, in the Augustan age, we forgive him the pain he suffers; but even Rome in all its splendor, except it be transfigured by the imagination, is a limited greatness, and therefore a subject unworthy of poetry, which, raised above every trace of the actual, ought only to mourn over what is infinite.

Thus the object of poetic complaint ought never to be an external object, but only an internal and ideal object; even when it deplores a real loss, it must begin by making it an ideal loss. The proper work of the poet consists in bringing back the finite object to the proportions of the infinite. Consequently the external matter of elegy, considered in itself, is always indifferent, since poetry can never employ it as it finds it, and because it is only by what it makes of it that it confers on it a poetic dignity. The elegiac poet seeks nature, but nature as an idea, and in a degree of perfection that it has never reached in reality, although he weeps over this perfection as something that has existed and is now lost. When Ossian speaks to us of the days that are no more, and of the heroes that have disappeared, his imagination has long since transformed these pictures represented to him by his memory into a pure ideal, and changed these heroes into gods. The different experiences of such or such a life in particular have become extended and confounded in the universal idea of transitoriness, and the bard, deeply moved, pursued by the increase of ruin everywhere present, takes his flight towards heaven, to find there in the course of the sun an emblem of what does not pass away.

I turn now to the elegiac poets of modern times. Rousseau, whether considered as a poet or a philosopher, always obeys the same tendency; to seek nature or to avenge it by art. According to the state of his heart, whether he prefers to seek nature or to avenge it, we see him at one time roused by elegiac feelings, at others showing the tone of the satire of Juneval; and again, as in his Julia, delighting in the sphere of the idyl. His compositions have undoubtedly a poetic value, since their object is ideal; only he does not know how to treat it in a poetic fashion. No doubt his serious character prevents him from falling into frivolity; but this seriousness also does not allow him to rise to poetic play. Sometimes absorbed by passion, at others by abstractions, he seldom if ever reaches aesthetic freedom, which the poet ought to maintain in spite of his material before his object, and in which he ought to make the reader share. Either he is governed by his sickly sensibility and his impressions become a torture, or the force of thought chains down his imagination and destroys by its strictness of reasoning all the grace of his pictures. These two faculties, whose reciprocal influence and intimate union are what properly make the poet, are found in this writer in an uncommon degree, and he only lacks one thing—it is that the two qualities should manifest themselves actually united; it is that the proper activity of thought should show itself mixed more with feeling, and the sensuous more with thought. Accordingly, even in the ideal which he has made of human nature, he is too much taken up with the limits of this nature, and not enough with its capabilities; he always betrays a want of physical repose rather than want of moral harmony. His passionate sensuousness must be blamed when, to finish as quickly as possible that struggle in humanity which offends him, he prefers to carry man back to the unintelligent uniformity of his primitive condition, rather than see that struggle carried out in the intellectual harmony of perfect cultivation, when, rather than await the fulfilment of art he prefers not to let it begin; in short, when he prefers to place the aim nearer the earth, and to lower the ideal in order to reach it the sooner and the safer.

Among the poets of Germany who belong to this class, I shall only mention here Haller, Kleist, and Klopstock. The character of their poetry is sentimental; it is by the ideal that they touch us, not by sensuous reality; and that not so much because they are themselves nature, as because they know how to fill us with enthusiasm for nature. However, what is true in general, as well of these three poets as of every sentimental poet, does not evidently exclude the faculty of moving us, in particular, by beauties of the simple genus; without this they would not be poets. I only mean that it is not their proper and dominant characteristic to receive the impression of objects with a calm feeling, simple, easy, and to give forth in like manner the impression received. Involuntarily the imagination in them anticipates intuition, and reflection is in play before the sensuous nature has done its function; they shut their eyes and stop their ears to plunge into internal meditations. Their souls could not be touched by any impression without observing immediately their own movements, without placing before their eyes and outside themselves what takes place in them. It follows from this that we never see the object itself, but what the intelligence and reflection of the poet have made of the object; and even if this object be the person itself of the poet, even when he wishes to represent to us his own feelings, we are not informed of his state immediately or at first hand; we only see how this state is reflected in his mind and what he has thought of it in the capacity of spectator of himself. When Haller deplores the death of his wife—every one knows this beautiful elegy— and begins in the following manner:—

"If I must needs sing of thy death,

O Marian, what a song it would be!

When sighs strive against words,

And idea follows fast on idea," etc.,

we feel that this description is strictly true, but we feel also that the poet does not communicate to us, properly speaking, his feelings, but the thoughts that they suggest to him. Accordingly, the emotion we feel on hearing him is much less vivid! people remark that the poet's mind must have been singularly cooled down to become thus a spectator of his own emotion.

Haller scarcely treated any subjects but the super-sensuous, and part of the poems of Klopstock are also of this nature: this choice itself excludes them from the simple kind. Accordingly, in order to treat these super-sensuous themes in a poetic fashion, as no body could be given to them, and they could not be made the objects of sensuous intuition, it was necessary to make them pass from the finite to the infinite, and raise them to the state of objects of spiritual intuition. In general, it may be said, that it is only in this sense that a didactic poetry can be conceived without involving contradiction; for, repeating again what has been so often said, poetry has only two fields, the world of sense and the ideal world, since in the sphere of conceptions, in the world of the understanding, it cannot absolutely thrive. I confess that I do not know as yet any didactic poem, either among the ancients or among the moderns, where the subject is completely brought down to the individual, or purely and completely raised to the ideal. The most common case, in the most happy essays, is where the two principles are used together; the abstract idea predominates, and the imagination, which ought to reign over the whole domain of poetry, has merely the permission to serve the understanding. A didactic poem in which thought itself would be poetic, and would remain so, is a thing which we must still wait to see.

What we say here of didactic poems in general is true in particular of the poems of Haller. The thought itself of these poems is not poetical, but the execution becomes so sometimes, occasionally by the use of images, at other times by a flight towards the ideal. It is from this last quality only that the poems of Haller belong to this class. Energy, depth, a pathetic earnestness —these are the traits that distinguish this poet. He has in his soul an ideal that enkindles it, and his ardent love of truth seeks in the peaceful valleys of the Alps that innocence of the first ages that the world no longer knows. His complaint is deeply touching; he retraces in an energetic and almost bitter satire the wanderings of the mind and of the heart, and he lovingly portrays the beautiful simplicity of nature. Only, in his pictures as well as in his soul, abstraction prevails too much, and the sensuous is overweighted by the intellectual. He constantly teaches rather than paints; and even in his paintings his brush is more energetic than lovable. He is great, bold, full of fire, sublime; but he rarely and perhaps never attains to beauty.

For the solidity and depth of ideas, Kleist is far inferior to Haller; in point of grace, perhaps, he would have the advantage—if, as happens occasionally, we did not impute to him as a merit, on the one side, that which really is a want on the other. The sensuous soul of Kleist takes especial delight at the sight of country scenes and manners; he withdraws gladly from the vain jingle and rattle of society, and finds in the heart of inanimate nature the harmony and peace that are not offered to him by the moral world. How touching is his "Aspiration after Repose"! how much truth and feeling there is in these verses!—

"O world, thou art the tomb of true life!

Often a generous instinct attracts me to virtue;

My heart is sad, a torrent of tears bathes my cheeks

But example conquers, and thou, O fire of youth!

Soon you dry these noble tears.

A true man must live far from men!"

But if the poetic instinct of Kleist leads him thus far away from the narrow circle of social relations, in solitude, and among the fruitful inspirations of nature, the image of social life and of its anguish pursues him, and also, alas! its chains. What he flees from he carries in himself, and what he seeks remains entirely outside him: never can he triumph over the fatal influence of his time. In vain does he find sufficient flame in his heart and enough energy in his imagination to animate by painting the cold conceptions of the understanding; cold thought each time kills the living creations of fancy, and reflection destroys the secret work of the sensuous nature. His poetry, it must be admitted, is of as brilliant color and as variegated as the spring he celebrated in verse; his imagination is vivid and active; but it might be said that it is more variable than rich, that it sports rather than creates, that it always goes forward with a changeful gait, rather than stops to accumulate and mould things into shape. Traits succeed each other rapidly, with exuberance, but without concentrating to form an individual, without completing each other to make a living whole, without rounding to a form, a figure. Whilst he remains in purely lyrical poetry, and pauses amidst his landscapes of country life, on the one hand the greater freedom of the lyrical form, and on the other the more arbitrary nature of the subject, prevent us from being struck with this defect; in these sorts of works it is in general rather the feelings of the poet, than the object in itself, of which we expect the portraiture. But this defect becomes too apparent when he undertakes, as in Cisseis and Paches, or in his Seneca, to represent men and human actions; because here the imagination sees itself kept in within certain fixed and necessary limits, and because here the effect can only be derived from the object itself. Kleist becomes poor, tiresome, jejune, and insupportably frigid; an example full of lessons for those who, without having an inner vocation, aspire to issue from musical poetry, to rise to the regions of plastic poetry. A spirit of this family, Thomson, has paid the same penalty to human infirmity.

In the sentimental kind, and especially in that part of the sentimental kind which we name elegiac, there are but few modern poets, and still fewer ancient ones, who can be compared to our Klopstock. Musical poetry has produced in this poet all that can be attained out of the limits of the living form, and out of the sphere of individuality, in the region of ideas. It would, no doubt, be doing him a great injustice to dispute entirely in his case that individual truth and that feeling of life with which the simple poet describes his pictures. Many of his odes, many separate traits in his dramas, and in his "Messiah," represent the object with a striking truth, and mark the outline admirably; especially, when the object is his own heart, he has given evidence on many occasions of a great natural disposition and of a charming simplicity. I mean only that it is not in this that the proper force of Klopstock consists, and that it would not perhaps be right to seek for this throughout his work. Viewed as a production of musical poetry, the "Messiah" is a magnificent work; but in the light of plastic poetry, where we look for determined forms and forms determined for the intuition, the "Messiah" leaves much to be desired. Perhaps in this poem the figures are sufficiently determined, but they are not so with intuition in view. It is abstraction alone that created them, and abstraction alone can discern them. They are excellent types to express ideas, but they are not individuals nor living figures. With regard to the imagination, which the poet ought to address, and which he ought to command by putting before it always perfectly determinate forms, it is left here much too free to represent as it wishes these men and these angels, these divinities and demons, this paradise and this hell. We see quite well the vague outlines in which the understanding must be kept to conceive these personages; but we do not find the limit clearly traced in which the imagination must be enclosed to represent them. And what I say here of characters must apply to all that in this poem is, or ought to be, action and life, and not only in this epopoeia, but also in the dramatic poetry of Klopstock. For the understanding all is perfectly determined and bounded in them—I need only here recall his Judas, his Pilate, his Philo, his Solomon in the tragedy that bears that name—but for the imagination all this wants form too much, and I must readily confess I do not find that our poet is at all in his sphere here. His sphere is always the realm of ideas; and he knows how to raise all he touches to the infinite. It might be said that he strips away their bodily envelope, to spiritualize them from all the objects with which he is occupied, in the same way that other poets clothe all that is spiritual with a body. The pleasure occasioned by his poems must almost always be obtained by an exercise of the faculty of reflection; the feelings he awakens in us, and that so deeply and energetically, flow always from super-sensuous sources. Hence the earnestness, the strength, the elasticity, the depth, that characterize all that comes from him; but from that also issues that perpetual tension of mind in which we are kept when reading him. No poet—except perhaps Young, who in this respect exacts even more than Klopstock, without giving us so much compensation —no poet could be less adapted than Klopstock to play the part of favorite author and guide in life, because he never does anything else than lead us out of life, because he never calls to arms anything save spirit, without giving recreation and refreshment to sensuous nature by the calm presence of any object. His muse is chaste, it has nothing of the earthly, it is immaterial and holy as his religion; and we are forced to admit with admiration that if he wanders sometimes on these high places, it never happened to him to fall from them. But precisely for this reason, I confess in all ingenuousness, that I am not free from anxiety for the common sense of those who quite seriously and unaffectedly make Klopstock the favorite book, the book in which we find sentiments fitting all situations, or to which we may revert at all times: perhaps even—and I suspect it—Germany has seen enough results of his dangerous influence. It is only in certain dispositions of the mind, and in hours of exaltation, that recourse can be had to Klopstock, and that he can be felt. It is for this reason that he is the idol of youth, without, however, being by any means the happiest choice that they could make. Youth, which always aspires to something beyond real life, which avoids all stiffness of form, and finds all limits too narrow, lets itself be carried away with love, with delight, into the infinite spaces opened up to them by this poet. But wait till the youth has become a man, and till, from the domain of ideas, he comes back to the world of experience, then you will see this enthusiastic love of Klopstock decrease greatly, without, however, a riper age changing at all the esteem due to this unique phenomenon, to this so extraordinary genius, to these noble sentiments—the esteem that Germany in particular owes to his high merit.

I have said that this poet was great specially in the elegiac style, and it is scarcely necessary to confirm this judgment by entering into particulars. Capable of exercising all kinds of action on the heart, and having graduated as master in all that relates to sentimental poetry, he can sometimes shake the soul by the most sublime pathos, at others cradle it with sweet and heavenly sensations. Yet his heart prefers to follow the direction of a lofty spiritual melancholy; and, however sublime be the tones of his harp and of his lyre, they are always the tender notes of his lute that resound with most truth and the deepest emotion. I take as witnesses all those whose nature is pure and sensuous: would they not be ready to give all the passages where Klopstock is strong, and bold; all those fictions, all the magnificent descriptions, all the models of eloquence which abound in the "Messiah," all those dazzling comparisons in which our poet excels,—would they not exchange them for the pages breathing tenderness, the "Elegy to Ebert" for example, or that admirable poem entitled "Bardalus," or again, the "Tombs Opened before the Hour," the "Summer's Night," the "Lake of Zurich," and many other pieces of this kind? In the same way the "Messiah" is dear to me as a treasure of elegiac feelings and of ideal paintings, though I am not much satisfied with it as the recital of an action and as an epic.

I ought, perhaps, before quitting this department, to recall the merits in this style of Uz, Denis, Gessner in the "Death of Abel"—Jacobi, Gerstenberg, Hoelty, De Goeckingk, and several others, who all knew how to touch by ideas, and whose poems belong to the sentimental kind in the sense in which we have agreed to understand the word. But my object is not here to write a history of German poetry; I only wished to clear up what I said further back by some examples from our literature. I wished to show that the ancient and the modern poets, the authors of simple poetry and of sentimental poetry, follow essentially different paths to arrive at the same end: that the former move by nature, individuality, a very vivid sensuous element; while the latter do it by means of ideas and a high spirituality, exercising over our minds an equally powerful though less extensive influence.

It has been seen, by the examples which precede, how sentimental poetry conceives and treats subjects taken from nature; perhaps the reader may be curious to know how also simple poetry treats a subject of the sentimental order. This is, as it seems, an entirely new question, and one of special difficulty; for, in the first place, has a subject of the sentimental order ever been presented in primitive and simple periods? And in modern times, where is the simple poet with whom we could make this experiment? This has not, however, prevented genius from setting this problem, and solving it in a wonderfully happy way. A poet in whose mind nature works with a purer and more faithful activity than in any other, and who is perhaps of all modern poets the one who departs the least from the sensuous truth of things, has proposed this problem to himself in his conception of a mind, and of the dangerous extreme of the sentimental character. This mind and this character have been portrayed by the modern poet we speak of, a character which with a burning sensuousness embraces the ideal and flies the real, to soar up to an infinite devoid of being, always occupied in seeking out of himself what he incessantly destroys in himself; a mind that only finds reality in his dreams, and to whom the realities of life are only limits and obstacles; in short, a mind that sees only in its own existence a barrier, and goes on, as it were, logically to break down this barrier in order to penetrate to true reality.

It is interesting to see with what a happy instinct all that is of a nature to feed the sentimental mind is gathered together in Werther: a dreamy and unhappy love, a very vivid feeling for nature, the religious sense coupled with the spirit of philosophic contemplation, and lastly, to omit nothing, the world of Ossian, dark, formless, melancholy. Add to this the aspect under which reality is presented, all is depicted which is least adapted to make it lovable, or rather all that is most fit to make it hated; see how all external circumstances unite to drive back the unhappy man into his ideal world; and now we understand that it was quite impossible for a character thus constituted to save itself, and issue from the circle in which it was enclosed. The same contrast reappears in the "Torquato Tasso" of the same poet, though the characters are very different. Even his last romance presents, like his first, this opposition between the poetic mind and the common sense of practical men, between the ideal and the real, between the subjective mode and the objective mode of seeing and representing things; it is the same opposition, I say, but with what a diversity! Even in "Faust" we still find this contrast, rendered, I admit—as the subject required—much more coarsely on both hands, and materialized. It would be quite worth while if a psychological explanation were attempted of this character, personified and specified in four such different ways.

It has been observed further back that a mere disposition to frivolity of mind, to a merry humor, if a certain fund of the ideal is not joined to it, does not suffice to constitute the vocation of a satirical poet, though this mistake is frequently made. In the same way a mere disposition for tender sentiments, softness of heart, and melancholy do not suffice to constitute a vocation for elegy. I cannot detect the true poetical talent, either on one side or the other; it wants the essential, I mean the energetic and fruitful principle that ought to enliven the subject, and produce true beauty. Accordingly the productions of this latter nature, of the tender nature, do nothing but enervate us; and without refreshing the heart, without occupying the mind, they are only able to flatter in us the sensuous nature. A constant disposition to this mode of feeling ends necessarily, in the long run, by weakening the character, and makes it fall into a state of passivity from which nothing real can issue, either for external or for internal life. People have, therefore, been quite right to persecute by pitiless raillery this fatal mania of sentimentality and of tearful melancholy which possessed Germany eighteen years since, in consequence of certain excellent works that were ill understood and indiscreetly imitated. People have been right, I say, to combat this perversity, though the indulgence with which men are disposed to receive the parodies of these elegiac caricatures— that are very little better themselves—the complaisance shown to bad wit, to heartless satire and spiritless mirth, show clearly enough that this zeal against false sentimentalism does not issue from quite a pure source. In the balance of true taste one cannot weigh more than the other, considering that both here and there is wanting that which forms the aesthetic value of a work of art, the intimate union of spirit with matter, and the twofold relation of the work with the faculty of perception as well as with the faculty of the ideal.

People have turned Siegwart ["Siegwart," a novel by J. Mailer, published at Ulm, 1776] and his convent story into ridicule, and yet the "Travels into the South of France" are admired; yet both works have an equal claim to be esteemed in certain respects, and as little to be unreservedly praised in others. A true, though excessive, sensuousness gives value to the former of these two romances; a lively and sportive humor, a fine wit, recommends the other: but one totally lacks all sobriety of mind that would befit it, the other lacks all aesthetic dignity. If you consult experience, one is rather ridiculous; if you think of the ideal, the other is almost contemptible. Now, as true beauty must of necessity accord both with nature and with the ideal, it is clear that neither the one nor the other of these two romances could pretend to pass for a fine work. And notwithstanding all this, it is natural, as I know it by my own experience, that the romance of Thummel should be read with much pleasure. As a fact it only wounds those requirements which have their principle in the ideal, and which consequently do not exist for the greater part of readers; requirements that, even in persons of most delicate feeling, do not make themselves felt at the moments when we read romances. With regard to the other needs of the mind, and especially to those of the senses, this book, on the other hand, affords unusual satisfaction. Accordingly, it must be, and will be so, that this book will remain justly one of the favorite works of our age, and of all epochs when men only write aesthetic works to please, and people only read to get pleasure.

But does not poetical literature also offer, even in its classical monuments, some analogous examples of injuries inflicted or attempted against the ideal and its superior purity? Are there not some who, by the gross, sensuous nature of their subject, seem to depart strangely from the spiritualism I here demand of all works of art? If this is permitted to the poet, the chaste nurseling of the muses, ought it not to be conceded to the novelist, who is only the half-brother of the poet, and who still touches by so many points? I can the less avoid this question because there are masterpieces, both in the elegiac and in the satirical kind, where the authors seek and preach up a nature quite different from that I am discussing in this essay, and where they seem to defend it, not so much against bad as against good morals. The natural conclusion would be either that this sort of poem ought to be rejected, or that, in tracing here the idea of elegiac poetry, we have granted far too much to what is arbitrary.

The question I asked was, whether what was permitted by the poet might not be tolerated in a prose narrator too? The answer is contained in the question. What is allowed in the poet proves nothing about what must be allowed in one who is not a poet. This tolerancy in fact reposes on the very idea which we ought to make to ourselves of the poet, and only on this idea; what in his case is legitimate freedom, is only a license worthy of contempt as soon as it no longer takes its source in the ideal, in those high and noble inspirations which make the poet.

The laws of decency are strangers to innocent nature; the experience of corruption alone has given birth to them. But when once this experience has been made, and natural innocence has disappeared from manners, these laws are henceforth sacred laws that man, who has a moral sense, ought not to infringe upon. They reign in an artificial world with the same right that the laws of nature reign in the innocence of primitive ages. But by what characteristic is the poet recognized? Precisely by his silencing in his soul all that recalls an artificial world, and by causing nature herself to revive in him with her primitive simplicity. The moment he has done this he is emancipated by this alone from all the laws by which a depraved heart secures itself against itself. He is pure, he is innocent, and all that is permitted to innocent nature is equally permitted to him. But you who read him or listen to him, if you have lost your innocence, and if you are incapable of finding it again, even for a moment, in a purifying contact with the poet, it is your own fault, and not his: why do not you leave him alone? it is not for you that he has sung!

Here follows, therefore, in what relates to these kinds of freedoms, the rules that we can lay down.

Let us remark in the first place that nature only can justify these licenses; whence it follows that you could not legitimately take them up of your own choice, nor with a determination of imitating them; the will, in fact, ought always to be directed according to the laws of morality, and on its part all condescending to the sensuous is absolutely unpardonable. These licenses must, therefore, above all, be simplicity. But how can we be convinced that they are actually simple? We shall hold them to be so if we see them accompanied and supported by all the other circumstances which also have their spring of action in nature; for nature can only be recognized by the close and strict consistency, by the unity and uniformity of its effects. It is only a soul that has on all occasions a horror of all kinds of artifice, and which consequently rejects them even where they would be useful—it is only that soul which we permit to be emancipated from them when the artificial conventionalities hamper and hinder it. A heart that submits to all the obligations of nature has alone the right to profit also by the liberties which it authorizes. All the other feelings of that heart ought consequently to bear the stamp of nature: it will be true, simple, free, frank, sensible, and straightforward; all disguise, all cunning, all arbitrary fancy, all egotistical pettiness, will be banished from his character, and you will see no trace of them in his writings.

Second rule: beautiful nature alone can justify freedoms of this kind; whence it follows that they ought not to be a mere outbreak of the appetites; for all that proceeds exclusively from the wants of sensuous nature is contemptible. It is, therefore, from the totality and the fulness of human nature that these vivid manifestations must also issue. We must find humanity in them. But how can we judge that they proceed in fact from our whole nature, and not only from an exclusive and vulgar want of the sensuous nature? For this purpose it is necessary that we should see—that they should represent to us—this whole of which they form a particular feature. This disposition of the mind to experience the impressions of the sensuous is in itself an innocent and an indifferent thing. It does not sit well on a man only because of its being common to animals with him; it augurs in him the lack of true and perfect humanity. It only shocks us in the poem because such a work having the pretension to please us, the author consequently seems to think us capable, us also, of this moral infirmity. But when we see in the man who has let himself be drawn into it by surprise all the other characteristics that human nature in general embraces; when we find in the work where these liberties have been taken the expression of all the realities of human nature, this motive of discontent disappears, and we can enjoy, without anything changing our joy, this simple expression of a true and beautiful nature. Consequently this same poet who ventures to allow himself to associate us with feelings so basely human, ought to know, on the other hand, how to raise us to all that is grand, beautiful, and sublime in our nature.

We should, therefore, have found there a measure to which we could subject the poet with confidence, when he trespasses on the ground of decency, and when he does not fear to penetrate as far as that in order freely to paint nature. His work is common, base, absolutely inexcusable, from the moment it is frigid, and from the moment it is empty, because that shows a prejudice, a vulgar necessity, an unhealthy appeal to our appetites. His work, on the other hand, is beautiful and noble, and we ought to applaud it without any consideration for all the objections of frigid decency, as soon as we recognize in it simplicity, the alliance of spiritual nature and of the heart.

Perhaps I shall be told that if we adopt this criterion, most of the recitals of this kind composed by the French, and the best imitations made of them in Germany, would not perhaps find their interest in it; and that it might be the same, at least in part, with many of the productions of our most intellectual and amiable poets, without even excepting his masterpieces. I should have nothing to reply to this. The sentence after all is anything but new, and I am only justifying the judgment pronounced long since on this matter by all men of delicate perceptions. But these same principles which, applied to the works of which I have just spoken, seem perhaps in too strict a spirit, might also be found too indulgent when applied to some other works. I do not deny, in fact, that the same reasons which make me hold to be quite inexcusable the dangerous pictures drawn by the Roman Ovid and the German Ovid, those of Crebillon, of Voltaire, of Marmontel, who pretends to write moral tales!—of Lacroix, and of many others—that these same reasons, I say, reconcile me with the elegies of the Roman Propertius and of the German Propertius, and even with some of the decried productions of Diderot. This is because the former of those works are only witty, prosaic, and voluptuous, while the others are poetic, human, and simple.

IDYL.

It remains for me to say a few words about this third kind of sentimental poetry—some few words and no more, for I propose to speak of it at another time with the developments particularly demanded by the theme.

This kind of poetry generally presents the idea and description of an innocent and happy humanity. This innocence and bliss seeming remote from the artificial refinements of fashionable society, poets have removed the scene of the idyl from crowds of worldly life to the simple shepherd's cot, and have given it a place in the infancy of humanity before the beginning of culture. These limitations are evidently accidental; they do not form the object of the idyl, but are only to be regarded as the most natural means to attain this end. The end is everywhere to portray man in a state of innocence: which means a state of harmony and peace with himself and the external world.

But a state such as this is not merely met with before the dawn of civilization; it is also the state to which civilization aspires, as to its last end, if only it obeys a determined tendency in its progress. The idea of a similar state, and the belief of the possible reality of this state, is the only thing that can reconcile man with all the evils to which he is exposed in the path of civilization; and if this idea were only a chimera, the complaints of those who accuse civil life and the culture of the intelligence as an evil for which there is no compensation, and who represent this primitive state of nature that we have renounced as the real end of humanity—their complaints, I say, would have a perfectly just foundation. It is, therefore, of infinite importance for the man engaged in the path of civilization to see confirmed in a sensuous manner the belief that this idea can be accomplished in the world of sense, that this state of innocence can be realized in it; and as real experience, far from keeping up this belief, is rather made incessantly to contradict it, poetry comes here, as in many other cases, in aid of reason, to cause this idea to pass into the condition of an intuitive idea, and to realize it in a particular fact. No doubt this innocence of pastoral life is also a poetic idea, and the imagination must already have shown its creative power in that. But the problem, with this datum, becomes infinitely simpler and easier to solve; and we must not forget that the elements of these pictures already existed in real life, and that it was only requisite to gather up the separate traits to form a whole. Under a fine sky, in a primitive society, when all the relations are still simple, when science is limited to so little, nature is easily satisfied, and man only turns to savagery when he is tortured by want. All nations that have a history have a paradise, an age of innocence, a golden age. Nay, more than this, every man has his paradise, his golden age, which he remembers with more or less enthusiasm, according as he is more or less poetical. Thus experience itself furnishes sufficient traits to this picture which the pastoral idyl executes. But this does not prevent the pastoral idyl from remaining always a beautiful and an encouraging fiction; and poetic genius, in retracing these pictures, has really worked in favor of the ideal. For, to the man who has once departed from simple nature, and who has been abandoned to the dangerous guidance of his reason, it is of the greatest importance to find the laws of nature expressed in a faithful copy, to see their image in a clear mirror, and to reject all the stains of artificial life. There is, however, a circumstance which remarkably lessens the aesthetic value of these sorts of poetry. By the very fact that the idyl is transported to the time that precedes civilization, it also loses the advantages thereof; and by its nature finds itself in opposition to itself. Thus, in a theoretical sense, it takes us back at the same time that in a practical sense it leads us on and ennobles us. Unhappily it places behind us the end towards which it ought to lead us, and consequently it can only inspire us with the sad feeling of a loss, and not the joyous feeling of a hope. As these poems can only attain their end by dispensing with all art, and by simplifying human nature, they have the highest value for the heart, but they are also far too poor for what concerns the mind, and their uniform circle is too quickly traversed. Accordingly we can only seek them and love them in moments in which we need calm, and not when our faculties aspire after movement and exercise. A morbid mind will find its cure in them, a sound soul will not find its food in them. They cannot vivify, they can only soften. This defect, grounded in the essence of the pastoral idyll, has not been remedied by the whole art of poets. I know that this kind of poem is not without admirers, and that there are readers enough who prefer an Amyntus and a Daphnis to the most splendid masterpieces of the epic or the dramatic muse; but in them it is less the aesthetical taste than the feeling of an individual want that pronounces on works of art; and their judgment, by that very fact, could not be taken into consideration here. The reader who judges with his mind, and whose heart is sensuous, without being blind to the merit of these poems, will confess that he is rarely affected by them, and that they tire him most quickly. But they act with so much the more effect in the exact moment of need. But must the truly beautiful be reduced to await our hours of need? and is it not rather its office to awaken in our soul the want that it is going to satisfy?

The reproaches I here level against the bucolic idyl cannot be understood of the sentimental. The simple pastoral, in fact, cannot be deprived of aesthetic value, since this value is already found in the mere form. To explain myself: every kind of poetry is bound to possess an infinite ideal value, which alone constitutes it a true poetry; but it can satisfy this condition in two different ways. It can give us the feeling of the infinite as to form, by representing the object altogether limited and individualizing it; it can awaken in us the feeling of the infinite as to matter, in freeing its object from all limits in which it is enclosed, by idealizing this object; therefore it can have an ideal value either by an absolute representation or by the representation of an absolute. Simple poetry takes the former road, the other is that of sentimental poetry. Accordingly the simple poet is not exposed to failure in value so long as he keeps faithfully to nature, which is always completely circumscribed, that is, is infinite as regards form. The sentimental poet, on the contrary, by that very fact, that nature only offers him completely circumscribed objects, finds in it an obstruction when he wishes to give an absolute value to a particular object. Thus the sentimental poet understands his interests badly when he goes along the trail of the simple poet, and borrows his objects from him—objects which by themselves are perfectly indifferent, and which only become poetical by the way in which they are treated. By this he imposes on himself without any necessity the same limits that confine the field of the simple poet, without, however, being able to carry out the limitation properly, or to vie with his rival in absolute definiteness of representation. He ought rather, therefore, to depart from the simple poet, just in the choice of object; because, the latter having the advantage of him on the score of form, it is only by the nature of the objects that he can resume the upper hand.

Applying this to the pastoral idyls of the sentimental poet, we see why these poems, whatever amount of art and genius be displayed in them, do not fully satisfy the heart or the mind. An ideal is proposed in it, and, at the same time, the writer keeps to this narrow and poor medium of pastoral life. Would it not have been better, on the contrary, to choose for the ideal another frame, or for the pastoral world another kind of picture? These pictures are just ideal enough for painting to lose its individual truth in them, and, again, just individual enough for the ideal in them to suffer therefrom. For example, a shepherd of Gessner can neither charm by the illusion of nature nor by the beauty of imitation; he is too ideal a being for that, but he does not satisfy us any more as an ideal by the infinity of the thought: he is a far too limited creature to give us this satisfaction. He will, therefore, please up to a certain point all classes of readers, without exception, because he seeks to unite the simple with the sentimental, and he thus gives a commencement of satisfaction to the two opposite exigencies that may be brought to bear on any particular part of a poem; but the author, in trying to unite the two points, does not fully satisfy either one or the other exigency, as you do not find in him either pure nature or the pure ideal; he cannot rank himself as entirely up to the mark of a stringent critical taste, for taste does not accept anything equivocal or incomplete in aesthetical matters. It is a strange thing that, in the poet whom I have named, this equivocal character extends to the language, which floats undecided between poetry and prose, as if he feared either to depart too far from nature, by speaking rhythmical language, or if he completely freed himself from rhythm, to lose all poetic flight. Milton gives a higher satisfaction to the mind, in the magnificent picture of the first human pair, and of the state of innocence in paradise;—the most beautiful idyl I know of the sentimental kind. Here nature is noble, inspired, simple, full of breadth, and, at the same time, of depth; it is humanity in its highest moral value, clothed in the most graceful form.

Thus, even in respect to the idyl, as well as to all kinds of poetry, we must once for all declare either for individuality or ideality; for to aspire to give satisfaction to both exigencies is the surest means, unless you have reached the terminus of perfection, to miss both ends. If the modern poet thinks he feels enough of the Greeks' mind to vie with them, notwithstanding all the indocility of his matter, on their own ground, namely that of simple poetry, let him do it exclusively, and place himself apart from all the requirements of the sentimental taste of his age. No doubt it is very doubtful if he come up to his models; between the original and the happiest imitation there will always remain a notable distance; but, by taking this road, he is at all events secure of producing a really poetic work. If, on the other hand, he feels himself carried to the ideal by the instinct of sentimental poetry, let him decide to pursue this end fully; let him seek the ideal in its purity, and let him not pause till he has reached the highest regions without looking behind him to know if the real follows him, and does not leave him by the way. Let him not lower himself to this wretched expedient of spoiling the ideal to accommodate himself to the wants of human weakness, and to turn out mind in order to play more easily with the heart. Let him not take us back to our infancy, to make us buy, at the cost of the most precious acquisitions of the understanding, a repose that can only last as long as the slumber of our spiritual faculties; but let him lead us on to emancipation, and give us this feeling of higher harmony which compensates for all his troubles and secures the happiness of the victor! Let him prepare as his task an idyl that realizes the pastoral innocence, even in the children of civilization, and in all the conditions of the most militant and excited life; of thought enlarged by culture; of the most refined art; of the most delicate social conventionalities—an idyl, in short, that is made, not to bring back man to Arcadia, but to lead him to Elysium.

This idyl, as I conceive it, is the idea of humanity definitely reconciled with itself, in the individual as well as in the whole of society; it is union freely re-established between inclination and duty; it is nature purified, raised to its highest moral dignity; in short, it is no less than the ideal of beauty applied to real life. Thus, the character of this idyl is to reconcile perfectly all the contradictions between the real and the ideal, which formed the matter of satirical and elegiac poetry, and, setting aside their contradictions, to put an end to all conflict between the feelings of the soul. Thus, the dominant expression of this kind of poetry would be calm; but the calm that follows the accomplishment, and not that of indolence—the calm that comes from the equilibrium re-established between the faculties, and not from the suspending of their exercise; from the fulness of our strength, and not from our infirmity; the calm, in short, which is accompanied in the soul by the feeling of an infinite power. But precisely because idyl thus conceived removes all idea of struggle, it will be infinitely more difficult than it was in two previously-named kinds of poetry to express movement; yet this is an indispensable condition, without which poetry can never act on men's souls. The most perfect unity is required, but unity ought not to wrong variety; the heart must be satisfied, but without the inspiration ceasing on that account. The solution of this problem is properly what ought to be given us by the theory of the idyl.

Now, what are the relations of the two poetries to one another, and their relations to the poetic ideal? Here are the principles we have established.

Nature has granted this favor to the simple poet, to act always as an indivisible unity, to be at all times identical and perfect, and to represent, in the real world, humanity at its highest value. In opposition, it has given a powerful faculty to the sentimental poet, or, rather, it has imprinted an ardent feeling on him; this is to replace out of himself this first unity that abstraction has destroyed in him, to complete humanity in his person, and to pass from a limited state to an infinite state. They both propose to represent human nature fully, or they would not be poets; but the simple poet has always the advantage of sensuous reality over the sentimental poet, by setting forth as a real fact what the other aspires only to reach. Every one experiences this in the pleasure he takes in simple poetry.

We there feel that the human faculties are brought into play; no vacuum is felt; we have the feeling of unity, without distinguishing anything of what we experience; we enjoy both our spiritual activity and also the fulness of physical life. Very different is the disposition of mind elicited by the sentimental poet. Here we feel only a vivid aspiration to produce in us this harmony of which we had in the other case the consciousness and reality; to make of ourselves a single and same totality; to realize in ourselves the idea of humanity as a complete expression. Hence it comes that the mind is here all in movement, stretched, hesitating between contrary feelings; whereas it was before calm and at rest, in harmony with itself, and fully satisfied.

But if the simple poet has the advantage over the sentimental poet on the score of reality; if he causes really to live that of which the other can only elicit a vivid instinct, the sentimental poet, in compensation, has this great advantage over the simple poet: to be in a position to offer to this instinct a greater object than that given by his rival, and the only one he could give. All reality, we know, is below the ideal; all that exists has limits, but thought is infinite. This limitation, to which everything is subject in sensuous reality, is, therefore, a disadvantage for the simple poet, while the absolute, unconditional freedom of the ideal profits the sentimental poet. No doubt the former accomplishes his object, but this object is limited; the second, I admit, does not entirely accomplish his, but his object is infinite. Here I appeal to experience. We pass pleasantly to real life and things from the frame of mind in which the simple poet has placed us. On the other hand, the sentimental poet will always disgust us, for a time, with real life. This is because the infinite character has, in a manner, enlarged our mind beyond its natural measure, so that nothing it finds in the world of sense can fill its capacity. We prefer to fall back in contemplation on ourselves, where we find food for this awakened impulse towards the ideal world; while, in the simple poet, we only strive to issue out of ourselves, in search of sensuous objects. Sentimental poetry is the offspring of retirement and science, and invites to it; simple poetry is inspired by the spectacle of life, and brings back life.

I have styled simple poetry a gift of nature to show that thought has no share in it. It is a first jet, a happy inspiration, that needs no correction, when it turns out well, and which cannot be rectified if ill turned out. The entire work of the simple genius is accomplished by feeling; in that is its strength, and in it are its limits. If, then, he has not felt at once in a poetic manner— that is, in a perfectly human manner—no art in the world can remedy this defect. Criticism may help him to see the defect, but can place no beauty in its stead. Simple genius must draw all from nature; it can do nothing, or almost nothing, by its will; and it will fulfil the idea of this kind of poetry provided nature acts in it by an inner necessity. Now, it is true that all which happens by nature is necessary, and all the productions, happy or not, of the simple genius, which is disassociated from nothing so much as from arbitrary will, are also imprinted with this character of necessity; momentary constraint is one thing, and the internal necessity dependent on the totality of things another. Considered as a whole, nature is independent and infinite; in isolated operations it is poor and limited. The same distinction holds good in respect to the nature of the poet. The very moment when he is most happily inspired depends on a preceding instant, and consequently only a conditional necessity can be attributed to him. But now the problem that the poet ought to solve is to make an individual state similar to the human whole, and consequently to base it in an absolute and necessary manner on itself. It is therefore necessary that at the moment of inspiration every trace of a temporal need should be banished, and that the object itself, however limited, should not limit the flight of the poet. But it may be conceived that this is only possible in so far as the poet brings to the object an absolute freedom, an absolute fulness of faculties, and in so far as he is prepared by an anterior exercise to embrace all things with all his humanity. Now he cannot acquire this exercise except by the world in which he lives, and of which he receives the impressions immediately. Thus simple genius is in a state of dependence with regard to experience, while the sentimental genius is forced from it. We know that the sentimental genius begins its operation at the place where the other finishes its own: its virtue is to complete by the elements which it derives from itself a defective object, and to transport itself by its own strength from a limited state to one of absolute freedom. Thus the simple poet needs a help from without, while the sentimental poet feeds his genius from his own fund, and purifies himself by himself. The former requires a picturesque nature, a poetical world, a simple humanity which casts its eyes around; for he ought to do his work without issuing from the sensuous sphere. If external aid fails him, if he be surrounded by matter not speaking to mind, one of two things will happen: either, if the general character of the poet-race is what prevails in him, he issues from the particular class to which he belongs as a poet, and becomes sentimental to be at any rate poetic; or, if his particular character as simple poet has the upper hand, he leaves his species and becomes a common nature, in order to remain at any rate natural. The former of these two alternatives might represent the case of the principal poets of the sentimental kind in Roman antiquity and in modern times. Born at another period of the world, transplanted under another sky, these poets who stir us now by ideas, would have charmed us by individual truth and simple beauty. The other alternative is the almost unavoidable quicksand for a poet who, thrown into a vulgar world, cannot resolve to lose sight of nature.

I mean, to lose sight of actual nature; but the greatest care must be given to distinguish actual nature from true nature, which is the subject of simple poetry. Actual nature exists everywhere; but true nature is so much the more rare because it requires an internal necessity that determines its existence. Every eruption of passion, however vulgar, is real—it may be even true nature; but it is not true human nature, for true human nature requires that the self-directing faculty in us should have a share in the manifestation, and the expression of this faculty is always dignified. All moral baseness is an actual human phenomenon, but I hope not real human nature, which is always noble. All the faults of taste cannot be surveyed that have been occasioned in criticism or the practice of art by this—confusion between actual human nature and true human nature. The greatest trivialities are tolerated and applauded under the pretext that they are real nature. Caricatures not to be tolerated in the real world are carefully preserved in the poetic world and reproduced according to nature! The poet can certainly imitate a lower nature; and it enters into the very definition of a satirical poet: but then a beauty by its own nature must sustain and raise the object, and the vulgarity of the subject must not lower the imitator too much. If at the moment he paints he is true human nature himself, the object of his paintings is indifferent; but it is only on this condition we can tolerate a faithful reproduction of reality. Unhappy for us readers when the rod of satire falls into hands that nature meant to handle another instrument, and when, devoid of all poetic talent, with nothing but the ape's mimicry, they exercise it brutally at the expense of our taste!

But vulgar nature has even its dangers for the simple poet; for the simple poet is formed by this fine harmony of the feeling and thinking faculty, which yet is only an idea, never actually realized. Even in the happiest geniuses of this class, receptivity will always more or less carry the day over spontaneous activity. But receptivity is always more or less subordinate to external impressions, and nothing but a perpetual activity of the creative faculty could prevent matter from exercising a blind violence over this quality. Now, every time this happens the feeling becomes vulgar instead of poetical.

No genius of the simple class, from Homer down to Bodmer, has entirely steered clear of this quicksand. It is evident that it is most perilous to those who have to struggle against external vulgarity, or who have parted with their refinement owing to a want of proper restraint. The first-named difficulty is the reason why even authors of high cultivation are not always emancipated from platitudes—a fact which has prevented many splendid talents from occupying the place to which they were summoned by nature. For this reason, a comic poet whose genius has chiefly to deal with scenes of real life, is more liable to the danger of acquiring vulgar habits of style and expression—a fact evidenced in the case of Aristophanes, Plautus, and all the poets who have followed in their track. Even Shakspeare, with all his sublimity, suffers us to fall very low now and then. Again, Lope De Vega, Moliere, Regnard, Goldoni worry us with frequent trifling. Holberg drags us down into the mire. Schlegel, a German poet, among the most remarkable for intellectual talent, with genius to raise him to a place among poets of the first order; Gellert, a truly simple poet, Rabener, and Lessing himself, if I am warranted to introduce his name in this category—this highly-cultivated scholar of criticism and vigilant examiner of his own genius—all these suffer in different degrees from the platitudes and uninspired movements of the natures they chose as the theme of their satire. With regard to more recent authors of this class, I avoid naming any of them, as I can make no exceptions in their case.

But not only is simple genius exposed to the danger of coming too near to vulgar reality; the ease of expression, even this too close approximation to reality, encourages vulgar imitators to try their hand in poetry. Sentimental poetry, though offering danger enough, has this advantage, to keep this crowd at a distance, for it is not for the first comer to rise to the ideal; but simple poetry makes them believe that, with feeling and humor, you need only imitate real nature to claim the title of poet. Now nothing is more revolting than platitude when it tries to be simple and amiable, instead of hiding its repulsive nature under the veil of art. This occasions the incredible trivialities loved by the Germans under the name of simple and facetious songs, and which give them endless amusement round a well-garnished table. Under the pretext of good humor and of sentiment people tolerate these poverties: but this good humor and this sentiment ought to be carefully proscribed. The Muses of the Pleisse, in particular, are singularly pitiful; and other Muses respond to them, from the banks of the Seine, and the Elbe. If these pleasantries are flat, the passion heard on our tragic stage is equally pitiful, for, instead of imitating true nature, it is only an insipid and ignoble expression of the actual. Thus, after shedding torrents of tears, you feel as you would after visiting a hospital or reading the "Human Misery" of Saltzmann. But the evil is worse in satirical poetry and comic romance, kinds which touch closely on every-day life, and which consequently, as all frontier posts, ought to be in safer hands. In truth, he less than any other is called on to become the painter of his century, who is himself the child and caricature of his century. But as, after all, nothing is easier than to take in hand, among our acquaintances, a comic character—a big, fat man—and draw a coarse likeness of him on paper, the sworn enemies of poetic inspiration are often led to blot some paper in this way to amuse a circle of friends. It is true that a pure heart, a well-made mind, will never confound these vulgar productions with the inspirations of simple genius. But purity of feeling is the very thing that is wanting, and in most cases nothing is thought of but satisfying a want of sense, without spiritual nature having any share. A fundamentally just idea, ill understood, that works of bel esprit serve to recreate the mind, contributes to keep up this indulgence, if indulgence it may be called when nothing higher occupies the mind, and reader as well as writer find their chief interest therein. This is because vulgar natures, if overstrained, can only be refreshed by vacuity; and even a higher intelligence, when not sustained by a proportional culture, can only rest from its work amidst sensuous enjoyments, from which spiritual nature is absent.

Poetic genius ought to have strength enough to rise with a free and innate activity above all the accidental hinderances which are inseparable from every confined condition, to arrive at a representation of humanity in the absolute plenitude of its powers; it is not, however, permitted, on the other hand, to emancipate itself from the necessary limits implied by the very idea of human nature; for the absolute only in the circle of humanity is its true problem. Simple genius is not exposed to overstep this sphere, but rather not to fill it entirely, giving too much scope to external necessity, to accidental wants, at the expense of the inner necessity. The danger for the sentimental genius is, on the other hand, by trying to remove all limits, of nullifying human nature absolutely, and not only rising, as is its right and duty, beyond finite and determinate reality, as far as absolute possibility, or in other terms to idealize; but of passing even beyond possibility, or, in other words, dreaming. This fault—overstraining—is precisely dependent on the specific property of the sentimental process, as the opposite defect, inertia, depends on the peculiar operation of the simple genius. The simple genius lets nature dominate, without restricting it; and as nature in her particular phenomena is always subject to some want, it follows that the simple sentiment will not be always exalted enough to resist the accidental limitations of the present hour. The sentimental genius, on the contrary, leaves aside the real world, to rise to the ideal and to command its matter with free spontaneity. But while reason, according to law, aspires always to the unconditional, so the sentimental genius will not always remain calm enough to restrain itself uniformly and without interruption within the conditions implied by the idea of human nature, and to which reason must always, even in its freest acts, remain attached. He could only confine himself in these conditions by help of a receptivity proportioned to his free activity; but most commonly the activity predominates over receptivity in the sentimental poet, as much as receptivity over activity in the simple poet. Hence, in the productions of simple genius, if sometimes inspiration is wanting, so also in works of sentimental poetry the object is often missed. Thus, though they proceed in opposite ways, they will both fall into a vacuum, for before the aesthetic judgment an object without inspiration, and inspiration without an object, are both negations.

The poets who borrow their matter too much from thought, and rather conceive poetic pictures by the internal abundance of ideas than by the suggestions of feeling, are more or less likely to be addicted to go thus astray. In their creations reason makes too little of the limits of the sensuous world, and thought is always carried too far for experience to follow it. Now, when the idea is carried so far that not only no experience corresponds to it—as is the case in the beau ideal—but also that it is repugnant to the conditions of all possible experience, so that, in order to realize it, one must leave human nature altogether, it is no longer a poetic but an exaggerated thought; that is, supposing it claims to be representable and poetical, for otherwise it is enough if it is not self-contradictory. If thought is contradictory it is not exaggeration, but nonsense; for what does not exist cannot exceed. But when the thought is not an object proposed to the fancy, we are just as little justified in calling it exaggerated. For simple thought is infinite, and what is limitless also cannot exceed. Exaggeration, therefore, is only that which wounds, not logical truth, but sensuous truth, and what pretends to be sensuous truth. Consequently, if a poet has the unhappy chance to choose for his picture certain natures that are merely superhuman and cannot possibly be represented, he can only avoid exaggeration by ceasing to be a poet, and not trusting the theme to his imagination. Otherwise one of two things would happen: either imagination, applying its limits to the object, would make a limited and merely human object of an absolute object—which happened with the gods of Greece—or the object would take away limits from fancy, that is, would render it null and void, and this is precisely exaggeration.

Extravagance of feeling should be distinguished from extravagance of portraiture; we are speaking of the former. The object of the feeling may be unnatural, but the feeling itself is natural, and ought accordingly to be shadowed forth in the language of nature. While extravagant feelings may issue from a warm heart and a really poetic nature, extravagance of portraiture always displays a cold heart, and very often a want of poetic capacity. Therefore this is not a danger for the sentimental poet, but only for the imitator, who has no vocation; it is therefore often found with platitude, insipidity, and even baseness. Exaggeration of sentiment is not without truth, and must have a real object; as nature inspires it, it admits of simplicity of expression and coming from the heart it goes to the heart. As its object, however, is not in nature, but artificially produced by the understanding, it has only a logical reality, and the feeling is not purely human. It was not an illusion that Heloise had for Abelard, Petrarch for Laura, Saint Preux for his Julia, Werther for his Charlotte; Agathon, Phanias, and Peregrinus —in Wieland—for the object of their dreams: the feeling is true, only the object is factitious and outside nature. If their thought had kept to simple sensuous truth, it could not have taken this flight; but on the other hand a mere play of fancy, without inner value, could not have stirred the heart: this is only stirred by reason. Thus this sort of exaggeration must be called to order, but it is not contemptible: and those who ridicule it would do well to find out if the wisdom on which they pride themselves is not want of heart, and if it is not through want of reason that they are so acute. The exaggerated delicacy in gallantry and honor which characterizes the chivalrous romances, especially of Spain, is of this kind; also the refined and even ridiculous tenderness of French and English sentimental romances of the best kind. These sentiments are not only subjectively true, but also objectively they are not without value; they are sound sentiments issuing from a moral source, only reprehensible as overstepping the limits of human truth. Without this moral reality how could they stir and touch so powerfully? The same remark applies to moral and religious fanaticism, patriotism, and the love of freedom when carried up to exaltation. As the object of these sentiments is always a pure idea, and not an external experience, imagination with its proper activity has here a dangerous liberty, and cannot, as elsewhere, be called back to bounds by the presence of a visible object. But neither the man nor the poet can withdraw from the law of nature, except to submit to that of reason. He can only abandon reality for the ideal; for liberty must hold to one or the other of these anchors. But it is far from the real to the ideal; and between the two is found fancy, with its arbitrary conceits and its unbridled freedom. It must needs be, therefore, that man in general, and the poet in particular, when he withdraws by liberty of his understanding from the dominion of feeling, without being moved to it by the laws of reason—that is, when he abandons nature through pure liberty—he finds himself freed from all law, and therefore a prey to the illusions of phantasy.

It is testified by experience that entire nations, as well as individual men, who have parted with the safe direction of nature, are actually in this condition; and poets have gone astray in the same manner. The true genius of sentimental poetry, if its aim is to raise itself to the rank of the ideal, must overstep the limits of the existing nature; but false genius oversteps all boundaries without any discrimination, flattering itself with the belief that the wild sport of the imagination is poetic inspiration. A true poetical genius can never fall into this error, because it only abandons the real for the sake of the ideal, or, at all events, it can only do so at certain moments when the poet forgets himself; but his main tendencies may dispose him to extravagance within the sphere of the senses. His example may also drive others into a chase of wild conceptions, because readers of lively fancy and weak understanding only remark the freedom which he takes with existing nature, and are unable to follow him in copying the elevated necessities of his inner being. The same difficulties beset the path of the sentimental genius in this respect, as those which afflict the career of a genius of the simple order. If a genius of this class carries out every work, obedient to the free and spontaneous impulses of his nature, the man devoid of genius who seeks to imitate him is not willing to consider his own nature a worse guide than that of the great poet. This accounts for the fact that masterpieces of simple poetry are commonly followed by a host of stale and unprofitable works in print, and masterpieces of the sentimental class by wild and fanciful effusions,—a fact that may be easily verified on questioning the history of literature.

Two maxims are prevalent in relation to poetry, both of them quite correct in themselves, but mutually destructive in the way in which they are generally conceived. The first is, that "poetry serves as a means of amusement and recreation," and we have previously observed that this maxim is highly favorable to aridity and platitudes in poetical actions. The other maxim, that "poetry is conducive to the moral progress of humanity," takes under its shelter theories and views of the most wild and extravagant character. It may be profitable to examine more attentively these two maxims, of which so much is heard, and which are so often imperfectly understood and falsely applied.

We say that a thing amuses us when it makes us pass from a forced state to the state that is natural to us. The whole question here is to know in what our natural state ought to consist, and what a forced state means. If our natural state is made to consist merely in the free development of all our physical powers, in emancipation from all constraint, it follows that every act of reason by resisting what is sensuous, is a violence we undergo, and rest of mind combined with physical movement will be a recreation par excellence. But if we make our natural state consist in a limitless power of human expression and of freely disposing of all our strength, all that divides these forces will be a forced state, and recreation will be what brings all our nature to harmony. Thus, the first of these ideal recreations is simply determined by the wants of our sensuous nature; the second, by the autonomous activity of human nature. Which of these two kinds of recreation can be demanded of the poet? Theoretically, the question is inadmissible, as no one would put the human ideal beneath the brutal. But in practice the requirements of a poet have been especially directed to the sensuous ideal, and for the most part favor, though not the esteem, for these sorts of works is regulated thereby. Men's minds are mostly engaged in a labor that exhausts them, or an enjoyment that sets them asleep. Now labor makes rest a sensible want, much more imperious than that of the moral nature; for physical nature must be satisfied before the mind can show its requirements. On the other hand, enjoyment paralyzes the moral instinct. Hence these two dispositions common in men are very injurious to the feeling for true beauty, and thus very few even of the best judge soundly in aesthetics. Beauty results from the harmony between spirit and sense; it addresses all the faculties of man, and can only be appreciated if a man employs fully all his strength. He must bring to it an open sense, a broad heart, a spirit full of freshness. All a man's nature must be on the alert, and this is not the case with those divided by abstraction, narrowed by formulas, enervated by application. They demand, no doubt, a material for the senses; but not to quicken, only to suspend, thought. They ask to be freed from what? From a load that oppressed their indolence, and not a rein that curbed their activity.

After this can one wonder at the success of mediocre talents in aesthetics? or at the bitter anger of small minds against true energetic beauty? They reckon on finding therein a congenial recreation, and regret to discover that a display of strength is required to which they are unequal. With mediocrity they are always welcome; however little mind they bring, they want still less to exhaust the author's inspiration. They are relieved of the load of thought; and their nature can lull itself in beatific nothings on the soft pillow of platitude. In the temple of Thalia and Melpomene—at least, so it is with us—the stupid savant and the exhausted man of business are received on the broad bosom of the goddess, where their intelligence is wrapped in a magnetic sleep, while their sluggish senses are warmed, and their imagination with gentle motions rocked.

Vulgar people may be excused what happens to the best capacities. Those moments of repose demanded by nature after lengthy labor are not favorable to aesthetic judgment, and hence in the busy classes few can pronounce safely on matters of taste. Nothing is more common than for scholars to make a ridiculous figure, in regard to a question of beauty, besides cultured men of the world; and technical critics are especially the laughing-stock of connoisseurs. Their opinion, from exaggeration, crudeness, or carelessness guides them generally quite awry, and they can only devise a technical judgment, and not an aesthetical one, embracing the whole work, in which feeling should decide. If they would kindly keep to technicalities they might still be useful, for the poet in moments of inspiration and readers under his spell are little inclined to consider details. But the spectacle which they afford us is only the more ridiculous inasmuch as we see these crude natures—with whom all labor and trouble only develop at the most a particular aptitude,—when we see them set up their paltry individualities as the representation of universal and complete feeling, and in the sweat of their brow pronounce judgment on beauty.

We have just seen that the kind of recreation poetry ought to afford is generally conceived in too restricted a manner, and only referred to a simple sensuous want. Too much scope, however, is also given to the other idea, the moral ennobling the poet should have in view, inasmuch as too purely an ideal aim is assigned.

In fact, according to the pure ideal, the ennobling goes on to infinity, because reason is not restricted to any sensuous limits, and only finds rest in absolute perfection. Nothing can satisfy whilst a superior thing can be conceived; it judges strictly and admits no excuses of infirmity and finite nature. It only admits for limits those of thought, which transcends time and space. Hence the poet could no more propose to himself such an ideal of ennobling (traced for him by pure (didactic) reason) any more than the coarse ideal of recreation of sensuous nature. The aim is to free human nature from accidental hinderances, without destroying the essential ideal of our humanity, or displacing its limits. All beyond this is exaggeration, and a quicksand in which the poet too easily suffers shipwreck if he mistakes the idea of nobleness. But, unfortunately, he cannot rise to the true ideal of ennobled human nature without going some steps beyond it. To rise so high he must abandon the world of reality, for, like every ideal, it is only to be drawn from its inner moral source. He does not find it in the turmoil of worldly life, but only in his heart, and that only in calm meditation. But in this separation from real life he is likely to lose sight of all the limits of human nature, and seeking pure form he may easily lose himself in arbitrary and baseless conceptions. Reason will abstract itself too much from experience, and the practical man will not be able to carry out, in the crush of real life, what the contemplative mind has discovered on the peaceful path of thought. Thus, what makes a dreamy man is the very thing that alone could have made him a sage; and the advantage for the latter is not that he has never been a dreamer, but rather that he has not remained one.

We must not, then, allow the workers to determine recreation according to their wants, nor thinkers that of nobleness according to their speculations, for fear of either a too low physical poetry, or a poetry too given to hyperphysical exaggeration. And as these two ideas direct most men's judgments on poetry, we must seek a class of mind at once active, but not slavishly so, and idealizing, but not dreamy; uniting the reality of life within as few limits as possible, obeying the current of human affairs, but not enslaved by them. Such a class of men can alone preserve the beautiful unity of human nature, that harmony which all work for a moment disturbs, and a life of work destroys; such alone can, in all that is purely human, give by its feelings universal rules of judgment. Whether such a class exists, or whether the class now existing in like conditions answers to this ideal conception, I am not concerned to inquire. If it does not respond to the ideal it has only itself to blame. In such a class—here regarded as a mere ideal—the simple and sentimental would keep each other from extremes of extravagance and relaxation. For the idea of a beautiful humanity is not exhausted by either, but can only be presented in the union of both.

THE STAGE AS A MORAL INSTITUTION.

Sulzer has remarked that the stage has arisen from an irresistible longing for the new and extraordinary. Man, oppressed by divided cares, and satiated with sensual pleasure, felt an emptiness or want. Man, neither altogether satisfied with the senses, nor forever capable of thought, wanted a middle state, a bridge between the two states, bringing them into harmony. Beauty and aesthetics supplied that for him. But a good lawgiver is not satisfied with discovering the bent of his people— he turns it to account as an instrument for higher use; and hence he chose the stage, as giving nourishment to the soul, without straining it, and uniting the noblest education of the head and heart.

The man who first pronounced religion to be the strongest pillar of the state, unconsciously defended the stage, when he said so, in its noblest aspect. The uncertain nature of political events, rendering religion a necessity, also demands the stage as a moral force. Laws only prevent disturbances of social life; religion prescribes positive orders sustaining social order. Law only governs actions; religion controls the heart and follows thought to the source.

Laws are flexible and capricious; religion binds forever. If religion has this great sway over man's heart, can it also complete his culture? Separating the political from the divine element in it, religion acts mostly on the senses; she loses her sway if the senses are gone. By what channel does the stage operate? To most men religion vanishes with the loss of her symbols, images, and problems; and yet they are only pictures of the imagination, and insolvable problems. Both laws and religion are strengthened by a union with the stage, where virtue and vice, joy and sorrow, are thoroughly displayed in a truthful and popular way; where a variety of providential problems are solved; where all secrets are unmasked, all artifice ends, and truth alone is the judge, as incorruptible as Rhadamanthus.

Where the influence of civil laws ends that of the stage begins. Where venality and corruption blind and bias justice and judgment, and intimidation perverts its ends, the stage seizes the sword and scales and pronounces a terrible verdict on vice. The fields of fancy and of history are open to the stage; great criminals of the past live over again in the drama, and thus benefit an indignant posterity. They pass before us as empty shadows of their age, and we heap curses on their memory while we enjoy on the stage the very horror of their crimes. When morality is no more taught, religion no longer received, or laws exist, Medea would still terrify us with her infanticide. The sight of Lady Macbeth, while it makes us shudder, will also make us rejoice in a good conscience, when we see her, the sleep-walker, washing her hands and seeking to destroy the awful smell of murder. Sight is always more powerful to man than description; hence the stage acts more powerfully than morality or law.

But in this the stage only aids justice. A far wider field is really open to it. There are a thousand vices unnoticed by human justice, but condemned by the stage; so, also, a thousand virtues overlooked by man's laws are honored on the stage. It is thus the handmaid of religion and philosophy. From these pure sources it draws its high principles and the exalted teachings, and presents them in a lovely form. The soul swells with noblest emotions when a divine ideal is placed before it. When Augustus offers his forgiving hand to Cinna, the conspirator, and says to him: "Let us be friends, Cinna!" what man at the moment does not feel that he could do the same. Again, when Francis von Sickingen, proceeding to punish a prince and redress a stranger, on turning sees the house, where his wife and children are, in flames, and yet goes on for the sake of his word—how great humanity appears, how small the stern power of fate!

Vice is portrayed on the stage in an equally telling manner. Thus, when old Lear, blind, helpless, childless, is seen knocking in vain at his daughters' doors, and in tempest and night he recounts by telling his woes to the elements, and ends by saying: "I have given you all,"—how strongly impressed we feel at the value of filial piety, and how hateful ingratitude seems to us!

The stage does even more than this. It cultivates the ground where religion and law do not think it dignified to stop. Folly often troubles the world as much as crime; and it has been justly said that the heaviest loads often hang suspended by the slightest threads. Tracing actions to their sources, the list of criminals diminish, and we laugh at the long catalogue of fools. In our sex all forms of evil emanate almost entirely from one source, and all our excesses are only varied and higher forms of one quality, and that a quality which in the end we smile at and love; and why should not nature have followed this course in the opposite sex too? In man there is only one secret to guard against depravity; that is, to protect his heart against wickedness.

Much of all this is shown up on the stage. It is a mirror to reflect fools and their thousand forms of folly, which are there turned to ridicule. It curbs vice by terror, and folly still more effectually by satire and jest. If a comparison be made between tragedy and comedy, guided by experience, we should probably give the palm to the latter as to effects produced. Hatred does not wound the conscience so much as mockery does the pride of man. We are exposed specially to the sting of satire by the very cowardice that shuns terrors. From sins we are guarded by law and conscience, but the ludicrous is specially punished on the stage. Where we allow a friend to correct our morals, we rarely forgive a laugh. We may bear heavy judgment on our transgressions, but our weaknesses and vulgarities must not be criticised by a witness.

The stage alone can do this with impunity, chastising us as the anonymous fool. We can bear this rebuke without a blush, and even gratefully.

But the stage does even more than this. It is a great school of practical wisdom, a guide for civil life, and a key to the mind in all its sinuosities. It does not, of course, remove egoism and stubbornness in evil ways; for a thousand vices hold up their heads in spite of the stage, and a thousand virtues make no impression on cold-hearted spectators. Thus, probably, Moliere's

Harpagon never altered a usurer's heart, nor did the suicide in Beverley save any one from the gaming-table. Nor, again, is it likely that the high roads will be safer through Karl Moor's untimely end. But, admitting this, and more than this, still how great is the influence of the stage! It has shown us the vices and virtues of men with whom we have to live. We are not surprised at their weaknesses, we are prepared for them. The stage points them out to us, and their remedy. It drags off the mask from the hypocrite, and betrays the meshes of intrigue. Duplicity and cunning have been forced by it to show their hideous features in the light of day. Perhaps the dying Sarah may not deter a single debauchee, nor all the pictures of avenged seduction stop the evil; yet unguarded innocence has been shown the snares of the corrupter, and taught to distrust his oaths.

The stage also teaches men to bear the strokes of fortune. Chance and design have equal sway over life. We have to bow to the former, but we control the latter. It is a great advantage if inexorable facts do not find us unprepared and unexercised, and if our breast has been steeled to bear adversity. Much human woe is placed before us on the stage. It gives us momentary pain in the tears we shed for strangers' troubles, but as a compensation it fills us with a grand new stock of courage and endurance. We are led by it, with the abandoned Ariadne, through the Isle of Naxos, and we descend the Tower of Starvation in Ugolino; we ascend the terrible scaffold, and we are present at the awful moment of execution. Things remotely present in thought become palpable realities now. We see the deceived favorite abandoned by the queen. When about to die, the perfidious Moor is abandoned by his own sophistry. Eternity reveals the secrets of the unknown through the dead, and the hateful wretch loses all screen of guilt when the tomb opens to condemn him.

Then the stage teaches us to be more considerate to the unfortunate, and to judge gently. We can only pronounce on a man when we know his whole being and circumstances. Theft is a base crime, but tears mingle with our condemnation, when we read what obliged Edward Ruhberg to do the horrid deed. Suicide is shocking; but the condemnation of an enraged father, her love, and the fear of a convent, lead Marianne to drink the cup, and few would dare to condemn the victim of a dreadful tyranny. Humanity and tolerance have begun to prevail in our time at courts of princes and in courts of law. A large share of this may be due to the influence of the stage in showing man and his secret motives.

The great of the world ought to be especially grateful to the stage, for it is here alone that they hear the truth.

Not only man's mind, but also his intellectual culture, has been promoted by the higher drama. The lofty mind and the ardent patriot have often used the stage to spread enlightenment.

Considering nations and ages, the thinker sees the masses enchained by opinion and cut off by adversity from happiness; truth only lights up a few minds, who perhaps have to acquire it by the trials of a lifetime. How can the wise ruler put these within the reach of his nation.

The thoughtful and the worthier section of the people diffuse the light of wisdom over the masses through the stage. Purer and better principles and motives issue from the stage and circulate through society: the night of barbarism and superstition vanishes. I would mention two glorious fruits of the higher class of dramas. Religious toleration has latterly become universal. Before Nathan the Jew and Saladin the Saracen put us to shame, and showed that resignation to God's will did not depend on a fancied belief of His nature—even before Joseph II. contended with the hatred of a narrow piety—the stage had sown seeds of humanity and gentleness: pictures of fanaticism had taught a hatred of intolerance, and Christianity, seeing itself in this awful mirror, washed off its stains. It is to be hoped that the stage will equally combat mistaken systems of education. This is a subject of the first political importance, and yet none is so left to private whims and caprice. The stage might give stirring examples of mistaken education, and lead parents to juster, better views of the subject. Many teachers are led astray by false views, and methods are often artificial and fatal.

Opinions about governments and classes might be reformed by the stage. Legislation could thus justify itself by foreign symbols, and silence doubtful aspersions without offence.

Now, if poets would be patriotic they could do much on the stage to forward invention and industry. A standing theatre would be a material advantage to a nation. It would have a great influence on the national temper and mind by helping the nation to agree in opinions and inclinations. The stage alone can do this, because it commands all human knowledge, exhausts all positions, illumines all hearts, unites all classes, and makes its way to the heart and understanding by the most popular channels.

If one feature characterized all dramas; if the poets were allied in aim—that is, if they selected well and from national topics—there would be a national stage, and we should become a nation. It was this that knit the Greeks so strongly together, and this gave to them the all-absorbing interest in the republic and the advancement of humanity.

Another advantage belongs to the stage; one which seems to have become acknowledged even by its censurers. Its influence on intellectual and moral culture, which we have till now been advocating, may be doubted; but its very enemies have admitted that it has gained the palm over all other means of amusement. It has been of much higher service here than people are often ready to allow.

Human nature cannot bear to be always on the rack of business, and the charms of sense die out with their gratification. Man, oppressed by appetites, weary of long exertion, thirsts for refined pleasure, or rushes into dissipations that hasten his fall and ruin, and disturb social order. Bacchanal joys, gambling, follies of all sorts to disturb ennui, are unavoidable if the lawgiver produces nothing better. A man of public business, who has made noble sacrifices to the state, is apt to pay for them with melancholy, the scholar to become a pedant, and the people brutish, without the stage. The stage is an institution combining amusement with instruction, rest with exertion, where no faculty of the mind is overstrained, no pleasure enjoyed at the cost of the whole. When melancholy gnaws the heart, when trouble poisons our solitude, when we are disgusted with the world, and a thousand worries oppress us, or when our energies are destroyed by over-exercise, the stage revives us, we dream of another sphere, we recover ourselves, our torpid nature is roused by noble passions, our blood circulates more healthily. The unhappy man forgets his tears in weeping for another. The happy man is calmed, the secure made provident. Effeminate natures are steeled, savages made man, and, as the supreme triumph of nature, men of all clanks, zones, and conditions, emancipated from the chains of conventionality and fashion, fraternize here in a universal sympathy, forget the world, and come nearer to their heavenly destination. The individual shares in the general ecstacy, and his breast has now only space for an emotion: he is a man.

ON THE TRAGIC ART.

The state of passion in itself, independently of the good or bad influence of its object on our morality, has something in it that charms us. We aspire to transport ourselves into that state, even if it costs us some sacrifices. You will find this instinct at the bottom of all our most habitual pleasures. As to the nature itself of the affection, whether it be one of aversion or desire, agreeable or painful, this is what we take little into consideration. Experience teaches us that painful affections are those which have the most attraction for us, and thus that the pleasure we take in an affection is precisely in an inverse ratio to its nature. It is a phenomenon common to all men, that sad, frightful things, even the horrible, exercise over us an irresistible seduction, and that in presence of a scene of desolation and of terror we feel at once repelled and attracted by two equal forces. Suppose the case be an assassination. Then every one crowds round the narrator and shows a marked attention. Any ghost story, however embellished by romantic circumstances, is greedily devoured by us, and the more readily in proportion as the story is calculated to make our hair stand on end.

This disposition is developed in a more lively manner when the objects themselves are placed before our eyes. A tempest that would swallow up an entire fleet would be, seen from shore, a spectacle as attractive to our imagination as it would be shocking to our heart. It would be difficult to believe with Lucretius that this natural pleasure results from a comparison between our own safety and the danger of which we are witnesses. See what a crowd accompanies a criminal to the scene of his punishment! This phenomenon cannot be explained either by the pleasure of satisfying our love of justice, nor the ignoble joy of vengeance. Perhaps the unhappy man may find excuses in the hearts of those present; perhaps the sincerest pity takes an interest in his reprieve: this does not prevent a lively curiosity in the spectators to watch his expressions of pain with eye and ear. If an exception seems to exist here in the case of a well-bred man, endowed with a delicate sense, this does not imply that he is a complete stranger to this instinct; but in his case the painful strength of compassion carries the day over this instinct, or it is kept under by the laws of decency. The man of nature, who is not chained down by any feeling of human delicacy, abandons himself without any sense of shame to this powerful instinct. This attraction must, therefore, have its spring of action in an original disposition, and it must be explained by a psychological law common to the whole species.

But if it seems to us that these brutal instincts of nature are incompatible with the dignity of man, and if we hesitate, for this reason, to establish on this fact a law common to the whole species, yet no experiences are required to prove, with the completest evidence, that the pleasure we take in painful emotions is real, and that it is general. The painful struggle of a heart drawn asunder between its inclinations or contrary duties, a struggle which is a cause of misery to him who experiences it, delights the person who is a mere spectator. We follow with always heightening pleasure the progress of a passion to the abyss into which it hurries its unhappy victim. The same delicate feeling that makes us turn our eyes aside from the sight of physical suffering, or even from the physical expression of a purely moral pain, makes us experience a pleasure heightened in sweetness, in the sympathy for a purely moral pain. The interest with which we stop to look at the painting of these kinds of objects is a general phenomenon.

Of course this can only be understood of sympathetic affections, or those felt as a secondary effect after their first impression; for commonly direct and personal affections immediately call into life in us the instinct of our own happiness, they take up all our thoughts, and seize hold of us too powerfully to allow any room for the feeling of pleasure that accompanies them, when the affection is freed from all personal relation. Thus, in the mind that is really a prey to painful passion, the feeling of pain commands all others notwithstanding all the charm that the painting of its moral state may offer to the hearers and the spectators. And yet the painful affection is not deprived of all pleasure, even for him who experiences it directly; only this pleasure differs in degree according to the nature of each person's mind. The sports of chance would not have half so much attraction for us were there not a kind of enjoyment in anxiety, in doubt, and in fear; danger would not be encountered from mere foolhardiness; and the very sympathy which interests us in the trouble of another would not be to us that pleasure which is never more lively than at the very moment when the illusion is strongest, and when we substitute ourselves most entirely in the place of the person who suffers. But this does not imply that disagreeable affections cause pleasure of themselves, nor do I think any one will uphold this view; it suffices that these states of the mind are the conditions that alone make possible for its certain kinds of pleasure. Thus the hearts particularly sensitive to this kind of pleasure, and most greedy of them, will be more easily led to share these disagreeable affections, which are the condition of the former; and even in the most violent storms of passion they will always preserve some remains of their freedom.

The displeasure we feel in disagreeable affections comes from the relation of our sensuous faculty or of our moral faculty with their object. In like manner, the pleasure we experience in agreeable affections proceeds from the very same source. The degree of liberty that may prevail in the affections depends on the proportion between the moral nature and the sensuous nature of a man. Now it is well known that in the moral order there is nothing arbitrary for us, that, on the contrary, the sensuous instinct is subject to the laws of reason and consequently depends more or less on our will. Hence it is evident that we can keep our liberty full and entire in all those affections that are concerned with the instinct of self-love, and that we are the masters to determine the degree which they ought to attain. This degree will be less in proportion as the moral sense in a man will prevail over the instinct of happiness, and as by obeying the universal laws of reasons he will have freed himself from the selfish requirements of his individuality, his Ego. A man of this kind must therefore, in a state of passion, feel much less vividly the relation of an object with his own instinct of happiness, and consequently he will be much less sensible of the displeasure that arises from this relation. On the other hand, he will be perpetually more attentive to the relation of this same object with his moral nature, and for this very reason he will be more sensible to the pleasure which the relation of the object with morality often mingles with the most painful affections. A mind thus constituted is better fitted than all others to enjoy the pleasure attaching to compassion, and even to regard a personal affection as an object of simple compassion. Hence the inestimable value of a moral philosophy, which, by raising our eyes constantly towards general laws, weakens in us the feeling of our individuality, teaches us to plunge our paltry personality in something great, and enables us thus to act to ourselves as to strangers. This sublime state of the mind is the lot of strong philosophic minds, which by working assiduously on themselves have learned to bridle the egotistical instinct. Even the most cruel loss does not drive them beyond a certain degree of sadness, with which an appreciable sum of pleasure can always be reconciled. These souls, which are alone capable of separating themselves from themselves, alone enjoy the privilege of sympathizing with themselves and of receiving of their own sufferings only a reflex, softened by sympathy.

The indications contained in what precedes will suffice to direct our attention to the sources of the pleasure that the affection in itself causes, more particularly the sad affection. We have seen that this pleasure is more energetic in moral souls, and it acts with greater freedom in proportion as the soul is more independent of the egotistical instinct. This pleasure is, moreover, more vivid and stronger in sad affections, when self-love is painfully disquieted, than in gay affections, which imply a satisfaction of self-love. Accordingly this pleasure increases when the egotistical instinct is wounded, and diminishes when that instinct is flattered. Now we only know of two sources of pleasure—the satisfaction of the instinct of happiness, and the accomplishment of the moral laws. Therefore, when it is shown that a particular pleasure does not emanate from the former source, it must of necessity issue from the second. It is therefore from our moral nature that issues the charm of the painful affections shared by sympathy, and the pleasure that we sometimes feel even where the painful affection directly affects ourselves.

Many attempts have been made to account for the pleasure of pity, but most of these solutions had little chance of meeting the problem, because the principle of this phenomenon was sought for rather in the accompanying circumstances than in the nature of the affection itself. To many persons the pleasure of pity is simply the pleasure taken by the mind in exercising its own sensibility. To others it is the pleasure of occupying their forces energetically, of exercising the social faculty vividly—in short, of satisfying the instinct of restlessness. Others again make it derived from the discovery of morally fine features of character, placed in a clear light by the struggle against adversity or against the passions. But there is still the difficulty to explain why it should be exactly the very feeling of pain,—suffering properly so called,—that in objects of pity attracts us with the greatest force, while, according to those elucidations, a less degree of suffering ought evidently to be more favorable to those causes to which the source of the emotion is traced. Various matters may, no doubt, increase the pleasure of the emotion without occasioning it. Of this nature are the vividness and force of the ideas awakened in our imagination, the moral excellence of the suffering persons, the reference to himself of the person feeling pity. I admit that the suffering of a weak soul, and the pain of a wicked character, do not procure us this enjoyment. But this is because they do not excite our pity to the same degree as the hero who suffers, or the virtuous man who struggles. Thus we are constantly brought back to the first question: why is it precisely the degree of suffering that determines the degree of sympathetic pleasure which we take in an emotion? and one answer only is possible; it is because the attack made on our sensibility is precisely the condition necessary to set in motion that quality of mind of which the activity produces the pleasure we feel in sympathetic affections.

Now this faculty is no other than the reason; and because the free exercise of reason, as an absolutely independent activity, deserves par excellence the name of activity; as, moreover, the heart of man only feels itself perfectly free and independent in its moral acts, it follows that the charm of tragic emotions is really dependent on the fact that this instinct of activity finds its gratification in them. But, even admitting this, it is neither the great number nor the vivacity of the ideas that are awakened then in our imagination, nor in general the exercise of the social faculty, but a certain kind of ideas and a certain activity of the social faculty brought into play by reason, which is the foundation of this pleasure.

Thus the sympathetic affections in general are for us a source of pleasure because they give satisfaction to our instinct of activity, and the sad affections produce this effect with more vividness because they give more satisfaction to this instinct. The mind only reveals all its activity when it is in full possession of its liberty, when it has a perfect consciousness of its rational nature, because it is only then that it displays a force superior to all resistance.

Hence the state of mind which allows most effectually the manifestation of this force, and awakens most successfully its activity, is that state which is most suitable to a rational being, and which best satisfies our instincts of activity: whence it follows that a greater amount of pleasure must be attached necessarily to this state. Now it is the tragic states that place our soul in this state, and the pleasure found in them is necessarily higher than the charm produced by gay affections, in the same degree that moral power in us is superior to the power of the senses.

Points that are only subordinate and partial in a system of final causes may be considered by art independently of that relation with the rest, and may be converted into principal objects. It is right that in the designs of nature pleasure should only be a mediate end, or a means; but for art it is the highest end. It is therefore essentially important for art not to neglect this high enjoyment attaching to the tragic emotion. Now, tragic art, taking this term in its widest acceptation, is that among the fine arts which proposes as its principal object the pleasure of pity.

Art attains its end by the imitation of nature, by satisfying the conditions which make pleasure possible in reality, and by combining, according to a plan traced by the intelligence, the scattered elements furnished by nature, so as to attain as a principal end to that which, for nature, was only an accessory end. Thus tragic art ought to imitate nature in those kinds of actions that are specially adapted to awaken pity.

It follows that, in order to determine generally the system to be followed by tragic art, it is necessary before all things to know on what conditions in real life the pleasure of the emotion is commonly produced in the surest and the strongest manner; but it is necessary at the same time to pay attention to the circumstances that restrict or absolutely extinguish this pleasure.

After what we have established in our essay "On the Cause of the Pleasure we derive from Tragic Objects," it is known that in every tragic emotion there is an idea of incongruity, which, though the emotion may be attended with charm, must always lead on to the conception of a higher consistency. Now it is the relation that these two opposite conceptions mutually bear which determines in an emotion if the prevailing impression shall be pleasurable or the reverse. If the conception of incongruity be more vivid than that of the contrary, or if the end sacrificed is more important than the end gained, the prevailing impression will always be displeasure, whether this be understood objectively of the human race in general, or only subjectively of certain individuals.

If the cause that has produced a misfortune gives us too much displeasure, our compassion for the victim is diminished thereby. The heart cannot feel simultaneously, in a high degree, two absolutely contrary affections. Indignation against the person who is the primary cause of the suffering becomes the prevailing affection, and all other feeling has to yield to it. Thus our interest is always enfeebled when the unhappy man whom it would be desirable to pity had cast himself into ruin by a personal and an inexcusable fault; or if, being able to save himself, he did not do so, either through feebleness of mind or pusillanimity. The interest we take in unhappy King Lear, ill-treated by two ungrateful daughters, is sensibly lessened by the circumstance that this aged man, in his second childhood, so weakly gave up his crown, and divided his love among his daughters with so little discernment. In the tragedy of Kronegk, "Olinda and Sophronia," the most terrible suffering to which we see these martyrs to their faith exposed only excites our pity feebly, and all their heroism only stirs our admiration moderately, because madness alone can suggest the act by which Olinda has placed himself and all his people on the brink of the precipice.

Our pity is equally lessened when the primary cause of a misfortune, whose innocent victim ought to inspire us with compassion, fills our mind with horror. When the tragic poet cannot clear himself of his plot without introducing a wretch, and when he is reduced to derive the greatness of suffering from the greatness of wickedness, the supreme beauty of his work must always be seriously injured. Iago and Lady Macbeth in Shakspeare, Cleopatra in the tragedy of "Rodogune," or Franz Moor in "The Robbers," are so many proofs in support of this assertion. A poet who understands his real interest will not bring about the catastrophe through a malicious will which proposes misfortune as its end; nor, and still less, by want of understanding: but rather through the imperious force of circumstances. If this catastrophe does not come from moral sources, but from outward things, which have no volition and are not subject to any will, the pity we experience is more pure, or at all events it is not weakened by any idea of moral incongruity. But then the spectator cannot be spared the disagreeable feeling of an incongruity in the order of nature, which can alone save in such a case moral propriety. Pity is far more excited when it has for its object both him who suffers and him who is the primary cause of the suffering. This can only happen when the latter has neither elicited our contempt nor our hatred, but when he has been brought against his inclination to become the cause of this misfortune. It is a singular beauty of the German play of "Iphigenia" that the King of Tauris, the only obstacle who thwarts the wishes of Orestes and of his sister, never loses our esteem, and that we love him to the end.

There is something superior even to this kind of emotion; this is the case when the cause of the misfortune not only is in no way repugnant to morality, but only becomes possible through morality, and when the reciprocal suffering comes simply from the idea that a fellow-creature has been made to suffer. This is the situation of Chimene and Rodrigue in "The Cid" of Pierre Corneille, which is undeniably in point of intrigue the masterpiece of the tragic stage. Honor and filial love arm the hand of Rodrigue against the father of her whom he loves, and his valor gives him the victory. Honor and filial love rouse up against him, in the person of Chimene, the daughter of his victim, an accuser and a formidable persecutor. Both act in opposition to their inclination, and they tremble with anguish at the thought of the misfortune of the object against which they arm themselves, in proportion as zeal inspires them for their duty to inflict this misfortune. Accordingly both conciliate our esteem in the highest sense, as they accomplish a moral duty at the cost of inclination; both inflame our pity in the highest degree, because they suffer spontaneously for a motive that renders them in the highest degree to be respected. It results from this that our pity is in this case so little modified by any opposite feeling that it burns rather with a double flame; only the impossibility of reconciling the idea of misfortune with the idea of a morality so deserving of happiness might still disturb our sympathetic pleasure, and spread a shade of sadness over it. It is besides a great point, no doubt, that the discontent given us by this contradiction does not bear upon our moral being, but is turned aside to a harmless place, to necessity only; but this blind subjection to destiny is always afflicting and humiliating for free beings, who determine themselves. This is the cause that always leaves something to be wished for even in the best Greek pieces. In all these pieces, at the bottom of the plot it is always fatality that is appealed to, and in this there is a knot that cannot be unravelled by our reason, which wishes to solve everything.

But even this knot is untied, and with it vanishes every shade of displeasure, at the highest and last step to which man perfected by morality rises, and at the highest point which is attained by the art which moves the feelings. This happens when the very discontent with destiny becomes effaced, and is resolved in a presentiment or rather a clear consciousness of a teleological concatenation of things, of a sublime order, of a beneficent will. Then, to the pleasure occasioned in us by moral consistency is joined the invigorating idea of the most perfect suitability in the great whole of nature. In this case the thing that seemed to militate against this order, and that caused us pain, in a particular case, is only a spur that stimulates our reason to seek in general laws for the justification of this particular case, and to solve the problem of this separate discord in the centre of the general harmony. Greek art never rose to this supreme serenity of tragic emotion, because neither the national religion, nor even the philosophy of the Greeks, lighted their step on this advanced road. It was reserved for modern art, which enjoys the privilege of finding a purer matter in a purer philosophy, to satisfy also this exalted want, and thus to display all the moral dignity of art.

If we moderns must resign ourselves never to reproduce Greek art because the philosophic genius of our age, and modern civilization in general are not favorable to poetry, these influences are at all events less hurtful to tragic art, which is based rather on the moral element. Perhaps it is in the case of this art only that our civilization repairs the injury that it has caused to art in general.

In the same manner as the tragic emotion is weakened by the admixture of conflicting ideas and feelings, and the charm attaching to it is thus diminished, so this emotion can also, on the contrary, by approaching the excess of direct and personal affection, become exaggerated to the point where pain carries the day over pleasure. It has been remarked that displeasure, in the affections, comes from the relation of their object with our senses, in the same way as the pleasure felt in them comes from the relation of the affection itself to our moral faculty. This implies, then, between our senses and our moral faculty a determined relation, which decides as regards the relation between pleasure and displeasure in tragic emotions. Nor could this relation be modified or overthrown without overthrowing at the same time the feelings of pleasure and displeasure which we find in the emotions, or even without changing them into their opposites. In the same ratio that the senses are vividly roused in us, the influence of morality will be proportionately diminished; and reciprocally, as the sensuous loses, morality gains ground. Therefore that which in our hearts gives a preponderance to the sensuous faculty, must of necessity, by placing restrictions on the moral faculty, diminish the pleasure that we take in tragic emotions, a pleasure which emanates exclusively from this moral faculty. In like manner, all that in our heart impresses an impetus on this latter faculty, must blunt the stimulus of pain even in direct and personal affections. Now our sensuous nature actually acquires this preponderance, when the ideas of suffering rise to a degree of vividness that no longer allows us to distinguish a sympathetic affection from a personal affection, or our own proper Ego from the subject that suffers,—reality, in short, from poetry. The sensuous also gains the upper hand when it finds an aliment in the great number of its objects, and in that dazzling light which an over-excited imagination diffuses over it. On the contrary, nothing is more fit to reduce the sensuous to its proper bounds than to place alongside it super-sensuous ideas, moral ideas, to which reason, oppressed just before, clings as to a kind of spiritual props, to right and raise itself above the fogs of the sensuous to a serener atmosphere. Hence the great charm which general truths or moral sentences, scattered opportunely over dramatic dialogue, have for all cultivated nations, and the almost excessive use that the Greeks made of them. Nothing is more agreeable to a moral soul than to have the power, after a purely passive state that has lasted too long, of escaping from the subjection of the senses, and of being recalled to its spontaneous activity, and restored to the possession of its liberty.

These are the remarks I had to make respecting the causes that restrict our pity and place an obstacle to our pleasure in tragic emotions. I have next to show on what conditions pity is solicited and the pleasure of the emotion excited in the most infallible and energetic manner.

Every feeling of pity implies the idea of suffering, and the degree of pity is regulated according to the degree more or less of vividness, of truth, of intensity, and of duration of this idea.

1st. The moral faculty is provoked to reaction in proportion to the vividness of ideas in the soul, which incites it to activity and solicits its sensuous faculty. Now the ideas of suffering are conceived in two different manners, which are not equally favorable to the vividness of the impression. The sufferings that we witness affect us incomparably more than those that we have through a description or a narrative. The former suspend in us the free play of the fancy, and striking our senses immediately penetrate by the shortest road to our heart. In the narrative, on the contrary, the particular is first raised to the general, and it is from this that the knowledge of the special case is afterwards derived; accordingly, merely by this necessary operation of the understanding, the impression already loses greatly in strength. Now a weak impression cannot take complete possession of our mind, and it will allow other ideas to disturb its action and to dissipate the attention. Very frequently, moreover, the narrative account transports us from the moral disposition, in which the acting person is placed, to the state of mind of the narrator himself, which breaks up the illusion so necessary for pity. In every case, when the narrator in person puts himself forward, a certain stoppage takes place in the action, and, as an unavoidable result, in our sympathetic affection. This is what happens even when the dramatic poet forgets himself in the dialogue, and puts in the mouth of his dramatic persons reflections that could only enter the mind of a disinterested spectator. It would be difficult to mention a single one of our modern tragedies quite free from this defect; but the French alone have made a rule of it. Let us infer, then, that the immediate vivid and sensuous presence of the object is necessary to give to the ideas impressed on us by suffering that strength without which the emotion could not rise to a high degree.

2d. But we can receive the most vivid impressions of the idea of suffering without, however, being led to a remarkable degree of pity, if these impressions lack truth. It is, necessary that we should form of suffering an idea of such a nature that we are obliged to share and take part in it. To this end there must be a certain agreement between this suffering and something that we have already in us. In other words, pity is only possible inasmuch as we can prove or suppose a resemblance between ourselves and the subject that suffers. Everywhere where this resemblance makes itself known, pity is necessary; where this resemblance is lacking, pity is impossible. The more visible and the greater is the resemblance, the more vivid is our pity; and they mutually slacken in dependence on each other. In order that we may feel the affections of another after him, all the internal conditions demanded by this affection must be found beforehand in us, in order that the external cause which, by meeting with the internal conditions, has given birth to the affection, may also produce on us a like effect. It is necessary that, without doing violence to ourselves, we should be able to exchange persons with another, and transport our Ego by an instantaneous substitution in the state of the subject. Now, how is it possible to feel in us the state of another, if we have not beforehand recognized ourselves in this other.

This resemblance bears on the totality of the constitution of the mind, in as far as that is necessary and universal. Now, this character of necessity and of universality belongs especially to our moral nature. The faculty of feeling can be determined differently by accidental causes: our cognitive faculties themselves depend on variable conditions: the moral faculty only has its principle in itself, and by that very fact it can best give us a general measure and a certain criterion of this resemblance. Thus an idea which we find in accord with our mode of thinking and of feeling, which offers at once a certain relationship with the train of our own ideas, which is easily grasped by our heart and our mind, we call a true idea. If this relationship bears on what is peculiar to our heart, on the private determinations that modify in us the common fundamentals of humanity, and which may be withdrawn without altering this general character, this idea is then simply true for us. If it bears on the general and necessary form that we suppose in the whole species, the truth of this idea ought to be held to be equal to objective truth. For the Roman, the sentence of the first Brutus and the suicide of Cato are of subjective truth. The ideas and the feelings that have inspired the actions of these two men are not an immediate consequence of human nature in general, but the mediate consequence of a human nature determined by particular modifications. To share with them these feelings we must have a Roman soul, or at least be capable of assuming for a moment a Roman soul. It suffices, on the other hand, to be a man in general, to be vividly touched by the heroic sacrifice of Leonidas, by the quiet resignation of Aristides, by the voluntary death of Socrates, and to be moved to tears by the terrible changes in the fortunes of Darius. We attribute to these kinds of ideas, in opposition to the preceding ones, an objective truth because they agree with the nature of all human subjects, which gives them a character of universality and of necessity as strict as if they were independent of every subjective condition.

Moreover, although the subjectively true description is based on accidental determinations, this is no reason for confounding it with an arbitrary description. After all, the subjectively true emanates also from the general constitution of the human soul, modified only in particular directions by special circumstances; and the two kinds of truth are equally necessary conditions of the human mind. If the resolution of Cato were in contradiction with the general laws of human nature, it could not be true, even subjectively. The only difference is that the ideas of the second kind are enclosed in a narrower sphere of action; because they imply, besides the general modes of the human mind, other special determinations. Tragedy can make use of it with a very intense effect, if it will renounce the extensive effect; still the unconditionally true, what is purely human in human relations, will be always the richest matter for the tragic poet, because this ground is the only one on which tragedy, without ceasing to aspire to strength of expression can be certain of the generality of this impression.

3d. Besides the vividness and the truth of tragic pictures, there must also be completeness. None of the external data that are necessary to give to the soul the desired movement ought to be omitted in the representation. In order that the spectator, however Roman his sentiments may be, may understand the moral state of Cato—that he may make his own the high resolution of the republican, this resolution must have its principle, not only in the mind of the Roman, but also in the circumstances of the action. His external situation as well as his internal situation must be before our eyes in all their consequences and extent: and we must, lastly, have unrolled before us, without omitting a single link, the whole chain of determinations to which are attached the high resolution of the Roman as a necessary consequence. It may be said in general that without this third condition, even the truth of a painting cannot be recognized; for the similarity of circumstances, which ought to be fully evident, can alone justify our judgment on the similarity of the feelings, since it is only from the competition of external conditions and of internal conditions that the affective phenomenon results. To decide if we should have acted like Cato, we must before all things transport ourselves in thought to the external situation in which Cato was placed, and then only we are entitled to place our feelings alongside his, to pronounce if there is or is not likeness, and to give a verdict on the truth of these feelings.

A complete picture, as I understand it, is only possible by the concatenation of several separate ideas, and of several separate feelings, which are connected together as cause and effect, and which, in their sum total, form one single whole for our cognitive faculty. All these ideas, in order to affect us closely, must make an immediate impression on our senses; and, as the narrative form always weakens this impression, they must be produced by a present action. Thus, in order that a tragic picture may be complete, a whole series is required of particular actions, rendered sensuous and connected with the tragic action as to one whole.

4th. It is necessary, lastly, that the ideas we receive of suffering should act on us in a durable manner, to excite in us a high degree of emotion. The affection created in us by the suffering of another is to us a constrained state, from which we hasten to get free; and the illusion so necessary for pity easily disappears in this case. It is, therefore, a necessity to fasten the mind closely to these ideas, and not to leave it the freedom to get rid too soon of the illusion. The vividness of sudden ideas and the energy of sudden impressions, which in rapid succession affect our senses, would not suffice for this end. For the power of reaction in the mind is manifested in direct proportion to the force with which the receptive faculty is solicited, and it is manifested to triumph over this impression. Now, the poet who wishes to move us ought not to weaken this independent power in us, for it is exactly in the struggle between it and the suffering of our sensuous nature that the higher charm of tragic emotions lies. In order that the heart, in spite of that spontaneous force which reacts against sensuous affections, may remain attached to the impressions of sufferings, it is, therefore, necessary that these impressions should be cleverly suspended at intervals, or even interrupted and intercepted by contrary impressions, to return again with twofold energy and renew more frequently the vividness of the first impression. Against the exhaustion and languor that result from habit, the most effectual remedy is to propose new objects to the senses; this variety retempers them, and the gradation of impressions calls forth the innate faculty, and makes it employ a proportionately stronger resistance. This faculty ought to be incessantly occupied in maintaining its independence against the attacks of the senses, but it must not triumph before the end, still less must it succumb in the struggle. Otherwise, in the former case, suffering, and, in the latter, moral activity is set aside; while it is the union of these two that can alone elicit emotion. The great secret of the tragic art consists precisely in managing this struggle well; it is in this that it shows itself in the most brilliant light.

For this, a succession of alternate ideas is required: therefore a suitable combination is wanted of several particular actions corresponding with these different ideas; actions round which the principal action and the tragic impression which it is wished to produce through it unroll themselves like the yarn from the distaff, and end by enlacing our souls in nets, through which they cannot break. Let me be permitted to make use of a simile, by saying that the artist ought to begin by gathering up with parsimonious care all the separate rays that issue from the object by aid of which he seeks to produce the tragic effect that he has in view, and these rays, in his hands, become a lightning flash, setting the hearts of all on fire. The tyro casts suddenly and vainly all the thunderbolts of horror and fear into the soul; the artist, on the contrary, advances step by step to his end; he only strikes with measured strokes, but he penetrates to the depth of our soul, precisely because he has only stirred it by degrees.

If we now form the proper deductions from the previous investigation, the following will be the conditions that form bases of the tragic art. It is necessary, in the first place, that the object of our pity should belong to our own species—I mean belong in the full sense of the term and that the action in which it is sought to interest us be a moral action; that is, an action comprehended in the field of free-will. It is necessary, in the second place, that suffering, its sources, its degrees, should be completely communicated by a series of events chained together. It is necessary, in the third place, that the object of the passion be rendered present to our senses, not in a mediate way and by description, but immediately and in action. In tragedy art unites all these conditions and satisfies them.

According to these principles tragedy might be defined as the poetic imitation of a coherent series of particular events (forming a complete action): an imitation which shows us man in a state of suffering, and which has for its end to excite our pity.

I say first that it is the imitation of an action; and this idea of imitation already distinguishes tragedy from the other kinds of poetry, which only narrate or describe. In tragedy particular events are presented to our imagination or to our senses at the very time of their accomplishment; they are present, we see them immediately, without the intervention of a third person. The epos, the romance, simple narrative, even in their form, withdraw action to a distance, causing the narrator to come between the acting person and the reader. Now what is distant and past always weakens, as we know, the impressions and the sympathetic affection; what is present makes them stronger. All narrative forms make of the present something past; all dramatic form makes of the past a present.

Secondly, I say that tragedy is the imitation of a succession of events, of an action. Tragedy has not only to represent by imitation the feelings and the affections of tragic persons, but also the events that have produced these feelings, and the occasion on which these affections are manifested. This distinguishes it from lyric poetry, and from its different forms, which no doubt offer, like tragedy, the poetic imitation of certain states of the mind, but not the poetic imitation of certain actions. An elegy, a song, an ode, can place before our eyes, by imitation, the moral state in which the poet actually is—whether he speaks in his own name, or in that of an ideal person—a state determined by particular circumstances; and up to this point these lyric forms seem certainly to be incorporated in the idea of tragedy; but they do not complete that idea, because they are confined to representing our feelings. There are still more essential differences, if the end of these lyrical forms and that of tragedy are kept in view.

I say, in the third place, that tragedy is the imitation of a complete action. A separate event, though it be ever so tragic, does not in itself constitute a tragedy. To do this, several events are required, based one on the other, like cause and effect, and suitably connected so as to form a whole; without which the truth of the feeling represented, of the character, etc.—that is, their conformity with the nature of our mind, a conformity which alone determines our sympathy

—will not be recognized. If we do not feel that we ourselves in similar circumstances should have experienced the same feelings and acted in the same way, our pity would not be awakened. It is, therefore, important that we should be able to follow in all its concatenation the action that is represented to us, that we should see it issue from the mind of the agent by a natural gradation, under the influence and with the concurrence of external circumstances. It is thus that we see spring up, grow, and come to maturity under our eyes, the curiosity of Oedipus and the jealousy of Iago. It is also the only way to fill up the great gap that exists between the joy of an innocent soul and the torments of a guilty conscience, between the proud serenity of the happy man and his terrible catastrophe; in short, between the state of calm, in which the reader is at the beginning, and the violent agitation he ought to experience at the end.

A series of several connected incidents is required to produce in our souls a succession of different movements which arrest the attention, which, appealing to all the faculties of our minds, enliven our instinct of activity when it is exhausted, and which, by delaying the satisfaction of this instinct, do not kindle it the less. Against the suffering of sensuous nature the human heart has only recourse to its moral nature as counterpoise. It is, therefore, necessary, in order to stimulate this in a more pressing manner, for the tragic poet to prolong the torments of sense, but he must also give a glimpse to the latter of the satisfaction of its wants, so as to render the victory of the moral sense so much the more difficult and glorious. This twofold end can only be attained by a succession of actions judiciously chosen and combined to this end.

In the fourth place, I say that tragedy is the poetic imitation of an action deserving of pity, and, therefore, tragic imitation is opposed to historic imitation. It would only be a historic imitation if it proposed a historic end, if its principal object were to teach us that a thing has taken place, and how it took place. On this hypothesis it ought to keep rigorously to historic accuracy, for it would only attain its end by representing faithfully that which really took place. But tragedy has a poetic end, that is to say, it represents an action to move us, and to charm our souls by the medium of this emotion. If, therefore, a matter being given, tragedy treats it conformably with this poetic end, which is proper to it, it becomes, by that very thing, free in its imitation. It is a right—nay, more, it is an obligation—for tragedy to subject historic truth to the laws of poetry; and to treat its matter in conformity with requirements of this art. But as it cannot attain its end, which is emotion, except on the condition of a perfect conformity with the laws of nature, tragedy is, notwithstanding its freedom in regard to history, strictly subject to the laws of natural truth, which, in opposition to the truth of history, takes the name of poetic truth. It may thus be understood how much poetic truth may lose, in many cases by a strict observance of historic truth, and, reciprocally, how much it may gain by even a very serious alteration of truth according to history. As the tragic poet, like poets in general, is only subject to the laws of poetic truth, the most conscientious observance of historic truth could never dispense him from his duties as poet, and could never excuse in him any infraction of poetic truth or lack of interest. It is, therefore, betraying very narrow ideas on tragic art, or rather on poetry in general, to drag the tragic poet before the tribunal of history, and to require instruction of the man who by his very title is only bound to move and charm you. Even supposing the poet, by a scrupulous submission to historic truth, had stripped himself of his privilege of artist, and that he had tacitly acknowledged in history a jurisdiction over his work, art retains all her rights to summon him before its bar; and pieces such as "The Death of Hermann," "Minona," "Fust of Stromberg," if they could not stand the test on this side, would only be tragedies of mediocre value, notwithstanding all the minuteness of costume—of national costume—and of the manners of the time.

Fifthly, tragedy is the imitation of an action that lets us see man suffering. The word man is essential to mark the limits of tragedy. Only the suffering of a being like ourselves can move our pity. Thus, evil genii, demons—or even men like them, without morals—and again pure spirits, without our weaknesses, are unfit for tragedy. The very idea of suffering implies a man in the full sense of the term. A pure spirit cannot suffer, and a man approaching one will never awaken a high degree of sympathy. A purely sensuous being can indeed have terrible suffering; but without moral sense it is a prey to it, and a suffering with reason inactive is a disgusting spectacle. The tragedian is right to prefer mixed characters, and to place the ideal of his hero half way between utter perversity and entire perfection.

Lastly, tragedy unites all these requisites to excite pity. Many means the tragic poet takes might serve another object; but he frees himself from all requirements not relating to this end, and is thereby obliged to direct himself with a view to this supreme object.

The final aim to which all the laws tend is called the end of any style of poetry. The means by which it attains this are its form. The end and form are, therefore, closely related. The form is determined by the end, and when the form is well observed the end is generally attained. Each kind of poetry having a special end must have a distinguishing form. What it exclusively produces it does in virtue of this special nature it possesses. The end of tragedy is emotion; its form is the imitation of an action that leads to suffering. Many kinds may have the same object as tragedy, of emotion, though it be not their principal end. Therefore, what distinguishes tragedy is the relation of its form to its end, the way in which it attains its end by means of its subject.

If the end of tragedy is to awaken sympathy, and its form is the means of attaining it, the imitation of an action fit to move must have all that favors sympathy. Such is the form of tragedy.

The production of a kind of poetry is perfect when the form peculiar to its kind has been used in the best way. Thus, a perfect tragedy is that where the form is best used to awaken sympathy. Thus, the best tragedy is that where the pity excited results more from the treatment of the poet than the theme. Such is the ideal of a tragedy.

A good number of tragedies, though fine as poems are bad as dramas, because they do not seek their end by the best use of tragic form. Others, because they use the form to attain an end different from tragedy. Some very popular ones only touch us on account of the subject, and we are blind enough to make this a merit in the poet. There are others in which we seem to have quite forgotten the object of the poet, and, contented with pretty plays of fancy and wit, we issue with our hearts cold from the theatre. Must art, so holy and venerable, defend its cause by such champions before such judges? The indulgence of the public only emboldens mediocrity: it causes genius to blush, and discourages it.

OF THE CAUSE OF THE PLEASURE WE DERIVE FROM TRAGIC OBJECTS.

Whatever pains some modern aesthetics give themselves to establish, contrary to general belief, that the arts of imagination and of feeling have not pleasure for their object, and to defend them against this degrading accusation, this belief will not cease: it reposes upon a solid foundation, and the fine arts would renounce with a bad grace the beneficent mission which has in all times been assigned to them, to accept the new employment to which it is generously proposed to raise them. Without troubling themselves whether they lower themselves in proposing our pleasure as object, they become rather proud of the advantages of reaching immediately an aim never attained except mediately in other routes followed by the activity of the human mind. That the aim of nature, with relation to man, is the happiness of man,— although he ought of himself, in his moral conduct, to take no notice of this aim,— is what, I think, cannot be doubted in general by any one who admits that nature has an aim. Thus the fine arts have the same aim as nature, or rather as the Author of nature, namely, to spread pleasure and render people happy. It procures for us in play what at other more austere sources of good to man we extract only with difficulty. It lavishes as a pure gift that which elsewhere is the price of many hard efforts. With what labor, what application, do we not pay for the pleasures of the understanding; with what painful sacrifices the approbation of reason; with what hard privations the joys of sense! And if we abuse these pleasures, with what a succession of evils do we expiate excess! Art alone supplies an enjoyment which requires no appreciable effort, which costs no sacrifice, and which we need not repay with repentance. But who could class the merit of charming in this manner with the poor merit of amusing? who would venture to deny the former of these two aims of the fine arts solely because they have a tendency higher than the latter.

The praiseworthy object of pursuing everywhere moral good as the supreme aim, which has already brought forth in art so much mediocrity, has caused also in theory a similar prejudice. To assign to the fine arts a really elevated position, to conciliate for them the favor of the State, the veneration of all men, they are pushed beyond their due domain, and a vocation is imposed upon them contrary to their nature. It is supposed that a great service is awarded to them by substituting for a frivolous aim—that of charming—a moral aim; and their influence upon morality, which is so apparent, necessarily militates against this pretension. It is found illogical that the art which contributes in so great a measure to the development of all that is most elevated in man, should produce but accessorily this effect, and make its chief object an aim so vulgar as we imagine pleasure to be. But this apparent contradiction it would be very easy to conciliate if we had a good theory of pleasure, and a complete system of aesthetic philosophy.

It would result from this theory that a free pleasure, as that which the fine arts procure for us, rests wholly upon moral conditions, and all the moral faculties of man are exercised in it. It would further result that this pleasure is an aim which can never be attained but by moral means, and consequently that art, to tend and perfectly attain to pleasure, as to a real aim, must follow the road of healthy morals. Thus it is perfectly indifferent for the dignity of art whether its aim should be a moral aim, or whether it should reach only through moral means; for in both cases it has always to do with the morality, and must be rigorously in unison with the sentiment of duty; but for the perfection of art, it is by no means indifferent which of the two should be the aim and which the means. If it is the aim that is moral, art loses all that by which it is powerful,—I mean its freedom, and that which gives it so much influence over us— the charm of pleasure. The play which recreates is changed into serious occupation, and yet it is precisely in recreating us that art can the better complete the great affair—the moral work. It cannot have a salutary influence upon the morals but in exercising its highest aesthetic action, and it can only produce the aesthetic effect in its highest degree in fully exercising its liberty.

It is certain, besides, that all pleasure, the moment it flows from a moral source, renders man morally better, and then the effect in its turn becomes cause. The pleasure we find in what is beautiful, or touching, or sublime, strengthens our moral sentiments, as the pleasure we find in kindness, in love, etc., strengthens these inclinations. And just as contentment of the mind is the sure lot of the morally excellent man, so moral excellence willingly accompanies satisfaction of heart. Thus the moral efficacy of art is, not only because it employs moral means in order to charm us, but also because even the pleasure which it procures us is a means of morality.

There are as many means by which art can attain its aim as there are in general sources from which a free pleasure for the mind can flow. I call a free pleasure that which brings into play the spiritual forces—reason and imagination—and which awakens in us a sentiment by the representation of an idea, in contradistinction to physical or sensuous pleasure, which places our soul under the dependence of the blind forces of nature, and where sensation is immediately awakened in us by a physical cause. Sensual pleasure is the only one excluded from the domain of the fine arts; and the talent of exciting this kind of pleasure could never raise itself to the dignity of an art, except in the case where the sensual impressions are ordered, reinforced or moderated, after a plan which is the production of art, and which is recognized by representation. But, in this case even, that alone here can merit the name of art which is the object of a free pleasure—I mean good taste in the regulation, which pleases our understanding, and not physical charms themselves, which alone flatter our sensibility.

The general source of all pleasure, even of sensual pleasure, is propriety, the conformity with the aim. Pleasure is sensual when this propriety is manifested by means of some necessary law of nature which has for physical result the sensation of pleasure. Thus the movement of the blood, and of the animal life, when in conformity with the aim of nature, produces in certain organs, or in the entire organism, corporeal pleasure with all its varieties and all its modes. We feel this conformity by the means of agreeable sensation, but we arrive at no representation of it, either clear or confused.

Pleasure is free when we represent to ourselves the conformability, and when the sensation that accompanies this representation is agreeable. Thus all the representations by which we have notice that there is propriety and harmony between the end and the means, are for us the sources of free pleasure, and consequently can be employed to this end by the fine arts. Thus, all the representations can be placed under one of these heads: the good, the true, the perfect, the beautiful, the touching, the sublime. The good especially occupies our reason; the true and perfect, our intelligence; the beautiful interests both the intelligence and the imagination; the touching and the sublime, the reason and the imagination. It is true that we also take pleasure in the charm (Reiz) or the power called out by action from play, but art uses charm only to accompany the higher enjoyments which the idea of propriety gives to us. Considered in itself the charm or attraction is lost amid the sensations of life, and art disdains it together with all merely sensual pleasures.

We could not establish a classification of the fine arts only upon the difference of the sources from which each of them draws the pleasure which it affords us; for in the same class of the fine arts many sorts of pleasures may enter, and often all together. But in as far as a certain sort of pleasure is pursued as a principal aim, we can make of it, if not a specific character of a class properly so called, at least the principle and the tendency of a class in the works of art. Thus, for example, we could take the arts which, above all, satisfy the intelligence and imagination— consequently those which have as chief object the true, the perfect, and the beautiful—and unite them under the name of fine arts (arts of taste, arts of intelligence); those, on the other hand, which especially occupy the imagination and the reason, and which, in consequence, have for principal object the good, the sublime, and the touching, could be limited in a particular class under the denomination of touching arts (arts of sentiment, arts of the heart). Without doubt it is impossible to separate absolutely the touching from the beautiful, but the beautiful can perfectly subsist without the touching. Thus, although we are not authorized to base upon this difference of principle a rigorous classification of the liberal arts, it can at least serve to determine with more of precision the criterion, and prevent the confusion in which we are inevitably involved, when, drawing up laws of aesthetic things, we confound two absolutely different domains, as that of the touching and that of the beautiful.

The touching and the sublime resemble in this point, that both one and the other produce a pleasure by a feeling at first of displeasure, and that consequently (pleasure proceeding from suitability, and displeasure from the contrary) they give us a feeling of suitability which presupposes an unsuitability.

The feeling of the sublime is composed in part of the feeling of our feebleness, of our impotence to embrace an object; and, on the other side, of the feeling of our moral power—of this superior faculty which fears no obstacle, no limit, and which subdues spiritually that even to which our physical forces give way. The object of the sublime thwarts, then, our physical power; and this contrariety (impropriety) must necessarily excite a displeasure in us. But it is, at the same time, an occasion to recall to our conscience another faculty which is in us—a faculty which is even superior to the objects before which our imagination yields. In consequence, a sublime object, precisely because it thwarts the senses, is suitable with relation to reason, and it gives to us a joy by means of a higher faculty, at the same time that it wounds us in an inferior one.

The touching, in its proper sense, designates this mixed sensation, into which enters at the same time suffering and the pleasure that we find in suffering. Thus we can only feel this kind of emotion in the case of a personal misfortune, only when the grief that we feel is sufficiently tempered to leave some place for that impression of pleasure that would be felt by a compassionate spectator. The loss of a great good prostrates for the time, and the remembrance itself of the grief will make us experience emotion after a year. The feeble man is always the prey of his grief; the hero and the sage, whatever the misfortune that strikes them, never experience more than emotion.

Emotion, like the sentiment of the sublime, is composed of two affections—grief and pleasure. There is, then, at the bottom a propriety, here as well as there, and under this propriety a contradiction. Thus it seems that it is a contradiction in nature that man, who is not born to suffer, is nevertheless a prey to suffering, and this contradiction hurts us. But the evil which this contradiction does us is a propriety with regard to our reasonable nature in general, insomuch as this evil solicits us to act: it is a propriety also with regard to human society; consequently, even displeasure, which excites in us this contradiction, ought necessarily to make us experience a sentiment of pleasure, because this displeasure is a propriety. To determine in an emotion if it is pleasure or displeasure which triumphs, we must ask ourselves if it is the idea of impropriety or that of propriety which affects us the more deeply. That can depend either on the number of the aims reached or abortive, or on their connection with the final aim of all.

The suffering of the virtuous man moves us more painfully than that of the perverse man, because in the first case there is contradiction not only to the general destiny of man, which is happiness, but also to this other particular principle, viz., that virtue renders happy; whilst in the second case there is contradiction only with regard to the end of man in general. Reciprocally, the happiness of the wicked also offends us much more than the misfortune of the good man, because we find in it a double contradiction: in the first place vice itself, and, in the second place, the recompense of vice.

There is also this other consideration, that virtue is much more able to recompense itself than vice, when it triumphs, is to punish itself; and it is precisely for this that the virtuous man in misfortune would much more remain faithful to the cultus of virtue than the perverse man would dream of converting himself in prosperity.

But what is above all important in determining in the emotions the relation of pleasure and displeasure, is to compare the two ends—that which has been fulfilled and that which has been ignored—and to see which is the most considerable. There is no propriety which touches us so nearly as moral propriety, and no superior pleasure to that which we feel from it. Physical propriety could well be a problem, and a problem forever unsolvable. Moral propriety is already demonstrated. It alone is founded upon our reasonable nature and upon internal necessity. It is our nearest interest, the most considerable, and, at the same time, the most easily recognized, because it is not determined by any external element but by an internal principle of our reason: it is the palladium of our liberty.

This moral propriety is never more vividly recognized than when it is found in conflict with another propriety, and still keeps the upper hand; then only the moral law awakens in full power, when we find it struggling against all the other forces of nature, and when all those forces lose in its presence their empire over a human soul. By these words, "the other forces of nature," we must understand all that is not moral force, all that is not subject to the supreme legislation of reason: that is to say, feelings, affections, instincts, passions, as well as physical necessity and destiny. The more redoubtable the adversary, the more glorious the victory; resistance alone brings out the strength of the force and renders it visible. It follows that the highest degree of moral consciousness can only exist in strife, and the highest moral pleasure is always accompanied by pain.

Consequently, the kind of poetry which secures us a high degree of moral pleasure, must employ mixed feelings, and please us through pain or distress,—this is what tragedy does specially; and her realm embraces all that sacrifices a physical propriety to a moral one; or one moral propriety to a higher one. It might be possible, perhaps, to form a measure of moral pleasure, from the lowest to the highest degree, and to determine by this principle of propriety the degree of pain or pleasure experienced. Different orders of tragedy might be classified on the same principle, so as to form a complete exhaustive tabulation of them. Thus, a tragedy being given, its place could be fixed, and its genus determined. Of this subject more will be said separately in its proper place.

A few examples will show how far moral propriety commands physical propriety in our souls.

Theron and Amanda are both tied to the stake as martyrs, and free to choose life or death by the terrible ordeal of fire—they select the latter. What is it which gives such pleasure to us in this scene? Their position so conflicting with the smiling destiny they reject, the reward of misery given to virtue—all here awakens in us the feeling of impropriety: it ought to fill us with great distress. What is nature, and what are her ends and laws, if all this impropriety shows us moral propriety in its full light. We here see the triumph of the moral law, so sublime an experience for us that we might even hail the calamity which elicits it. For harmony in the world of moral freedom gives us infinitely more pleasure than all the discords in nature give us pain.

When Coriolanus, obedient to duty as husband, son, and citizen, raises the siege of Rome, them almost conquered, withdrawing his army, and silencing his vengeance, he commits a very contradictory act evidently. He loses all the fruit of previous victories, he runs spontaneously to his ruin: yet what moral excellence and grandeur he offers! How noble to prefer any impropriety rather than wound moral sense; to violate natural interests and prudence in order to be in harmony with the higher moral law! Every sacrifice of a life is a contradiction, for life is the condition of all good; but in the light of morality the sacrifice of life is in a high degree proper, because life is not great in itself, but only as a means of accomplishing the moral law. If then the sacrifice of life be the way to do this, life must go. "It is not necessary for me to live, but it is necessary for Rome to be saved from famine," said Pompey, when the Romans embarked for Africa, and his friends begged him to defer his departure till the gale was over.

But the sufferings of a criminal are as charming to us tragically as those of a virtuous man; yet here is the idea of moral impropriety. The antagonism of his conduct to moral law, and the moral imperfection which such conduct presupposes, ought to fill us with pain. Here there is no satisfaction in the morality of his person, nothing to compensate for his misconduct. Yet both supply a valuable object for art; this phenomenon can easily be made to agree with what has been said.

We find pleasure not only in obedience to morality, but in the punishment given to its infraction. The pain resulting from moral imperfection agrees with its opposite, the satisfaction at conformity with the law. Repentance, even despair, have nobleness morally, and can only exist if an incorruptible sense of justice exists at the bottom of the criminal heart, and if conscience maintains its ground against self-love. Repentance comes by comparing our acts with the moral law, hence in the moment of repenting the moral law speaks loudly in man. Its power must be greater than the gain resulting from the crime as the infraction poisons the enjoyment. Now, a state of mind where duty is sovereign is morally proper, and therefore a source of moral pleasure. What, then, sublimer than the heroic despair that tramples even life underfoot, because it cannot bear the judgment within? A good man sacrificing his life to conform to the moral law, or a criminal taking his own life because of the morality he has violated: in both cases our respect for the moral law is raised to the highest power. If there be any advantage it is in the case of the latter; for the good man may have been encouraged in his sacrifice by an approving conscience, thus detracting from his merit. Repentance and regret at past crimes show us some of the sublimest pictures of morality in active condition. A man who violates morality comes back to the moral law by repentance.

But moral pleasure is sometimes obtained only at the cost of moral pain. Thus one duty may clash with another. Let us suppose Coriolanus encamped with a Roman army before Antium or Corioli, and his mother a Volscian; if her prayers move him to desist, we now no longer admire him. His obedience to his mother would be at strife with a higher duty, that of a citizen. The governor to whom the alternative is proposed, either of giving up the town or of seeing his son stabbed, decides at once on the latter, his duty as father being beneath that of citizen. At first our heart revolts at this conduct in a father, but we soon pass to admiration that moral instinct, even combined with inclination, could not lead reason astray in the empire where it commands. When Timoleon of Corinth puts to death his beloved but ambitious brother, Timophanes, he does it because his idea of duty to his country bids him to do so. The act here inspires horror and repulsion as against nature and the moral sense, but this feeling is soon succeeded by the highest admiration for his heroic virtue, pronouncing, in a tumultuous conflict of emotions, freely and calmly, with perfect rectitude. If we differ with Timoleon about his duty as a republican, this does not change our view. Nay, in those cases, where our understanding judges differently, we see all the more clearly how high we put moral propriety above all other.

But the judgments of men on this moral phenomenon are exceedingly various, and the reason of it is clear. Moral sense is common to all men, but differs in strength. To most men it suffices that an act be partially conformable with the moral law to make them obey it; and to make them condemn an action it must glaringly violate the law. But to determine the relation of moral duties with the highest principle of morals requires an enlightened intelligence and an emancipated reason. Thus an action which to a few will be a supreme propriety, will seem to the crowd a revolting impropriety, though both judge morally; and hence the emotion felt at such actions is by no means uniform. To the mass the sublimest and highest is only exaggeration, because sublimity is perceived by reason, and all men have not the same share of it. A vulgar soul is oppressed or overstretched by those sublime ideas, and the crowd sees dreadful disorder where a thinking mind sees the highest order.

This is enough about moral propriety as a principle of tragic emotion, and the pleasure it elicits. It must be added that there are cases where natural propriety also seems to charm our mind even at the cost of morality. Thus we are always pleased by the sequence of machinations of a perverse man, though his means and end are immoral. Such a man deeply interests us, and we tremble lest his plan fail, though we ought to wish it to do so. But this fact does not contradict what has been advanced about moral propriety,—and the pleasure resulting from it.

Propriety, the reference of means to an end, is to us, in all cases, a source of pleasure; even disconnected with morality. We experience this pleasure unmixed, so long as we do not think of any moral end which disallows action before us. Animal instincts give us pleasure—as the industry of bees—without reference to morals; and in like manner human actions are a pleasure to us when we consider in them only the relation of means to ends. But if a moral principle be added to these, and impropriety be discovered, if the idea of moral agent comes in, a deep indignation succeeds our pleasure, which no intellectual propriety can remedy. We must not call to mind too vividly that Richard III., Iago, and Lovelace are men; otherwise our sympathy for them infallibly turns into an opposite feeling. But, as daily experience teaches, we have the power to direct our attention to different sides of things; and pleasure, only possible through this abstraction, invites us to exercise it, and to prolong its exercise.

Yet it is not rare for intelligent perversity to secure our favor by being the means of procuring us the pleasure of moral propriety. The triumph of moral propriety will be great in proportion as the snares set by Lovelace for the virtue of Clarissa are formidable, and as the trials of an innocent victim by a cruel tyrant are severe. It is a pleasure to see the craft of a seducer foiled by the omnipotence of the moral sense. On the other hand, we reckon as a sort of merit the victory of a malefactor over his moral sense, because it is the proof of a certain strength of mind and intellectual propriety.

Yet this propriety in vice can never be the source of a perfect pleasure, except when it is humiliated by morality. In that case it is an essential part of our pleasure, because it brings moral sense into stronger relief. The last impression left on us by the author of Clarissa is a proof of this. The intellectual propriety in the plan of Lovelace is greatly surpassed by the rational propriety of Clarissa. This allows us to feel in full the satisfaction caused by both.

When the tragic poet has for object to awaken in us the feeling of moral propriety, and chooses his means skilfully for that end, he is sure to charm doubly the connoisseur, by moral and by natural propriety. The first satisfies the heart, the second the mind. The crowd is impressed through the heart without knowing the cause of the magic impression. But, on the other hand, there is a class of connoisseurs on whom that which affects the heart is entirely lost, and who can only be gained by the appropriateness of the means; a strange contradiction resulting from over-refined taste, especially when moral culture remains behind intellectual. This class of connoisseurs seek only the intellectual side in touching and sublime themes. They appreciate this in the justest manner, but you must beware how you appeal to their heart! The over-culture of the age leads to this shoal, and nothing becomes the cultivated man so much as to escape by a happy victory this twofold and pernicious influence. Of all other European nations, our neighbors, the French, lean most to this extreme, and we, as in all things, strain every nerve to imitate this model.

Made in United States
North Haven, CT
21 February 2022

16339628R00130